THE PAPERS OF

James Madison

VOLUME 2

20 March 1780—23 February 1781

This second volume opens with Madison, in his thirtieth year, beginning his long national career by entering the Continental Congress as one of the delegates from Virginia.

During his first year in Congress, Madison emerged as a leader on issues relating to finance, the trans-Allegheny West, and Spain. He was foremost in insisting that an alliance with Spain was not worth the cost of surrendering the right of Americans to free use of the Mississippi River.

Interstate disputes over the ownership of western lands were, at this time, hampering Congress in concentrating upon winning the war and delaying the ratification of the Articles of Confederation. This delay seemingly restrained France from sending more military aid during the dark year of 1780. Madison joined with other far-sighted Virginians in persuading the General Assembly of their commonwealth to offer to cede to the United States its territory north of the Ohio River.

With the inauguration of the central government under the Articles of Confederation, the present volume appropriately closes.

THE PAPERS OF
James Madison

SPONSORED BY

The University of Chicago

AND

The University of Virginia

INDEPENDENCE HALL

THE PAPERS OF

James Madison

VOLUME 2

20 MARCH 1780—23 FEBRUARY 1781

EDITED BY

WILLIAM T. HUTCHINSON AND WILLIAM M. E. RACHAL

EDITORIAL STAFF

JEAN SCHNEIDER   ROBERT L. SCRIBNER

RALPH L. KETCHAM   DONALD O. DEWEY

THE UNIVERSITY OF CHICAGO PRESS

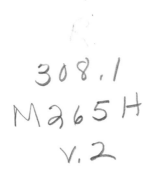

Library of Congress Catalog Card Number: 62-9114

The University of Chicago Press, Chicago & London
The University of Toronto Press, Toronto 5, Canada

To
LEONARD D. WHITE
1891–1958

CONTENTS

CONTENTS

CONTENTS

1781

CONTENTS

ILLUSTRATIONS

EDITORIAL METHOD

ABBREVIATIONS

FC   File copy. Any version of a letter or other document retained by the sender for his own files and differing little if at all from the completed version. A draft, on the other hand, is a preliminary sketch, often incomplete and varying frequently in expression from the finished version.

JM   James Madison.

LC   Library of Congress.

MS   Manuscript. A catchall term describing numerous reports and other papers written by Madison, as well as items sent to him which were not letters.

NA   National Archives.

PCC   Papers of the Continental Congress, a collection in the National Archives.

RC   Recipient's copy. The copy of a letter intended to be read by the addressee. If its handwriting is not that of the sender, this fact is mentioned in the headnote.

TR   Transcript. A copy of a manuscript, or a copy of that copy, usually handwritten, made considerably later than the date of the manuscript and ordinarily not by its author or by the person to whom the original was addressed. The "Force Transcripts," made under the direction of Peter Force in the mid-nineteenth century, are those most frequently used in the present series.

SHORT TITLES FOR BOOKS

Only those books used very frequently, and a few whose titles are so long as to necessitate an abbreviation, have been given short titles. This list applies only to Volume II; succeeding volumes will contain lists of titles abbreviated in them.

Boyd, *Papers of Jefferson.* Julian P. Boyd *et al.*, eds., *The Papers of Thomas Jefferson* (16 vols. to date; Princeton, N.J., 1950——).

Brant, *Madison.* Irving Brant, *James Madison* (6 vols.; Indianapolis and New York, 1941–61).

Burnett, *Letters.* Edmund C. Burnett, ed., *Letters of Members of the Continental Congress* (8 vols.; Washington, D.C., 1921–36).

Doniol, *Histoire*. Henri Doniol, *Histoire de la participation de la France à l'établissement des États-Unis d'Amérique* (5 vols.; Paris, 1886–92).

Fitzpatrick, *Writings of Washington*. John C. Fitzpatrick, ed., *The Writings of George Washington, from the Original Sources, 1745–1799* (39 vols.; Washington, D.C., 1931–44).

Hening, *Statutes*. William Waller Hening, ed., *The Statutes at Large; being a Collection of all the Laws of Virginia, from the First Session of the Legislature, in the Year 1619* (13 vols.; Richmond and Philadelphia, 1819–23).

Journal of the House of Delegates. *Journal of the House of Delegates of the Commonwealth of Virginia; Begun and Held At the Capitol, in the City of Williamsburg.* Beginning in 1780, the portion after the semicolon reads, *Begun and Held in the Town of Richmond. In the County of Henrico.* The journal for each session has its own title page and is individually paginated. The edition used, unless otherwise noted, is the one in which the journals for 1777–1781 are brought together in one volume, with each journal published in Richmond in 1827 or 1828, and often called the "Thomas W. White reprint."

Madison, *Letters* (Cong. ed.). [William C. Rives and Philip R. Fendall, eds.], *Letters and Other Writings of James Madison* (published by order of Congress; 4 vols.; Philadelphia, 1865).

Madison, *Papers* (Gilpin ed.). Henry D. Gilpin, ed., *The Papers of James Madison* (3 vols.; Washington, D.C., 1840).

Madison, *Writings* (Hunt ed.). Gaillard Hunt, ed., *The Writings of James Madison* (9 vols.; New York, 1900–1910).

New Jersey Archives. William A. Whitehead *et al.*, eds., *Documents Relating to the Colonial History of the State of New Jersey* (1st ser., 42 vols.; Newark, Trenton, Paterson, 1880–1949).

Pennsylvania Archives. Samuel Hazard *et al.*, eds., *Pennsylvania Archives* (9 ser., 138 vols.; Philadelphia and Harrisburg, 1852–1949).

Wharton, *Revolutionary Diplomatic Correspondence*. Francis Wharton, ed., *The Revolutionary Diplomatic Correspondence of the United States* (6 vols.; Washington, D.C., 1889).

MADISON CHRONOLOGY

1780 (January–March)	At home in Orange County.
1780 (20 March)	Took his seat in Continental Congress in Philadelphia.
1780 (22 March–6 June)	Served as member of Board of Admiralty.
1780 (6 September)	Co-sponsored with Joseph Jones resolutions on western lands.
1780 (17 October)	Adoption of Instructions to John Jay, Madison's first important state paper in Congress.
1780 (23 October)	Appointed to committee to correspond with General Nathanael Greene.
1780 (23 December)	Madison's draft of commission to John Laurens approved by Congress.
1781 (1 March)	Formal ratification of the Articles of Confederation on behalf of each state by its delegation in the Continental Congress.

THE PAPERS OF

James Madison

To James Madison, Sr.

FC (LC: Madison Papers). In this retained copy, JM omitted "Hon'd Sir," his usual salutation when writing to his father.

PHILADELPHIA Monday March 20th. 1780.

The extreme badness of the roads and frequency of rains rendered my journey so slow that I did not reach this place till saturday last.[1] The only public intelligence I have to communicate is that the great and progressive depreciation of the paper currency had introduced such disorder and perplexity into public affairs for the present and threatened to load the United States with such an intolerable burden of debt, that Congress have thought it expedient to convert the 200,-000,000 of Dollars now in circulation into a real debt of 5,000,000 by establishing the exchange at 40 for 1. and taxes for calling it in during the ensuing year, are to be payable at the option of the people in specie or paper according to that difference. In order to carry on public measures in future money is to be emitted under the combined faith of Congress and the several States, secured on permanent and specific fun[ds] to be provided by the latter. This scheme was finally resolved on on saturday last.[2] It has not yet been printed but will be immediately. I shall transmit a copy to you by the first opportunity. The little time I have been here makes it impossible for me to enter into a particular delineation of it. It will probably create great perplexity and complaints in many private transactions. Congress have recommended to the States to repeal their tender laws, and to take measures for preventing injustice as much as possible. It is probable that in the case of loans to the public, the state of depreciation at the time they were made will be the rule of payment, but nothing is yet decided on that point. I expect to be more at leisure to write fully by next post. Yrs. &c. &c.

JAMES MADISON JUNR.

[1] JM's expense account, dated 20 September 1780 (q.v.), indicates that he was twelve days on his journey from Montpelier to Philadelphia.
[2] See essay on "Money," September 1779–March 1780, n. 1.

Election to Board of Admiralty

Printed text (*Journals of the Continental Congress,* XVI, 277).

[22 March 1780]

Resolved, That a member be elected for the Board of Admiralty, in the room of Mr. [James][1] Forbes, who by reason of sickness cannot attend.

Congress proceeded to an election, and the ballots being taken, Mr. [James] Madison was elected.[2]

[1] All brackets are in printed text. Forbes (b. *ca.* 1731) of Charles City County, Md., died on 25 March 1780 after serving in Congress for a little over two years.

[2] JM's service on the Board of Admiralty, created by Congress on 28 October 1779 in the stead of its Marine Committee, extended from 22 March until 6 June 1780, when, at his own request, he was excused from further attendance (Worthington Chauncey Ford *et al.,* eds., *Journals of the Continental Congress, 1774–1789* [34 vols.; Washington, D.C., 1904–37], XVI, 277; XVII, 490). During this period, his colleagues on the Board were the chairman, Francis Lewis, a New York merchant, and William Ellery, a delegate to Congress from Rhode Island. As the Board's junior member, young in years and inexperienced in maritime affairs, JM probably contributed little to shaping the correspondence, reports, and motions emanating from the Board. While he was a member, it dispatched at least forty letters (Charles Oscar Paullin, ed., *Out-Letters of the Continental Marine Committee and Board of Admiralty* [2 vols.; New York, 1914], II, 168–208), and brought sundry reports and resolutions before Congress. The originals of these latter documents are among the Papers of the Continental Congress in the National Archives. Many of them are in the hand of the Board's secretary, John Brown. No one of them, either on the score of its handwriting or content, can be attributed with assurance to JM. For this reason, the present volume includes merely samples of the matters submitted to Congress by the Board and of its outgoing letters during JM's membership on it. These samples will at least illustrate the Board's activities which were of concern to JM in the spring of 1780.

Board of Admiralty to Abraham Whipple

FC (NA: PCC, Marine Committee Letter Book, fol. 271).

March 24th. 1780

SIR[1]

We wrote you the 26th february in answer to your letter of the 7th January, since which we are favoured with yours of the 14th february.[2] In your letter of the 7th. January you request that a quantity of Bread and flour may be sent you from hence, this is not in our power at present to accomplish and if it were the dificulty of Procuring Vessels to transport it together with the probabiltity of its falling into the enemys hands is such that it would be very imprudent at this time to attempt it. We are also informed by the South Carolina Delegates that the State can furnish the Squadron with A Substitute for those Articles[3]

The Board have an high opinion of your Zeal for the Service of your Country and doubt not your exerting it on every Occasion relying on your prudence and Oeconomy, We are

Sir Your very Hble servants   By Order

JOHN BROWN Secy[4]

[1] Captain Abraham Whipple (1733–1819) of Providence, R.I.

[2] John Brown's letter to Whipple of 26 February is in Charles O. Paullin, ed., *Out-Letters of Board of Admiralty*, II, 163. Whipple's two letters have not been found. On 23 December 1779, Whipple's fleet, consisting of the frigates "Providence," "Boston," and "Queen of France" and sloop of war "Ranger," reached Charleston to co-operate with General Benjamin Lincoln in defending that city against the British forces comprising ships and General Clinton's army. With the exception of the "Queen of France," which had been sunk to help block the Cooper River against the enemy, Whipple's vessels were surrendered to the British when they captured Charleston on 12 May 1780 (Gardner W. Allen, *A Naval History of the American Revolution* [2 vols.; Boston, 1913], II, 403, 495, 497).

[3] On 29 February 1780 the North Carolina delegates in Congress informed Governor Richard Caswell of that state that "North Carolina assumed [the obligation to furnish] the flower because South Carolina could furnish none, and the Troops from Virginia and north Carolina cannot be Subsisted upon Rice" (Burnett, *Letters*, V, 58).

[4] John Brown (1748–1833) of Pennsylvania became secretary of the Marine Committee soon after its establishment on 14 December 1775 and, when the Board of Admiralty succeeded the Marine Committee in 1779, he continued as secretary. When Robert Morris became agent of marine in September 1781, he sent Brown to Boston as naval agent. The Navy Board at Boston continued to operate, however, and did not turn over its records to Brown until the spring of 1782 (information from Rear Admiral E. M. Eller, Director of Naval History, Department of the Navy; Emelin Knox Parker, "A Biographical Sketch of John Brown," typescript, March 1929, in Historical Society of Pennsylvania).

To Thomas Jefferson

RC (LC: Madison Papers).

PHILADELPHIA March 27th. 1780

DEAR SIR

Nothing under the title of news has occurred since I wrote last week by express[1] except that the Enemy on the 1st. of March remained in the neighbourhood of Charlestown in the same posture as when the preceding account came away. From the best intelligence from that quarter there seems to be great encouragement to hope that Clinton's operations will be again frustrated.[2] Our great apprehensions at present flow from a very different quarter. Among the various conjunctures of alarm and distress which have arisen in the course of the revolution, it is with pain I affirm to you Sir, that no one can be singled out more truly critical than the present. Our army threatened with an immediate alternative of disbanding or living on free quarter; the public treasury empty; public credit exhausted, nay the private credit of purchasing Agents employed, I am told, as far as it will bear, Congress complaining of the extortion of the people; the people of the improvidence of Congress, and the army of both; our affairs requiring the most mature & systematic measures, and the urgency of occasions admitting only of temporizing expedients, and those expedients generating new difficulties. Congress from a defect of adequate Statesmen more likely to fall into wrong measures and of less weight to enforce right ones, recommending plans to the several states for execution and the states separately rejudging the expediency of such plans, whereby the same distrust of concurrent exertions that has damped the ardor of patriotic individuals, must produce the same effect among the States themselves. An old system of finance discarded as incompetent to our necessities, an untried & precarious one substituted, and a total stagnation in prospect between the end of the former & the operation of the latter: These are the outlines of the true picture of our public situation. I leave it to your own imagination to fill them up. Believe me Sir as things now stand, if the States do not vigorously proceed in collecting the old money and establishing funds for the credit of the new, that we are undone; and let them be ever so expeditious in doing this[,] still the intermediate distress to our army and hindrance to public affairs are a subject of melancholy reflection. Gen Washington writes that a failure of bread has already commenced in the army, and that for any thing he sees, it must unavoidably increase. Meat they have only for a short season and as the whole dependance is on provisions now to be procured, without a shilling for the purpose, and without credit for a shilling, I look forward with the most pungent apprehensions.[3] It will be attempted I believe to purchase a few supplies with loan office Certificates; but whether they will be received is perhaps far from being certain; and if received will certainly be a most expensive & ruinous expedient. It is not without some reluctance I trust this information to a conveyance by post, but I know of no better at present, and I conceive it to be absolutely necessary to be known to those who are most able and zealous to contribute to the public relief.

March 28.

Authentic information is now recd. that the Enemy in their passage to Georgia lost all their Horse, the Defiance of 64 guns which foundered at sea, three transports with troops, although it is pretended these troops and the men of the Defiance were saved, and 1 transport with Hessians of which nothing has been heard.[4] By a letter from Mr. Adams dated Corunna 16 Decr. there seems little probability that Britain is yet in a humour for peace. The Russian Ambassador at that Court has been lately changed, and the new one on his way to London made some stop at Paris whence a rumor has spread in Europe that Russia was about to employ her mediation for peace. Should there be any reality in it, Mr. Adams says it is the opinion of the most intelligent [persons] he had conversed with that the independance of the United [States] would be insisted on as a preliminary: to which G. B. would accede with much greater repugnance than the cession of Gibraltar which Spain was determined to make a sine qua non.[5]

With respect and regard I am Dr Sir, yrs. sincerely

JAMES MADISON JR

His Excellency T. Jefferson

[1] Letter not found.

[2] Seven weeks earlier, the troops under General Henry Clinton (ca. 1738–1795) disembarked thirty miles south of Charleston. Two days after the date of this letter they crossed the Ashley River. Helped by eight British frigates, they besieged the city until 12 May, when it and the nearly 5,500 patriot troops within it surrendered.

[3] Washington's letter of 17 March was read to Congress four days later (Journals of the Continental Congress, XVI, 274; Fitzpatrick, Writings of Washington, XVIII, 121–22).

[4] This information, conveyed by Washington in his letter of 23 March, was made known to Congress on the 27th (Journals of the Continental Congress, XVI, 288–89). The British fleet, convoying transports from New York City to Savannah, encountered a severe storm off Cape Hatteras. One ship, loaded with Hessian troops, was blown far out to sea and never reached its destination. The "Defiance" of sixty-four guns foundered at the entrance of Tybee River, Ga. (William B. Willcox, ed., The American Rebellion: Sir Henry Clinton's Narrative of his Campaigns, 1775–1782 [New Haven, Conn., 1954], pp. 159–62).

[5] On 27 March, Congress listened to John Adams' letter of 16 December 1779, addressed to its president (Journals of the Continental Congress, XVI, 288; Wharton, Revolutionary Diplomatic Correspondence, III, 427–28).

Report of Board of Admiralty

MS (NA: PCC, No. 37, fol. 211).

March 29th 1780

The Board of Admiralty beg leave to lay the enclosed Papers before Congress, and to receive their Instruction thereon.[1]

By Mr Langdons letter and estimate it will appear that to compleat the 74 gun Ship building under his agency he requires an immediate supply of Money.[2] That his funds are totally exhausted and by letters of a late date from the Commissioners of the Navy Board in the Eastern department this Board are also informed that they "will soon be drained of the last shilling."

The Board would also inform Congress that the Bourbon building in Connecticut is almost ready for Launching, and her sails, and a principal part of her rigging & other Materials provided; and that unless they can have a Supply of Money she must remain on the Stocks unfinished to the great injury of the public.[3]

In this Situation the Board can conceive no other mode of Supply than by Warrant issuing on the Continental treasurer or upon the State treasurers of Massachusetts Bay and New Hampshire payable out of the Money arising from taxes; or that part of the Sugars and Rum in the hands of the Continental Agent in Boston[4] Should be Sold and the Monies arising from the Sale be applied for fitting out the Bourbon and to prepare the 74 gun Ship for launching.

Beside the injury the 74 gun Ship will receive by remaining on the Stocks from the weather, She is, from her situation exposed to be destroyed by the enemy unless a gaurd is constantly kept up at considerable expence for her protection; Whereas if she can be so far compleated as to be launched, She may then if we Should not be in A Capacity to fit her for Sea be moved up the River to a place of Safety.

As the Board conceive the last will be the most eligible mode of Supply, they therefore beg leave to report, "that the Board of Admiralty be authorized to cause such part of the Sugars and Rum in the hands of the Continental agent at Boston to be disposed of as shall be necessary to compleat the 74 gun Ship now building at Portsmouth for launching and also for fitting out the Bourbon.["][5]

---

[1] The "enclosed papers" have not been identified.
[2] In 1780 John Langdon (1741–1819) of Portsmouth, N.H., was continental

agent in his home town. He would later be a member of the Constitutional Convention of 1787, a United States senator, and governor of his state. His letter, referred to in the text, was dated 2 February 1780, but has not been found (Marine Committee to Langdon, 17 March 1780, NA: PCC, Marine Committee Letter Book, 1776–80, fols. 268–69; Charles O. Paullin, ed., *Out-Letters of Board of Admiralty*, II, 166). The "74 gun ship," the "America," remained unfinished until 5 November 1782, when it was launched at Portsmouth and presented to King Louis XVI of France as a testimonial to "his generous exertions in behalf of the United States." The "America" replaced the "Magnifique," wrecked in Boston harbor earlier that year (*Journals of the Continental Congress*, XXIII, 543; Burnett, *Letters*, VI, 468, n. 2).

3 The "Bourbon" was finally launched at Middletown, Conn., on 31 July 1783. Shortly thereafter Congress sold the ship to a private purchaser (Gardner W. Allen, *A Naval History of the American Revolution*, II, 615).

4 Captain John Bradford, shipmaster, local officeholder, and prominent Boston patriot during the decade before the Revolution, was appointed by Congress as the continental agent in Boston on 23 April 1776 (Robert Francis Seybolt, ed., *The Town Officials of Colonial Boston, 1634–1775* [Cambridge, 1939], pp. 321–63, passim; *Journals of the Continental Congress*, IV, 301).

5 Congress took no action on this report, probably for the reasons mentioned in the Board of Admiralty to the Navy Board at Boston, 12 May 1780 (*q.v.*).

Virginia Board of Trade to Virginia Delegates in Congress

Letter not found.

EDITORIAL NOTE

1 April 1780. Under this date, on page 30 of a bound manuscript volume entitled "Board of Trade Minute Book, 27 November 1779–7 April 1780," in the Virginia State Library, is recorded: "Ordered that a Letter be written to the Hons. The Delegates from Virginia in Congress, requesting them to aid Mr. Moss."

John Moss, an agent of Virginia for equipping its continental line, expected to visit Philadelphia, under orders from the Board of Trade, to sell three hundred hogsheads of tobacco owned by the Commonwealth, because of "the most pressing Necessity for securing the deficient supplies for the Officers & Troops, now on the Southern Expedition" sent to compel the British to abandon their siege of Charleston. Since the editors have found no conclusive reference either to the letter or to Moss's mission, they are not certain that the dispatch was ever sent to JM and his fellow delegates. Although a letter dated 13 August 1781 indicates that Moss had once visited Baltimore or Philadelphia for a similar purpose, it is not clear that this trip was made in the spring of 1780. Moss (1750–1809) was from Fairfax County (William P. Palmer et al., eds., *Calendar of Virginia State Papers and Other Manuscripts* [11 vols.; Richmond, 1875–93], II, 326).

Board of Admiralty to Messrs.
Hewes, Smith, and Allen

FC (NA: PCC, Marine Committee Letter Book, fols. 275–76).

April 7th. 1780

GENTLEMEN[1]

We received by the last Post your letters of the 1st. January and the 6th of March last,[2] giving us an Account that on the 25th of December some villans with false keys had entered the ware House where the public Canvass was stored and carried away the whole except three Bolts—that they likewise[3] carried away a large Quantity of Salt from you; that you had found out some of the Offenders had hanged two and were in pursuit of a third. The hanging all that were concerned in perpetrating this Villany would indeed be a poor compensation to you or to us for any losses we have sustained. Perhaps by writing to Virginia to some proper persons you may discover with whom the goods were lodged there for Sale, and may be able to recover a part & perhaps the whole value of them. Doubtless there was a gang concerned in this business and part of it reside in Virginia.

As you are interested in this matter we trust that you will take the best measures for the detection of these Robbers and the recovery of the Goods or the value of them.

Considering the circumstances of this Roberry we cannot forbear taxing you with neglect, but we have still a greater reason to blame you when we consider that if you had complied with requisition made for the Canvass in pursuance of the Commercial Committees Order by William Bennett of Edenton, who writes to Francis Lewis Esquire then of the Commercial Committee, now of this Board in his Letter dated Edenton Decemr. 1779, "I applied to Messrs. Hewes Smith & Allen for the 37 pieces sail Duck, but they could give me no account of them till they had *overhawled their Books*" the Duck would have been safe.[4] That *overhawling of Books* could be necessary in Order to the delivery of the 37 Pieces of Duck we cannot conceive when by a return of the Continental Stores that have been received by Hewes, Smith & Allen, made by Hewes Smith & Allen dated Edenton Augt. 28th. 1778 and rendered in October 1779 it appears that they were in your possession. If the Duck had been delivered to Order which you ought to have complied with, it would not have been lost.

If you thought it was not our property when demanded you will not, we hope, think it our loss now it is stolen. We should be glad upon an explanation of this dark business to have reason to continue that confidence we once placed in your constant Attention to Public Charges.

We desire you will transmit to us by the first safe opportunity the balance of your Accounts with the Marine & Commercial Committees being $\left. \begin{array}{l} £\,2493.13.4 \\ 3953.\ 8.5 \end{array} \right\}$ £6447.1.9 No. Carrolina Currency agreeably to accounts furnished & settled by your Mr.[?] Hewes

I am Gentlemen Your Hble servant   By Order

J BROWN Secy

---

[1] Joseph Hewes (1730–1779), of Edenton, N.C., merchant-shipowner and signer of the Declaration of Independence, had been prominent in naval affairs when in Congress (1774–1777, 1779). He had left instructions in his will that the firms of Hewes and Smith and of Hewes, Smith, and Allen were to be dissolved upon his death. Robert Smith wrote George Washington on 3 March 1780 that Hewes, Smith, and Allen had been dissolved, but Hewes's name was still used by the other firm as late as 1785 (Edward W. Sikes and Samuel A. Ashe, eds., *Biographical History of North Carolina* [8 vols.; Greensboro, N.C., 1905–7], III, 172–80; Walter Clark, ed., *The State Records of North Carolina, 1777–1790* [16 vols.; Winston and Goldsboro, 1895–1905], XXII, 632; *North Carolina Historical Review*, XII [1935], 153). One of his partners, Robert Smith (d. 1787), was a brother of James Smith of Kirkcudbright, Scotland, a friend of John Paul Jones (Samuel Eliot Morison, *John Paul Jones: A Sailor's Biography* [Boston, 1959], p. 27). The third partner, Nathaniel Allen (d. 1805), a nephew of Hewes and executor of his estate, was a member of the North Carolina Convention of 1788 which rejected the United States Constitution (*North Carolina Historical and Genealogical Register*, I [1900], 517 n.). The partners had served as continental agents.

[2] Not found.

[3] Word is "likewisewise" in document.

[4] At this time William Bennett (d. 1801) was the commissioner to buy provisions for troops in the Edenton district; earlier he had been an army contractor (*State Records of North Carolina*, XIV, 12–13; XV, 200; XVI, 1019). Francis Lewis (1713–1803) had emigrated from Wales in 1735 to establish mercantile houses in New York and Philadelphia. He had served as a New York delegate to the Stamp Act Congress in 1765. As a member of the Continental Congress, 1774–1779, he signed the Declaration of Independence. In 1779 he became a commissioner of the Board of Admiralty. The letter from Bennett has not been found.

Report of Board of Admiralty

MS (NA: PCC, No. 37, fol. 221).

April 10th 1780

The Board of Admiralty beg leave to inform Congress that they are about to order the Mercury a Continental packet from Boston to this Port, and as that vessel is a very fast Sailer they are of opinion that it would be expedient to bring round in her some of Sugar belonging to the Public at that place, and request that they may be Authorized to order 20 hhds of it to be put on board of her.[1]

[1] Congress having sanctioned this request, the Board of Admiralty wrote John Bradford, continental agent in Boston, to dispatch the "Mercury" with sugar and as much rum and other liquors, taken from captured British ships, as she could carry. The packet reached Philadelphia safely in mid-June (*Journals of the Continental Congress*, XVI, 344; Charles O. Paullin, ed., *Out-Letters of Board of Admiralty*, II, 182–84, 211).

Board of Admiralty to John M. Nesbitt and John Nixon

FC (NA: PCC, Marine Committee Letter Book, fol. 278).

April 12th 1780

GENTLEMEN[1]

Congress having impowered and directed this Board to call upon the Several Agents for A settlement of their respective Accounts relative to the Continental Prizes you are therefore requested to furnish the Board with an Account of the disposition of all such Prizes under your Agency.[2]

I am Gentlemen Your Obedt Hble sert   By Order

JOHN BROWN Sec:

[1] Continental agents, Philadelphia. John Maxwell Nesbitt (*ca.* 1730–1802) was the senior member of a firm of merchants. John Nixon (1733–1808) served not only as a continental agent but also from 1776 to 1778 as a commissioner of the Navy Board, Middle Department.

[2] On 14 August 1780 the Board of Admiralty recommended to Congress that Nesbitt and Nixon be discharged as continental agents, since the Board "have not been able to induce them to exhibit their accounts" (*Journals of the Continental Congress*, XVII, 743–44; NA: PCC, No. 13, fol. 80).

Report of Board of Admiralty

MS (NA: PCC, No. 37, fol. 223).

[12 April 1780]

The Board of Admiralty beg leave to represent to Congress that the Continental ship Saratoga has been lately launched at this place, and may be speedily fitted for Sea, if the board had Money for that purpose. As the Saratoga in all probability will be a very fast Sailing Vessel, and considerable advantages may arise to the public from her being Speedily fitted out—the Board would therefore recommend.

That the balance of Money in their hands arising from the Sale of Wines Sold under their direction be applyed in fitting with despatch the Ship Saratoga.[1]

agreed

[1] The eighteen-gun sloop of war "Saratoga" was ordered to sea on 11 August under the command of Captain John Young. About seven months later, sailing north from the West Indies, she failed to reach her destination and her fate remains unknown (Charles O. Paullin, ed., *Out-Letters of Board of Admiralty*, II, 238–39, 245–46, 269–71; Gardner W. Allen, *A Naval History of the American Revolution*, II, 507, 556).

Virginia Delegates in Congress
to George Washington

RC (LC: Papers of George Washington). Docketed "Philada. 12th April 1780 from Cyrus Griffin & James Maddison Esqrs."

April 12th[, 1780][1]

We have the honor to enclose your excellency a letter from Governor Jefferson[2] and am with the highest respect

your most obedient & very humble Servant

C GRIFFIN[3]

JAMES MADISON JUN

[1] This note of referral was almost certainly written in 1780, not only because it was so docketed but also because that year was the only one during Jefferson's governorship of Virginia when Griffin and JM were together in Congress.

[2] Possibly the letter of 19 March from Jefferson to Washington (Boyd, *Papers of Jefferson*, III, 321).

[3] Cyrus Griffin (1748–1810), a delegate of Virginia in Congress, 1778–1780; a member of Congress' Court of Appeals in Cases of Capture, 1780–1787; president of Congress, 1788–1789; and judge of the United States District Court of Virginia, 1789–1810.

Board of Admiralty to John Langdon

FC (NA: PCC, Marine Committee Letter Book, fol. 279).

April 14th. 1780

SIR

We have been favoured with your letters of the 5th and 18th Ulto., wherein you inform us that unless you are supplied with Money either from the Navy Board or Admiralty, it will not be in your power to Ship the Masts &c for Martinico.[1] We are sorry to say that such is still the low state of the Treasury; that it will be impossible for us at this juncture to Obtain Money from thence, so that our sole relyance Must be on the Navy Board at Boston to supply you. In Order to Obtain some Money for the Military Chest Congress has been necessitated to risque a large quantity of their Sugar and Rum from Boston by water, induced thereto by knowing that those Articles will yield above 100 per Cent more at this place than at Boston, which proceeds from the imprudent management of sending nearly all Continental prizes into that Port,[2] to the emolument of some individuals but of great detriment to the Public and Army as by the distance of places the latter can reap no benefit from those Articles so essentially necessary for the Army.

I am Sir Your very hble servant   By Order

JOHN BROWN Sec:

[1] To refit the dismasted U.S. frigate "Confederacy" (JM to Page, 8 May 1780, n. 6). The ship appeared in the Delaware River about 28 April, having managed to limp home from Martinique without aid from the Board of Admiralty (Charles O. Paullin, ed., *Out-Letters of Board of Admiralty*, II, 188–89).

[2] See Report of Board of Admiralty, 10 April 1780, n. 1; Board of Admiralty to Navy Board, Boston, 12 May 1780, n. 3.

Board of Admiralty to James Nicholson

FC (NA: PCC, Marine Committee Letter Book, fol. 280).

April 17th 1780

SIR[1]

The Board were this day favoured with your letter of the 27th Ultimo[2] by which they find the frigate Trumbull is compleatly rigged, wooded, & Watered with 120 Men on board officers included, and that she only waited for some additional provision & Cannon which you have no doubt will be on board in three weeks.

As the Continental Ship Saratoga Captain John Young is now launched and fitting with the utmost expedition[3] the Board intend that Ship to Cruize in concert with the Trumbull, therefore you are hereby directed to take a Short Cruize in such latitudes as you think will be most likely to annoy the enemy,[4] and afterwards come into Delaware towards the latter end of the Month of June, in Order to join the Saratoga and any other of the Continental Ships which may be here at that time. On your arrival at the capes[5] send an express to advise the Board thereof and the State of your Ship, who (Should there be Occasion) will give Orders for compleating your complement of Men & Provision from hence. Any Prizes you may take you are to send into this port, if from your situation and other circumstance it may be deemed the most convenient.

The Board have reason to expect the Continental frigates Alliance & Confederacy soon on this Coast, therefore they hope to have a Squadron of respectable force, especially if the Deane & Bourbon can be added.[6]

I am Sir &c &c   By Order

JOHN BROWN Secy

[1] Captain James Nicholson (*ca.* 1736–1804) of Maryland commanded the frigate "Trumbull," then at New London, Conn.

[2] Not found.

[3] See Report of Board of Admiralty, 12 April 1780, n. 1.

[4] For the outcome of this cruise, see Board of Admiralty to Navy Board, Boston, 12 May 1780, n. 5.

[5] Entrance of Delaware Bay.

[6] The "Alliance" reached Boston from France in mid-August 1780 (Charles O. Paullin, ed., *Out-Letters of Board of Admiralty*, II, 260). For the "Confederacy," see Board of Admiralty to Langdon, 14 April 1780, n. 1, and to Harding, 2 May 1780, n. 1; for the "Deane," see Board of Admiralty to Navy Board, Boston, 12 May 1780, n. 6; and for the "Bourbon," see Report of Board of Admiralty, 29 March 1780, n. 3, and Board of Admiralty to Trumbull, 30 May 1780. The Board of Admiralty intended Captain Nicholson, as senior officer of the navy, to command this fleet. For the fate of the plan, see Board of Admiralty to Nicholson, 22 May 1780, n. 3.

Board of Admiralty to Seth Harding

FC (NA: PCC, Marine Committee Letter Book, fol. 281).

May 2d. 1780

S<small>IR</small>

The Board are favoured with your letter of the 28th Ultimo informing them of the arrival of the frigate Confederacy.

As the Masts & Spars wanted for the Confederacy can be furnished here, you are directed immediately to proceed up with the Ship to this place where the most speedy measures will be taken for fitting her out again with all expedition.[1]

I am Sir Your very Hble servant   By Order

J<small>OHN</small> B<small>ROWN</small> secy

[1] Shortage of money delayed the refitting and resupplying of the "Confederacy" until the winter of 1781. Then, under the command of Captain Seth Harding (1734–1814), it cruised in West Indian waters in concert with the U.S. frigates "Deane" and "Saratoga." On 15 April 1781, while returning to the United States, the "Confederacy" was captured by two British men-of-war. After he was freed, Harding served on the "Alliance" until the end of the war (Gardner W. Allen, *A Naval History of the American Revolution*, II, 556; James L. Howard, *Seth Harding, Mariner: A Naval Picture of the Revolution* [New Haven, 1930], pp. 157–61).

Seal for the Admiralty of the United States

Printed text (*Journals of the Continental Congress*, XVI, 412).

[4 May 1780]

The Board of Admiralty reported the device of a seal for the Admiralty of the United States: the arms, thirteen bars mutually supporting each other, alternate red and white, in a blue field, and surmounting an anchor proper. The crest a ship under sail. The motto S<small>USTENTANS</small> E<small>T</small> S<small>USTENTATUS</small>. The legend U. S. A. Sigil. Naval.

Ordered, That the same be engraved, and used as the seal of the Board of Admiralty of the United States of America.[1]

[1] This seal remained unaltered until 1798. The motto is translated, "Upholding and Upheld."

William Ellery and JM to the Committee of Congress at Washington's Headquarters

Printed text (John Sanderson, ed., *Biography of the Signers to the Declaration of Independence* [2d ed.; 5 vols.; Philadelphia, 1828], I, 388–89). Nothing is said there of its source except that it had "fallen into our hands." References to the existence of the letter are made in Brant, *Madison*, I, 90; Burnett, *Letters*, V, 178; and *Pennsylvania Magazine of History and Biography*, XII (1888), 501.

In Congress, *May 5th*, 1780.

Ye poor devils![1] shivering on the bleak hills of Morris, how we pity you!—Ho! soldier with your canteen; view that poor committee man—see him trembling. Hark!—hear his teeth chatter—unable to support himself under the chilling blasts, which, unclothed and unfed, you have endured with invincible perseverance and fortitude:—see him expiring!—he was nursed under a fervid sun, and exposes himself to your nipping gales to bring you some relief. For the sake of G—d, one drop of whiskey for poor Matthews!

As for ye, sons of the North, ye can get along well enough, especially if ye can find, now and then, a cup of beer and a little New England.

As for our illustrious general, if it were in our choice, for him the rich Madeira should flow in copious streams;—and as for the gallant officers, and faithful brave soldiers under his command, if we had the powers of conversion, we would turn water into wine, the camp should overflow with that exhilarating and invigorating liquor.

The last bottle had been broached.—We addressed congress, and used every argument in our power to induce them to order a couple of pipes to be sent to head-quarters, and told them that the general's wine was entirely exhausted. They doubted. We informed them that we had received a letter from the committee giving us that information. They still doubted, and desired that the letter might be produced. We delivered it with the utmost reluctance. Upon reading it, congress immediately concluded that any persons who would dare to charge us with niggardliness, and threaten to run congress "d—ly" in debt, must be d—ly drunk, and utterly refused to send any wine to head-quarters until you should have returned. We wish you had been more guarded in your expressions.—However, we shall for once stretch our power, and send forward two pipes immediately.—You will be pleased

17

to consider soberly the business you have undertaken, and the expectations of congress, and not drink more than three glasses of wine at dinner, and six at supper; and whenever you write to us, do it before breakfast.

We return your "word to the wise," and are your's as you conduct,

W. ELLERY,

Js. MADISON, JR.[2]

[1] On 13 April 1780 Congress elected Philip Schuyler (N.Y.), John Mathews (S.C.), and Nathaniel Peabody (N.H.) as a committee to consult with Washington and his principal officers in devising ways to improve and enforce methods of recruiting, paying, and supplying the army (*Journals of the Continental Congress*, XVI, 362).

[2] Although both JM and William Ellery (1727–1820) signed this letter, it is probable that the latter was its principal author. It is unlikely that anyone who had been in Congress less than two months and was not a close friend of the members of the Committee at Headquarters would write to them in this jocular, informal way. JM's natural reserve increases the probability that he did not draft the letter. Ellery, on the other hand, was a veteran of four years' service in the Congress and doubtless was well acquainted with the committee members.

The content of the letter reflects the circumstances existing in the spring of 1780. Ellery and JM, the two congressional members of the Board of Admiralty, were addressing the committee on a subject of keen interest to the Board and important personages at army headquarters—the disposal of wine and other liquors from captured vessels. On 2 May 1780 Congress adopted the Board of Admiralty's draft of a code of instructions for observance by each master of a privateer. The fifth of these instructions warned him against "selling, spoiling, wasting or diminishing the same [a captured vessel and its cargo], or breaking the bulk thereof, nor suffering any such thing to be done" (*Journals of the Continental Congress*, XVI, 407–8).

The out-letters of the Board frequently urged the continental agents at the port cities either to sell their prize cargoes for the public interest or to forward them to Philadelphia for disposal by the Board (Charles O. Paullin, ed., *Out-Letters of Board of Admiralty*, II, 182–83, 198). These agents, the Board of Admiralty, and members of Congress, however, were adept at requisitioning choice wine for private purposes, often with the honorable intention of rewarding those who labored in the patriot cause. Washington was the recipient of such a favor on 13 May 1780, when he acknowledged to the Board of Admiralty that he had just received two pipes of Madeira and had been favored with two others during the previous winter (Fitzpatrick, *Writings of Washington*, XVIII, 352).

Although the Ellery-JM letter suggests that a communication from the committee to the Board of Admiralty about the scarcity of liquor at headquarters had been laid before Congress, no message of this kind, or mention of such a message, has been found in the Papers of the Continental Congress or in its printed journal. "New England," in the letter's second paragraph, was often used as a synonym of rum.

To Thomas Jefferson

RC (LC: Madison Papers). The manuscript is much faded and barely legible. In his old age JM evidently selected this letter for inclusion in the first printed edition of his papers. With this purpose in mind he added at the beginning of the first paragraph and at the close of the long final one a bracket and quotation mark. Apparently at eight places in the letter he crossed out a word or re-inked a word or part of a word which had become indistinct. Insofar as can be determined, these revisions did not alter the meaning of the letter as originally written.

PHILADA. May 6th. 1780

DEAR SIR

I am sorry I can give you no other account of our public situation than that it continues equally perplexed & alarming as when I lately gave you a sketch of it.[1] Our army has as yet been kept from starving, and public measures from a total stagnation, by draughts on the States for the unpaid requisitions. The great amount of these you may judge of, from the share that has fallen to Virginia. The discharge of debts due from the purchasing departments has absorbed a great proportion of them, and very large demands still remain. As soon as the draughts amount to the whole of the monthly requisitions up to the end of March, they must cease according to the new scheme of finance.[2] We must then depend wholly on the emissions to be made in pursuance of that scheme, which can only be applied, as the old emissions are collected & destroyed. Should this not be done as fast as the current expenditures require, or should the new emissions fall into a course of depreciation, both of which may but too justly be feared, a most melancholy crisis must take place. A punctual compliance on the part of the States with the specific supplies will indeed render much less money necessary than would otherwise be wanted, but experience by no means affords satisfactory encouragement that due and unanimous exertions will be made for that purpose not to mention that our distress is so pressing that it is uncertain whether any exertions of that kind can give relief in time. It occurs besides, that as the ability of the people to comply with the pecuniary requisitions is derived from the sale of their commodities, a requisition of the latter must make the former proportionally more difficult and defective: Congress have the satisfaction however to be informed that the legislature of Connecticut have taken the most vigorous steps for supplying their quota both of money & commodities; and that a body of their principal merchants have associated for supporting the credit of the new paper, for which purpose they have in a public address pledged their faith to the Assembly to sell their merchandise on the same terms for it as if they were to be paid in specie.[3] A Similar vigor throughout the Union may perhaps produce effects as far exceeding our present hopes as they have heretofore fallen short of our wishes.

It is to be observed that the situation of Congress has undergone a total change from what it originally was. Whilst they exercised the indefinite power of emitting money on the credit of their constituents they had the whole wealth & resourses of the continent within their command, and could go on with their affairs independently and as they pleased. Since the resolution passed for shutting the press,[4] this power has been entirely given up and they are now as dependent on the States as the King of England is on the parliament. They can neither enlist pay nor feed a single soldier, nor execute any other pu[r]pose but as the means are first put into their hands. Unless the legislatures are sufficiently attentive to this change of circumstances and act in conformity to it, every thing must necessarily go wrong or rather must come to a total stop. All that Congress can do in future will be to administer public affairs with prudence vigor and oeconomy. In order to do which they have sent a Committee to Head Quarters with ample powers in concert with the Commander in chief and the Heads of the departments to reform the various abuses which prevail and to make such arrangements, as will best guard against a relapse into them.[5]

The papers inclosed herewith contain all the news we have here.[6]

With great regard, I am Dr Sir Yr Obt Servt

JAMES MADISON JNR

His Excelly Thomas Jefferson Esqr.

[1] Probably JM's letter of 27–28 March 1780.

[2] At the bottom of the first page of the letter the words, "the 40 for 1 scheme," are added in JM's hand. Thereby he apparently intended to clarify this sentence for editing.

[3] Although it was not mentioned in the *Journals of the Continental Congress* until 11 May 1780, Congress was informed of Connecticut's action a week earlier (James Duane to George Washington, 4 May 1780, in Burnett, *Letters*, V, 126). Duane added that Massachusetts had also "cheerfully adopted the new plan of Finance." See Jefferson to JM, 26 July 1780, n. 2.

[4] On 18 March 1780 (*Journals of the Continental Congress*, XVI, 262–67).

[5] The "Committee to Head Quarters" received its instructions from Congress on 12 April and, after beginning its investigations in Philadelphia, left for Morristown, N.J., thirteen days later (*ibid.*, XVI, 354–57; Burnett, *Letters*, V, 123, n. 2).

[6] The inclosures, not found, were probably recent issues of Philadelphia newspapers.

To John Page[?]

RC (University of Chicago Library). Docketed: "James Madison, Philadelph[ia,] May 8th 1780" in a hand which resembles that of John Page.

PHILADELPHIA May 8th. 1780

DEAR SIR

By yesterday's post I had the pleasure of receiving your favor of the 27th. Ulto.[1] The price of Dunlap's paper[2] I understand will be 204 Drs. per annum besides the gratification to the Post which will be not much less. But if there were less objection against the expence, the uncertainty of the conveyance is such that I scarcely think it would be worth your while to become a subscriber. Should that still be your wish however your instructions shall be immediately executed.

Our public affairs still continue in a very confused and critical state owing to the distress of public credit. Nor can they be well put into a better one till the new arrangement of finance and the requisition of specific supplies are complied with by the States. It appears that this is likely to be done with great decision and energy in the Eastern States. And if Virginia fulfils the expectation[3] and hopes of the public, I flatter myself that however objectionable past[?] measures may be thought we shall in future stand on firmer ground than we have ever done. The terms on which the new money is to be emitted will certainly give it a more substantial and intrinsic value than the old ever had, and the experienced folly of tampering with public credit, will it is to be hoped prevent any mischief to it from that source. Our great danger at present arises from the dilatory proceedings of the States and the real difficulty of drawing forth those resources which the new System is to operate upon. The Treasury and the Army both require immediate relief; and every thing must be in a state of stagnation, to say the lea[s]t, till the contributions of Money & Stores arrive. It is not to be expected that Congress can do any thing further of themselves. The only real power they ever had of supporting the war was that of emitting money on the faith of their Constituents. Their vote for stopping the press was a voluntary relinquishment of that.[4] They are now totally dependent on the supplies from the States. They can not execute a single measure but as the means are first put into their hands. It is absolutely necessary that the States should attend to this change of circumstances and regulate their conduct accordingly. Any further reliance on the separate[5] resources of Congress will infallibly end in disappointment & ruin.

A Vessel from the West Indies brings information that Mr Gerard & Mr Jay had arrived at Cales [Cadiz?] in 22 days from their leaving Martinique. The English fleet at St. Lucia consists of 22 Ships of the line and a few frigates. They had collected their force at that place in order to make an attempt on Grenada & St. Vincents. But the french reinforcement has stopped that enterprize. The Marquis de Bouillé has also strengthened those places with 800 troops sent to one and 600 to the other.[6]

The Enemy at N. York have received late despatches from Europe. But a profound silence is as yet observe[d] with regard to the news in them. An Opinion prevails there that Paul Jones is on the Coast with a small squadron They say in their papers that the Galatea has been chased by it and that a 74 & some other ships are going out in search of it.[7] The Marquis de la Fayette is arrived at Boston and probably will be here in a few days. His return was not expected and is considered as an omen not unfavorable.[8]

I suppose you must have heard of the death of your friend Don Juan de Miralles. We were this morning on the invitation of [the] Minister of France, at the celebration of the service for the repose of his Soul. He died at Head Quarters whither he attended the Minister on a visit to the Genl & the Army. Every mark of sincere regret is visible in all those who were acquainted with him. The lying genius of Rivington has converted his death into that of the Chevalr. de la Luzerne who he says was obliged to fly to the Army for protection against the vengeance of the people.[9] With very sincere esteem & regard I am Dr Sir [Yr.] Obt. & humble Servt

JAMES MADISON JNR.[10]

[1] Not found. A letter from John Page to JM, dated 27 April 1780, is mentioned in a list of correspondence probably compiled by Peter Force and now in the Madison Miscellany collection of the Library of Congress. The present editors have not discovered any other communication to JM on that date. For this reason, as well as for that given in the headnote, they believe that JM's addressee was John Page of Rosewell, Gloucester County, Va. The two men had served together at Williamsburg—Page as lieutenant governor and both men as members of the council of the state of Virginia. When Don Juan de Miralles, mentioned in the final paragraph of this letter, visited Williamsburg in the spring of 1778, he met Governor Patrick Henry and other state officials, probably including Page (*Virginia Gazette* [Williamsburg, Purdie], 29 May 1778).

[2] *The Pennsylvania Packet or the General Advertiser*, published in Philadelphia by John Dunlap, had changed from a triweekly to a semiweekly newspaper on 8 April 1780 (Clarence S. Brigham, *History and Bibliography of American Newspapers*,

1690–1820 [2 vols.; Worcester, Mass., 1947], II, 942). "Dunlap's" was apparently JM's favorite news sheet.

³ Immediately following this word, JM crossed out a line of script so heavily that it cannot now be read.

⁴ Here JM refers to Congress' decision of 18 March 1780 to stop printing more paper money (*Journals of the Continental Congress*, XVI, 264).

⁵ This word is written above a deleted "independent."

⁶ Conrad Alexandre Gérard (1729–1790), lately French minister to the United States, and John Jay, appointed U.S. minister to Spain on 27 September 1779, took passage for France on the U.S. frigate "Confederacy" about one month later. Dismasted and left rudderless by a gale on 7 November, the ship limped into the port of St. Pierre, Martinique, on 18 December. From there Gérard and Jay were taken to Spain in a French frigate, arriving at Cadiz on 22 January 1780 (Gardner W. Allen, *A Naval History of the American Revolution*, II, 405–7; James L. Howard, *Seth Harding, Mariner*, pp. 105–18). François Claude Amour, Marquis de Bouillé (1739–1800), was the governor general of the French West Indies. A letter from him to the president of Congress, and a further dispatch from Martinique, were laid before Congress on 1 and 8 May, respectively (*Journals of the Continental Congress*, XVI, 401; XVII, 415).

⁷ The thirty-two-gun frigate "Alliance," in which Congress expected Captain John Paul Jones to bring military supplies from France, arrived at Nantucket, Mass., 16 August 1780 under the nominal command of First Lieutenant James Degge (Charles O. Paullin, ed., *Out-Letters of Board of Admiralty*, II, 260). Jones finally arrived back in the United States from France on 18 February 1781, and then as captain of "Ariel," a twenty-gun sloop lent to America by France (*Journals of the Continental Congress*, XIX, 175; Samuel E. Morison, *John Paul Jones*, p. 309). The twenty-eight-gun frigate "Galatea" was a unit of the British fleet centered at New York (Fitzpatrick, *Writings of Washington*, XVIII, 393–94).

⁸ Lafayette, returning to the patriot army from France, reached Boston on 27 April, visited Washington at his Morristown, N.J., headquarters from 10 to 14 May, and arrived in Philadelphia on 15 May (Louis Gottschalk, *Lafayette and the Close of the American Revolution* [Chicago, 1942], pp. 77–83).

⁹ Miralles (b. *ca.* 1717), Spain's unofficial agent in the United States, died at Morristown, 28 April, while visiting Washington in company with Anne César, Chevalier de La Luzerne (1741–1791), French minister to the United States from 1779 to 1784. JM and La Luzerne were friends. JM's attendance at the requiem mass in the Catholic chapel in Philadelphia was probably a new experience for him, as it was for other members of Congress (Burnett, *Letters*, V, 131). Tory editors like James Rivington of the *Royal Gazette* (New York) tried to use Miralles' and La Luzerne's Catholicism, and the attendance by Continental Congress delegates at the mass, to injure the patriot cause by stirring up the anti-Catholic prejudices of many Americans. See also *Virginia Gazette* (Richmond, Dixon and Nicolson), 4 October 1780.

¹⁰ The Peter Force list, mentioned at the beginning of n. 1, above, refers to a four-page letter from John Page to JM, dated 30 September 1780. The contents of this document and its location are unknown.

Motion on Letter from J. M. P. Le Gras

MS (NA: PCC, No. 19, III, 537). This motion of the Virginia delegates is in the hand of Joseph Jones. A copy of the motion (now in the Henry E. Huntington Library) written by Charles Thomson, together with the letter of Le Gras and its inclosures, was forwarded by Samuel Huntington on 11 May 1780 to Governor Jefferson (Boyd, *Papers of Jefferson*, III, 373).

[9 May 1780]

The Delegates of Virginia[1] to whom were referred the Letter and papers inclosed of P. Legras[2] Report that the same are proper for the consideration of the general Assembly of Virginia and in their opinion ought to be transmitted to the Executive of that State.[3]

[1] JM, Joseph Jones, Cyrus Griffin, and James Henry.

[2] Not found but dated 22 March 1780. Congress had referred them to the Virginia delegates on 14 April 1780 (*Journals of the Continental Congress*, XVI, 362). Lieutenant Colonel Jean Marie Philippe Le Gras or Legrace (*ca.* 1740–*ca.* 1788), a merchant of Vincennes serving under a commission from Colonel George Rogers Clark, had been acting for at least six months prior to the date of this motion as one of the principal purchasers in the Illinois country of military supplies for Clark and his troops. The mercantile firms of New Orleans appear to have been his main source of supply (William Hayden English, *Conquest of the Country Northwest of the River Ohio, 1778–1783: and Life of Gen. George Rogers Clark* [2 vols.; Indianapolis and Kansas City, 1896], I, 356; Boyd, *Papers of Jefferson*, III, 270–71, 274, 316, 328–29).

[3] Congress adopted this motion on 9 May 1780 (*Journals of the Continental Congress*, XVII, 416–17). On 5 June, after Jefferson submitted a copy of the motion, together with the Le Gras letter and its inclosures, to the Virginia House of Delegates, it referred them to a committee. The report of this committee on 20 June probably reflects the matter which had led Le Gras to appeal to Congress. Judging from the report, the military and civil officials of Virginia in the Illinois country had been paying for goods and services in continental currency which had already been called in by Congress. Following instructions, these officials then sequestered the obsolete emissions but gave the holders no currency in exchange. To remedy this injustice, the House of Delegates adopted the recommendation of its committee by resolving that, "the called in emissions of continental money, sealed up by the county or district commandants in Illinois, and certified, ought to be exchanged for other emissions." The Senate agreed to this resolution on 24 June (*Journal of the House of Delegates*, May 1780, pp. 35, 55–56, 62).

Board of Admiralty to Nathaniel Shaw, Jr.

FC (NA: PCC, Marine Committee Letter Book, fol. 283).

May 9th 1780

SIR[1]

The Board have this day received your letter of the 26th ultimo announcing the arrival of a Polacca laden with Wine & fruits, Prize to the Deane frigate Captain Nicholson.[2]

You are directed to cause the Cargo to be divided and the Continental Moiety reserved until the farther orders of this Board;[3] but should the fruit from its present state be liable to perish soon, we would in that case have the fruit sold, unless you could procure a small fast sailing Vessel to bring it round to this port on freight. As Anchors, Cables and other Cordage are much wanted for the Navy, if any such can be spared from the Polacca we would advise the selling them seperate from the vessel, and purchased for the Navy. If it be practicable, we wish you to send to General Washington about a dozen Boxes Lemons which we shall inform him of by Post. You will also inform the Board by the first opportunity with an exact Invoice of the Polacca's Cargo & condition of the Vessel. We are sir Your Hble serts.

[1] Nathaniel Shaw, Jr. (1735–1782), was continental agent at New London, Conn. For an amendment of the orders in this letter, see Board of Admiralty to Shaw, 22 May 1780.

[2] Samuel Nicholson (1743–1811) of Maryland, the commander of the U.S. frigate "Deane," was a brother of Captain James Nicholson. A polacca or polacre usually had two or three masts, square-rigged.

[3] If a U.S. naval ship captured an enemy privateer or man-of-war, its captain and crew owned the prize completely. On the other hand, if the prize was a transport, storeship, or, as in this instance, a merchantman, one-half of the vessel and cargo, or of the money realized from their sale, belonged to the United States. Because the United States was entitled to no return from captures made by privateers, the Continental Congress was seriously handicapped in recruiting officers and crew to man the ships of its navy (*Journals of the Continental Congress*, VI, 913).

Board of Admiralty to John Bradford

FC (NA: PCC, Marine Committee Letter Book, fols. 284–85).

May 12th 1780

SIR

The foregoing is a Copy of our last[1] since which we have not been favoured with any of yours. Within these few days your Packet relative to the Lord Sandwich packet Boat was handed to us by Lieutenant Brown which was immediately lodged with the Secretary of Congress and Council retained in the Cause when determined by the Court of Appeals shall advise you.[2] As the Navy Board is directed to fit out the Dean frigate to proceed to this Bay with the utmost expedition, you are directed to put on board of her as much of the Humes Cargo of prize Rum as she can conveniently take in, reserving 60 hhds which you are directed to sell, and deliver the Money arising therefrom to the Commissioners of the Navy Board at Boston.[3] The enclosed are Copies of Major Lees application for a pipe of Maderia Wine which he aledges was by Mr. Henley engaged for with you.[4] We have answered that as you were not Authorized to sell any of the Continental Wines, and we had no information from you respecting this Matter we did not think proper to deliver a pipe of those in our possession, nor to decide respecting any engagement you may have made.

We are Sir Your Hble servts.

[1] Probably the letter of 14 April from the Board of Admiralty to Bradford, continental agent at Boston, requesting information about the disposal of prize cargoes (Charles O. Paullin, ed., *Out-Letters of Board of Admiralty*, II, 184).

[2] The frigates "Deane" (Captain Samuel Nicholson) and "Boston" (Captain Samuel Tucker) captured the sixteen-gun packet "Lord Sandwich" in the late summer of 1779 (Gardner W. Allen, *A Naval History of the American Revolution*, II, 402). In 1780 the Continental Congress created the Court of Appeals in Cases of Capture. The letter was probably delivered by Lieutenant Philip Brown of Massachusetts, who served as first lieutenant of the sloop "Providence" and then was given command of the captured brig "Diligent." He commanded this ship in the Penobscot expedition of 1779, under Commodore Dudley Saltonstall (information from Rear Admiral E. M. Eller, Director of Naval History, Department of the Navy). There was also a Lieutenant John Brown, who was commissioned on "Private Service at Boston" on 12 October 1776 (NA: PCC, No. 37, fol. 473).

[3] See Board of Admiralty to Navy Board, Boston, 12 May 1780, n. 3.

[4] These men were probably Major Henry ("Light-Horse Harry") Lee (1756–1818) of the Continental Dragoons and David Henley (1748–1823) of the Boston mercantile firm of Otis and Henley (*Journals of the Continental Congress*, XVII, 569; Charles O. Paullin, ed., *Out-Letters of Board of Admiralty*, II, 193, 299; Burnett, *Letters*, V, 96 n.).

Board of Admiralty to Commissioners of the Navy Board at Boston

FC (NA: PCC, Marine Committee Letter Book, fol. 285).

May 12th 1780

GENTLEMEN[1]

We are favoured with your letter of the 18th. ultimo acknowledging the receipt of ours dated the 7th & 31 March[.] we have since wrote you of the 7th & 11th ultimo which we presume were not then received. We observe you intend to send the Box with types and papers to the Treasury Board, and that your next will inform us with the result of your inquiry relative to the conduct of the privateer Brig Revenges Crew.[2] you say you are pleased with the prospect of being supplied with money thro Captain Bradfords hands by the Sale of Rum and Sugar; In consequence we suppose of a plan reported by us to Congress for that purpose which we are sorry to say is rejected, the Commissary Genl. of Purchases being previously empowered to dispose of All the Sugar & Rum in Captain Bradfords hands in order to furnish a fund for purchasing provisions for the Army—and having given Mr Bradford directions not to sell any of the Rum imported in Hume, we presume that the Rum and Sugar supplied Colonel Langdon, was part of the 20 & 30 hhds deliver'd your Board by an Order to Mr Bradford the 20th November last.[3]

In our letter of the 11th ultimo we requested the Mercury Packet should be immediately fitted to receive Sugar and Rum which Captain Bradford is directed to put on board for this place, least that letter should miscarry it is now repeated.[4] Our letter of the 18th Ultimo & 2d instant informed you that we had Ordered Captain James Nicholson with the Trumbull on a short Cruize and to return to this Bay by the latter end of June;[5] and as the Deane is Arrived at Boston we would have her fitted out with the utmost expedition so as to be here also by the latter end of June, we presume you can furnish the Deane with wet provision sufficient for a four Months Cruize—the Bread kind can be furnished here.[6] We shall direct Captain Bradford to sell 60 hhds of the Prize ship Humes Rum and deliver the Money into your hands. We shall also direct him to put on board the Deane as much of the remainder of said Rum as she can conveniently carry. If the Copper Bottomed Snow[7] prize to the Deane be in your opinion fit for a Cruizer you are directed to purchase her for the Public service. The Board disaprove the Idea of Concerting their frigates with Privateers the public having already suffered thereby.[8] We are pleased to find that your general Accounts will be forwarded in a few days. As we are very anxious to have all our Accounts adjusted.

We are Gentn Your hble servts

P: S: the Confederacy having lost some of her Anchors & Cables[9] the following are wanted for her, which if they can be procured you are directed to ship on board the Deane for this place if they cannot be had with you or any part of them please to Advise by Post.

[1] The members of the Navy Board of the Eastern Department were James Warren of Plymouth, Mass., William Vernon of Providence, R.I., and John Deshon of New London, Conn. (Charles O. Paullin, ed., *Out-Letters of Board of Admiralty*, I, xxvii).

[2] The senior British officer at Halifax charged Captain Alexander Murray, commanding the eighteen-gun privateer "Revenge," with unlawfully capturing a schooner, not subject to seizure (Board of Admiralty to the Navy Board of the Eastern Department, 31 March 1780, *ibid.*, II, 175). In this same letter, the Board of Admiralty inquired about "a Box of types, Paper and other Materials for Counterfeiting the Currency," captured by the "Deane" (Captain Samuel Nicholson) and turned over to the Navy Board at Boston.

[3] The British merchantman "Hume," bound from Jamaica to New York with a cargo mainly of rum, was captured by the "Deane" south of Sandy Hook. Instead of taking the prize into the Delaware River, as the navy regulations prescribed, Captain Samuel Nicholson had his prize crew sail the "Hume" to Boston (*ibid.*, II, 182–83).

[4] *Ibid.*, II, 181.

[5] *Ibid.*, II, 187–88, 189–90. On 1 June, a few days after leaving New London, the "Trumbull" was so badly damaged in a hard-fought, drawn battle with the British privateer "Watt" that it with difficulty reached Boston harbor on 14 June. Refitting held the frigate in port there until August (*ibid.*, II, 216–17; Gardner W. Allen, *A Naval History of the American Revolution*, II, 499–504, 508).

[6] When the "Deane" finally went to sea in September, it cruised off the South Carolina coast with little success insofar as taking prizes was concerned (*ibid.*, II, 510).

[7] A "snow" was a square-rigged vessel somewhat resembling a brig.

[8] Acrimonious disputes over the allocation of prize money frequently occurred when enemy vessels were captured by United States naval ships and privateers working in concert (Board of Admiralty to Shaw, 9 May 1780, n. 3).

[9] See JM to Page [?], 8 May 1780, n. 6.

From David Jameson

RC (LC: Rives Collection of Madison Papers).

RICHMOND May 21. 1780

DR SIR[1]

I had the pleasure to receive two letters from you the 15th, one dated the 2d by Post & the other the 9th by the return messenger I am sorry to find one of my letters has not got to your hands[2]—in it I told you I applied to Mr Blair and the Attorney and offered to pay for the Books you had from Dunmores Estate Mr Blair referred to the Attorney and the latter said he did not know how to act—he concluded however with saying that he would pay for the Books and let you or me know the amount when he had done so.[3] I think I sent the Letter by Cap Harrison, if you set out for Phila. before his return, it may now be in Orange.[4] The Maryland & Delawar[e] troops arrived at Petersburg the 17th. every effort has been made and is making for their March & accomodation on the Route[.] yesterday the Assembly passed a resolution impowering the Executive to impress Waggons Teems &c if needful on the occasion Also one of a more extraordinary import— to impress Horses Saddles &c. to mount the Men[.] this last I think it will be impossible to execute in time to answer the end. it will distress the people from whom the Horses are taken very much; and when collected I doubt if it will be possible to find forage for them in so little time as it would take to March the men on foot, however the attempt will be made, at least as much will be put in motion as the Quarter Master thinks can be effected[.] every person is anxious to give every possible aid to So. Carolina. The Assembly have voted 2500 Militia to be sent on. We have lent to North Carolina 2000 Arms toward equipg. their Militia to be sent to So. Carolina. Col Porterfield with about 500 of our State Regulars will I expect get to Chas. Town (or to the place of Rendezvous on this side) by the last of the Month.[5] I am sorry to inform you that yesterday was the first meeting of the Senate for the Session, they could not before get a sufficient number of members*

The Members of our board are much confined. we have but four; which makes the attendance fatiguing. in a few days we are to have three vacancies filled up[.] the persons are not yet proposed in Assembly. those talked of are Mr Ambler, G Webb, R. Adams, T. Randolph, B Stark & some others I do not recollect[6] There is a Bill carried in, to put down the boards of War & Trade—it is proposed to have a Military Commissioner to act in the first & an Agent in the other.[7]

Mr. Bee[8] is now here and sets out to day for Phila. he has been some time from Chas. Town but from his Accot. of their strength &ca I have hope that pla[ce] will not fall. Much—perhaps all, depends on the ability of our forces (collecting on this side Cooper River) to keep the communication open

* it was the 8th[9] of the month before the Delegates had Members enough for a House

Richmond must one day or other be a great Town and were we in Peace I should think it a proper place for the Seat of Government. at present I do not think it so I believe I shall never be reconciled to it as a desirable place of residence. half the mornings since I have been here the Town has been covered with Fog. if so at this Season, what may we not dread in August? and who not used to it, can stand the thin putrid state of the Air? I have been long used to the Salt Air and think I cannot enjoy health without it I think with you no Man has a right to withdraw himself altogether from the service of his Country at this critical time, but you will allow he may make room for a better Man to fill his place. Your letter mi[gh]t raise an idea too flattering on this subject A sacrifice ought to be made, but of time, (a risk) of health, and of fortune too, is too much. three days allowance will not pay more than one days expence as we now stand And to give salaries to all equal to the depreciation would exaust a Treasury. I am very glad when I hear of a prize taken by our Conl. Vessels[.] I think we ought to see some of them but all our share has been as you know, to see and feed some of the prisoners[10] I am with real respect and esteem Dr Sir Yr mo. Obedt Serv

DAVID JAMESON

[1] David Jameson's friendship with JM probably dated from their service together on the Council of State.

[2] Neither the two letters from JM to Jameson nor the earlier one from Jameson to JM have been found.

[3] The "Attorney" was Edmund Randolph (1753–1813), the attorney general of Virginia, 1776–1786. His later service as governor, member of the Federal Constitutional Convention, Attorney General of the United States, and Secretary of State is well known. John Blair and Randolph were two of the five commissioners named on 15 June 1776 by the Virginia Convention "to sell at publick auction [on twelve months' credit] the Slaves and personal Estate of Lord *Dunmore*" located in or near Williamsburg. The commissioners announced that the auction would be on 25 June 1776 (Peter Force, ed., *American Archives*, 4th ser. [6 vols.; Washington, D.C., 1837–46], VI, 1573; *Virginia Gazette* [Williamsburg, Purdie], 21 June 1776). In presenting his claims to the British government, Dunmore declared that he had at the governor's palace in Williamsburg "a valuable Library consisting of upwards of 1500 volumes" ("American Loyalists Transcripts, 1783–1790," LVIII, 202, in New York Public Library). What volumes JM purchased is not known.

[4] Probably Benjamin Harrison, Jr. (1755–1799), Richmond merchant, business associate of Robert Morris, and brother of William Henry Harrison. During the Revolution he was deputy paymaster general of Virginia for continental troops.

[5] This military activity, including the dispatch of about fourteen hundred Delaware and Maryland troops under Major General Johann Kalb, had as its immediate aim the relief of General Benjamin Lincoln's troops, besieged by the British in Charleston, S.C. (Christopher L. Ward, *The Delaware Continentals, 1776–1783* [Wilmington, Del., 1941], pp. 326–27; *Journal of the House of Delegates,*

May 1780, pp. 10, 11, 16, 17, 20; Hening, *Statutes,* X, 221-26). Colonel Charles Porterfield (1750-1781), quartermaster general of the Virginia state line, died 10 January 1781 of wounds received at the Battle of Camden, S.C., 16 August 1780 (Boyd,
Papers of Jefferson, IV, 497). Although Charleston fell to the British nine days before Jameson wrote this letter, word of the disaster did not reach Richmond until
5 June (*ibid.*, III, 403 n.).

[6] On 24 May 1780, Andrew Lewis (1720-1781), George Webb (1729-*ca.* 1786),
and Jacquelin Ambler (1742-1798) were chosen by the Assembly as members of the
Council of State. Richard Adams (1726-1800), Thomas Mann Randolph (1741-
1793), and Bolling Stark had also been given consideration (*Journal of the House
of Delegates*, May 1780, p. 21).

[7] This bill, introduced on 12 May, was passed on 8 July 1780 (*ibid.*, pp. 8, 79;
Hening, *Statutes,* X, 291-92).

[8] Thomas Bee (1725-1812) was on his way to Philadelphia to begin two years of
service in Congress as a delegate from South Carolina. Arriving at his destination
about 6 June, he may have had with him Jameson's letter to JM (*Journals of the
Continental Congress,* XVII, 490).

[9] In fact it was the 9th (*Journal of the House of Delegates,* May 1780, p. 4).

[10] This sentence and the five preceding sentences probably disclose at least some
of the matters mentioned to Jameson by JM in his now missing letters of 2 and 9
May (above, n. 2).

Board of Admiralty to James Nicholson

FC (NA: PCC, Marine Committee Letter Book, fol. 288).

May 22d 1780

SIR

The Board are favoured with your letter of the 3d instant[1] acknowledging the receipt of theirs of the 17th ultimo, wherein the[y] expressly directed you to proceed with the Trumbull on A short Cruize
so as to return to the Delaware by the latter end of June in Order to
join the Confederacy Saratoga & Deane for the execution of a particular plan concerted by this Board.[2]

The Board are concerned to find your last letter seems to indicate an
intention of your concerting with the private ship of war Mifflin upon
a different plan. We now repeat our former Order viz. that you make
A short Cruize so as to return to the Delaware as above directed.[3] We
are

Your Hble servants by Order

JOHN BROWN sec

[1] Not found.

[2] The "particular plan," namely, for these four ships to cruise in concert and also
in company with French warships, never went into effect. The "Saratoga" (Captain

31

John Young), the "Deane" (Captain Samuel Nicholson), and the "Trumbull" finally worked together more or less as a squadron in the early autumn of 1780, but even by then the "Confederacy" was not ready for sea (Charles O. Paullin, ed., *Out-Letters of Board of Admiralty*, II, 247–71, *passim*).

[3] Captain Nicholson obeyed these orders by sailing from New London late in May (Board of Admiralty to Navy Board, Boston, 12 May 1780, n. 5). For the privateer "General Mifflin" of Boston, commanded by George W. Babcock, see Gardner Weld Allen, *Massachusetts Privateers of the Revolution* (Boston, 1927), p. 149.

Board of Admiralty to Nathaniel Shaw, Jr.

FC (NA: PCC, Marine Committee Letter Book, fol. 287).

May 22d. 1780

SIR

By letter from the Board dated the 9th instant you were directed to reserve the Continental Moiety of the prize Wines until farther Orders and to send the fruit by water to this place. but from the present scarcity of money here, and the urgent necessity for the same in Order to fit out and man two Ships of war now in this port[1] we are compelled to direct that the Wines be immediately sold for ready money together with the Polacca &c as also the Fruit, if not already shipped pursuant to the former Order (excepting 12 Boxes to be reserved for the General) and that the whole Money Arising from the said sale be immediately sent to this Board and under a Safe gaurd if necessary. Mr. Ephraim Bill 2d Lieutenant of Marines to the Confederacy[2] will deliver you this, who is directed at his return to call upon you, by whom we hope you will send us A[s] much Money as you can possibly collect, for without an immediate Assistance from you the Confederacy &c cannot be fitted for Sea.[3]

We are sir Your Hble servts by Order.

JOHN BROWN secy

[1] The U.S. frigates "Confederacy" and "Saratoga" (Board of Admiralty Report, 12 April 1780; Board of Admiralty to Langdon, 14 April 1780, n. 1; Charles O. Paullin, ed., *Out-Letters of Board of Admiralty*, II, 187, 211–12).

[2] That is, the ship "Confederacy." Ephraim Bill (1719–1802) of Norwich, Conn., had also acted as a messenger to Philadelphia in 1779. During the Revolution he was a military and marine agent for Connecticut. In August 1775 he was appointed to oversee the building of a battery at Waterman's Point, and in the following February he was sent to Saybrook to superintend the building of the warship "Defense" (Ledyard Bill, ed., *History of the Bill Family* [New York, 1867], *passim*).

[3] See Board of Admiralty to Harding, 2 May 1780, n. 1.

Patrick Henry to Virginia
Delegates in Congress

RC (NA: PCC, No. 71, I, 339–40, 342).

RICHMOND May 23d. 1780
GENTLEMEN.

I take the Liberty of introducing to you the Bearer Mr. George Anderson.[1] A Ratification of the French Alliance,[2] together with some other State Papers were sent to me very early while I was in Office & I put them all into Mr. Andersons Hands to go to Paris, but he was unfortunately taken by the Enemy & cary'd into Lisbon where he became acquainted with Mr. Arnold Henry Dorman a Gentleman of the first Distinction & Importance in his profession viz. that of a Merchant, & of whose Attachment to America you will be informed.[3] The great Numbers of Seamen & others our Friends who are carry'd to Lisbon in Captivity, & who must suffer extreme Misery if left unnoticed in that remote Country, seems to be an Object that calls for Attention. The Appointment of some proper Person as Agent at that Place, I am persuaded would have a very salutary Effect in the present State of Things. I will not trouble you with an Enumeration of the Reasons for such an appointment, but only just mention, that the generous Interposition of Mr. Dorman would have been more efficacious in relieving & emancipating our distressed Countrymen, If those in power had seen Credentials authorizing his Demands in their Behalf. This Gentleman requires no Salary & from his eagerness to be connected with our Country, his great Wealth & willingness to advance Money for the States, I have no Doubt Congress may find the Means of availing themselves for the public Good.

Mr. Anderson will lay before you some proposals for interesting Mr. Dorman in a Scheme of War & Comerce with our States, & I can only say in Mr. Andersons Behalf that I think he's worthy of your Confidence & that the proposed Agency of Mr. Dorman will answer many valuable purposes.[4]

I beg your Excuse for giving you this Trouble & with the greatest Regard, I am,

Gentn. Your most obedient & very humble Servant

P. HENRY

33

¹ Probably the George Anderson (1755–1816) of Henry's home county of Hanover, who became a tavern keeper in Cumberland County after the Revolution and eventually the owner of Newington plantation there. He was a brother of Lieutenant Colonel Richard Clough Anderson, prominent in the military and political life of Kentucky after moving there about 1783 (Anonymous [Edward L. Andrews], *The Andersons of Gold Mine, Hanover County, Virginia* [Cincinnati, 1913], pp. 36–38). On 26 February 1796 Arnold Henry Dohrman, writing from New York City to JM, mentioned "a number of embarrassments into which George Anderson by dissapating my property has thrown me, & out of which I am now gradually emerging." Also see n. 4 below.

² The legislature of Virginia in June 1779 ratified the treaties of alliance and commerce between the United States and France (*Journal of the House of Delegates,* May 1779, p. 37).

³ William Lee, commissioner of Congress for the courts of Vienna and Berlin and Virginia's official agent in France, referred to "John Henry Dohrman" as his commercial representative in Lisbon (Boyd, *Papers of Jefferson,* III, 92). No other reference to a "John" Dohrman has been found. Perhaps the "John" should have been either "Arnold Henry" or his brother "Jacob" (Frank Landon Humphreys, *Life and Times of David Humphreys* [2 vols.; New York, 1917], II, 91, 103, 143).

⁴ This letter, upon being presented to Congress by the Virginia delegates on 12 June 1780, was referred to the Committee of Foreign Affairs. In accord with its report, Congress appointed Arnold Henry Dohrman (1749–1813) on 21 June to be the agent of the United States in Portugal "for the transaction of such affairs . . . as may be committed to his direction" (*Journals of the Continental Congress,* XVII, 504, 538, 541–42). On 11 July 1780 James Lovell and William C. Houston wrote to Dohrman, informing him of his appointment and of what he might do for the relief of captives, etc. (Wharton, *Revolutionary Diplomatic Correspondence,* III, 845; IV, 106, 388). On 21 June, Congress referred Anderson's "scheme of war" to the Board of Admiralty and his proposals about "Commerce with our States" to the Committee of Commerce. Anderson's two undated statements about these matters are in NA: PCC, No. 71, I, 343–45, 347–48. In the statement entitled "Facts Relative to the behavior and Conduct of Arnold Henry Dohrman Esqr (Merchant in Lisbon) to which I have been an Eye Witness," Anderson told of Dohrman's kind treatment of him and many other Americans engaged in ocean trade who had been captured by the British and put ashore penniless on the Portuguese coast. Using these stranded seamen as crews, Dohrman had sought to send needed supplies, "of which I had the Consignments," to the patriot army and had fitted out a schooner as a privateer to prey upon British ships in the Atlantic Ocean off Lisbon. In his second statement, after remarking that he had the consent of Dohrman to seek for him from Congress an appointment as U.S. consul general in Portugal, Anderson reported Dohrman's belief that by his financial and other aid, eagerly offered because of his "Conviction of the Justice of their Cause," the United States could develop a profitable trade, certainly with Lisbon and Cadiz, and even with France and Holland. Late in the 1780's Dohrman was in serious straits, owing money to Philip Mazzei and others. Helped by Thomas Jefferson, Nathaniel Macon, and JM, Dohrman received from Congress a grant of money and a township of the public domain in Ohio. He and his numerous family moved in 1809 to Steubenville in that state (Boyd, *Papers of Jefferson,* IX, 257; XI, 402, 601; XII, 104; *Annals of the United States,* 6th Cong., 2d sess., cols. 1050, 1052 [February 1801]; Dohrman to JM, 26 February 1796, New York Public Library, and 4 March 1809, LC: Madison Papers).

Report and Resolution of Board of Admiralty

FC (NA: PCC, No. 37, fol. 247).

May 26th 1780

The board beg leave to represent to Congress, That the Hull of the seventy four gun ship[1] now building at Portsmouth in New Hampshire might, if money could be procured for that purpose, be completely finished the ensuing summer, and in that case, if the expected fleet of our ally[2] could furnish out the stores necessary for her equipment, she might cooperate with the said fleet and give it a decided superiority over the enemy;

The board would further represent that they have the best reason to believe that it is the earnest wish of the honble the minister of France[3] that the hull of the said ship might be finished and such materials collected for her as may be in the power of the board to procure; and also that our frigates may be prepared for sea with all possible expedition.

In order to accomplish these important objects the board beg leave to propose the following resolution.

That the board of Admiralty be and they are hereby authorized to receive three hundred hogsheads of the sugar and thirty hogsheads of the rum remaining in the hands of John Bradford Esqr. Continental agent in Boston, and to dispose of the same in such manner as they shall judge proper, for completing the Hull of the 74 gun ship building at Portsmouth in New Hampshire, and collecting such materials for her equipment as can be procured; and also for finishing and equipping the Bourbon,[4] and fitting the other frigates for sea with all possible dispatch.[5]

---

[1] The frigate "America" (above, Report of Board of Admiralty, 29 March 1780, n. 2).

[2] On 11 July 1780 seven French warships, commanded by Admiral de Ternay and convoying five thousand troops under General Rochambeau, arrived at Newport (Burnett, *Letters*, V, 265, n. 2). Within two weeks these vessels were blockaded there by British men-of-war commanded by Admiral Thomas Graves (*ibid.*, V, 304).

[3] The Chevalier de La Luzerne.

[4] Above, Report of Board of Admiralty, 29 March 1780, n. 3.

[5] On 27 May 1780 Congress decided to postpone consideration of this resolution. Every southern delegate except JM voted for the motion to that effect. Congress thereupon directed Bradford to sell the sugar and to send posthaste to "the continental treasury" all cash he received from its sale. In other words, a majority of the state delegations in Congress concluded that naval requirements must yield

priority to reinforcing with men and matériel the patriot troops in the Carolinas in their faltering efforts to stem the advance of the British army under General Clinton (*Journals of the Continental Congress*, XVII, 469–71; NA: PCC, No. 136, IV, 413).

Board of Admiralty to Jonathan Trumbull

FC (NA: PCC, Marine Committee Letter Book, fol. 289).

SIR[1]   May 30th 1780

Pursuant to the Resolutions of Congress passed the 27th inst. relative to the Navy[2] which will be transmitted to your Excellency by their Secretary, I am directed by the Board to Solicit every assistance in your power, by furnishing money and otherwise towards preparing the frigate Bourbon for launching and compleating her for Sea.[3]

As from the distance of place it is impossible for this Board to be acquainted with the situation of the Bourbon from time to time and supply what may be wanted we have directed John Deshon Esquire a Commissioner of the Eastern Navy Board[4] to apply to your Excellency for assistance and we request that his application may be regarded as made by this Board. It is unnecessary to inform your Excellency of the utility of having our Naval force in readiness to act in conjunction with A Squadron of our Allies which may be shortly expected.[5]

I have the Honor to be Sir Your Obedt servant

F Lewis per Order

[1] Jonathan Trumbull (1710–1785), governor of Connecticut, 1769–1783. Letters of the same tenor were written on 30 May to President Meshech Weare of New Hampshire, and to James Bowdoin, president of the Massachusetts Council (Charles O. Paullin, ed., *Out-Letters of Board of Admiralty*, II, 203–6).

[2] In this series of resolutions, Congress urged the states to render "every assistance to the Board of Admiralty" in fitting "for sea, with the utmost expedition, the several ships of war and frigates now in port" (*Journals of the Continental Congress*, XVII, 466–69).

[5] See Report of Board of Admiralty, 26 May 1780, n. 2.

[4] John Deshon (1727–1794) was appointed to the "board of assistants to the Marine Committee . . . in the eastern department" on 6 May 1777. He also served during the Revolutionary War as an agent to erect fortifications at New London, Conn., as a commissary, and on his town's Committee of Correspondence. He was a state representative in 1783–1784, 1787–1788, and 1791 (*Journals of the Continental Congress*, VII, 331; Frances Manwaring Caulkins, *History of New London, Connecticut . . .* [New London, 1895], pp. 503, 506, 619; Charles J. Hoadly et al. comps., *The Public Records of the State of Connecticut* [9 vols.; Hartford, 1894 1953], V, 5, 316; VI, 280, 396; VII, 309).

[5] See Report of Board of Admiralty, 26 May 1780, n. 2.

To Thomas Jefferson

RC (LC: Madison Papers).

Philadelphia, June 2d 1780

Dear Sir

I have written several private letters to you since my arrival here, which as they contained matters that I should be sorry should fall into other hands, I could wish to know had been received. If your Excellency has written any acknowledgments of them, they have never reached me.[1]

Mr. Griffin tells me he has seen several letters just recd. by Mr. Bingham from Martinique[2] which give information that three successive engagements have taken place between the Fleets in the W. Indies, the two first of which were indecisive but that the third was so far in favor of the French that the English had gone into port and left the former entirely master of those Seas: that they were gone in consequence of that, inside Barbadoes, and that the general expectation was that both that Island and St Kitts would speedily be in their possession.[3]

It appears from sundry accounts from the Frontiers of N. York and other N. States that the Savages are making the most distressing incursions under the direction of British Agents, and that a considerable force is assembling at Montreal for the purpose of wresting from us Fort Schuyler which covers the N. Western frontiers of N. York.[4] It is probable the Enemy will be but too successful this campaign in exciting their vindictive spirit against us throughout the whole frontier of the United States. The Expedition of Genl. Sullivan agst. the six nations seems by its effects rather to have exasperated than to have terrified or disabled them.[5] And the example of those nations will add great weight to the exhortations addressed to the more Southern tribes.

Rivington has published a positive and particular account of the Surrender of Charlestown on the 12 U[l]to. said to be brought to N. York by the Iris which left Charleston five days after. There are notwithstanding some circumstances attending it which added to the notorious character for lying of the Author, leave some hope that it is fictitious. The true state of the matter will probably be known at Richmond before this reaches you.[6]

We have yet heard nothing further of the Auxiliary Armament from France:[7] However anxiously its arrival may be wished for it is much to be feared we shall continue to be so unprepared to co-operate with them, as to disappoint their views, and to add to our distress & disgrace. Scarce a week, and sometimes scarce a day, but brings us a most lamentable picture from Head Quarters. The Army are a great part of their time on short allowance, at some times without any at all, and constantly depending on the precarious fruits of momentary expedients. General Washington has found it of the utmost difficulty to repress the mutinous spirit engendered by hunger and want of pay: and all his endeavours could not prevent an actual eruption of it in two Connecticut Regts. who assembled on the parade with their arms and resolved to return home or satisfy their hunger by the force of the Bayonet.[8] We have no permanent resource and scarce even a momentary one left but in the prompt & vigorous supplies of the States. The State of Pennsylvania has it in her power to give great relief in the present crisis, and a recent act of its Legislature shews, they are determined to make the most of it. I understand they have invested their Executive with a dictatoreal Authority from which nothing but the *lives* of their Citizens are exempted. I hope the good resulting from it will be such as to compensate for the risk of the precedent.[9]

With great respect I am Yr. Excellency's Most Ob. & humb Servt

JAMES MADISON JUNR.

[1] If JM wrote other "private letters" to Jefferson than those of 27–28 March and 6 May, their present location is unknown; nor have any replies been found.

[2] Cyrus Griffin. William Bingham (1752–1804), U.S. agent in Martinique, 1776–1780, returned to his home in Philadelphia, 30 April 1780 (Margaret L. Brown, "William Bingham, Agent of the Continental Congress in Martinique," *Pennsylvania Magazine of History and Biography,* LXI [1937], 79).

[3] JM's information was overly sanguine. Between mid-April and mid-May, the French and English fleets, commanded by Admiral Luc Urbain du Bouexic, Comte de Guichen and Admiral George B. Rodney, respectively, met three times without either gaining a decisive advantage over the other. Guichen appeared unwilling to come firmly to grips with his opponent and before long returned to Brest to refit (Doniol, *Histoire,* IV, 353, 498–99).

[4] Washington's letter of 27–28 May, reporting this ominous news, was read in Congress on 31 May 1780 (Fitzpatrick, *Writings of Washington,* XVIII, 428–32; *Journals of the Continental Congress,* XVII, 473). Fort Schuyler, formerly Fort Stanwix, was at the present site of Rome, N.Y. The "British agents" were chiefly Sir John Johnson, Colonel John Butler, and Captain Joseph Brant.

[5] The momentarily successful expedition of Major General John Sullivan (1740–1795) of New Hampshire against the hostile Iroquois tribes in central New York had occurred during the summer and early autumn of 1779 (Christopher Ward, *The War of the Revolution,* ed. by John Richard Alden [2 vols.; New York, 1952], II, 638–45).

[6] James Rivington's report in his *Royal Gazette* (New York) was correct.

[7] See Report of Board of Admiralty, 26 May 1780, n. 2.

[8] Above, n. 4.

[9] Act of 1 June 1780, empowering the governor to commandeer supplies for the army (*Pennsylvania Archives,* 1st ser., VIII, 287–88).

To Thomas Jefferson

RC (LC: Madison Papers).

PHILADELPHIA Jun 6th. 1780

DEAR SIR

A Vessel from West Florida has brought to the President of Congress intelligence from Govr. Galvez of the surrender of Mobile. No other particulars than those contained in the inclosed paper are mentioned, except the verbal report of the Capt. that the Garrison consisted of about 800 including inhabitants &c.[1] Seven or eight vessels have just arrived from the W. Indies as you will also observe in the inclosed paper but they bring no satisfactory information concerning the late engagements between the two fleets.[2] The Address from the Genl. Assembly was yesterday immediately on its receipt laid before Congress and referred to a Special Committee, on whose report it will probably be considered in a committee of the whole.[3] I flatter myself that the arrival of the French Armament which is hourly expected will place our affairs in a less melancholy situation than their apprehensions seem to paint them.[4] There is little doubt but the Conquest of the Southern States was the object of the operations of the present Campain, but I can not think the Enemy will pursue that object at the manifest risk of N. York. It is more probable they will leave a strong Garrison in Charleston, and carry back to N. York the residue of their forces. If they should endeavour to extend their acquisitions in the Southern States, it must proceed from an Assurance from England that a superior naval force will follow the french fleet to frustrate their views on the American Coast. I cannot suppose that however intent they may have been on taking post at Portsmouth,[5] that they will venture in the present prospect to spread themselves out in so exposed a situation.

With great respect & sincerity I am Dr Sir Yr. friend & Servt.

JAMES MADISON JUNR

[1] In a letter dated 8 May, read in Congress on 6 June, Bernardo de Gálvez, Spanish governor and captain general of Louisiana (1777–1781), told of his capture of Mobile from the British on 13 March 1780 (*Journals of the Continental Congress*, XVII, 490).

[2] See JM to Jefferson, 2 June 1780, n. 3. The "inclosed paper" was probably the *Pennsylvania Packet* (Philadelphia) of 6 June 1780.

[3] Congress on 5 June referred to a committee the "Address" of 24 May from the General Assembly of Virginia relating to the defense of the southern states. The committee's report on 7 June led to a wide-ranging debate on the subject (Hening, *Statutes*, X, 539–41; *Journals of the Continental Congress*, XVII, 487, 493–94).

4 See Report of Board of Admiralty, 26 May 1780, n. 2.

5 Probably Portsmouth, Va. The British captured it on 11 May 1779, and used it often thereafter as a naval depot supplementary to the one at New York, and as a base from which to raid into Virginia (H. R. McIlwaine, ed., *Official Letters of the Governors of the State of Virginia* [3 vols.; Richmond, 1926–29], I, 367–68).

Credentials as a Delegate to Continental Congress

MS (NA: PCC, Credentials of Virginia Delegates, fol. 47).

In the House of Delegates.
the 21st: of June 1780

Resolved that Theodorick Bland jn: Esquire[1] be appointed a Delegate to represent this Commonwealth in Congress until the first Monday in November next in the room of Cyrus Griffin Esqr: who hath resigned; Also that Joseph Jones, James Madison jn: Theodorick Bland jn: James Henry, and Meriwether Smith Esquires[2] be appointed Delegates to represent this Commonwealth in Congress for one Year from the first Monday in November next; they having been so elected by joint Ballot of both Houses of Assembly.

June 22d: 1780
Agreed to by the Senate   Teste   JOHN BECKLEY C. h. d.
   WILL: DREW: C. S.   A Copy JOHN BECKLEY C. h. d.

1 Bland presented these credentials upon taking his seat in Congress on 30 August 1780 (*Journals of the Continental Congress*, XVII, 792).

2 Meriwether Smith (1730–1790) was in Congress from 1778 to 1782 and in the House of Delegates in 1776–1778, 1781, 1782, 1785, and 1788. He also attended the Virginia Convention of 1788 that ratified the Federal Constitution.

To Thomas Jefferson

RC (LC: Madison Papers).

PHILADELPHIA June 23d. 1780.

DEAR SIR

Nothing material has taken place since my last. The fact is confirmed that Clinton has returned to N.Y. with part of the Southern army, and has joined Kniphausen. They are at present manoeuvering for purposes not absolutely known, but most probably in order to draw Gnl Washington to an action in which they suppose he may be disabled to give the necessary co-operation to the french armament.[1] Could they succeed in drawing him from his strong position, the result indeed ought to be exceedingly feared. He is weak in numbers beyond all suspicion, and under as great apprehension from famine as from the Enemy. Unless very speedy & extensive reinforcements are recvd. from the Eastern States which I believe are exerting themselves, the issue of the Campain must be equally disgraceful to our Councils & disgus[t]ful to our Allies. Our greatest hopes of being able [to] feed them are founded on a patriotic scheme of the opulent Merchts of this City who have already subscribed nearly £3,000,000 and will very soon complete that sum, the immediate object of which is to procure and transport to the Army 3,000,000,000 of rations and 300 Hhds of rum.[2] Congress for the support of this bank and for the security and indemnification of the Subscribers, have pledged the faith of the United States & agreed to deposit Bills of Exchange in Europe to the Amount of £150,000 Sterling, which are not however to be made use of unless other[3] means of discharging this Debt shd. be inadequate.[4] With sincere regard I am Yr. Obt Servt

J MADISON JUNR

[1] Turning over the command of the British forces in the South to General Charles Cornwallis, General Henry Clinton and a large portion of those troops sailed from Charleston early in June 1780 and reached Staten Island on the 17th and 18th of that month. General Wilhelm von Knyphausen (1716–1800) had been in immediate command of the British in the New York City area during Clinton's six months' absence in the South. The "manoeuvering" was mostly along the western shore of the Hudson River from its mouth north to the American stronghold at West Point. On the date of JM's letter, a strong British patrol attacked an outpost of Washington's army at Springfield, N.J. (Harry Miller Lydenberg, ed., *Archibald Robertson, Lieutenant-General Royal Engineers: His Diaries and Sketches in America, 1762–1780* [New York, 1930], pp. 230–33).

[2] JM should have written £300,000 and 3,000,000 rations.

[3] JM inadvertently wrote "other" twice.

[4] Although Elbridge Gerry had suggested an association of merchants throughout the United States to assure adequate food supplies for the army, Robert R. Livingston apparently was the first to propose the co-operation of Philadelphia merchants and bankers for this purpose. By 17 June, under the leadership of James Wilson, Thomas Willing, and Robert Morris, they had five hundred barrels of flour on their way to Washington's troops. On 22 June, Congress unanimously accepted the "liberal offer" of the "associators" as "a distinguished proof of their patriotism" and guaranteed to reimburse them within six months. The five congressional resolutions on this subject do not mention the payment of 6 per cent interest per annum on the money advanced, but a pledge to this effect seems to have been a part of the bargain (*Journals of the Continental Congress*, XVII, 548–50; Burnett,

Letters, V, 205, 220, 223, 225, 239, 255, 273, 277; Charles Page Smith, *James Wilson: Founding Father, 1742–1798* [Chapel Hill, 1956], pp. 142–45). In a letter of 18 June 1780 to Washington, Philip Schuyler mentioned a promise made to him by the Virginia delegates to tell Jefferson that most of Washington's army could not move unless Virginia supplied it with sixty thousand bushels of corn (Burnett, *Letters,* V, 224). No known letter from the delegates to Jefferson refers to this promise.

Instructions from Virginia General Assembly to Its Delegates in Congress

Printed text (*Journal of the House of Delegates,* May 1780, p. 84).

[12 July 1780]

Resolved, That the delegates of this Commonwealth in Congress, be desired and expressly required regularly to transmit quarterly accounts of their respective expenses to the auditors, according to law. And that the auditors be directed to lay the same before every session of Assembly at its first meeting; and that they moreover lay before the next session of Assembly, a state of the accounts which any members of Congress have heretofore settled with their board, and also, of all sums of money which have been paid, by virtue of any warrant from the President of Congress, to any of the Virginia delegates or their order.[1]

Resolved, also, That it be an instruction to the said delegates to collect from the continental treasury, exact accounts of all the several sums of money, which have at any time been paid or advanced to the delegates of this Commonwealth, or any of them, from the treasury of the United States, distinguishing for what particular purpose, or on what account such sums have been respectively paid or advanced, and transmit the same, authenticated and certified by the treasurer of the United States, to the Governor before the first day of October next, with a certificate also from the said treasurer of the United States, that such accounts contain the whole of the payments which have at any time been made at the treasury to any of the Virginia delegates or their order, that the same may be laid before the General Assembly; and that it be a further instruction to the said delegates to transmit to the Governor, before the first day of October next, an account, certified by themselves, of the expenditure of all public money heretofore entrusted to the Virginia delegates, as the same shall appear to them in the account book of such expenditures kept by the said delegates.[2]

1 The auditors abided by their directive except that they did not lay the quarterly accounts of the delegates before the next session of the assembly "at its first meeting" (*Journal of the House of Delegates*, October 1780, pp. 24, 58).

2 JM's conformance with these instructions may be noted by referring to JM to Virginia Auditors, 25 September 1780 and n. 3, and Expense Account as Delegate in Congress of the same date.

Instruction from Virginia General Assembly to Its Delegates in Congress

RC (NA: PCC, No. 71, I, 391).

Virginia to wit.
In the House of Delegates
the 12th of July 1780

Resolved that the Virginia Delegates to Congress be informed that the people of this Commonwealth are alarmed at the omission of the Yeas and Nays in the Monthly publication of the proceedings of Congress, as the publication of them best ascertains the conduct of their delegates in every important debate

Resolved that it be an instruction to the Virginia delegates in Congress to use their best endeavors to have the Yeays and Nays on every important question printed in the Journals of Congress as formerly:[1]

Teste   JOHN BECKLEY C.h.d.

July the 13th. 1780.
Agreed to by the Senate
WILL: DREW C.S.   A Copy   JOHN BECKLEY C.h.d.

1 When the Virginia delegation laid its "instruction" before Congress on 22 August 1780, it was "referred to the committee appointed to superintend the printing the Journal" (*Journals of the Continental Congress*, XVII, 755). The committee's report, if any, is apparently not on record. By authorization of Congress and the President in 1799, the Folwell Press of Philadelphia published the following year a reprint of the original edition of the journals of the Continental Congress, under the title, *Journals of Congress: Containing Their Proceedings*. Volume V of this edition, covering 1779, records how each delegate voted on many motions, resolutions, and bills, while the next volume, covering 1780, omits these listings altogether. Hence the reason for the Virginia legislature's request becomes evident (see also Burnett, *Letters*, V, 371). On 1 March 1781, due to Maryland's ratification, the Articles of Confederation went into effect. Article IX of this document required Congress to "publish the Journal of their proceedings monthly" and, except on matters requiring secrecy, "the yeas and nays of the delegates of each state on any question shall be entered on the Journal. . . ." Conforming with this mandate, Congress on 16 March 1781 resumed the publication of the yeas and nays.

43

Committee Report on Letter
from Nathanael Greene

FC (NA: PCC, No. 19, II, 449–51). This report is in JM's hand.

[22 July 1780]

The Committee to whom was referred the letter of the 19th. of June last from General Greene, desiring the sense of Congress on his responsibility as Q. M. General for the expenditures of his Agents[1] submit the following report.

They conceive it to be essential to the public interest as well as incident to the nature of all offices entrusted with money for public uses, that those who exercise them should be accountable for its due application; nor can it make any substantial difference whether the advances be immediately disbursed by the Principal himself to whom they are made, or by agents appointed by and amenable to him, since it is always in his power and is manifestly his duty to take the precaution of sufficient securities.

That this has been the idea of Congress appears not only from the express condition on which every particular advance of money has been made to the several departments, but from a resolution of Congress of March 2d. 1778 subsequent to the appointment of Genl Greene, "enacting that the forage masters, waggon masters and other officers in the department be in the appointment of the Q. M. General, who is to be *responsible for their conduct*."[2] In this general responsibility no doubt can exist, that the faithful expenditure of public money is included. On the contrary it is rather to be supposed, that this branch of their duty was most immediately pointed at.

The Committee however in searching the Journals find two instances in which it appears that Congress have been disposed to qualify the strictness of this doctrine in favor of the Heads of the Departments. The first is a resolution passed April 16th. 1778 respecting the Commissary Genls Department, which as far as the expenditure of money is concerned, is perfectly analogous to that of the Q. Mr. General. It is in these words "That nothing contained in the system of the Commissary Generals department shall be construed to make the Commissary General liable for the misapplication of money for the use of his department by any inferior officer in that department, provided that he shall take bonds from the deputy Commissary General and Assistant Commissary General respectively appointed by him, with not less than two good and sufficient securities in the sum of twenty thousand dollars, to be by him lodged in the Treasury Office; and the said deputy Commissaries shall be exonerated of all sums of money by them respectively paid to the purchasing commissaries, provided they shall take bonds from the said purchasing commissaries respectively with not less than two good & sufficient securities in the sum of 10,000 Dollars, which bonds they shall lodge in the said Treasury Office.["]³

The other instance is the report of a Committee on a letter from General Mifflin agreed to in Congress May 19th. 1778, in the words following: "That they had had a conference with Majr. Genl Mifflin and the Auditor General on the subject of the said letter and having heard Genl Mifflin's observations on his peculiar situation as Q. M. General and his objections to being held strictly to account in cases where from the nature of the business and particular circumstances attending it, he was incapable of direct agency & the necessary superintendence that the Committee delivered to him and to the Auditor General, their opinion that the great servants of the public are *generally* to be accountable; that if in the course of adjusting the public accts. deficiences shall appear, Congress will in every special case determine upon the circumstances as they arise whether the party shall or shall not be discharged, that the Committee had no doubt but such favorable allowances would be made as justice should require; but that Congress could not consistent with their duty to the United States by any general resolution hold up the maxim that payment of money to deputies or assistants in a department should discharge the principal.["]⁴

From this view of the subject, The Committee recommend the following resolution, "That General Greene be informed in answer to his letter of the 19th. of June last, that Congress conceiving it to be essential to the public interest as well as incident to the nature of all offices entrusted with the disbursement of public monies, that those who exercise them should be responsible for such disbursement whether it be made immediately by themselves or by Agents appointed by and responsible to them, cannot consistently with their duty to their Constituents by any general resolution hold up a contrary maxim; but as they wish not to expose the faithful servants of the public to any unreasonable risks or losses, and are sensible that in the various branches of the Q. Masters department, abuses and frauds may possibly happen, notwithstanding all the customary precautions, that in all such cases they will determine on the circumstances as they arise and make such favorable allowances as justice may require.["]⁵

¹ On 29 June, Congress referred General Nathanael Greene's (1742–1786) eleven-page letter of 19 June (NA: PCC, No. 155, I, 303) to a committee composed of Oliver Ellsworth (Conn.), James Duane (N.Y.), and JM. When the first two men left Congress on 1 July, Congress named to the committee in their stead Samuel Adams (Mass.) and Robert R. Livingston (N.Y.). Although much their junior in political experience and prestige, JM was their senior in tenure on this committee and hence, under the congressional rules of procedure, became its chairman. The matter at issue was important and divisive. In his letter Greene called the rule of the Treasury Board that the quartermaster general be held accountable for all improper expenditures of public funds by his appointees both unjust and impracticable. Scattered as they were in many army posts, he obviously could not closely supervise them. "No man," Greene wrote, "can with safety to himself, be subject to a greater degree of responsibility than that of calling the under Agents to account, but not to be accountable for them. Nor would I hold the office a moment upon any other footing.... If I have ever betrayed my trust let me suffer."

² *Journals of the Continental Congress*, X, 210. Congress appointed Greene quartermaster general on this date.

³ *Ibid.*, X, 356–57.

⁴ *Ibid.*, XI, 511. General Thomas Mifflin (1744–1800) had been quartermaster general from 1775 to 1777. He was twice a member of Congress and in 1783 was its president. He attended the Federal Convention of 1787 and was governor of Pennsylvania from 1790 to 1799.

⁵ This report, with its appended resolution, was adopted by Congress on 24 July (*ibid.*, XVII, 656–58). Charles Thomson's endorsement, "Passed July 24," is on the wrapper of the report. Although the report is in JM's hand, it seems to agree in its rejection of Greene's requests with the views of his two colleagues on the committee more than with his own. Samuel Adams always expressed concern about the lowly status of the privates and the lofty status of the officers in the patriot army, while Livingston apparently felt that the personnel of the quartermaster's department enjoyed too high salaries and too many perquisites (Burnett, *Letters*, V, 281). In view of the adverse report, Greene wrote a bitter letter on 26 July, resigning as quartermaster general (George Washington Greene, *The Life of Nathanael Greene* [3 vols.; New York, 1871], II, 314–16). On 5 August, after debating about this letter and committee reports on it almost daily since 29 July, Congress accepted Greene's resignation, without releasing him from financial accountability, and named Timothy Pickering of Massachusetts in his stead (*Journals of the Continental Congress*, XVII, 680–98, *passim*).

From David Jameson

RC (LC: Rives Collection of Madison Papers).

RICHMOND July 26. 1780

DR. SIR

In my last I inclosed you the Journals so far as they were printed, and some other papers, since that I have recd. your favour of the 11th., and now agreable to your request inclose you the papers last published at our printing offices. it will be very agreable to me to continue this weekly[1] Although our Capes & Bay are infested with privateers several Vessels have lately arrived from the W. Indies. indeed they were pretty well armed and three of them had kept company. they retook two Vessels that had sailed but a few days before from our Bay. they bring no late news[2] We have reports here that Augustine and Savanah are taken by the French and Spaniards I most heartily wish a confirmation of these reports but confess I fear I shall not have that pleasure[3] The New Money is not yet ready wch. I am sorry for as Col Bland is to set out tomorrow, and would be a good hand to send it by.[4] Very considerable quantities of Bacon and Corn has been and will be siezed under the provision Act.[5] I wish it could be safely sent up the Bay, but there are so many Privateers it would be imprudent to attempt it: And to our great reproach we have not a Vessel to guard the provs.[6] or drive away the picaroons. We have indeed three or four Vessels, but the time of service of the Men is expired, and we have not yet been able to recruit more. private Vessels give very high wages and such other inducements, as Room for ventures, payment in the W Indies &ca., that we have little hope of prevailing on them to enter into pub. service[7]

adieu Yr Ob

D. JAMESON

[1] At this time, Jameson appears to have written every week to JM, inclosing Williamsburg newspapers and, in his missing letter of 19[?] July, a copy of the Virginia legislative journals, probably for the session which adjourned on 14 July. No letters from JM to Jameson are known to exist.

[2] On 2 July 1780 Governor Jefferson asked Samuel Huntington, president of the Continental Congress, whether the United States could not "find means of clearing our bay of the privateers which have for some weeks infested it," so as to expedite the collection of supplies in Virginia for forwarding to the armies in the Carolinas and New Jersey (Boyd, *Papers of Jefferson*, III, 477). Governor Thomas S. Lee of Maryland made a similar appeal. Congress, however, not only had no ships available for this purpose but through its Board of Admiralty had asked Jefferson on 19 June to furnish naval protection for army supplies moving down Chesapeake Bay on their way to North Carolina (Charles O. Paullin, ed., *Out-Letters of Board of Admiralty*, II, 213; Burnett, *Letters*, V, 319-20).

[3] These rumors were untrue.

[4] Act of Virginia legislature on 12 July, "for calling in and redeeming the money now in circulation, and for emitting and funding new bills of credit, according to the resolutions of Congress of the eighteenth of March last" (Hening, *Statutes*, X, 241-54; *Journals of the Continental Congress*, XVI, 262-66). JM and the other Virginia delegates in Congress, as well as other officials of that state, were in sore need of their salaries (JM to Virginia Auditors, 25 September 1780). Contrary to Jameson's statement, Theodorick Bland did not leave Virginia for Philadelphia until early in August.

[5] "An act for procuring a supply of provisions and other necessaries for the use

of the army" (Hening, *Statutes*, X, 233–37). Under this act, JM's father in August and September 1780 provided 262 pounds of bacon, 785 pounds of beef, and 24 gallons of brandy. For these he was given promissory notes totaling about £2,033, signed by "Johnny Scott, Commissioner" (Virginia State Library: Public Service Claims, Orange County, Certificates).

6 Provisions.

7 For further comment by Jameson upon shipping difficulties on Chesapeake Bay, see his letter to JM, 13 August 1780.

From Thomas Jefferson

Printed text (Boyd, *Papers of Jefferson*, III, 506–7).

DEAR SIR   RICHMOND July 26. 1780.

With my letter to the President[1] I inclose a copy of the bill for calling in the paper money now in circulation, being the only copy I have been able to get. in my letter to the delegates I ask the favor of them to furnish me with authentic advice when the resolutions of Congress shall have been adopted by five other states.[2] in a private letter I may venture to urge great dispatch & to assign the reasons. the bill on every vote prevailed but by small majorities, & on one occasion it escaped by two voices only. it's friends are very apprehensive that those who disapprove of it will be active in the recess of assembly to produce a general repugnance to it, and to prevail on the assembly in October to repeal it. they therefore think it of the utmost consequence to get it into a course of execution before the assembly meets. I have stated in my public letter to you what we shall consider as *authentic advice* lest a failure in that article should increase the delay. if you cannot otherwise get copies of the bill, it would be worth while to be at some extraordinary expence to do it.

Some doubt has arisen here to which quarter our 3000 draughts are to go? as Congress directed 5000 militia to be raised & sent to the Southward including what were ordered there, & these 3000 (which I think will be 3500) draughts are raised in lieu of so many militia, the matter seems clear enough. when we consider that a fourth or fifth of the enemy's force are in S. Carolina, it could not be expected that N. Carolina, which contains but a tenth of the American militia should be left to support the Southern war alone; more especially when the regular force to the Northward & the expected aids are taken into the scale.[3] I doubt more whether the balance of the 1,900,000 Doll. are meant by Congress to be sent Northwardly, because in a resolution of

June 17. subsequent to the requisition of the sum before mentioned they seem to appropriate *all* the monies from Maryland Southward to the Southern military chest. we shall be getting ready the balance, in which great disappointments have arisen from an inability to sell our tobacco; and in the mean time wish I could be advised whether it is to go Northward or Southward.[4] the aids of money from this state through the rest of the present year will be small, our taxes being effectually anticipated by certificates issued for want of money, & for which the sheriffs are glad to exchange their collections rather than bring them to the treasury. Congress desired N. Carolina & Virginia to recruit remount, & equip Washington's & White's horse. the whole has been done by us except as to 200 saddles which the Q. M. expects to get from the Northward.[5] this draws from us about six or seven hundred thousand pounds, the half of which I suppose is so much more than was expected from us. we took on us the whole, because we supposed N. Carolina would be considerably burthened with calls for occasional horse, in the present low state of our cavalry; & that the disabled horses would be principally to be exchanged there for fresh.

Our troops are in the utmost distress for clothing, as are also our officers. what we are to do with the 3000 draughts when they are raised I cannot foresee.

Our new institution at the college has had a success which has gained it universal applause. Wythe's school is numerous. they hold weekly courts & assemblies in the capitol the professors join in it; and the young men dispute with elegance, method & learning. this single school by throwing from time to time new hands well principled & well informed into the legislature will be of infinite value.[6]

I wish you every felicity & am Dr. Sir Your friend & sert.

TH: JEFFERSON

P.S. you have not lost sight of the map I hope.[7]

[1] Letter of 27 July 1780 to Samuel Huntington, president of the Continental Congress (Boyd, *Papers of Jefferson*, III, 508–13).

[2] Jefferson's "letter to the [Virginia] delegates," presumably dated 26 or 27 July, has not been found. By "the resolutions of Congress" he meant those of 18 March 1780 (*Journals of the Continental Congress*, XVI, 262–67), passed by a close vote over the opposition of the delegations from the southern states, including Virginia. These resolutions asked each state to emit new bills of credit to an amount proportionate to its usual quota of money (Virginia's was 16⅔ per cent of the total expected from all the states) due to be paid monthly into the continental treasury. Every state, up to a total equivalent to its quota, might use each $1.00 of its new currency to redeem $40.00 of the approximately $200,000,000 of the depreciated congres-

sional issues then outstanding; and Congress resolved not to emit any more paper money. The new issue by each state was not to exceed 5 per cent of the old issues to be called in and burned. Each new bill would pay an annual interest of 5 per cent to the holder and be redeemable in specie not later than 31 December 1786. To prevent these new bills from depreciating and to prepare for this redemption day, Congress urged each state to levy additional taxes and accumulate a sinking fund, presumably in specie. In token of the fact that Congress pledged to redeem the new currency in specie, in case any state could not do so, every new paper note issued by a state was to bear the signature of the *continental* loan officer for that state, as well as the signatures of its own loan officers. Of the new emissions, 40 per cent were to be at the disposal of Congress, and 60 per cent at that of the issuing state.

"The bill," which Jefferson inclosed in his letter to "the President," was one of the two on this subject, passed by the Virginia legislature in July 1780 after much debate (*Journal of the House of Delegates*, May 1780, p. 84; Hening, *Statutes*, X, 241–54, 279–86). Designed to enforce the resolutions of Congress, mentioned above, these statutes provided for a sinking fund, a variety of new taxes, and the emission of $1,666,666.67 in new bills. This equaled 5 per cent of $33,333,333.34, which was Virginia's quota (16⅔ per cent) to redeem, at $1.00 to $40.00 of the outstanding $200,000,000 of continental paper currency. One provision, however, stipulated that the new system was not to become operative until the governor had received "authentick advices" that a majority of the states, not counting enemy-occupied Georgia and South Carolina, had "actually or conditionally approved of . . . the said resolutions of congress of the eighteenth of March last" (Hening, *Statutes*, X, 254). On 4 August President Samuel Huntington, on 7 August Charles Lee, secretary to the Board of Treasury of Congress, and on 5 September 1780 the Virginia delegation in Congress, dispatched to Jefferson these required "authentick advices" (Boyd, *Papers of Jefferson*, III, 527–28, 531–32; Jameson to JM, 23 August 1780, n. 3; and Certification of Virginia Delegates in Congress, 5 September 1780). Because of the delay which would be caused by this proviso in the law of Virginia, and because of its need for emergency funds, the legislature in July 1780 provided for the issuance of not over "two millions of pounds" of treasury notes "for supplying the present urgent necessities of this commonwealth" (Hening, *Statutes*, X, 279–86).

³ On 17 June 1780 Congress urged Virginia to have five thousand of its militia in the hard-pressed patriot army in South Carolina by sending there "with all possible despatch" whatever additional number was needed to bring its total up to that figure. On the same day, Congress also asked Virginia to ready for instant call three thousand more men (*Journals of the Continental Congress*, XVII, 523–24). Thereupon the Assembly enacted three statutes—two to have 2,500 militiamen dispatched with all speed as a three-month reinforcement of the southern army, and the other to raise three thousand men for service until 31 December 1781 (Hening, *Statutes*, X, 221–26, 229, 257–62). In order to recruit these three thousand soldiers, each county lieutenant was directed to raise one-fifteenth of the total number of militia in his county, either by calling for volunteers who would be given money bounties for enlisting, or, if need be, by resorting to a draft. He could count as part of this quota whatever men had already gone from his county to the southern army or to the army defending the western frontier. Jefferson assumed that the men so raised would probably number 3,500 rather than three thousand, and that they would also be allocated by Congress to the army in the South—especially since the congressional troop table had fixed Virginia's obligation at 6,070 men and North Carolina's at only 3,640 (*Journals of the Continental Congress*, XVI, 150).

4 Of the $1,953,200 which Congress, on 19 May 1780, requested from Virginia within thirty days, the state dispatched $1,430,239⅝ to Philadelphia on 30 June 1780. On 17 June, however, Congress asked all states from Maryland south, until further notice, to send their money quotas directly to the headquarters of the southern army. Jefferson was in doubt whether this directive applied to the balance of $522,960⅛ still owed by Virginia under the resolution of 19 May (*ibid.*, XVII, 437, 524; Boyd, *Papers of Jefferson*, III, 510).

5 In April 1780, in fighting at Monck's Corner and Lanneau's (Lenud's) Ferry, the British in South Carolina had decimated the cavalry of Colonel Anthony Walton White (1751–1803) and of Lieutenant Colonel William Augustine Washington (1752–1810) of the 3d Continental Dragoons (*Journals of the Continental Congress*, XVII, 527–28; *Journal of the Virginia House of Delegates*, May 1780, p. 89; William B. Willcox, ed., *The American Rebellion*, pp. 168–69).

6 As a member of the Board of Visitors of the College of William and Mary, Jefferson had been instrumental in reforming its curriculum and in establishing a chair of "Law and Police," with George Wythe (1726–1806) as its first incumbent (Boyd, *Papers of Jefferson*, II, 535–43; Dumas Malone, *Jefferson the Virginian* [Boston, 1948], pp. 284–85; Robert M. Hughes, "William and Mary, the First American Law School," *William and Mary Quarterly*, 2d ser., II [1922], 40–43).

7 See JM to Jefferson, 26 September 1780.

Committee Report on Letter
from Jonathan Trumbull

MS (NA: PCC, No. 20, I, 261). In JM's hand. Docketed by Charles Thomson "Report of the Comee on the letter of May 1. 1780 from Govr Trumbull–Delivered July 29. 1780 passd."

[29 July 1780]

The Committee to whom was referred the letter from Governor Trumbull of May 1. 1780, report as their opinion that Jeremiah Wadsworth late commissary general be directed to make sale of the public sugars stated in the said letter to be in his hands, and report to Congress the amount thereof.[1]

1 On 1 May 1780 Governor Jonathan Trumbull of Connecticut wrote President Samuel Huntington asking, among other things, that Wadsworth (1743–1804), commissary general in 1778 and 1779, be allowed to sell sugar, mainly in a prize ship at New London, to pay certain long overdue U.S. debts. These debts were chiefly owed to "Fatners of Cattle." Trumbull requested this authorization "*without the Loss of a moment*," because "this Failure of payment not only retards the Collection of our Taxes, but also renders the Growers unable to purchase lean Cattle to put into their Pastures, by which the Army will fail of its necessary supplies. We tremble in fear of such an Event" (NA: PCC, No. 66, II, 41). On 11 May, Congress referred the matter to James Duane, Nathaniel Folsom (N.H.), and JM. Their recommendation, written by JM, was adopted by Congress, apparently without a dissenting vote (*Journals of the Continental Congress*, XVII,

423, 680, 783). JM drafted this brief report probably because Duane was not in Congress during July, and Folsom lacked skill with his pen.

Why Trumbull's plea for fast action was ignored is unknown. The delay, coupled with the requirement that Wadsworth report the amount of the sugar receipts to Congress rather than use them to pay the overdue debts, may reflect the suspicions of some members of Congress that he and his agents had profiteered (Edmund Cody Burnett, *The Continental Congress* [New York, 1941], pp. 395–99). Following the Revolution, Wadsworth was prominent in banking, manufacturing, insurance, and as a Federalist in Connecticut politics.

From George Mason

RC (LC: Madison Papers).

GUNSTON-HALL, August 2d. 1780

DEAR SIR

By late Letters from Europe I[1] understand a Treaty of Alliance will soon be concluded between his Catholic Majesty & the United American States, upon which it is presumed Congress will find it necessary to appoint a Consul in Spain, for the Superintendance & protection of our Trade: Shou'd this be the Case, I beg leave to recommend Mr. Richard Harrison as a very proper person for the Office. This Gentleman is a native of Maryland, but about the Beginning of the present Troubles, removed to the Island of Martinique, where He resided about two Years, learned the french Language, & transacted a good deal of Business for Virginia & some other of the United States, in a Manner that gave general Satisfaction. He is now setled at Cadiz, but when I heard from him last was in Madrid, & I am authorised to say will undertake the Office, if he is appointed to it; presuming that Congress will think Cadiz the most proper place for the Residence of an American Consul. I have always been cautious in giving Recommendations for public Offices; but my Knowledge of Mr. Harrison's Diligence, Integrity & commercial Knowledge, from a personal Acquaintance with him, convinces me He will discharge such an Office with Reputation to himself, & Advantage to the Commercial Interest of America.[2]

I have written a long letter to Mr. Jones (who desired my Sentiments) upon the Subject of our back Lands; not doubting the Harmony and Confidence subsisting between him & his Colleagues in the Delegation, I have desired him to communicate the Contents, & must beg Leave to recommend the Subject to your particular Attention.[3]

Our Assembly considered Mr. Griffin's Appointment to the Office of a Judge in the new Court of Admiralty established by Congress, not only as vacating his Seat in Congress, but rendering him ineligible, during his Continuance in [office][4] and therefore elected Colo. The: Bland to succeed him; who has accepted the Appointment, & will soon attend Congress.[5]

I am Dr. Sir Yr. most obdt. Sert.

G. MASON

[1] As a member of the Virginia House of Delegates, Mason (1725–1792) had been in Richmond until the adjournment of the Assembly on 14 July. He then returned to his Potomac River plantation not far from Alexandria.

[2] Richard Harrison (1750–1841), a merchant in Cadiz, performed all the duties of a consul from 1780 to 1786 without being formally appointed by Congress (Boyd, *Papers of Jefferson*, IX, 223). JM nominated him for the office on 7 May 1781, according to Charles Thomson's records, but apparently no final action was ever taken (NA: PCC, No. 186, fol. 2). In June 1790, with the consent of the Senate, President Washington appointed Harrison, then a merchant at Alexandria, Va., as consul "for the port of Cadiz." Whether he returned to that city is unknown, but on 29 November 1791 the Senate confirmed his appointment as auditor in the Treasury Department of the United States (*Journal of the Executive Proceedings of the Senate of the United States of America* [Washington, D.C., 1828 ——], I, 47, 49, 90–91). He continued in this office until 1836 (*ibid.*, IV, 579).

[3] The original letter of 27 July 1780 from Mason to Joseph Jones, a delegate from Virginia in Congress, is apparently lost, but at least a considerable portion of what Mason wrote is in Charles Campbell, ed., *The Bland Papers, Being a Selection from the Manuscripts of Colonel Theodorick Bland, Jr., of Prince George County, Virginia* (2 vols.; Petersburg, Va., 1840–43), II, 125–30. Mason's letter was of importance in the sequence of steps leading to Virginia's offer to cede most of her western lands to the United States, to Maryland's consequent ratification of the Articles of Confederation (thus inaugurating the first legal union of the thirteen states), to the eventual agreement between the United States and Virginia (1784) over the terms of cession, and to the growth of the Confederation and later federal Union through the admission of states formed west of the Appalachians (Ordinances of 1784, 1785, and 1787). In Mason's view, the recent solution of the long-standing dispute between Pennsylvania and Virginia over their common boundary (*Journal of the House of Delegates*, May 1780, p. 74; and Hening, *Statutes*, X, 239) made it opportune for Congress to propose that if Virginia would cede to the United States the "panhandle" between the western boundary of Pennsylvania and the Ohio River, and the vast area north and west of that stream and east of the Mississippi River, which were claimed under the London Company's charter of 1609, the United States would agree to a number of stipulations very similar to those finally accepted in 1784. The United States was (*a*) to guarantee that at least two states would be made from this "Old Northwest"; (*b*) to confirm titles given by Virginia to land privately owned in the ceded area; (*c*) to recompense Virginia for its military and other expenses in that area during the Revolution; (*d*) to confer liberal land grants there upon George Rogers Clark and his troops; (*e*) to protect the French and Canadian inhabitants in their rightful liberties and possessions; (*f*) to allow the bounty land promises to the troops of Virginia to be satisfied in the ceded territory, if the state's reserve in Kentucky for this purpose proved to be too small; and (*g*) to forbid individuals or companies to purchase land in the area from Indians. Furthermore, Mason asked that the area ceded by Virginia "be considered as a common fund for the use and benefit" of the present

and future states of the United States "and for no other use or purpose whatsoever." He admitted that many Virginians would resist his proposals, but he believed that if Congress would offer them in time to be laid before the session of
the Assembly of Virginia beginning on 6 November 1780, his influence as a member
of that body would be sufficient to gain their acceptance. He closed by stating—
probably as a warning for Congress not to delay—that since he expected to withdraw from the state legislature after the coming session, he was "anxious" before
then "to do this last piece of service to the American union." Mason's leadership
in this matter was the more creditable because of his membership in a group of
Virginian speculators claiming land north of the Ohio. If control of that area were
transferred to Congress, the claims of Maryland and Pennsylvania speculators to
the same area would more likely be acquiesced in than if the title remained in Virginia. See Jones-Madison resolutions of 6 September 1780.

4 Manuscript torn.

5 *Journal of the House of Delegates*, May 1780, pp. 55, 57. On 27 April 1780,
Congress appointed Cyrus Griffin one of the three judges of the recently established
Court of Appeals from the various courts of Admiralty. His last recorded vote in
Congress was on 13 June, and he apparently left Philadelphia for Virginia shortly
thereafter. Bland replaced him in Congress, beginning on 30 August (*Journals of
the Continental Congress*, XVI, 61–62, 397; XVII, 507, 554, 792).

From Reverend James Madison

RC (LC: Madison Papers).

August 3d. 1780[1]

I recd. your last of ye 18th. July, as well as ye preceeding, enclosing
ye European Intelligence.[2] I hope at last ye Blessings of peace cannot
be far from us. If Russia adheres to her Memorial, and ye. Dutch have
not lost their antient spirit, if ye Irish too proceed in their reasonable
& just Demands, wh. I have no Doubt they will, because they are reasonable & just, I think ye. Pride of Britain cannot much longer induce
them to prosecute so destructive a War.[3] We are here in perfect
Repose at present. The Arrival of ye. French Fleet has dissipated our
apprehensions, and I doubt not, but ye lethargic Spirit of Virginia will
enjoy her Slumbers. There is indeed a little Stir about ye. Troops to
be raised, but it is rather ye. Stirring of a Man between sleeping &
waking, than ye. vigorous Exertions of ye. more northern States, who
seem to resemble ye Giant that has been refreshed with Wine.[4]

I expect about ye middle of this Month to set out for ye Mountains,
so that I will not trouble you with writing, untill ye first of October.[5]
But is it true that I had like to have lost my valuable Correspondent &
Friend. We hear that you have refused an important Place in a foreign

Embassy. If so—ye Refusal does you Honour, but at ye same Time, I think, it wd. have been ye. highest Gratification to a Person who wd. have viewed ye. Improvements & ye Sta[tesmen?][6] with a philosophical Eye. And no Doubt all ye Honours America could confer wd. in Time have succeeded. I am glad however that you have preferred your *Natale Solum*, tho' I do not think, I shd. have had Resolution to have withstood so alluring a Prospect. Not that I suppose ambitious motives ought to have or cd. have any Influence with you but ye. knowledge to be obtained from such an Appointment, wd. have had real weight.[7]

I have attempted to give a Course of Lectures upon Nat. History, with ye assistance of Buffon,[8] and find ye Study both pleasing & useful. I think also that a useful Course of such Lectures might be published, and have serious Thoughts of preparing them for ye Press, if it can be done without Cost to myself of any Thing but my own Labour. Will you then be so good as to make Enquiry whether such a Publication, wh. will make but a small Vol. wd. meet with ye. Approbation of any of ye Philadelphia Printers so far as to undertake it, Whether they wd. allow me any Thing for ye Copy Right,—or if they will not do that, whether they will print reserving to myself a certain Nr of Copies.[9]

If I receive yr. Answer by ye. last of September, when I shall have returned, it will be Time eno'. If they will undertake ye Business, it shall be ready in ye Winter or Spring.

Having recd. a Letter from Dr Stiles of Yale Coll. I have taken ye liberty of enclosing one to him, wh. I must beg you wd. deliver to a Connecticut Member.[10]

Our Heat here, wh. I inclose you has been almost intolerable on Acct. of ye preceeding Temperature. I shall either write to Mr. Rittenhouse by this or ye next Post.[11] But is there any Impropriety in inclosing a Letter to Members of Congress? I wish you wd mention, as I am unacquaint[ed] with ye Regulations.

I am, with ye. greatest Esteem

J. MADISON

I hear by Majr. Nelson from ye. Southward, that a small advantage has been gained by ye No C. Militia over a Party of ye. Loyal Americans, new Levies in So Carolina.[12]

Some of ye Charlestown Families are fled here for Refuge.[13]

Will you mention to Ma. Mayard,[14] if he shd. fall in yr. Way, that his Package is still here, and that I have had no oppy. of sending it, and almost despair of getting one.

¹ The letter was probably written at Williamsburg.

² Not found.

³ As a protection against French, and especially against British, interference with neutral commerce, Empress Catherine the Great of Russia issued a Proclamation of Armed Neutrality on 29 February 1780. The Estates General of the Netherlands, after somewhat equivalent action on 24 April, joined Russia in the League of Armed Neutrality in November of that year. Other western European powers declared their adherence to the League in 1782 or 1783. It was designed to protect, by force if necessary, neutral ships and non-contraband cargoes against capture and confiscation by belligerents (Samuel Flagg Bemis, *A Diplomatic History of the United States* [rev. ed.; New York, 1942], pp. 37–41). Unrest in Ireland, in part stimulated by the American Rebellion, led Parliament between 1777 and 1782 to ease or remove entirely some of the religious, economic, and political disabilities against which the Irish had protested for many years.

⁴ See Board of Admiralty Report, 26 May 1780, n. 2. In view of Governor Jefferson's and the Assembly's measures to reinforce the patriot army in South Carolina with Virginia troops, these remarks seem to exaggerate the lethargy. Madison was probably referring to the people of Virginia rather than to the commonwealth officials at Richmond.

⁵ Probably he intended to go to his father's and brother's homes in Rockbridge County, Va.

⁶ Manuscript torn.

⁷ Except for Richard Henry Lee's suggestion in October 1778 that JM serve as secretary to Philip Mazzei on his proposed mission to the Italian states to borrow money for Virginia's use (Boyd, *Papers of Jefferson*, II, 215), this letter appears to be the only recorded mention of a possible overseas appointment for JM during the Revolution. Perhaps he was thought of in connection with one or another of the consulships, secretaryships, or special missions discussed in Congress during the summer of 1780. If JM really had an opportunity to go abroad on government service at that time, he may have declined to leave his "Natale Solum" (native soil) for the cryptic reason mentioned by him on 27 April 1785, in a letter to Jefferson: "I have some reason also to suspect that crossing the Sea would be unfriendly to a singular disease of my constitution" (Boyd, *Papers of Jefferson*, VIII, 115). Furthermore, JM had a number of short periods of illness during the summer of 1780 (Jameson to JM, 13 September 1780, n. 1).

⁸ Georges Louis Leclerc, Comte de Buffon (1707–1788), *Histoire naturelle, générale et particulière* (44 vols.; Paris, 1749–1804).

⁹ These lectures were apparently never published. "Copy Right" must have meant merely an author-publisher agreement, because no state had a copyright law until Connecticut enacted one in 1783 (Thorvald Solberg, comp., *Copyright Enactments of the United States, 1783–1906*, Copyright Office Bulletin No. 3 [2d ed., rev.; Washington, 1906], p. 11).

¹⁰ Reverend Ezra Stiles (1727–1795), president of Yale College from 1778 until his death, wrote on 12 July 1780 to establish a "fraternal communication, espy in Literary matters." He was striving at this time to promote friendly relations among the various American colleges. Madison answered on 1 August, writing what Stiles described as a "learned Letter, giving an account of that College." Both letters are in Franklin Bowditch Dexter, ed., *The Literary Diary of Ezra Stiles* (3 vols.; New York, 1901), II, 445–49. Roger Sherman, the Connecticut delegate who lived in New Haven, was the intermediary for both letters (*ibid.*, II, 464).

¹¹ David Rittenhouse (1732–1796), Philadelphia scientist, inventor, and leading member of the American Philosophical Society, shared with Jefferson and Reverend James Madison a lively interest in meteorology. For a communication of the latter,

accompanied by his "Meteorological Observations" during 1777–1778, see *Transactions of the American Philosophical Society*, II (Philadelphia, 1786), 141–58.

[12] Probably Major John Nelson (*ca.* 1748–1827) of York County, Va., a cavalry officer with General Gates's army in the Carolinas. The "small advantage" may have been the victory at Ramsour's Mill late in June 1780 of a force of about four hundred North Carolina militia under Colonel Francis Locke over twice that number of Tories led by John Moore (Christopher Ward, *War of the Revolution*, II, 706–9).

[13] In July 1780 the legislature of Virginia enacted a measure "to authorize the citizens of South Carolina and Georgia to remove their slaves into this state" (Hening, *Statutes*, X, 307–8). Refugees from Georgia and South Carolina were thus exempted from the law of Virginia "for preventing the farther importation of slaves."

[14] Unidentified, but possibly a Major Maynard was meant. The Maynard family of Virginia apparently had at least five members in the patriot army (*Eighth Annual Report of the Library Board of the Virginia State Library, 1910–1911* [Richmond, 1912], p. 304).

From David Jameson

RC (LC: Rives Collection of Madison Papers).

RICHMOND Augt. 13. 1780

DR S[IR]

I recd. your favour by Mr Webb the moment I was setting out for York. I did not return from thence till a few days ago, is the reason you have not heard from me[1]

When I left Richmond I deld. the wart. I had obtained for £20,000 to the Governor who promised to get the money as soon as it was struck and send it on if a safe conveya. offered. Col Bland had not left Virga. and by him it seems the money was sent.[2] Mr Dixon tells me he sent on your papers in my absence agreable to my directions.[3] I shall again receive and forward them by the Post. The Privateers continue to come in and go out of our Bay at pleasure. they have made many Captures and will put an entire stop to our Trade if some measures cannot be fallen on to drive them away. they have taken *some* provision Vessels that attempted to go up the Bay. The time of Service of all our Seamen is out, and we cannot now man the Brig Jefferson—indeed if we could she would not be sufficient to convoy the provision Vessels There being several Brigs & Sloops each equal in strength to her that constantly cruise within or near the Capes. The Ship Thetis is at last launched and will be fitted in a few weeks, but I fear we shall not get Men. The Traders by paying their Seamens wages in the West Indies and giving them priviledges in the Vessels make their allowance so much beyond the Bounty & wages given aboard our Armed Vessels that we have little hope of keeping or rather of getting Men. Ought not Congress to send a Frigate or two here to protect our Trade and that of our Allies, and to convoy the provision Vessels?[4]

The Act for recruiting, or drafting the Militia will prove a very heavy tax. I think I sent you one of the Acts before however lest I should be mistaken I now inclose one. You will see the Counties are to be laid off in divisions, each division to recruit its Men or stand a draft. All the taxable property of the division to pay the bounty given to the recruit. I am told some divs. have already given £5000., and I shall not be surprised if I hear of £10,000, for who will run the risk of being drafted if he can by taxing his Neighbours procure a Man.[5] We have heard nothing worth relating from the Southward. Are we to expect a second division of the French Fleet or not?[6] I shall write again by Post and in the mean time with sincere esteem I am dr Sir Yr Obt. Servt

DAVID JAMESON

[1] Jameson presumably left Richmond for his York County plantation on or about 14 July, the day when the legislature adjourned. Foster Webb (1733–1795), the state treasurer of Virginia, had started from Richmond on 30 June to carry a letter from Jefferson to Congress; therefore Webb may well have brought back with him the now missing letter to Jameson from JM. Since Jameson was a member of the Council of State, his early return to Richmond probably was occasioned by the convening of that body on or about 9 August (*Journal of the House of Delegates*, May 1780, p. 89; *Journals of the Continental Congress*, XVIII, 910–11; Boyd, *Papers of Jefferson*, III, 90, 92, 471, 487, 536).

[2] For the act authorizing the emission of the new currency, see Jefferson to JM, 26 July 1780, n. 2. Upon his arrival in Philadelphia late in August, Bland gave the warrant for £20,000 salary-and-expense money to the three Virginia delegates (JM, Joseph Jones, and John Walker) then in Congress (Expense Account as Delegate, 25 September 1780, notation for 30 August 1780; Jefferson to Virginia Delegates, 14 November 1780).

[3] John Dixon (d. 1791), printer, who with various associates published the *Virginia Gazette* (its title was lengthened after 1781) in Williamsburg up to 8 April 1780, and thereafter in Richmond, during most of the years from 1766 until his death. The paper was continued by his son of the same name.

[4] See Jameson to JM, 26 July 1780, n. 2. On 13 July the Virginia Assembly, in order to defend this "eastern frontier," passed an act to arm a force of militia, to recruit three hundred marines, and to man and equip a half-dozen armed ships (Hening, *Statutes*, X, 296–99). For an analysis by Jefferson of the privateer problem in Chesapeake Bay, see his letter to Richard H. Lee on 13 September 1780, in Boyd, *Papers of Jefferson*, III, 642–43.

[5] See Jefferson to JM, 26 July 1780, n. 3.

[6] See JM to Jefferson, 2 June 1780, n. 3.

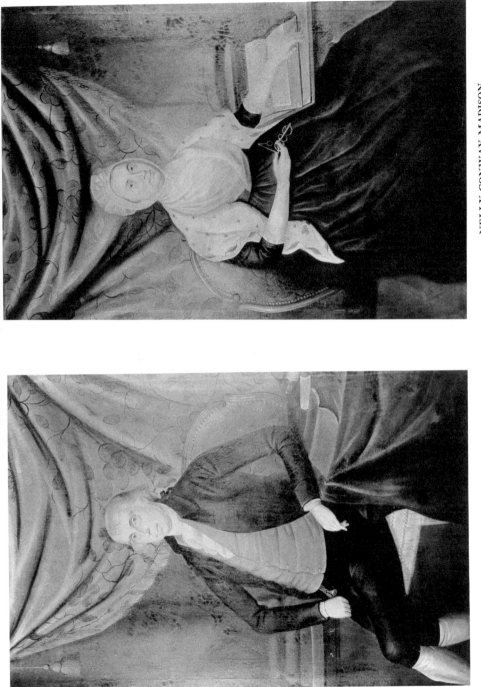

JAMES MADISON, SR.

NELLY CONWAY MADISON

The War in the South
1780-1781

From David Jameson

RC (LC: Rives Collection of Madison Papers).

RICHMOND Aug 16th. 1780

DR SIR

I wrote to you the 12t. or 13t. by a private hand, since which I am favoured with yours of the 1st.[1] I acquainted you with the reason of my silence for sometime past and mentioned to you that the £20,000 for which I had taken out a wart. was sent by Col Bland for the Virga Delegates By a letter from the French Minister to the Govr. I find reason to expect that Court will give us further aid.[2] I am sorry the whole force intended for No. America had not come out at the same time. I fear the British are so reinforced as to prevent the Ships at Rhode Island doing us the service we hoped and should a few Ships be sent from France they may be intercepted by Greaves[3]

The two Millions now making is paid away as fast as it is Signed— was the whole now done it would not carry us beyond the end of this month. Much of it goes for Continental purposes.[4] What we are to do when this is gone I really do not know. I think we shall be in a miserable situation, for I believe most of the tax to be collected in next Month, will be paid off by Certificates given for Waggons, Horses, provs. Rum, Salt &c &c &c impressed and siezed[5]

By Letters from our Southern Army (on Pee dee) under date from the 3d to the 8t. Inst. We are informed that the Enemy have evacuated their posts on Pee dee, & Lynch's Creek and were retreating to Cambden Col Armand & Col Porterfield hung on their Rear—had taken some of their Sick, two Waggons & Teams, and a large Medicine Chest. It is supposed Ld. Cornwallis is gone to Savanah, that Ld Rawden commands at their princ. post Cambden, and that he has there no very considerable force[6]

Have you recd. quantities of Clothing through the Interest of Mr Gerard? I believe I did not tell you we some time ago entered into Contract with Mr Francy. He is to furnish us with Clothing &c &c. against the next Spring at 7/. Sterl for Tobo. deld. here*[7]

I am Dr Sir Yr afft. hb. Sert

DAVID JAMESON

*he is to deliver the Goods here free of cost or damage & receive Tobo. in payment on their arrival at 7/ Sterl. PCt—Livre 10½d Sterl.[8]

[1] Not found.

[2] The present whereabouts of the letter of 27 July 1780 by the French minister, Chevalier de La Luzerne, to Jefferson is unknown (Boyd, *Papers of Jefferson*, III, 578).

[3] Admiral Thomas Graves (1725–1802). See Report of Board of Admiralty, 26 May 1780, n. 2.

[4] See Jefferson to JM, 26 July 1780, last two sentences of n. 2.

[5] In other words, the tax, instead of bringing in much money, would largely be paid in promissory notes issued previously by the state government to citizens who had been obliged to yield up their property for military use.

[6] Jameson evidently knew not only of General Horatio Gates's letter of 3 August (Boyd, *Papers of Jefferson*, III, 524–25), but also of a later dispatch or dispatches not known to the editors. Colonel Charles Armand, Marquis de La Rouërie (1756–1793), commanded the Pulaski Legion, the first to be assailed by the British at the Battle of Camden, S.C. Lord Rawdon (Francis Rawdon-Hastings [1754–1826]), at the head of the British troops centered in that town, was faced by Gates with about 3,050 men fit for duty. On 6 August, Rawdon withdrew from his position on Lynch's Creek. Shortly thereafter, reinforcements raised his force to about 2,300 men, and Lord Cornwallis (1738–1805) arrived from Charleston to take over their command. On the day that Jameson wrote this letter, Cornwallis severely defeated Gates in the Battle of Camden. In this engagement, Colonel Charles Porterfield was mortally wounded.

[7] The Continental Congress had reason to expect that, upon his return to France, Conrad Alexandre Gérard, the first minister from that country to the United States, would use his influence to expedite the shipment of military supplies to the patriot army, to encourage more trade between the merchants of the two countries, and to effect additional loans of money from the French crown. Although Gérard left the United States on 18 October 1779, his virtual shipwreck at sea (JM to Page, 8 May 1780, n. 6) and further delay in Spain held up his arrival at Versailles until late in February 1780 (Fitzpatrick, *Writings of Washington*, XVIII, 24; John J. Meng, ed., *Despatches and Instructions of Conrad Alexandre Gérard, 1778–1780* [Baltimore, 1939], pp. 120, 905–8). The business transactions in Virginia of Jean Baptiste Lazarus Théveneau de Francy (d. 1783), agent of Pierre Augustin Caron de Beaumarchais in his efforts to assist the patriot cause with money and goods from France, began in 1778 during the governorship of Patrick Henry. De Francy claimed that he had delivered supplies worth more than the value of the tobacco he had received for them. Jameson's reference is to a new agreement made between Governor Jefferson and de Francy on 11 May 1780 (Boyd, *Papers of Jefferson*, III, 372–73).

[8] That is, seven shillings per hundredweight of tobacco, with a livre equated as 10½ pence.

Committee Report on Letter to Rochambeau

Draft (NA: PCC, No. 78, XVIII, 319–20). Proposed reply to be made by the president of Congress to the Comte de Rochambeau's letter to him of 3 August 1780. Except for minor amendments noted below, the letter was drafted by JM between 12 and 17 August 1780.

[17? August 1780]

The Committee[1] to whom was referred the letter of the 3d. inst: from le Compte de Rochambeau, report the following answer to be given by the President:[2]

Sɪʀ

Congress have recd. with Satisfaction[3] your letter of the 3d inst: which besides exhibiting the zeal of the troops under your command for the service of their allies, and the vigilance of their chief in providing agst. the enterprises of the Enemy, conveys fresh assurances from your illustrious sovereign of his benevolent views towards the United States; assurances which can not fail to make the deepest impression, because they are attended with the most solid proofs of their sincerity.

If any difficulties have retarded a part of the succour generously destined to Co-opperate in[4] the expulsion of the Enemy from these states, or have rendered the preparations on our part less complete than was Intended, We persu[a]de ourselves[5] that sufficient Amends will be made by the vigor of the combined operations, and by the mutual emulation that must be felt by the allied troops, fighting side by side, in a cause so honorable and with an object of such magnitude immediately before them. Under circumstances like these, any impediments, that may arise from the strength or position of the enemy can have no other effect than to increase the Ardor[6] to overcome them.

Should Genl Clinton resume his projected attack on your armament Congress have the highest confidence that the adjacent militia will[7] again evinc[e] their zealous attachment to their friends & brethren as well as that the latter will give equal proof that their intrepid valour which has so often displayed itself against the British arms in Europe is no less formidable when opposed to her ambitious designs against this Country; And that the result will be a happy presage of a successful issue to the campaign: a[s] this must be of a successful issue to the war.

The Citizens of the United States and the French nation, already bound together by the ties of interest, of honor and the most solemn engagements, want nothing to perfect their coalition, but t[he] endearing circumstance of having mutually contributed to acquire for each other the glory of triumphing over a restless and powerful enemy to the rights of Mankind.

With sentiments of the most perfect consideration & respect I have the hono[r] to be your most Obedient & very humble Servant.

S. H. Pt.[8]

[1] JM, Samuel Adams, and James Lovell, appointed on 12 August (*Journals of the Continental Congress*, XVII, 723).

[2] Lieutenant General Jean Baptiste Donatien de Vimeur, Comte de Rochambeau (1727–1807), arrived at Newport, R.I., in command of six thousand French troops on 11 July. For many months thereafter the fleet in which they had come, commanded by the admiral Chevalier de Ternay, was blockaded in Narragansett Bay by British warships under Admiral Thomas Graves. Believing that these beleaguered French ships might need the aid of his soldiers, Rochambeau remained in Rhode Island a full year before joining his forces with those of Washington near New York City. Rochambeau's letter to President Samuel Huntington (NA: PCC, No. 78, XVIII, 315–16) explained his delay in paying his respects on the score of pressing duties, expressed his belief that New York City would be restored to patriot control if General Henry Clinton and his ten thousand troops should attack him, mentioned his eagerness to serve under Washington's orders, referred to the fine discipline and health of his own troops and to the continuing aid given him by Massachusetts and Rhode Island militia, and assured Huntington that Louis XVI was determined to render all possible aid and to make common cause with the United States until Great Britain had been defeated.

[3] Before this word, "sincere" was originally written and later crossed out either by JM or by Samuel Adams. To Adams, Edmund C. Burnett (*Letters*, V, 333–34) attributes, no doubt correctly, all the word substitutions in JM's draft.

[4] The original "for" was replaced by "to Co-opperate in." Rochambeau's reference in his letter to the delayed arrival of additional military and naval aid from France because of a lack of transportation facilities really meant that these reinforcements were bottled up in the harbor of Brest by British men-of-war (*ibid.*, V, 357).

[5] Although in the above text JM first wrote "their," "they," and "themselves," instead of the corresponding "our," "we," and "ourselves," he jotted these first-person equivalents in the left-hand margin, evidently inviting his committee colleagues to decide which were preferable. "Intended" is written over a deleted "wished."

[6] Here again, although JM first wrote "inspire an inflexibility" instead of "increase the Ardor," he noted this latter phrase in the margin, thus leaving the choice between them to the committee.

[7] Following this word, there is crossed out "by the promptitude of their support."

[8] Abbreviations for "Samuel Huntington, President." The following resolution, adopted by Congress on 17 August in lieu of this letter, was forwarded to Rochambeau two days later, accompanied by a brief covering note from Huntington (*Journals of the Continental Congress*, XVII, 742; Burnett, *Letters*, V, 335):

"*Resolved*, That Congress have a just sense of the vigilance and prudence of the commanders of the fleet and army of our ally, in taking the precautions mentioned in the letter of Monsieur the Count de Rochambeau, of the 3d of August, as well as of his attention to the ease and convenience of the militia of these states. The spirit, good order, and discipline of the troops under his command, deserve their warmest approbation."

From David Jameson

RC (LC: Rives Collection of Madison Papers).

RICHMOND Aug 23. 1780

DR SIR

I have to acknowledge your favour of the 8th. mentioning the reports from the West Indies.[1] Notwithstanding our Bay is so closely watched by the Enemy's private armed Vessels we have had some arrivals, and they give us reason to believe Jamaica is invested by the combined Fleets. If it is, I must suppose so great an Armament will find little difficulty in taking it.[2] The Governor went last week to Albemarle, and will not return till Monday or tuesday next. before he set out he recd a letter from the President of Congress acquainting him what States had acceded to the Act of Congress of the 18t. of March. This notification he did not think sufficient for him to put our Act in execution, And I suppose the certificate you inclosed from the board of Treasury will have no greater weight. In his letter to Congress on this subject he required authentic copies of the Acts of the several States, and until he has such I doubt if he will issue his proclamation. You will see by our Act of Assembly Assessors are to be appointed, and the property valued in October, and unless this matter is soon put in motion, the distant Counties will not be able to execute the Law in proper time. several other ills will attend a delay. I wish authenticated copies of the several Acts to be sent as soon as possible[3] By the last Post Mr Thompson sent some letters of Marque directed to the Governor. on the packet he wrote "on public service" and undersigned "Charles Thompson". The postmaster says nothing is free of postage by authority of Mr Thompson. The charge on this packet is £149.6.8. there was in another packet the Journals of Congress for July, postage £7.13.4. And on the letter from the Treasury office, a charge of £5.6.8. I supposed *all* letters & packets from the public offices of Congress were free, and mention the matter to you that the postMaster may be called to Accot.[4] I am very sorry to inform you we have nearly issued the two Millions. what we are to do from this time to the setting of the Assembly is out of my power to say—indeed what can or will be done then, is not easy to foresee We are really in most deplorable condition. We have no Blankets nor Tents for the 3000 recruits and very little clothing—not enough for our old Soldiers—no Money—no Credit. The subject is too affecting to dwell on[5]

Adieu   Your affe. hum. Servt

DAVID JAMESON

We have nothing from the South since my last.[6]

[1] The present whereabouts of JM's letter of 8 August is unknown. It probably mentioned the apparent threat of the combined French and Spanish fleets to the British island of Jamaica, as reported in a letter of 7 July from Martinique to William Bingham of Philadelphia (Burnett, *Letters*, V, 315, 316).

[2] Contrary to Jameson's expectation, the Comte de Guichen, with fourteen French warships, sailed from the West Indies on 16 August for home, arriving at Brest in late September. The British squadron under Admiral George B. Rodney had crippled but not decisively defeated Guichen's force in several engagements, but the official French explanation of the latter's departure from the Caribbean was the flat refusal of the Spanish admiral there to co-operate in the capture of any British island in the West Indies (Doniol, *Histoire*, V, 498–99; Vicomte de Noailles, *Marins et soldats français en Amérique pendant la guerre de l'indépendance des États-Unis, 1778–1783* [Paris, 1903], p. 126). This depletion of the French naval force in the West Indies allowed Rodney, with a dozen of his ships, to leave the area temporarily. He reached New York on 14 September.

[3] Jefferson left Richmond on 15 August. Thirteen days later, following his return, he issued a proclamation declaring in force the Virginia statute passed earlier in the summer for carrying into effect the act of Congress of 18 March 1780. Contrary to what Jameson states, Jefferson in his letter of 27 July to President Samuel Huntington (Boyd, *Papers of Jefferson*, III, 510) did not request "authentic copies" of the statutes of at least five other states for carrying out that act of Congress, but merely, as the Virginia legislature stipulated, "authentic advices" that five other states had already complied. Before releasing the proclamation mentioned above, he had received these "advices." See Jefferson to JM, 26 July 1780, n. 2.

[4] Charles Thomson (1729–1824) of Philadelphia was secretary of Congress from 1774 to 1789. For his circular letter of 28 July 1780 to Jefferson and the other state governors, see Boyd, *Papers of Jefferson*, III, 515. Jameson's complaint about the postage due on official mail may have been relayed by JM to Congress. In any event, Congress on 19 September resolved: "That all the Journals of Congress and other public papers transmitted by the secretary of Congress to the supreme executive or general assembly of any of the United States shall go free of postage, and that they be accordingly franked by the secretary" (*Journals of the Continental Congress*, XVIII, 837).

[5] See Jefferson to JM, 26 July 1780, n. 3.

[6] See Jameson to JM, 16 August 1780, and n. 6.

Motion of Virginia Delegates on Kentucky

Printed text (*Journals of the Continental Congress*, XVII, 763–64).

[24 August 1780]

A petition from a number of the inhabitants of Kentucke[1] was read; on which

A motion was made by the delegates of Virginia, that this petition, together with that read yesterday,[2] from a number of inhabitants of the said country, be transmitted to the governor of Virginia; which on the question, passed in the negative.[3]

[1] The petition, dated 19 May 1780 and addressed to Congress, contained about five hundred signatures. It asked separate statehood for Kentucky, principally on the grounds that its settlers were ineffectively governed by Virginia, that Virginia's taxes were oppressive, and that Virginia had granted large tracts of Kentucky land to absentee owners who made no efforts to cultivate it (NA: PCC, No. 48, fols. 237–44).

[2] A similar petition, undated, and addressed to the president of Congress. This memorial, signed by some four hundred Kentuckians, asked to be allowed to govern themselves as citizens only of the United States. If their prayer was not granted, they would probably choose, in preference to remaining as "slaves" of the Virginia land engrossers and courts, either to move west of the Mississippi River under Spain or north of the Ohio River (NA: PCC, No. 48, fols. 247–48; *Journals of the Continental Congress*, XVII, 760).

[3] The vote of the state delegations on the motion is not known. Judging from the printed journals, no new petition asking separate statehood for Kentucky came before Congress until 27 August 1782. It then touched off an animated debate in which JM prominently shared (*ibid.*, XXIII, 532; Burnett, *Letters*, VI, 456–59).

From Edmund Pendleton

Tr (LC: Force Transcripts). Although the originals of this letter and, with few exceptions, the more than one hundred others which Pendleton wrote to JM are probably no longer extant, three partial collections (of which at least one is independent of the other two) are available. About 1890, Frederick B. McGuire of Washington, D.C., who had in his possession a considerable portion of Pendleton's side of the correspondence, permitted Worthington C. Ford to make copies of some and perhaps all of it. Ford published these in the *Proceedings of the Massachusetts Historical Society*, 2d ser., XIX (1905), 107–67. On 6–7 December 1892, Stan. V. Henkels, a prominent manuscript dealer of Philadelphia, auctioned off the large

McGuire collection of the papers of JM, including 135 "Autograph Letters" of Pendleton to JM, dated "from August 31, 1752 to December 1812 [1802?]," as well as "fifteen documents relating to transactions at law between James Madison and Carter Braxton, mostly in the handwriting of Edmund Pendleton" (Stan. V. Henkels Catalogue No. 694, p. 79). On pages 80–96 of this same catalogue are printed excerpts from sixty-two of these letters. Since he dated the beginning of this correspondence back to 1752, when JM was only one year of age, Henkels evidently failed to distinguish JM from his father. The "Lowdermilk," to whom Henkels sold the Pendleton letters for $315, was most probably Will H. Lowdermilk, the well-known Washington, D.C., bookdealer. What he did with them remains a mystery. James C. McGuire, father of Frederick McGuire, had acquired this collection of JM papers in 1850, the year following Dolley Madison's death.

Although Peter Force of Washington, D.C., editor of the *American Archives* and other United States source documents, may have had his clerks make transcripts of seventy of Pendleton's letters to JM when they were in Dolley Madison's possession or, what is much less likely, before JM's death in 1836, he probably prepared the copies after his friend James C. McGuire obtained the originals. A notation, reading "Mss McGuire" on page 8561 of the transcripts, supports this conclusion. Thus the transcripts, made under Force's direction, are not only the earliest known copies of the original Pendleton letters but also are the most complete. Therefore the letters from Pendleton published in this work will follow, whenever possible, the copies in the Force transcripts. A variant reading in either or both of the other versions will be pointed out whenever the difference seems significant. For comment about the letters written by JM to Pendleton, see headnote, 12 September 1780.

EDMUNDSBURY,[1] Augt. 27. 1780

DEAR SIR:

When you first went to Congress I should have bespoke your correspondence, but knew your acquaintance was extensive & nearer relations very numerous, from whence I judged such a request would give you too much trouble, and declined it, as I was happy enough then to have other[2] two valuable friends, who handed me all the important intelligence which was allowed to be made public. They have since retired from Congress,[3] & I must starve for want of news at this interesting crisis, unless you can drop me a line now & then without interfering too much with yr business or ease, for happy as it would make me,

I can't agree to accept it upon the terms of Interrupting either. It is fair to let you know that the benefits arising from the correspondence will be unequal, since tho' you will find me dilligent & punctual in it, yet placed as I am in a Forest, occurrences will not enable me to give you much entertainment. Thus you have a fair state of the case on my side & will exercise the Rights of Friendship in declining it altogether, if you find it will subject you to any inconvenience. I am sorry to open this proposed Intercourse with condoling you on the unhappy affair to the Southward, the particulars of which you will know better than I, as I hear an Aid has passed wth. Genl Gates Letter to Congress, & our accounts here are much confused;[4] we have been unfortunate in that quarter hither[to] but I hope we shall persevere til we catch the lucky moment for success; and that you will hand us something comfortable from the Northward 'ere long. I am with great regard Dr Sr

Yr Affecte. & Obd. Servt.

EDMD PENDLETON

1 Pendleton's country seat in Caroline County, Va. Following more than twenty years of political prominence in that colony before the Revolution, Edmund Pendleton (1721–1803) became president of the Virginia Convention of 1776, advocated independence from England, and helped to draft the first constitution of his state and to revise its laws. After serving as speaker of the House of Delegates of the General Assembly of Virginia, he was president of the state Supreme Court of Appeals from 1779 until his death. In 1788 he presided over the Virginia Convention which ratified the Federal Constitution.

2 Although the copyist wrote "friends" after "other," and then crossed it out, he probably should also have transferred "other" to follow "two." The W. C. Ford version, however, in the *Proceedings of the Massachusetts Historical Society*, cited above, reads "to have two valuable friends."

3 Cyrus Griffin and James Henry, delegates from Virginia, left Congress during the summer of 1780, and Joseph Jones, also a delegate, returned to that state in early September.

4 On 31 August, Congress read the letter of 20 August from Horatio Gates (*ca.* 1728–1806), reporting his disastrous defeat at Camden, S.C. (*Journals of the Continental Congress*, XVII, 797). The aide-de-camp was Major Charles Magill.

From David Jameson

RC (LC: Rives Collection of Madison Papers).

RICHMOND, Aug 30. 1780

DR. SIR

I have not had the favour of a letter from you by this weeks post As Col Senf & Maj Magill went on with Gen. Gates's letter to Congress giving accot. of our disaster in Carolina, and could give you the particulars I did not write on the occasion.[1] Since they left this place we have recd. a letter from Gen. Stevens, he dates from Spinks's about 70 miles from Hillsborough the 22d. where he then was and where he had collected some Men—how many he does not mention, or what Men —he had a few Arms. he gives nearly the same accot. of the action we had from Gen Gates. he adds that he had been informed Col Sumpter shared their fate[2]

We have had no other information from the Southward. We have just now been informed by a Vessel from Eusta that some British Ships went to St. Martins and demanded all the American Vessels & threatened to burn the Town unless they were deld. up. The Vessels were deld. up to the amount of six or seven it is said & among them some of considerable value[3]

If we do not hear soon that we are able to collect a good many of our scattered Army I fear we must call some Militia to send on in aid of the 3000 recruits & how we are to equip & March even the recruits, I am at loss to tell for we have none of the two Millions left and very little chance of receiving any Money for the tax now payable. there will be Certificates to discount the greater part if not the whole[4]

About 400 regulars March Saturday last from Chesterfield Courthouse. they are those of the sevl. Regiments who were left in the Hospital, those who were out on furlow, the remains of Bufords, and some of the former drafts.[5] I beleive there will be 150 more sent on in a few days. How soon any of the new recruits will March is still uncertain. I am with esteem dr Sir

Yr mo hb Servt,

DAVID JAMESON

[1] Colonel John Christian Senf (*ca.* 1754–1806) of South Carolina was a Swedish-or Danish-born engineer who had emigrated to that province. He was serving at this time with General Gates. In 1781 he refused an appointment as state engineer of Virginia. After the war he was prominent in the construction of South Carolina canals (*South Carolina Historical and Genealogical Magazine*, XXVIII [1927], 8; Boyd, *Papers of Jefferson*, IV, 11 n.; V, 13–14). Major Charles Magill (1760–1827) of Winchester, Va., was commissioned in the Virginia militia, and on 9 August 1780 he was attached to Gates's staff (*ibid.*, III, 563; F. B. Heitman, *Historical Register of Officers of the Continental Army during the War of the Revolution* [Washington, D.C., 1893], p. 277).

[2] Jameson's account mirrors the information contained in the 20 (not 22) August letter of General Edward Stevens (1745–1820) of the Virginia militia to Governor Jefferson (Boyd, *Papers of Jefferson*, III, 558–59). On 18 August 1780, three days after his victory at the Wateree Ford, S.C., General (not Colonel) Thomas Sumter (1734–1832) of that state was decisively defeated by Lieutenant Colonel Banastre

Tarleton at Fishing Creek, S.C. (Henry B. Dawson, *Battles of the United States by Sea and Land* [2 vols.; New York, 1858], 612, 622–24).

[3] Jameson's news was probably derived from a letter of 11 August from St. Eustatius, published in the 6 September 1780 issue of the *Virginia Gazette* (Richmond, Dixon and Nicolson). St. Eustatius and St. Martin are among the Leeward Islands in the West Indies. The Netherlands owned the former but divided control of the latter with France.

[4] See Jefferson to JM, 26 July 1780, n. 3; Jameson to JM, 16 August 1780, n. 5.

[5] The 11th Virginia Regiment, commanded by Colonel Abraham Buford (1749–1833), was cut to pieces on 29 May 1780 at the Waxhaws, S.C., by a force of British and Tories led by Lieutenant Colonel Tarleton (Christopher Ward, *War of the Revolution*, II, 705–6).

Thomas Jefferson to Virginia Delegates in Congress

FC (Photostat in Virginia State Library of copy in British Museum: Addington MSS 38,650).

RICHMOND August 31. 1780.

GENTLEMEN

We agree to employ mr. Dunlap according to his proposals inclosed in your Letter of the 15th instant[1] except that we must adhere to our requisition that a complete sheet of his weekly paper shall be kept clear of advertisements, and reserved for intelligence, essays, &c., except that advertisements from the Legislature or Executive shall be put into the same sheet with the intelligence. The standing salary is to be fixed by the assembly, not by the executive, and we will recommend to them in settling it to consider the utility of the weekly paper and make liberal allowance for that over and above mr. Dunlaps services in printing the public acts, journals, proclamations, advertisements, &c. and this we can venture to undertake will be done. As to money which you say mr. Dunlap will want as soon as he comes we are not in a condition to make him any advances between this and the meeting of assembly but immediately after their meeting we have no doubt it will be in our power. I hope his press will be got to work before they meet. we will give him any aid in our power in procuring a house here, and if we should have any vessels coming from the head of Elk[2] down the bay they shall take in any thing he pleases to have lodged here without charge.[3] I wou'd recommend strongly to mr. Dunlap that his manager here obtain the postmaster's office of the place besides that it will carry custom to his shop it will give him an exemption from militia duties which may otherwise be a considerable interruption.[4] I have the honor to be with every sentiment of respect Gents., Your mo obedient servant,

TH: JEFFERSON

[1] Not found.

[2] Elkton, Md.

[3] By this letter, Jefferson sought to render effective a legislative authorization to him, "with the advice of council," "to engage with, and employ, at the publick expense, and for the publick service, a good and able printer, of firm and known attachment to the independence of the United States, who may be willing to bring a good and well provided press into this commonwealth." This authorization was embodied in a lengthy statute enacted at the most recent session of the Assembly and entitled, "An act for giving farther powers to the governor and council, and for other purposes" (Hening, *Statutes*, X, 309–15). In his now missing letter of *ca.* 26 July 1780 to the Virginia Delegates, Jefferson had probably initiated his effort to induce John Dunlap (1747–1812), publisher of the *Pennsylvania Packet* of Philadelphia and, for a time, of *Dunlap's Maryland Gazette* of Baltimore and Annapolis, to become the public printer at Richmond. Although the negotiations were quickly successful, the loss of his "costly printing apparatus" by shipwreck and capture by the British delayed the appearance of the first issue of the *Virginia Gazette or Weekly Advertiser* until December 1781. Its publisher was James Hayes, Jr., with whom Dunlap had been associated between 1775 and 1778 in publishing the *Maryland Gazette*. For further details, see Boyd, *Papers of Jefferson*, III, 580.

[4] On 8 July 1776 Congress resolved, "That the post masters, while in office, be excused from all military duty" (*Journals of the Continental Congress*, V, 526).

From Robert Forsyth

Letter not found.

EDITORIAL NOTE

1 September 1780. In the Madison Miscellany in the Library of Congress are lists, probably prepared under the direction of Peter Force, which mention a one-page letter from Forsyth to JM on this date. The writer in all likelihood was Major Robert Forsyth (1754–1794), continental deputy commissary of purchases from Virginia, and soon for Greene's southern army, who became a U.S. marshal in Georgia in 1789. In a letter of 17 August 1780 to him, Lieutenant Governor Dudley Digges refers to Forsyth's going "very soon" to Philadelphia where he would let Congress or the commissary general know "how impracticable it will be for this state to engage to make further advances in your department, whilst the demands for the southern troops occur so frequently as totally to exhaust . . . our abilities to comply with any future requisitions, at least until the next meeting of the general Assembly" (H. R. McIlwaine, ed., *Official Letters of Virginia Governors*, II, 169; Jennie Forsyth Jeffries, comp., *A History of the Forsyth Family* [Indianapolis, 1920], pp. 49–50).

Certification That Six States Have Complied with 18 March 1780 Resolutions of Congress

MS (Virginia State Library). The text is in JM's hand.

PHILADELPHIA Septr. 5th. 1780

We, Delegates from the Commonwealth of Virginia do certify that Congress have received authenticated copies of Acts of the Legislatures of the following States, complying with their resolutions of the 18th. of March last relative to the public finances, viz.[1]

1. An Act of the Legislature of Maryland passed the 12th. day of June 1780. entitled "An Act for sinking the Quota required by Congress of this State of the bills of credit emitted by Congress."

2. An Act of the Legislature of New Jersey passed the 9th. day of June 1780 entitled "An Act for establishing a fund for sinking and redeeming the proportion of the bills of credit of the United States assigned as the quota of this State."

3. An Act of the Legislature of New York passed the 15th. of June 1780 entitled "An Act approving of the Act of Congress of the 18th. day of March 1780, relative to the finances of the United States, and making provision for redeeming the proportion of this State of the bills of credit to be emitted in pursuance of the said Act of Congress.["]

4. An Act of the Legislature of Massachussets bay passed the 5th. day of May 1780. entitled an "An Act making provision for calling in to be destroyed this State's Quota according to the present apportionment of all the public bills of credit, which have been emitted by Congress, and for making and emitting on the credit of this State other bills of credit not to exceed the sum of four hundred and sixty thousand pounds, and for establishing funds sufficient to secure the redemption of the bills so emitted by the last day of december 1786. as recommended by a resolution of Congress of the 18th. day of March of the present year and in conformity thereto; also for paying annually in specie the interest arising on notes which have been issued upon the credit of the province Colony or now State of Massachussets bay promising to be paid in gold or silver.["]

5. An Act of the Legislature of New Hamshire passed April 29th. 1780 entitled "An Act for complying with and carrying into execution certain resolutions of Congress of the 18th of March 1780 for sinking the bills of public credit now current and for issuing other bills in their stead."

71

6. A Conditional Act of the Legislature of Pennsylvania passed the first day of June 1780 entitled "An Act for funding and redeeming the bills of credit of the United States of America and for providing means to bring the present war to a happy conclusion.["][2]

Jos: Jones
James Madison Jun
Jn. Walker

[1] See Jefferson to JM, 26 July 1780, n. 2; and Jameson to JM, 23 August 1780, n. 3. As required by the suspending section of the enforcement act of Virginia (Hening, *Statutes*, X, 254), the delegates probably sent this certification directly to Governor Jefferson, or may have inclosed it for him in JM's now missing letter of 5 September to David Jameson.

[2] Although the delegates might also have certified that the legislatures of Connecticut and Rhode Island had taken similar action (Burnett, *Letters*, V, 264, No. 314, n. 2), Jefferson had interpreted the Virginia statute to require him to delay proclaiming it in force until he had "authentic" knowledge of the compliance by only five other states with the 18 March 1780 resolutions of Congress (Jefferson to JM, 26 July 1780).

Motion Regarding the Western Lands

MS (NA: PCC, No. 36, I, 97–98). In the hand of Joseph Jones.

EDITORIAL NOTE

On 26 June 1780 Congress referred the long-standing and complicated issue of the "western frontiers" to a committee composed of James Duane, John Henry (Md.), Joseph Jones, Roger Sherman, and Willie Jones (N.C.). Its "report and resolve," written by Duane, was laid before Congress on 30 June, debated on 2 September, and adopted on the sixth of that month, immediately before the introduction of Joseph Jones's motion (*Journals of the Continental Congress*, XVII, 559–60, 580, 586, 802, 806–8). Pointing out how "indispensibly necessary" an early ratification of the Articles of Confederation was to the "public credit," "the support of our army," "the vigour of our councils and success of our measures," "our tranquillity at home, and our reputation abroad," "our present safety and our future prosperity," and to "our very existence as a free, sovereign and independent people," the committee in its "resolve" called, on the one hand, upon the states claiming "western country" to enable their delegates "to effectually remove the only obstacle to a final ratification of the articles," and upon Maryland, on the other hand, to authorize its delegates "to subscribe" to those Articles.

Although the committee declined to judge which of the parties had the stronger case in law and in precedent, its resolution virtually asked Virginia to surrender its position, no matter how well justified it may have been, for the sake of the common cause. The reasons for Virginia's stand, however, and for that of Maryland also, must be recalled in order to clarify the role of JM in the matter during the next three or four years. Until he seconded Jones's motion, he apparently had concerned himself very little, if at all, with the western lands issue. Immediately after introducing his motion, Jones left for Virginia in order to be with his ailing wife and to persuade the Virginia legislature to accede to the request of Congress. Jones's departure obliged JM to share prominently for the first time in the congressional deliberations about the West.

At its simplest, the controversy over this vast area west of the Appalachians was between the seven "landed" states (Massachusetts, Connecticut, New York, Virginia, North Carolina, South Carolina, and Georgia) holding more or less valid titles to territory there, and the other six states lacking such titles. Each of the seven, with the exception of New York, based its claim upon a royal charter which extended its western limit to the Pacific Ocean, or at least to the Mississippi River. South of the Ohio River, these jurisdictions of Virginia, the Carolinas, and Georgia did not seriously overlap, but between that stream and the Great Lakes and from the poorly defined western boundary of Pennsylvania to the Mississippi, Virginia claimed all, and New York, Massachusetts, and Connecticut claimed some, of the area. The alleged legality of Virginia's title stemmed from the charter of King James I in 1609 to the London Company, granting that corporation two hundred miles north and south of Cape Comfort along the Atlantic Coast and "up into the Land, throughout from Sea to Sea, West, and Northwest." Although this territory had been given to a company and not to its colony, although the charter had been rescinded by the Court of the King's Bench in 1624, although later sovereigns by grants to other proprietors had encroached upon the seaboard frontage of Virginia, and although that colony made no vigorous protest on the strength of "its" old charter when Parliament in 1774 extended the southern limits of the Province of Quebec to the Ohio River, Virginians contended early in the Revolution that since their ancestors had never consented to the rescinding of "their" charter (which they declared to have been a contract between the King and the people of the colony, unalterable except by mutual consent) their ancient bounds "north and northwest of the Ohio" were still valid, or at least were more so than those of Massachusetts, Connecticut, or New York.

In their origin, the claims of these three colonies all postdated 1609. Connecticut's charter of 1662 extended the colony "to the South Sea [Pacific Ocean] on the West parte," while Massachusetts' of 1691 was similarly generous. New York's claim may have been as well grounded, but at least it was more vague about how far it extended toward the west. By the late seventeenth century, the five tribes of Iroquois Indians whose homes were within the province of New York exercised suzerainty over numerous groups of Algonquin Indians living between Lake Erie and the Ohio River. In 1684 Governor Thomas Dongan, in furtherance of New York's economic and political rivalry with the French in Canada, declared the Iroquois to be subjects of the English Crown and under the immediate protection of his provincial government. Thus the geographic range of New York's control became elastic toward the west, embracing the Iroquois (six rather than five "nations" by 1730), their vassal tribes, and, presumably, the territory over which they roamed.

During the Revolution, although these overlapping claims of four "landed" states, and the simultaneous dispute among New York, New Hampshire, and Massachusetts over the Vermont country, complicated the issue of the western territory, the heart of that controversy involved Virginia on the one side and the "landless" states of Rhode Island, New Jersey, Pennsylvania, Delaware, and Maryland on the other. Virginians were much the more insistent upon their legal right to the area north of the Ohio River because their own economic advantage and that of their commonwealth were heavily involved. As individual investors or as members of land companies, some of the "first gentlemen" of Virginia, including Washington and George Mason, owned, claimed to own, or wanted to own, vast tracts of land in that region. If their titles were not unassailable, the Virginia legislature could make them so. Before the Revolution, at a considerable expense of "blood and treasure," Virginia had sent troops against offending Indians living north of the Ohio. During the Revolution, at a much heavier cost, the state was maintaining against the British in that region the forces commanded by Colonel George Rogers Clark. Furthermore, Virginia counted upon her public domain, both in Kentucky and in the Northwest, to make good her bounty-land pledges to her soldiers, preserve her financial credit, and pay her war debt.

Opponents of Virginia's claim to the Northwest could not deny that "the United States in Congress Assembled" possessed no land of their own, but they argued with considerable force that "the landed states" should cede to the central government all or most of the territory west of the Appalachians. Although these opponents had no charters or other legal documents to cite in support of their position, they could defend it on grounds of justice, necessity, and patriotism. The title of Virginia would be worthless unless independence from Britain were won. The attainment of this goal hinged upon military victory, and it, in turn, upon the efforts and sacrifices of all the states, and not of Virginia alone. If a defeated Britain were compelled to withdraw from the West, it necessarily would cede its sovereignty over, and title to, that territory to the United States rather than to one or another of the "landed states." And fortunately so, because the bond of common ownership thus created would come most opportunely to replace the broken tie of a common danger to hold the discordant states together. The United States might also be able to use this public domain to restore its financial credit and pay its huge war debt.

Furthermore, a union of states would more likely be lasting if they were nearer alike in size. Although each of the thirteen declared itself to be sovereign, and hence equal one to another, the leaders of Rhode Island, New Jersey, Pennsylvania, Delaware, and, above all, Maryland, were not blind to the gap between political theory and actuality. If success in the war merely resulted in exchanging a master across the Atlantic Ocean for several master-states close at hand, the "fruit" of the Revolution would hardly be true independence. Not a few of these leaders, however, masked without much success a personal financial stake behind these high-level arguments on behalf of a gift by the "landed states" of their western territories to the United States. These leaders singly, or organized in companies, had speculated in trans-Allegheny lands, including large tracts which conflicted in their vague boundaries with those claimed by Virginians. These speculators from the Middle States, centered largely in Philadelphia and in Maryland, could not hope to have their titles validated by the legislature of Virginia but might influence Congress in their favor if the territory in question became the property of the United States.

Early in the Revolution many of these crosscurrents converged with two other important subjects of discussion in the Continental Congress—(a) upon what terms a legal union of the states might be created; and (b) upon what terms patriots might be induced to enlist in the army for the duration of the war. In harmony with the sovereignty of each state, the Articles of Confederation provided not only that it would not go into effect until every state had ratified it (Preamble and Art. XIII) but also that "no State shall be deprived of territory for the benefit of the United States" (Art. IX). The latter guarantee was included upon the insistence of the delegates from "the landed" states and over the opposition of those from Maryland and other "landless" states. In September 1776 Congress passed the first of several acts promising bounties in land to men who would enlist in the "continental line" for the duration of the war. Having no territory of its own, Congress apparently relied for the fulfillment of these pledges upon state generosity. In the autumn of 1778 the Virginia legislature (*Journal of the House of Delegates*, October 1778, pp. 124–25) offered to make available from its western territory its due proportion of lands needed for this purpose but reserved its right of political jurisdiction over the promised acreage. Owing to this proviso, spokesmen for the small states spurned a proffer which would drain away many of their best young men and reduce their own land values and income from taxes, all for the benefit of a commonwealth which even then was the most populous and reputedly the most wealthy of the thirteen.

In November 1777, sixteen months after the original form of the Articles of Confederation was laid before Congress, that body adopted a much revised draft and asked each state to authorize its delegates to sign it (*Journals of the Continental Congress*, IX, 806–8, 842–43, 916, 918). By June of the next year, all states except Maryland, Delaware, and New Jersey had ratified the document. The main objection of these three was embodied in an amendment, submitted by the Maryland delegation but voted down by Congress, to empower that body to appoint commissioners "fully authorized ... to ascertain and restrict the boundaries of ... states which claim to extend to the river Mississippi, or South Sea" (*ibid.*, XI, 631–32, 637). Notwithstanding this rebuff, New Jersey gave its assent to the Articles in November 1778, and Delaware in February of the next year (*ibid.*, XII, 1161–64; XIII, 150, 186–88). Thereafter for two more years no legal union could be effected because of Maryland's refusal to ratify. Its proximity to Virginia, its friction with its neighbor for 150 years over the control of Chesapeake Bay, and the interests of its land speculators combined with more statesman-like considerations to account for its obstinacy.

On 20 May 1779, under instructions from their state legislature, the Virginia delegates in Congress tried without avail to have the Articles of Confederation go into effect for the twelve states which had agreed to the document (*ibid.*, XIV, 617–18). The following day the Maryland delegates countered by making known the mandate from their state assembly forbidding them to sign the Articles until an amendment was added granting Congress discretionary power to create "free, convenient and independent governments" in the "common property" won "by the blood and treasure of the thirteen states" (*ibid.*, XIV, 619–22). A month later the Virginia legislature, led by George Mason, took a similarly uncompromising stand by creating a land office to issue warrants for, and to sell, the state's "waste and unappropriated lands" (Hening, *Statutes*, X, 50–65; Boyd, *Papers of Jefferson*, II, 136–38). In reprisal, the Maryland delegates on 30 October 1779 carried through Congress by a decisive vote, in spite of the protest of the representatives from Virginia and North Carolina, a resolution calling upon Virginia to stop selling land (*Journals of the Continental Congress*, XV, 1226–30).

As the year ended, the Virginia legislature adopted a "Remonstrance ... to the delegates of the United American States in Congress Assembled," written by George Mason, and transmitted it to the state's delegates in Philadelphia for their use on an opportune occasion. After mentioning that, in deference to Congress' request, the legislature had taken steps "to prevent present Settlements on the North West Side of the Ohio River," this document reminded Congress that it had no land of its own and that it must not invade Virginia's sovereignty by giving heed to petitions from land speculator companies (Vandalia and Indiana companies) asserting claims to territory in the West (Boyd, *Papers of Jefferson*, III, 630–32). Over seven weeks before the Virginia delegation, on 28 April 1780, presented this Remonstrance to Congress (*Journals of the Continental Congress*, XVI, 398), New York had moved the dispute into a new phase by offering both its "western lands" and its jurisdiction over them to the United States in order "to accelerate the foederal alliance" (*ibid.*, XVI, 236; Burnett, *Letters*, V, 21–22).

Other circumstances attending this "darkest year" of the Revolution worked more directly than New York's cession toward ending the impasse between Virginia and Maryland. By the spring of 1780, with a British army moving northward from South Carolina and the foe raiding inward from Chesapeake Bay, Virginia for the first time since 1776 was in dire need of military aid from the middle seaboard states. La Luzerne, the French minister to the United States, took pains to make clear to Marylanders and others that his country would be the more eager to supply ships and soldiers to aid the hard-pressed patriots if they would complete their union by ratifying the Articles of Confederation. This military crisis brought converts to Jefferson's view, advanced as early as 1776, that Virginia should create "colonies," free and independent of its control, in the territory west of the mountains (Boyd, *Papers of Jefferson*, I, 353). John Walker, Richard Henry Lee, Joseph Jones, and especially George Mason, whose land speculations in that area would normally incline him to oppose its cession to the United States, rallied to Jefferson's side (Jones to Jefferson, 30 June 1780, *ibid.*, III, 472–75; Mason to JM, 2 August 1780, and n. 3).

Now that the much altered military outlook had fostered this change of opinion, these men readily discovered many reasons why Virginia's own future advantage harmonized with an action so well calculated to promote the welfare of the United States. The western lands were too distant and too vast in extent to be governed effectively by Virginia. The expense to be expected from fighting the Indians there or from clearing their titles, and from surveying and administering the area, would exceed for years in the future the income flowing from it into the state treasury. Furthermore, by reducing through cession the size of its domain and the number of its inhabitants, Virginia would correspondingly lessen the financial quota apportioned to it by Congress. That body encouraged the Virginia legislature to be more conciliatory by referring to a committee on 23 May 1780, when the Maryland delegates were absent, a resolution stating that although the United States owned no land Congress was "bound to employ the common forces and common powers in support of the jurisdiction of the said states [over their land] whenever the same shall be invaded or infringed" (*Journals of the Continental Congress*, XVII, 452). On 2 June 1780, although somewhat contrary to the spirit of the recent Remonstrance of Virginia, its delegates helped to carry a resolution, over the opposition of Maryland and Rhode Island, to have Congress adjudicate the Vermont lands issues involving New York, New Hampshire, and Massachusetts (*ibid.*, XVII, 482–84, 499). Later that month, Congress appointed the committee mentioned at the beginning of this note.

[6 September 1780]

A motion was made by Mr. [Joseph] Jones, seconded by Mr. [James] Madison, respecting the lands that may be ceded in pursuance of the foregoing report and resolve.[1]

That in case the recommendation of Congress to the States of Virginia North Carolina and Georgia to cede to the United States a portion of the unappropriated western Territory shall be complied with in such manner as to be approved of by Congress—the Territory so ceded shall be laid out in separate and distinct States at such time and in such manner as Congress shall here after direct, so as that no State be less than one hundred or more than one hundred and fifty miles square or as near thereto as circumstances will admit—and that upon such cession being approved of and accepted by Congress the United States will guaranty the remaining Territory to the said States respectively.

That such of the said States as have been at expence in subduing any of the British Posts [within] the Territory proposed to be ceded and in maintaining Garrisons and supporting civil Govern[ment] therein since the reduction of such Posts shall be reimbursed by the Continent the amount of such expence

That all the Lands to be ceded to the United States and not appropriated or disposed of in bounties to the American Army shall be considered as a common Fund for the use and benefit of such of the United States as have become or shall become Members of the Confederation according to their usual proportions or quotas of general charge and expenditure and shall be applied and disposed of For that purpose and no other whatsoever. And therefore all purchases and Deeds from any Indian or Indians or any Indian Nation or Nations for any Lands within any part of such ceded Territory which shall have been or shall be made for the use of any private person or persons whatsoever shall be deemed and taken as absolutely void.[2]

[1] This introductory paragraph is not a part of the motion as found in the Papers of the Continental Congress, but is taken from *Journals of the Continental Congress*, XVII, 808.

[2] Action upon this motion was postponed until 9 September, when Congress referred it to a committee composed of Roger Sherman, Artemas Ward (Mass.), Whitmell Hill (N.C.), John Henry, and JM (*ibid.*, XVIII, 816; Jones to JM, 2 October 1780, n. 2).

Virginia Delegates in Congress to Virginia Auditors of Public Accounts

RC (Virginia State Library). The note appears to be in John Walker's hand.

GENTLEMEN:[1]   PHILADA. Sepr. 11th. 1780.

Please to pay to Mr. Michael Gratz[2] or order Thirty Thousand Dollars & charge the same to our Acct. as Delegates to Congress.[3]

JAMES MADISON JUNR.
JN WALKER
THEOK BLAND

To The Gentn. Auditors of public Accts.
Virginia[4]

[1] By a law enacted in December 1778 the legislature of Virginia created a Board of Auditors, comprising three men to be elected by joint ballot of the two houses

of the Assembly. In September 1780 the auditors were Harrison Randolph, Leighton Wood, and Edward Archer, Jr. (*Journal of the House of Delegates,* October 1778, p. 111; Hening, *Statutes,* IX, 536–40; *Calendar of Virginia State Papers,* I, 355, 414). Harrison Randolph (*ca.* 1740–*ca.* 1801) of Brunswick County became a state auditor in May 1780 and remained on the board until 1784. In 1793 he was appointed clerk of the Virginia district court for his district (Brunswick County Court Records, Deed Book, No. 15, p. 183, microfilm in Virginia State Library; Brunswick County Property Tax Books, 1801–1802). Leighton Wood (1740–1805) of Hanover County had been a commissioner to investigate accounts of public trade in 1777–1778. His tenure as auditor was only seven months, for he became state solicitor general on 29 December 1780 (*Journal of the House of Delegates,* October 1777, p. 116; May 1780, p. 21; October 1780, pp. 76, 78). Edward Archer, Jr. (*ca.* 1741–1807), a merchant from Norfolk, was named to the Board of Auditors in 1779 and remained until 1781. He was a member of the Norfolk County Committee of Safety in 1775 and the state Board of Naval Commissioners from 1776 to 1779. With the establishment of the federal government he became a supporter of the first Bank of the United States (*St. Paul's Church, 1832, originally the Borough Church, 1739, Elizabeth River Parish, Norfolk, Virginia* [Norfolk, 1934], p. 90; *Virginia Magazine of History and Biography,* LXIII [1955], 333; *Journal of the House of Delegates,* October 1776, p. 104; May 1779, pp. 53, 64; October 1781, p. 17).

2 Michael Gratz (1740–1811), a prominent Philadelphia merchant who for a time had lived and traded in Virginia. He frequently handled the business of members of Congress.

3 For a detailed statement of JM's financial accounts during his first six months in Congress, see below, 25 September 1780 and 20 December 1780.

4 Below the text of this note is written, probably by one of the auditors, "30,000 Dollars a[t] 75 for 1 is £120." That is, $30,000 divided by 75 (the depreciation rate in September 1780 was 75 to 1) equals $400. One pound Virginia currency was equated as $3.33 continental currency. Hence, $400 divided by $3.33 is £120. Beneath the sentence in quotation marks appears the following, apparently written at least four years later:

"NB.

"Mr. Maddison has credited his third part of the above[.] Colo Bland render'd an acct. of his third part, but it was not charged to him & the settlemt. consequently the public is not answerable for it[.] Mr. Walker is charged with his third part July 21, 1784, but had not rendered any acct as Delegate in Congress at that period[.]"

Motion in Congress

Printed text (*Journals of the Continental Congress,* XVIII, 818–19). Motion seconded by Samuel Adams.

[11 September 1780]

Ordered, That the Committee of Foreign Affairs cause to be printed at the expence of the United States 1200 copies of a correct translation of a memorial published by the Court of France, entitled "Observations sur le memoire justificatif de la cour de Londres;"[1] and distribute the same to such public bodies throughout the states, and in such proportions as they shall judge expedient.[2]

[1] This brochure of eighty-four pages was published in Paris in 1780. Its anonymous author was Joseph Mathias Gérard de Rayneval. John Adams wrote from Paris to President Samuel Huntington on 11 May 1780 that the pamphlet "contains many points of serious information respecting France, Spain, and America" (Wharton, *Revolutionary Diplomatic Correspondence*, III, 670). Perhaps this comment and the fact that on 1 May 1780 the British House of Commons had manifested an interest in the essay (*Journals of the House of Commons*, XXXVII [1778–80], 812) led JM to introduce his motion. Rayneval's work was an answer to Edward Gibbon's tract, written under governmental auspices and entitled, *Mémoire justificatif pour servir de réponse à l'exposé, &c. de la cour de France* (London, 1779).

[2] In accordance with this directive, the Committee for Foreign Affairs had the brochure translated and published in Philadelphia in 1781, under the title, *Observations on the Justificative Memorial of the Court of London*. "Col. Madison" is written in ink on the title page of the copy in the Alderman Library, University of Virginia.

To Edmund Pendleton

RC (LC: Madison Papers). The address sheet is missing, but Pendleton wrote on the letter: "James Maddison, Esqr. Sepr. 12. 1780." Although the originals of most of the letters from Pendleton to JM have not been found (see headnote to Pendleton to JM, 27 August 1780), JM's letters to Pendleton, insofar as their present location is known, are with one exception in two repositories—the Library of Congress and the New York Public Library. Thirty-nine letters dating between 12 September 1780 and 2 April 1782, and thirty-five between 30 November 1786 and 7 February 1796, are in the Library of Congress. Retrieved by JM from Pendleton or his heirs, many of these letters appear to have been carefully scanned by JM in his old age or by some members of his family with a view to preparing them, or extracts from them, for publication. Whenever possible, the present editors will point out these emendations as well as the original wording. Of the fifteen letters in the New York Public Library from JM to Pendleton, all except one were written between 9 April and 4 November 1782. Unlike the other group, this one gives no evidence of having been revised, and hence may not have been recovered by JM. And yet, Stan. V. Henkels sold both sets in 1892 without suggesting that they had been merged after being acquired from different owners (Catalogue No. 694, "Washington-Madison Papers"). Pendleton acknowledged in his replies to JM the receipt of many more letters from the latter than are now known to exist. These lost letters have been missing for many years and were apparently unknown even to the earliest biographers of JM and the first editors of his papers.

PHILA. Sepr. 12th. 1780

DEAR SIR

I received your favor of the 27th. of August by last week's post and should not have failed to testify the pleasure with which I embrace your correspondence by an immediate answer had I not understood from Mr. Jones that he proposed to write you the news, and enclose you the paper of the day.[1] In future I shall endeavor to drop you a line by every post, or at least as often as any thing material occurs.

The delay of Ternay's 2d. division and the report of its being shut up in Brest have brought our hopes from the present campaign very low.[2] They have been a little revived within a few days by sundry concurring information, that a large French fleet from the West Indies is on our coast. This story is the more credible, as pretty certain intelligence has been recd. that the French & Spanish fleets in that quarter[,] instead of going to Jamaica as every body expected and their own movements announced, had separated from each other, and gone into different ports, and as there is no other place after such an event where the former could act with so much advantage as on our coast in conjunction with Ternay.[3] Should this goo[d] news prove true it is to be regretted that Graves did not stay a little longer off Rhode Island, unless he should return to Sandy Hook of which no notice has been received, where[,] as his large ships cannot get into the harbour, they must be an easy prey to the superior force of our Allies.

We have the comfort to find from every successive account from the Southward that the late unfortunate affair in that quarter, although truly distressing, is by no means so fata[l] as was at first held up to us. Our scattered troops are again embodying, and as a sense of shame is now joined to a sense of public danger in the Militia it is to be hoped they will endeavour to cancel their disgrace by extraordinary exertions.[4] Congress have recommended it to Virga. & N. Carolina to form Magazines for a large army, to the former to hasten the march of her new levies, & the latter to take immediate measures for filling her continental line.[5]

Congress have also at length entered seriously on a plan for finally ratifying the confederation. Convinced of the necessity of such a measure, to repress the hopes with which the probable issue of the campaign will inspire our Enemy, as well as to give greater authority & vigor to our public councils, they have recommended in the most pressing terms to the States claiming unappropriated back lands, to cede a liberal portion of them for the general benefit. As these exclusive claims formed the only obstacle with Maryland there is no doubt that a compliance with this recommendation will bring her into the confederation. How far the States holding the back lands may be disposed to give them up cannot be so easily determined. From the sentiments of the most intelligent persons which have come to my knowledge, I own I am pretty sanguine that they will see the necessity of closing the union in too strong a light to oppose the only expedient that can accomplish it.[6]

Another circumstance that ought greatly to encourage us under disappointed expectations from the campaign is the combination of ye maritime powers in support of their neutral rights, and particularly the late insolent and provoking violation of those rights by the English Ships at St. Martin's[.][7] It is not probable that the injured will be satisfied without reparations & acknowledgement which the pride of Britain will not submit [to], and if she can ever be embroiled in an altercation with so formidable a league, the result must necessarily be decisively in our favour. Indeed It is not to be supposed after the amazing resources which have been seen in G. Britain when not only deprived of but opposed by her antient colonies, and ye success of the latter in resisting for so long a time the utmost exertion of their resources against her,[8] that the Maritime powers who appear to be so jealous of their rights will ever suffer an event to take place which must very soon expose them to be trampled on at pleasure of G. Britain.

I must beg you once for all to excuse the inaccuracies with which the hurry of the post day will deface my letters.

With sincere regard I am Dr Sir yr. Obt friend and servt.

JAMES MADISON JUNR.

[1] Before Joseph Jones left Philadelphia for Virginia on 7 September, he evidently told JM he would get in touch with Pendleton.

[2] Admiral Charles Louis D'Arsac, Chevalier de Ternay (1723–1780). For the blockade of his fleet, see above, Report of Board of Admiralty, 26 May 1780, n. 2; and Committee Report on Rochambeau's Letter, 17 August 1780, nn. 2 and 4.

[3] See JM to Jefferson, 2 June 1780, n. 3; and Jameson to JM, 23 August 1780, nn. 1 and 2.

[4] JM here refers to the Battle of Camden, S.C., on 16 August, where the defeat of Gates's army was due largely to the disgraceful conduct of Brigadier General Edward Stevens' Virginia militia and of Major General Richard Caswell's North Carolina militia (Christopher Ward, *War of the Revolution*, II, 726–28).

[5] For these recommendations, adopted on 8 and 11 September, and including also a call upon Maryland to complete filling its troop quota and send it to the southern army, see *Journals of the Continental Congress*, XVIII, 812–13, 818.

[6] Above, Motion regarding the Western Lands, 6 September 1780. Many years later, JM inclosed this paragraph and the succeeding one in brackets and quotation

marks, evidently designating them for publication with other portions of his early letters.

[7] See Reverend James Madison to JM, 3 August 1780, and n. 3; Jameson to JM, 30 August 1780, and n. 3.

[8] JM probably intended to write, "the utmost exertion of her resources against them."

From David Jameson

RC (LC: Rives Collection of Madison Papers).

RICHMOND Sep 13. 1780

DR. SIR

I have recd your two favours of the 23d & 29th. ult. since my last, and am very glad to find you were getting into better health[1]

We have had nothing lately from the Southward but what you will find mentd. in Dixons Paper.[2] We are very anxious to hear something more from Chas. Town. should there be a French or Spanish Fleet there, something may yet be done, but the defeat of Gen. Gates will in all probability prevent the speedy retaking the place and the capture of the whole british force there. had he proceeded with caution, as he would have been joined by Men from both South & No. Carolina, The Enemy must have retreated to Chas. Town[,] And he would have found himself in a condition with a foreign aid to have compleated the Work[3] I am very sorry to find Congress are disapointed in their expectation of small Arms.[4] they will be wanted to the Southward, and I fear from your Accot. none can be spared from the Northern operations. We are quite drained, and should the Enemy make us a visit we shall be in very poor condition to oppose them. We have not yet recd those we expected from France.[5] You may remember we were served in the same manner you have lately been—Cannon sent & small Arms left behind.

The Consul has taken Station at Cape Henry and seems to think the 2d divn. of the French Fleet will probably appear there.[6]

I am dr Sir Yr obt Servt.

DAVID JAMESON

Commodore Barron is gone with the Jefferson & the Boats Liberty & Patriot up to Baltimore to join some Vessels there. they expect to clear the Bay of all the piccaroons & Open a safe passage for the provision Vessels. Considerable qtys of Bacon and Corn lie ready for transportation.[7]

¹ These two letters from JM have not been found. Although he was evidently feeling well enough to write the letters, JM is not mentioned in the journal of Congress between mid-August and 6 September.

² See Jameson to JM, 13 August 1780, n. 3.

³ No French or Spanish fleet was in the Charleston neighborhood at this time (JM to Jefferson, 2 June 1780, n. 3; Jameson to JM, 23 August 1780, n. 2). For Gates's defeat at Camden, see Jameson to JM, 16 August 1780, n. 6; and JM to Pendleton, 12 September 1780, n. 4.

⁴ The "Alliance" reached Boston from France in mid-August but, contrary to Congress' expectation, it brought no munitions (Board of Admiralty to Nicholson, 17 April 1780; JM to Page [?], 8 May 1780, n. 7).

⁵ See Jameson to JM, 16 August 1780, n. 7.

⁶ The vice-consul of France for Virginia was Charles François, Chevalier d'Anmours. He had gone on his futile mission to Cape Henry on 9 September (Boyd, *Papers of Jefferson*, III, 84, 624).

⁷ Commodore James Barron, Sr. (1740–1787), of Hampton had recently been appointed to command the navy of Virginia. With the brig "Jefferson," fourteen guns, and the swift, armed boats "Liberty" and "Patriot," he sailed from York on 12 September to co-operate with Maryland ships in clearing Chesapeake Bay of picaroons and in convoying vessels loaded with stores for the southern army (*ibid.*, III, 579, 590–91, 642).

Notes on Territorial Claim of New Hampshire

MS (LC: Madison Papers, Vol. 91). Undated memorandum docketed by JM, "Livermore's state[ment] of the Territorial claim of N Hampshire." To give this memorandum even an approximate date depends upon what JM meant by "state[ment]." If it signifies an oral statement to which JM listened and upon which he took this obviously hurried note, it must date between 20 March 1780, when he first entered Congress, and 8 April 1780, when Livermore left Congress, or between 14 May 1781 and 29 April 1782 (Burnett, *Letters*, V, 110, n. 2; VI, xlvii) when both men were again members of that body and the subject of the memorandum was frequently discussed. On the other hand, if JM's note was upon a written statement filed with Congress by Livermore during either of his two periods of service as a delegate, JM might have made these jottings at any time between 20 March 1780 and a decade later, since the controversy came to the fore now and again until the admission of Vermont as a state in 1791. If, however, Livermore presented a written brief, it apparently is not among the Papers of the Continental Congress in the National Archives. Perhaps he took it back to New Hampshire when he returned there early in April 1780 (*ibid.*, V, 170). Being unable to date the memorandum, the editors have placed it immediately preceding JM's resolutions upon the Vermont issue. Samuel Livermore (1732–1803), who had been the attorney general of New Hamp-

shire and would be its chief justice, and a United States con-
gressman and senator, arrived in Philadelphia on 5 February
1780 as a special delegate to Congress from his state to defend
its title to the Vermont area against the rival claims of New
York, Massachusetts, and the *de facto* independent government
organized by many of Vermont's settlers in the winter of 1776–
1777 (*ibid.*, V, 28, n. 3).

About the year 1630 a grant was made by Chas I to Capt. Mason,[1]
of a tract of Country call'd by him N. H. beginning at the mouth of
Piscataqua river & to extend 60 miles into the Country about north.
Then to begin at the head of Nahumkeeg river[2] & to extend 60 miles
abt west into the country & so to cross over to the end of the 60 miles
aforesd. without jurisdiction,[3] wch Till about the 1680 was exercised
with the acquiescence of the inhabitants by Massachussetts, over the
grant itself & such parts of the country back of it as was from time to
time settled. About this time civil Govt. was established over N.
Hamshire by the King without specifying its limits.[4] About the 1738.
a line was settled between N. H. & Mass: by Commisrs. appointed by
the Crown, according to their present possessions; extending Westward till it should meet with his Majesty's other Govts. The Comissrs.
to the Governors of the former have since been conformable to the
sd. settlement; by which as well as by other acts of the Crown & especially that relating to fort Drummer it appears that the territory of
N. H. should extend to the twenty mile line.[5] prior the year 1764. the
Govr. of N. H.[6] had granted upwards of 130 townships 6 miles square
each in the territory thence called N. H. grants, lying between Connecticut river & the 20 Mile line upon wch. not less than 10,000 souls
settled. In the year 1764 on an exparte hearing at the instance [of]
L. Govr. Colden[7] of N. Y. who wished to regrant the land & made
imme[n]se sums therefrom. a decree of the King in Council extended
the jurisdiction of that State to Connecticut river.[8] The Govt. of N. H.
was prior to the revolution taking measure[s] in conjunction wth. the
Inhabts. west of the River to obtain a reversal of the decree, and had
made such progress therein, that a prohibition agst. further grants had
issued to the Govt. of N. Y.[9]

[1] By virtue of its royal charter, the Council for New England, not King Charles I,
issued several patents to John Mason (1586–1635) between 1622 and his death. The
one here referred to was dated 7 November 1629.

[2] Naumkeag or Salem River.

[3] That is, having merely grants of land from the New England council and no
charter from the Crown, Mason and his heirs lacked constitutional authority to

govern their holdings (Herbert Levi Osgood, *The American Colonies in the Seventeenth Century* [3 vols.; New York, 1904–7], III, 320).

4 On 18 September 1679, King Charles II created the royal province of New Hampshire without designating its geographic limits. Thereafter the area was in the main a separate jurisdiction, although from 1699 to 1741 the governor of Massachusetts Bay Colony, acting under a distinct commission, was also the governor of New Hampshire.

5 The blockhouse of Fort Dummer, erected in 1724, in the present site of Brattleboro, was the earliest English settlement in the disputed area. Following the determination of New Hampshire's southern and eastern boundary with Massachusetts in 1738, New Hampshire's principal boundary quarrel was with New York on the west. By "twenty mile line" is meant twenty miles east of the Hudson River, so as to make New Hampshire's western boundary conform with the western limits of Massachusetts and Connecticut. JM probably meant "Commissions of" rather than "Comissrs. to."

6 JM's confused punctuation, capitalization, and verb forms suggest the haste with which he made these notes. The intended reading here is probably, "Prior [to] the year 1764, the Govr. of N. H." "The Govr." was Benning Wentworth (1696–1770), who held that office for twenty-five years, ending in 1767.

7 Cadwallader Colden (1688–1776), lieutenant governor of New York from 1761 until his death.

8 The meaning of this sentence and the preceding one would be clarified if "make" were substituted for "made," and a comma for the period after "therefrom." The date of the Order in Council was 20 July 1764 (Nathaniel Bouton, comp. and ed., *Documents and Records Relating to the Province of New-Hampshire from 1764 to 1776*, VII [Nashua, N.H., 1873], 62).

9 The matter was again before the King's Commissioners for Trade and Plantations in the spring of 1775 (*The Letters and Papers of Cadwallader Colden* [9 vols.; New-York Historical Society, 1918–37], VII, 279–81).

Resolutions Respecting Vermont Lands

MS (NA: PCC, No. 20, II, 249–52).

EDITORIAL NOTE

These resolutions were merely one episode in an exceedingly difficult and prolonged controversy into which Congress was first drawn on 8 May 1776 (*Journals of the Continental Congress*, IV, 334–35, 405). During the war, the concern of Congress about the dispute among New Hampshire, New York, and, to a lesser degree, Massachusetts over jurisdiction and land titles in the Vermont area, and between each of these three states and the *de facto* independent government created by many of the Vermont settlers, was the greater because the matters at issue often diverted these states from concentrating upon, and from co-operating fully with the other ten states in, the main business of winning the Revolution. Furthermore, the efforts by Congress to solve the divisive issue of the western lands, and thereby to secure the ratification of the Articles of Confederation, were hampered by the "jockeying" of the delegations from each of these three disputants to gain votes in support of the claim of its state to Vermont (above, Motion of 6 September 1780 regarding the Western Lands, editorial note).

By mid-1780, Congress had at least made clear (*a*) that it would not recognize the independence of Vermont (*Journals of the Continental Congress,* VIII, 508–11); (*b*) that, despite the insistence of the New York delegation, it would not accept the King's Order in Council of 1764 as settling the jurisdictional issue (above, notes on Livermore's statement, n. 8); and (*c*) that, as soon as nine states other than the three at loggerheads were amply represented, it would, with the consent of the three, "hear and examine into and finally determine the disputes and differences relative to jurisdiction." The resolutions summing up this position were adopted on 2 June 1780, with eight state delegations, including JM and his Virginia colleagues, voting for them and with those of Maryland and Rhode Island opposed. The delegates from North Carolina and Delaware were absent, and those from Massachusetts were evenly divided (*ibid.*, XVII, 482–85). One week later a motion, introduced by George Walton of Georgia and seconded by Nathaniel Folsom of New Hampshire, to postpone the hearing until 12 September carried without a recorded vote but in spite of the opposition of the delegation from New York (*ibid.*, XVII, 499). On 16 September, the second day of the hearing, the resolutions printed below were offered by JM and seconded by Francis Kinloch of South Carolina (*ibid.*, XVIII, 832–33).

Why JM should suddenly have assumed this active role in the matter is not answered by the sources. Neither he nor Kinloch was then, nor had either of them been before, on any committee assigned to deal with the Vermont issue. Perhaps of relevance are the facts that Folsom had left for home on 15 September (Burnett, *Letters*, V, lviii, 386) and Walton would do so later that month (*ibid.*, V, lvi). Except for Walton and certain delegates from the three states primarily affected by the controversy, no member who had been prominently identified with it during the past three years was in Congress when JM submitted his resolutions. Furthermore, earlier in September he had replaced the absent Joseph Jones as Virginia's main spokesman on the western lands question—an issue with which the Vermont problem interlocked.

[16 September 1780]

Resolved that it appears to Congress from the evidence stated to them by the Delegates of New Hamshire and New York, as well as from former resolutions of Congress defining the general boundary of the United States,[1] that the territory commonly called the New Hamshire Grants is within the limits of some one or more of the United States.[2]

Resolved that every attempt by force to set up a separate and independent jurisdiction within the limits of any one of the United States is a direct violation of the rights of such state, and subversive of the Union of the whole under the superintending authority of Congress.

Resolved that it be earnestly recommended to the people who have assumed an independent jurisdiction over the district aforesaid immediately to desist from the exercise thereof; and to remain, untill a final determination shall take place, subject to such of the states contending for jurisdiction over them, as a major part of the inhabitants of each of the townships shall on an election for that purpose respectively prefer.

Resolved that Congress, will immediately proceed to the appointment of commissioners, agreeably to their resolutions of the 24 day of September last, to hear and determine the claims of New Hamshire and New York to the country commonly called the New Hamshire Grants.[3]

Resolved that it be recommended to the State or States within whose jurisdiction the same shall fall to confirm the titles of the inhabitants to the lands they respectively hold notwithstanding any defect in the grants on which such titles depend.

Resolved that a special Committee be appointed to prepare and report an Address to the inhabitants of the district in question, explaining to them the principles and reasons on which the foregoing resolutions are founded, and urging them to a ready and peaceable submission to them[4]

[1] Resolutions of 4 August 1779, defining the boundaries of the United States (*Journals of the Continental Congress*, XIV, 920–21).

[2] After debate, the states (with the delegations from New Hampshire, Massachusetts, and New York abstaining) equally divided in their vote upon this first resolution on 16 September, and a further consideration of it was postponed (*ibid.*, XVIII, 832).

[3] *Ibid.*, XV, 1095–99. The words "and will enforce the decrees of the said Commissioners" originally ended this sentence in the manuscript, but they seem to have been crossed out by JM himself (*ibid.*, XVIII, 833).

[4] Apparently this "special Committee" was never appointed. After debating the Vermont issue on 19, 20, and 27 September and 6 October without reaching agreement (*ibid.*, XVIII, 839, 843, 868, 908–9), Congress dropped the matter for the rest of the year and, in fact, until 20 July 1781 (*ibid*, XX, 770–72). What JM is reported to have said when his 16 September 1780 motion was debated on 6 October is printed below, under that date.

To Joseph Jones

RC (LC: Madison Papers). Wishing to recover his letters to Jones, JM wrote for them on 21 October 1817 to James Monroe, the nephew of Jones and custodian of his papers. Monroe returned eleven, all dated in 1780. Of these, the one given below is the earliest. JM, or some other person at an undetermined time, bracketed portions of these letters for publication. The last two paragraphs of this one were so marked. Monroe seems to have failed to comply with a second request by JM to forward his letters to Jones written after 1780. These letters were later destroyed or lost. Apparently only one letter written after 1780 from JM to Jones has been preserved.

DEAR SIR

Sepr. 19th. 1780.

Instead of a confirmation of the good news respecting the french fleet mentioned in my last, I have the mortification to inform you that it is pretty certain that Rodney has arrived at the Hook with 12 sail of the line from the W. Indies & 4 frigates. The report however still continues that a french fleet is somewhere on the coast. The arrival of Rodney is a proof that it had left the W. Indies and was conjectured to be coming hither.[1] It is further said that 5 or 6000 Troops would embark at N. York on the 25th. inst: either for Virga. or S. Carolina. This is by no means probable. The danger of such a measure is too obvious not to deter them from it. It is given out at N. York that a reinforcement of 4000 troops are expected next month from England.[2]

Yesterday was employed by Congress in discussing the resolutions you left with them. The first and second were passed after undergoing sundry alterations. The clause in the 2d for allowing the expence of maintaining civil govt within the ceded territory was struck out by the committee, and an attempt to get it reinserted in the house was negatived. It was surmised that so indefinite an expression might subject Congress to very exorbitant claims. With respect to Virga. I believe that expence has not been so considerable as to be much worth insisting on. The principal expences may properly be included under the military head. The consideration of the last resolution annulling Indian purchases was postponed, with an intention I believe of not resuming it. It is supposed by some to be unnecessary, by others to be improper, as implying that without such previous assurance Congress would have a right to recognize private claims in a territory expressly given up to them for the common benefit. These motives prevailed, I am persuaded with more than the real view of gratifying private interest at the public expence. The States may annex what conditions they please to their cessions, and by that means guard them agst. misapplication[,] or if they only annul all pretended purchases by their own laws before the cessions are made, Congress are sufficiently precluded by their general assurance that they shall be applied to the common benefit from admiting any private claims which are opposed to it.[3]

The Vermont business has been two days under agitation and nothing done in it except rejecting a proposition for postponing the determination of Congress till Commissioners should enquire into the titles & boundaries of N. Hampshire & N. York. Congress have bound themselves so strongly by their own act to bring it to an issue at this time and are pressed by N. York so closely with this engagement, that it is not possible any longer to try evasive expedients. For my own part if a final decision must take place, I am clearly of opinion that it ought to be made on principles that will effectually discountenance the erection of new Governments without the sanction of proper Authority, and in a style marking a due firmness and dicision in Congress.[4]

With sincere regard I am Dr Sir
Yr. friend & Servt.

J. Madison Junr.

[1] See JM to Jefferson, 2 June 1780, n. 3; Jameson to JM, 23 August, n. 2, and 13 September 1780, n. 3. On 4 October 1780, in a letter to Horatio Gates, Jefferson wrote: "The Extracts of letters which you will see in our Paper of this day are from Genl. Washington, President Huntington and our Delegates in Congress to me" (Boyd, *Papers of Jefferson*, IV, 11). In the *Virginia Gazette* (Richmond, Dixon and Nicolson) of 4 October, there are three brief extracts from as many letters written at Philadelphia on 16, 18, and 19 September, respectively. If any one of them is from the Virginia delegates to Jefferson, that letter has been lost. The extract of 19 September closely resembles what JM wrote to Jones and Pendleton on that day. Admiral George Brydges Rodney (1719–1792) had been governor of Newfoundland and a member of Parliament before returning to active service.

[2] JM was overly sanguine. On 16 October 1780 Major General Alexander Leslie with about 3,500 troops sailed from New York for Virginia to destroy military stores there, especially at Petersburg, and to divert pressure from Cornwallis' army in North Carolina. After a little over a month in Virginia, Leslie and most of his force embarked at Portsmouth about 15 November for the Carolinas to reinforce Cornwallis. On 15 October a British fleet arrived in New York from England "with Recruits and Stores" (Benjamin Franklin Stevens, ed., *The Campaign in Virginia, 1781; An exact Reprint of Six rare Pamphlets on the Clinton-Cornwallis Controversy* . . . [2 vols.; London, 1888], I, 271, 281–82, 294, 298, 313).

[3] This paragraph refers to Jones's motion of 6 September (above, Motion regarding the Western Lands) and serves to illuminate the following laconic entry in the printed journal for 18 September: "Congress took into consideration the report of the committee on the motion of the delegates of Virginia, and made some

progress." The debate on the report was not resumed until 10 October (*Journals of the Continental Congress*, XVIII, 836, 915–16; JM to Jones, 17 October 1780, n. 2).

4 Above, Notes on Territorial Claim of New Hampshire, and Resolutions respecting Vermont Lands, 16 September 1780. In assuring Jones of the inability of the delegates in Congress to prolong "evasive expedients" with regard to the Vermont issue, JM was again overly optimistic in this letter.

From Joseph Jones

RC (LC: Madison Papers).

VIRGA. 19th. Sep. 1780[1]

DR. SR.

I must Request you will so far oblige me as to enclose me every week Dunlaps paper or either of the others containing any thing worth reading. Mr. Dunlap told me he would furnish you with the papers for me.[2] I must also request you to send me the monthly Jou[r]nals as soon as printed and such information of the proceedings from time to time as you may think necessary. particularly be pleased to inform me of the Fate of the resolutions left on the Table when I cam[e] off respective the Confederation & the objections that governed the House if any of them are rejected.[3] I should also be glad to know whether the Report respecting the Mississippi has been considered.[4] Mr. Hill told me he wod. not forget to propose to the Commrs. of the Admirelty the ordering the Frigates to call in and scour the Chesapeake Bay. I fear it was forgot as they have not yet done it and the Enemies armed vessels still swarm there.[5] In return for your Communications I shall from time to time give you whatever may be new and worth mentioning. The recomn to the States for filling up the deficiencies in the army and laying up in time the necessary Magazines if not already shod. be despatched and forwarded withot. delay.[6] I did not get the Copy of the Report passed the day before I came away respecting the Cession of the back Lands. pray send it me and the resolutions if passed.[7]

Pray present my Compliments to the worthy Mistress and Gentlemen of the Family at the House the corner of fifth Street in Market Street—to the old Lady if she is returned and inform me whether my Friend the General and *his Friend* Buckley have finished th[eir] dispute and whether there is any hope for the old Lady's geting rid of her plague.[8] very truly I am

Yr. Obt Servt.

JOS. JONES

P.S. From Wilmington I inclosed you a [Letter?] for Gen Washington wch. I omitted to leave with [you?] for the [post?].[9] I also had two Letters from Col. Meade for Fitzhugh but [left?] them behind I think as I cannot find them. if they are fou[nd] pray enclose them.[10] Griffin requested me to send you the letters in[closed?][11]

    Compliments to Walker & Bland.[12]

[1] Owing to Jones's blurred dating at the close of this letter, Worthington C. Ford in his edition of the *Letters of Joseph Jones of Virginia, 1777–1787* (Washington, D.C., 1889), pp. 8–9, erroneously assumed that it had been written on 19 April 1780.

[2] John Dunlap's *Pennsylvania Packet*. Jones was a member both of the House of Delegates of Virginia and of the Continental Congress. Mistakenly believing that the legislature of his state would convene on 2 rather than on 16 October, he had returned from Philadelphia earlier than was necessary in order to induce his fellow assemblymen to cede Virginia's lands north and west of the Ohio River to Congress (W. C. Ford, ed., *Letters of Joseph Jones*, p. 33).

[3] Above, editorial note to Motion regarding the Western Lands, 6 September 1780. The resolutions to which Jones refers were adopted in amended form on 10 October 1780 (*Journals of the Continental Congress*, XVIII, 915–16).

[4] On 21 August 1780 Congress appointed Jones, George Walton, and Thomas McKean (Del.) a committee to make recommendations about the free use of the Mississippi River by American citizens—an issue raised by the Virginia legislature in its instructions of 5 November 1779 to its delegates and by a letter of 26 May 1780 to Congress from John Jay, U.S. minister to Spain. The committee reported on 2 September, but over a month elapsed before the recommendations were adopted by Congress (*ibid.*, XVII, 754–55, 802; XVIII, 873, 900–902).

[5] See Jameson to JM, 13 September 1780, n. 7. Whitmell Hill (1743–1797), of North Carolina, was one of the congressional members of the Board of Admiralty.

[6] Congress' action of 8 and 11 September on these matters was made known to Governor Jefferson in a dispatch from President Huntington on 12 September (*ibid.*, XVIII, 812–13, 818; Boyd, *Papers of Jefferson*, III, 640).

[7] Above, n. 3.

[8] JM and Jones, together with other delegates to Congress, principally from Virginia and New York, lived in a boarding house at the corner of Fifth and Market Streets in Philadelphia. The "Family at the House" comprised Mrs. Mary House ("old Lady" and widow), her daughter Eliza ("the worthy Mistress"), Eliza's husband Nicholas Trist, their young son Hore Browse, and Eliza's brother Samuel House. The "Gentlemen of the Family" included the boarders. Most likely the "General" was John Morin Scott (*ca.* 1730–1784), a delegate from New York (Brant, *Madison*, II, 16–17). When in Philadelphia, JM continued to live in the House-Trist home until his marriage in September 1794. See JM to Jones, 10 October 1780, n. 6, for comments upon the dispute involving "the General," "Buckley," and "the old Lady."

[9] If this means that Jones wrote JM from Wilmington, Del., his letter has not been found. Jones's letter to Washington of 6 September 1780, written in Philadelphia, is in W. C. Ford, ed., *Letters of Joseph Jones*, pp. 27–29.

[10] Jones may refer to letters from Washington's aide-de-camp, Colonel Richard Kidder Meade (1746–1805), to his relative by marriage, William Fitzhugh. If JM found these letters, he made no mention of the fact, insofar as is known.

[11] These letters from Cyrus Griffin have not been identified.

[12] John Walker and Theodorick Bland were members of the Virginia delegation in Congress.

To Edmund Pendleton

RC (LC: Madison Papers).

PHILADA. Sepr. 19[t]h. 1780

DEAR SIR

I was in hopes when I wrote my last that I should be able by this post to congratulate you on the arrival of the french fleet from the W. Indies But so far is this from being the case, that it comes from authority which seems to have a just claim to our faith that Admiral Rodney is actually at the Hook with 12. Sail of the line & 4 frigates. It is still said however that a french fleet is somewhere on the coast. The arrival of Rodney is certainly an evidence that it had quited the Islands and was suspected to be coming hither. It is also given out at New York that a reinforcement of 4000 troops will arrive next mont[h] from England. Another part of our reports is that 5 or 6000 troops will embark at N. York on the 25th. inst. for Virga. or S. Carolina: but it is not to be supposed that such a measure will be hazarded in the present ticklish state of things. 22 Sail of the Quebeck fleet are carried prizes into N. England.[1]

I am Dr Sir with sincere respect Yr. Obt friend & Servt.

J. MADISON JNR.

P.S. The mortality in this place exceeds any thing ever remembered. The only person of note that occurs at present is the Lady of President Reid who fell a victim to it yesterday morning.[2]

[1] With the exception of what JM notes in his last sentence, the news in this paragraph is identical with that in his letter on the same day to Joseph Jones (*q.v.*). On 17 August 1780, in a letter to Governor William Livingston of New Jersey, George Washington remarked: "I have just recd. advice from Newport that the greater part of the fleet of Victuallers and Merchant men bound from England to Quebec had been taken by the Eastern privateers. Sixteen of the prizes had arrived in the different ports" (Fitzpatrick, *Writings of Washington*, XIX, 388). A report of this success had probably reached Philadelphia before Washington's letter of 9 September to the president of Congress, casually mentioning it, was presented to that body three days later (*ibid.*, XX, 21; *Journals of the Continental Congress*, XVIII, 819). In any event, Pendleton could have read about the capture in the *Virginia Gazette* (Richmond, Dixon and Nicolson) of 13 and 20 September 1780. From these accounts it appears that the prizes had been taken in July and that the privateers were the "Brutus," "Essex," "Jack," "America," and "Stark."

[2] Esther DeBerdt Reed (1747–1780), wife of President Joseph Reed (1741–1785) of Pennsylvania, died in Philadelphia on 18 September, a victim of "the flux" which was epidemic there during the first three weeks of that month (William B. Reed, ed., *Life and Correspondence of Joseph Reed* [2 vols.; Philadelphia, 1847], II, 269 n.; *Pennsylvania Magazine of History and Biography*, XLI [1917], 308–9).

From David Jameson

RC (LC: Rives Collection of Madison Papers).

Rᴵᴄʜᴍᴏɴᴅ Sep 20th. 1780

Dʀ Sɪʀ

I was favoured with yours of the 5th.¹ by Post. It may not be amiss to mention to you that the post comes to Newcastle within eighteen Miles of this place on Wednesday, and we do not get the letters till the Monday following—after the rider has been down to Wmsburg. The Governor had a promise that there should be an alteration in the post route, or the days, but none has as yet taken place. If they will not order the rider to come from Fredsbg directly to this place by Hanover Court House, they might at least order one to bring the letters from Newcastle immediately here, and that would give us an opporty of sending you intelligence near a week sooner.² We have had nothing from the Southward since the riders were set in motion with Gen. Gates's Letter to Congress giving the information he had recd. of Ld. Cornwallis's intention to go to Cape Fear &ca.³ Col Morgan left Richmond this morning on his way to join the Southern Army. I have good dependance on his abilities to harass the Enemy and hope they will give him a proper Corps.⁴ I am very sorry to tell you the people do not like the New Money (the 2 Millions). many have already refused to take it, principally because it will pay no tax but that laid for its redemption. this must be altered by the Assembly.⁵

The Governor has had many letters from Mr. Mezzei. he appears by dint of —— to have worked himself into notice at Paris, where he still was in May. His letters are very clever and his remarks judicious and entertaining. I fear he will not succeed in his grand Errand.⁶ Our eighteen Months recruts are assembling. what pity it is they are not for the War.⁷ they have recd. bounty enough for-life—I had like to have said—from two to eight thousand pounds has been given. Several Vessels have lately come in cleared from different ports, but the Men and cargoes the produce of Ireland.⁸ Tobacco at these Warehouses has risen to £70 Pbl. The Jefferson is gone up the Bay as Convoy to several provision Vessels. The Bay is not yet clear of the piccaroons. I hope when the Jefferson joins the Maryland Armed Vessels (wch she is to do) they will make a sweep.⁹ I am Dr Sir

Yr mo. Ob Set

Dᴀᴠɪᴅ Jᴀᴍᴇꜱᴏɴ

94

¹ Not found.

² In a letter of 9 June 1780 to President Samuel Huntington of Congress, Governor Jefferson requested that the post route in Virginia be altered to pass directly through Richmond, the new capital city of the state (Boyd, *Papers of Jefferson*, III, 427).

³ Jameson refers to Gates's letter of 9 September, received by Jefferson about five days later (*ibid.*, III, 620–21). Gates was mistaken about Cornwallis' intention to move his troops to the North Carolina coast, but not in his information, given in the same letter, that Cornwallis had asked General Clinton "to send a reinforcement to take immediate possession of Portsmouth, in Your State" (JM to Jones, 19 September 1780, n. 2).

⁴ On 16 June 1780, Congress ordered Colonel Daniel Morgan (1736–1802) of the Virginia line to return to military service. He had resigned in 1779 after serving with conspicuous distinction since 1775. Upon joining General Gates at Hillsboro, N.C., in late September 1780, he was placed in command of a corps of light infantry. Although the Board of War asked on 14 July that he be commissioned a brigadier general, Congress delayed adopting this recommendation until 13 October 1780 (*Journals of the Continental Congress*, XVII, 519, 612–13; XVIII, 921).

⁵ See Jameson to JM, 26 July, n. 4, and 16 August 1780, n. 5; Jefferson to JM, 26 July 1780, n. 2.

⁶ Philip Mazzei's fourteen letters to Jefferson, written from Paris in the spring and early summer of 1780, are in Boyd, *Papers of Jefferson*, III, 305–460, *passim*. Jameson probably expected JM, who knew Mazzei, to fill in the blank with an uncomplimentary word such as "aggressiveness" or "obtrusiveness." Mazzei had arrived in France in the autumn of 1779 under a commission from the governor and council of Virginia to borrow money and purchase supplies for the use of the state (Mazzei to JM, 13 June 1779, n. 3).

⁷ That is, they could not be held in service for the duration of the war (Jefferson to JM, 26 July 1780, n. 3).

⁸ Jameson's meaning is uncertain. Perhaps he wished JM to infer that the vessels had not brought the hoped-for supplies either from Mazzei or in accordance with the agreement of 11 May 1780 made by Governor Jefferson with Theveneau de Francy (Boyd, *Papers of Jefferson*, III, 372–73; Jameson to JM, 16 August 1780, n. 7).

⁹ See Jameson to JM, 13 September 1780.

Thomas Jefferson to Virginia Delegates in Congress

Letter not found.

EDITORIAL NOTE

22 September 1780. A letter, now missing, from Governor Jefferson to the Virginia delegates on 22 September 1780, was presented by them to Congress on 4 October. Since Congress thereupon resolved to appropriate money for "providing and transporting arms for the troops raising in Virginia for continental service," Jefferson's letter probably had requested these military supplies (*Journals of the Continental Congress*, XVIII, 899).

To Virginia Auditors of Public Accounts

RC (Mrs. Henry M. Sage, Albany, N.Y., 1958).

PHILADELPHIA Sepr. 25th. 1780

GENTLEMEN

The inclosed is a state of my receipts and expences from the 20 of March to the 20 of Sepr. being two complete quarters.[1] I am sensible that the law directs that it should have been transmitted at the end of the first quarter, but my account of extra expences, being mixed with that of some Gentlemen of the family who were absent,[2] I could not then do it with the precision I wished, and as no particular inconveniency seemed to attend it I postponed the settlement till the end of the second quarter. As I find by a resolution past the last session of Assembly that they make a point of it I shall not fail in future to conform punctually to the law.[3]

You will observe from the account that there is a ballance in favor of the State of 9962⅓. The contrary being the case with Mr. Jones when he left this place, I advanced him upwards of that sum which he is to replace from the Treasury. I mention this circumstance, that my being out of money may expedite a compliance with his draughts.[4]

I am Gentlemen with due respect Yr. obt & humble Servt.

JAMES MADISON JUNR.

[1] For the inclosure, see the following expense account for 20 March to 20 September 1780.

[2] By "Gentlemen . . . absent," JM probably meant Cyrus Griffin, who had resigned early in June (before JM's first quarter ended on the 20th) as a Virginia delegate, and also some of JM's fellow boarders with whom he needed to apportion certain of the incidental expenses mentioned in his account below.

[3] Resolutions of the House of Delegates, 12 July 1780 (*Journal of the House of Delegates,* May 1780, p. 84).

[4] The letter from Joseph Jones to JM on 9 October 1780 (*q.v.*), in which this financial transaction is clarified, also indicates that JM had written Jones about 25 September, inclosing the present letter to the auditors and his appended accounts. This letter to Jones has not been found.

Expense Account as Delegate in Congress
(Headnote on page 98)

James Madison Junr. in account with the Commo[n]wealth of Virginia

[25 September 1780]

Dr.

Date	Particulars	Dollars
1779 December	To cash received from the Treasury of Virginia.	6666⅔
1780 April 7	To the moity of a draught on the Auditors for 30,000 dollars in favor of S. C. Morris[1] by C. Griffin & J. Madison Jr.	15000
June 23	To cash received from the Continental Treasury on warrant from Congress dated April 12[2] for 15 000 dollars in favor of C. Griffin and J. Madison Junr., the remainder of the moity being received by Mr. J. Walker	2500
June	To one third of a draught on the Auditors for 23312 dollars by Jos: Jones Jas. Henry & J. Madison Junr. in favor of Col. Balard negociated by Levi Hollingsworth[3]	7770⅔
Augst. 30	To one fourth of a draught on the Auditors for £20 000 Virginia currency by Jos: Jones, J. Madison Junr, and John Walker, received from Theo: Bland Junr	16666⅔[4]
		48604⅔

Philada. Sepr. 20. 1780[8]
J. Madison Junr.

E E[9]

Cr.

Date	Particulars	Dollars
1780 March 20	By ferriages in travelling to Philadelphia	122
	By allowance of 2 dollars per mile for do[5]	520
	By expences in Philadelphia prior to fixed lodgings	320⅔
	By expence of boarding from 20 of March to 20 of Septemr	21373⅓
	By incidental expences for liquors sugar fruit not included in board	2459
	By expence of 3 horses from 20 of March to 30 of June and of 2 to the 20 of September at the continental Stables	6034
	By extra expences for do. during a scarcity of forage there	577
	By expence for washing	1776
	By expence to Barber	1020
	By expence in wood[6]	605
Sepr. 20	By allowance of 20 drs. per day for attendance at Congress from the 20 of March to the 20 of Sepr. being 183 days[7]	3660
		38467⅓
June 15	By cash advanced to an Express returning to Virginia	175
		38642⅓
		9962⅓
	Ballance	
		48604⅔

Expense Account as Delegate in Congress

MS (Virginia State Library). Expense account of JM, for 20 March to 20 September 1780, inclosed in preceding letter. To the extent that a fragmentary copy of this account, in the Madison Papers, Library of Congress, can be read, it duplicates what he submitted to the auditors. In the Virginia State Library is the ledger sheet itemizing the debits and credits of JM's account with the state from 16 December 1779 to 31 December 1782. Accompanying this double page are three large sheets, divided by horizontal lines of ink into three-month periods, on which JM listed his receipts and expenses as a delegate in Congress from 16 December 1779 to 20 March 1782. The entries on these sheets correspond with his quarterly statements, and hence will not be reproduced in this volume unless one of the quarterly statements is missing.

[1] Samuel Cadwalader Morris (1743–1820), a leading patriot and merchant of Philadelphia.

[2] The authorization by Congress was on 10 April 1780 (*Journals of the Continental Congress*, XVI, 343; NA: PCC, No. 136, III, 175).

[3] "Col. Balard" was probably Colonel Robert Ballard (*ca.* 1742–*ca.* 1803) of Mecklenburg County and of the 4th Virginia Regiment. Late in the Revolution, or shortly after its close, he moved to Baltimore, Md. Levi Hollingsworth (1739–1824) of Philadelphia was a well-known merchant and speculator. John Walker evidently did the negotiating with Hollingsworth (Walker to Jefferson, 13 June 1780, in Boyd, *Papers of Jefferson*, III, 441).

[4] Multiplying £20,000 by 3.33 and dividing the result by four equals the $16,666\frac{2}{3}$ (Virginia Delegates to Auditors, 11 September 1780, n. 4).

[5] In December 1779 the Virginia legislature fixed the salary of delegates at $20.00 a day, their travel allowance at $2.00 a mile plus ferry costs, and guaranteed to reimburse each delegate for the living costs of himself and family at Philadelphia, including his expenses for rent, fuel, food, and a maximum of three servants and four horses (Hening, *Statutes*, X, 163).

[6] JM's consolidated expense sheets for 1779–1782, mentioned in the headnote, state that the amount of wood was two cords.

[7] Above, n. 5.

[8] On their ledger sheets mentioned in the headnote, the auditors not only divided each of the sums listed by JM by 3.33, in order to arrive at the value in Virginian rather than continental paper currency, but also reduced the latter to its specie equivalent by applying a depreciation ratio. Thus between December 1779 and June 1780 this ratio was 62 for 1. By August of that year it had grown to 75 for 1.

[9] Probably stands for "Errors Excepted," an expression sometimes found at the close of the accounts of other delegates. The law, mentioned in n. 5, required the delegates to submit only "a general account of all their disbursements" and apparently did not oblige them to file supporting receipts.

From Edmund Pendleton

Tr (LC: Force Transcripts).

EDMUNDSBURY, Sepr. 25. 1780

DEAR SIR:

I am made very happy by yr obliging favr of the 12th promising to indulge me in the desireable correspondence; since I requested it I have been informed you have ill health,[1] I cordially wish its speedy restitution, but intreat you'l not Injure it by devoting to me too much of that small portion of time which health as well as vigor of mind requires should be emploied in relaxation from the severe duties of your appointment. And on these terms I shall thankfully accept the favr you so kindly offer.

Our sanguine hopes of redeeming our Ill luck to the Southward, by a great Stroke Eastward, have lately been fluctuating; since the account of the fleet with the 2d division Intended for our Assistance by our Illustrious allies being lock'd up at Brest, we had Intelligence by a Vessel from Cape Francois that he sail'd from thence with a French Fleet of 24 sail of the line for America, which he parted with to the So ward. comparing this with the Account of our two prisoners escap'd from Charles Town that they were Alarm'd there by the Arrival of a French Fleet; Genl. Gates's information that St. Augustine was attack'd, & the various Accounts of a Fleet of about 18 sail having passed our Capes[,] a mind sanguine as mine, will draw hopes of very important events yet taking place before the close of this Campaign.[2]

The affair to the Southward was indeed unfortunate, not only in the loss of some of the bra[ve] Maryland line & the Baggage, but in the disappointme[nt] we met of a great Victory, which every circumstance promised. I feel no part of it more sensibly than its having added another article to the *blushing* Honours of poor Virginia;[3] what will she come to? Her new levies are gathering, they would have form'd but a weak line at best, but their numbers considerably lessen'd by too many excuses of inability being admitted from the Militia, & their quality impaird by accepting substitutes unequal to the person drafted; there are however some very clever fellows & I should be satisfied with them if they were engaged for the War, but by the time they learn the duty tolerably, they return, and we are to incur again the ruinous expence of recruiting which on this Occasion has been enormous, I believe by Accounts I have had, the men inlisted have cost on an average £5000, each, besides the Public bounty of a hhd. tobo., a sum which at any rate of depreciation must exceed the ability of any countrey frequently to repeat.[4]

I have thought long agoe that 'twas high time the confederation was completed, & feared some foreign Powers might entertain from its delay, suspicions of some secret disunion amongst the States, or a latent intention in Congress to keep it open for purposes unworthy of them; I am happy to hear it is resumed & think it becoming and indeed an indispensable duty in this, as in all other social Compacts, for the contracting members to yield points to each other, in order to meet as near the Centre of General good as the different jarring Interests can be brought, And did it depend upon my Opinion I would not hesitate to yield a very large Portion of our back lands to accomplish this purpose, except for the reason wch Shakespeare has put into the mouth of his Hotspur.[5] In reason & Justice the title of Virginia to her Western Territory can no more be questioned than to any other spot in it. The point was fully & warmly agitated in congress & determined in her favr. 12 States were satisfied & agreed to confederate & yet one stops the whole business, setting up her Judgment in Opposition to so many? yield to her in this, may she not play the same game to gain any future point of Interest? I am told that Maryland Insists upon one of our Delegates having in a manner promised, when the point of declaring Independence was in debate, that the back lands should be a fund for supporting the War. I have heard that a Rhetorical expression to that purpose was used by a Gentn on that Occasion, but can ballance that account at least by a very serious question more in point, debated in Congress in 1775, when the Delegates from Pennsylvania & Virga. proposed a Garrison of 400 men rais'd & kept at common expence at Pitsburg to awe the Indians. It was warmly opposed from *Maryland*, upon this ground that it was a [duty?] of those two states merely to guard their own Frontiers in which the others were not concern'd & therefore the expence must be incurr'd by the former. their objections prevailed, the motion was rejected, & the two states raised the 200 men [for?] that service soon afterwards:[6] However with the Assembly it must rest to determine what they will yield to Harmonize & cement the Union, & it must be acknowledged that in other respects, particularly in the Field, Maryland has maintain'd a very worthy character in the Contest. For my own part I never was anxious about our back lands as a valuable fund. I was against the Sale of them at all, but for putting them into the hands of the people upon the terms, & in the mode accustomed, being of Opinion that the consequence of allowing purchases of unlimited quantities & that without the obligation of Culture, would introduce more disputes & confusion than the money would recompence. the small experience I have had of the business since, has rather confirmed than changed this opinion, however as I was then, & perhaps am yet singular in this Opinion, I am very ready to suppose I am mistaken in it.

Whilst I am on this subject permit me to suggest that I have heard it surmised that this mighty earnestness in Maryland proceeds from 5 or 6 Gentn. there being concerned in an Indian Grant of great part of the countrey between the Ohio & the Lakes, which they hope to preserve by having it thrown into the share of that Countrey in case they can make it a common stock. this Our Assembly will never agree to, as it would be most unreasonable to expect them to yield their territory in order to form Principalities for a few Individuals of other states. It is time for me to leave it to those whose province it is to decide on it. it shall be mine to acquiesce.[7]

I have much more reason to intreat you to cast a vale over inaccuracies. I am not much hurried indeed, but alwa[y]s was a very careless writer. I send you a paper.[8] I wish it was more entertaining. I am with great respect,

Dr Sr Yr obliged & affe friend

EDMD. PENDLETON

[1] See Reverend James Madison to JM, 3 August 1780, n. 7; and Jameson to JM, 13 September 1780, n. 1.

[2] See JM to Jefferson, 2 June 1780, n. 3; Jameson to JM, 23 August, n. 2, and 13 September 1780, n. 3. It may be that the vessel from Cape François, Haiti, had fallen in with the fleet homeward bound and that the "18 Sail" off the Chesapeake capes had been, in reality, Rodney's command on its way north to New York (Jones to JM, 2 October 1780). No dispatch from Gates mentioning an attack on St. Augustine has been found, but Pendleton could have read about this, along with what the "two prisoners" said, in the *Virginia Gazette* (Richmond, Dixon and Nicolson), 13 September 1780.

[3] Pendleton was referring to the cowardice of the Virginia militia at the Battle of Camden on 16 August (JM to Pendleton, 12 September 1780).

[4] In the summer of 1780, the Virginia legislature by its "act to embody militia for the relief of South Carolina, and for other purposes" provided for raising 2,500 infantrymen on three months' service. Their pay was to be in tobacco in amounts proportioned to their rank. Thus, the brigadier general would receive 125 pounds a day, each major fifty, each sergeant ten, and each private seven and one-half pounds. On enlistment, a private would be given £50 "to be hereafter deducted from his pay, at the rate of twelve shillings per pound" of tobacco due him (Hening, *Statutes,* X, 221–26). A "clever" fellow was one who was active and healthy.

⁵ Shakespeare, *King Henry IV, Part I,* Act III, scene 1, lines 137–40:

> I'll give thrice so much land
> To any well-deserving friend;
> But in the way of bargain, mark ye me,
> I'll cavil on the ninth part of a hair.

⁶ Neither the printed journal of the Continental Congress during 1775 nor the letters of its members, as compiled by Edmund C. Burnett, mention this debate. Thomas Perkins Abernethy in his *Western Lands and the American Revolution* (New York, 1937), p. 140, questions the accuracy of Pendleton's recollection. There is no doubt, however, that the Virginia Convention in the summer of 1775 provided for the stationing of one hundred soldiers and their officers at Pittsburgh (Hening, *Statutes,* IX, 13).

⁷ For the general subject of this paragraph and the next preceding one, see Mason to JM, 2 August 1780, n. 3; and Motion regarding the Western Lands, 6 September 1780, editorial note.

⁸ Not found. This last paragraph and the complimentary close are omitted in the version of the letter printed in *Proceedings of the Massachusetts Historical Society,* 2d ser., XIX (1905), 114.

To Thomas Jefferson

RC (LC: Madison Papers). Although the cover sheet is missing with the name of the addressee, "Madison Jas." is written above the date in Jefferson's hand.

PHILADA. Sepr. 26[t]h. 1780

DEAR SIR

I am at length able to give you some answer on the subject of the map in the hands of Dr. Smith. As the Docr. lived out of Town and it was difficult to know when he was to be found in it, and as I supposed the request would go with greater weight through Mr. Rittenhouse[1] I asked the favor of him to speak to the Docr. on the Subject. Through forgetfulness or want of opportunity he failed to do it till lately and brought me for answer that the Docr. although anxious to oblige you was unwilling to let it go out of his hands, but wd. suffer any transcript to be taken from it at his house and would even assist in it himself. Yesterday evening I had an opportunity of being introduced to him and renewed the application, that he would spare it till I could get a copy taken; which he again declined by politely assuring me that he was proud of an opportunity of obliging you and that he would have a correct & authentic copy made out by his son for you.

I am Dr. Sir Yrs respectfully

JAMES MADISON JR

[1] William Smith, formerly provost of the College of Philadelphia, whose home was at the falls of the Schuylkill River, and David Rittenhouse, an astronomer, were prominent members of the American Philosophical Society. As late as 1782, Jefferson was still waiting for Smith to fulfill his promise to send a copy of what was probably Nicholas, John, and Virginia Ferrar's "Faithfull Map of Virginia in America," dating from 1651. Although Smith was a "difficult" man with whom to deal, his unreliability in this instance may have been occasioned by his move, shortly after JM saw him, from Philadelphia to Chesterton, Md., where he established Kent School and continued as its rector for several years (*Dictionary of American Biography*, XVII, 353–57). On 18 March 1782, JM informed Jefferson that a copy of the Ferrar map was in the book collection of the Library Company of Philadelphia (Boyd, *Papers of Jefferson*, VI, 169–70). For further information on this map, see Coolie Verner, "The First Maps of Virginia, 1590–1673," *Virginia Magazine of History and Biography*, LVIII (1950), 13–14.

To Edmund Pendleton

RC (LC: Madison Papers).

PHILADA. Sepr. 26[t]h. 1780

DEAR SIR

Yesterday's post disappointed me of the expected pleasure of a line from you. I hope the next will not fail to make amends for it.

I have nothing to add to the inclosed paper[1] except that Ternay is yet unreinforced, Graves at Sea no one knows where or for what purpose, and Rodney with 10 Ships of the line still at the Hook, though according to some private accounts he also is gone to Sea.[2] In this state of uncertainty conjectures & speculations abound as usual[.] I shall not trouble you with them, because, as far as they are founded in reason they will be much better formed by yourself. We hear nothing further of an intended visit from N.Y. to Virginia.[3] With sincere respect & regard

I am Dr. Sr. Yrs. &c.

J. MADISON JUNR.

Edmd. Pendleton Esqr.

[1] Not found, but perhaps it was the 26 September issue of the *Pennsylvania Packet* (Philadelphia).

[2] The ships of Admiral Thomas Graves or Admiral Marriot Arbuthnot still blockaded Admiral Ternay's fleet in Narragansett Bay. Admiral Rodney and his war vessels remained in New York harbor or its vicinity until 9 November 1780 (Harry M. Lydenberg, ed., *Archibald Robertson: Diaries and Sketches*, pp. 235, 241–42).

[3] JM doubtless refers to the rumored descent of a British expeditionary force upon Virginia from New York (JM to Jones, 19 September 1780, n. 2).

From Edmund Pendleton

Tr (LC: Force Transcripts).

EDMUNDSBURY, October 1, 1780

DEAR SIR:

Since my last I have yr favr of the 19th & can't conceive where the great Fleet of our Allies are? they must have left the Windward Islands, & Rodney have been deceived by them if they did not come to America, As he would not otherwise have ventured to leave those seas: We hear nothing further of them to the Southward.[1]

I hope they are not in a state of such perfect security at New York, as to induce them to spare 5 or 6000 men to invade us. Our people, however, promise if they should pay Us such a Visit, to fight them hard,[2] I hope at least they will do better than those who met Ld. Cornwallis, at Cambden, I mean the Militia, for the Maryland Regulars did Honr to themselves & countrey.

I am sorry to hear of the Mortality which rages in yr city. it is pretty General & might indeed be expected after so very hot a summer, even our healthy Forrests are not exempt from the Ague & fever, tho' scarce ever known in them before. I hope you & my other friends from Virginia escape the Contagion, which low habits have generally the best chance to do.[3]

We have just received an Account that Colo. Clarke has had a battle with the Indians at one of their Towns about 170 miles from the falls of Ohio—he had 16 killed & 12 wounded—& found abt 15 of their dead—he made them run, burnt up two Towns & destroyed all their corn there about 300 acres of very fine, my Informant who was in the action thinks it would have made 20 Barrels to the Acre. Colo Clarke did not pursue them, having intelligence that the Indians had somehow got notice of his Attack, & had sent to Detroit for a powerful reinforcement which they daily expected.[4] I am

My Dr Sr Yr very afft & obt Servt

EDMD PENDLETON

I have taken the liberty to inclose a letter for my Nephew. if he should have left Phila. pray return it.[5]

---

[1] See JM to Jefferson, 2 June 1780, n. 3; Jameson to JM, 23 August, n. 2, and 13 September 1780, n. 3.

[2] See JM to Jones, 19 September 1780, n. 2.

[3] The meaning of "low habits" in this connection is doubtful. Perhaps he in-

tended to signify the opposite of "high living" or that persons accustomed to living on low ground, as along one of the many rivers in Virginia, gained an immunity from malaria.

⁴ A letter of Colonel George Rogers Clark to Governor Jefferson on 22 August 1780, published in the *Virginia Gazette* (Richmond, Dixon and Nicolson) of 4 October 1780, stated that, after destroying crops and buildings at Chillicothe, Ohio, he and his men on 8 August fought the Indians at their Pickaway settlements on the Great Miami River. In the battle Clark lost "about 14 killed and thirteen wounded, theirs at least tripple that number." Before returning to Louisville, Clark destroyed the Indians' vegetable gardens and "upward of 800 acres" of their corn.

⁵ This postscript is omitted in the version printed in the *Proceedings of the Massachusetts Historical Society*, 2d ser., XIX (1905), 115. In his reply on 10 October, JM remarked that he had delivered this inclosure to "Mr. Pendleton." Edmund Pendleton had many nephews, but the one in question was Judge Henry Pendleton of South Carolina (1750–1789), a son of Edmund's brother Nathaniel. On 6 October 1780 Judge Pendleton presented a memorial to Congress, asking for an advance of money as a charge against his state, because the occupancy of South Carolina by the British had cut off his salary and other sources of income and thereby threatened him with "distress little better than a prison ship or a dungeon." On 23 October Congress tabled his memorial but, on the application of South Carolina delegates the same day, may have heeded his plea by granting to them "a warrant . . . for twenty thousand dollars for the special and particular use of the said State, which is to be accountable" (NA: PCC, No. 41, VIII, 136; *Journals of the Continental Congress*, XVIII, 908, 965). In the *Pennsylvania Packet* (Philadelphia) of 2 September 1780 is Judge Pendleton's letter of 20 July to Cornwallis, explaining why he had felt justified in leaving Charleston, thereby breaking his parole given at the time of the surrender of that city to the British.

From Joseph Jones

RC (LC: Madison Papers).

2d. Octr. 1780

DEAR SR.

I thank you for your favour of the 19th. ult. and the inclosures. It was really a mortifying circumstance to find the French Fleet converted into twelve British Ships of the line and four Frigates from which nothing can effectually relieve us but the arrival of a superior number of French Battle Ships and unless these come I fear many of our people not only here but in other States will entertain unfavourable opinions of the ability at least, if not the inclination of our ally to give us effective support.¹ The alteration of ye. resolutions I left are not I think mater[i]al excepting the one postponed not to be taken up which I am certain will be made a Condition by Virga. in any Cession she may make as there are jealousies entertained of certain Individuals greatly interested in that question.² Congress cannot in honor or Justice delay their determination on the Virmont dispute. Had the Territorial claims of N. Y. & N. Hampshire been settled in the first instance the State of Vermont would not at this Day have been known—delay has given them a name and made them formidable. such excrescencies should be taken off on their first appearance as then the work is easy and less Dangerous than when they have grown to a head. We know not what may be the consequences if Congress shall countenance by precedent the dismembering of States because the people blown up into discontents by designing ambitious Men shall ask or demand it. fix the boundaries of these States and let the people who live within their respective limits know they are their Citizens and must submit to their Government.[3] I was one of a Com: to whom the Generals long Letter on very important matters was referred[.][4] we had come to some resolutions before I left Congress but no Report made. pray inform me what has been done and whether any recommendation has gone to the States to fill up their Battalions immediately and lay up Magazines in time.[5] I was also of a Com: to arrange or reform the civil departments of Congress and it was in contemplation to place at the head of the Foreign affairs the Admiralty and Treasury some respectable persons to conduct the Business and be responsible. has any thing been done in these matters[?] they are important and should not be forgotten. we shall never have these great departments well managed untill something of this kind is done. I cannot forget Mr. L—ls very *candid* confession respecting Dr. Franklins complaint of want of information of our affairs.[6] Is there a Report made respecting the Medical Departmt. And is there any hope of geting that branch reformed[?] If any removals are to take place and persons shall be wanting to fill the higher offices of that Department, there are two Gentlemen mentioned to me who from their long and fait[h]full Services deserve the attention of Congress[.] I mean Dr. Craig and Dr. Cochran.[7] Col. Mason wrote to us abt. Mr. Harrison in Case a Consull should be wanting for Spain[.] I have since received a Letter from Col. Meade upon the Same Subject and have assured him should any such appointment take place Mr. Harrison should be recommended but that there was no reason to expect this wod. soon be the case.[8] this reminds me of the report respecting the Mississippi. what has been done with it?[9] Has Dr. Lee made his appearance and does he attempt to revive the old disputes?[10] would not the publication of extracts of the several Acts of the States that have adopted the Scheme of Finance specifying the Funds established for support & redemption of the money be of use, as the money is to circulate through all the States; all the States should be properly and fully informed of the solidity of the Funds; much very much depends on our supporting the Credit of the new money.[11]

The Assembly adjourned to the 3d. Monday of this month instead of the first their usual time of meeting. had I known it I might have staid a week or two longer with you.[12] I have heard nothing of Mr. Henry and cannot inform you when he intends to Congress.[13] I found Mrs. Jones and my little Boy in bad health when I got Home. she has been so ever since July and still in a low state[.] he is something better though not quite well. I sha[ll] prevail on her for her Health sake if nothing else to visit the North next Spring if I do so myself of which I shall soon inform you and give you the trouble of securing either Mr. Pembertons or Mr. Pleasants House as she will not take the small pox by inoculation and by living in the Country she may avoid it.[14]

We have a Report that the French Fleet is arrived at Newport. I hope for a confirmation of it by the Post Tomorrow. Make my Compliments to Genl. Scott and the other Gentlemen of the Family of my acquaintance, also to the good Lady of the House[15] and be assured I am

D. Sir. Yr. Friend & Servt.

Jos: Jones

[1] See Jameson to JM, 23 August 1780, n. 2.

[2] The report of the committee appointed on 9 September (above, Motion regarding the Western Lands, 6 September 1780, n. 2) was submitted to Congress on 15 September and debated for the first time three days later (*Journals of the Continental Congress*, XVIII, 828, 836). In his letter of 19 September (*q.v.*), JM acquainted Jones with the results of this discussion. Following further debate on the report, a vote was taken on 10 October—that is, eight days after Jones wrote the present letter (*ibid.*, XVIII, 915–16; and JM to Jones, 17 October 1780 and n. 2). Since the vote resulted in a tie, the report was tabled for later consideration.

[3] Above, Notes on Territorial Claim of New Hampshire, and Resolutions respecting Vermont Lands, 16 September 1780.

[4] Punctuation is supplied in brackets in six cases in this letter to clarify the meaning.

[5] On 8 September Congress substituted Theodorick Bland for Jones on this committee, and added two more members to it four days later. It was instructed not only to make recommendations upon Washington's "long letter" of 20 August but also upon several other dispatches from him of a later date. On 14, 15, and 21 September the committee reported plans to secure beef for the army and to fill the troop quotas of the states by December, and on 3 October it submitted its important recommendations for the reorganization of the regular army of the United States (*Journals of the Continental Congress*, XVIII, 812, 817, 825–30, 836, 843–44, 893–97). In the meantime, on 8, 11, and 20 September, following the recommendations of another committee, Congress had called upon Maryland, Virginia, and North Carolina to "furnish magazines of forage, flour, and salted provisions," to complete their troop quotas, and to hasten them to the southern army (*ibid.*, XVIII, 812–13, 818–19, 842–43).

[6] On 29 August 1780 Jones had seconded Robert R. Livingston's motion to

create a committee "to report a plan for the revision and new arrangement of the civil executive departments." Congress named both men to the committee, together with James Lovell (Mr. L—l) and two others (*ibid.*, XVII, 791). Lovell (1737–1814), who since 25 May 1777 had been a member of the harassed Committee for Foreign Affairs (*ibid.*, VIII, 385), was, on 15 May 1780, named chairman of a committee to "report a proper arrangement for the department of foreign affairs" (*ibid.*, XVII, 428). Lovell's "*candid* confession" is not on record but its probable equivalent is in his letters to Benjamin Franklin of 4 May and to John Jay of 11 July 1780 (Burnett, *Letters*, V, 124–25, 259). Congress, following the recommendations of the Committee on the Civil Executive Departments, agreed on 7 February 1781 to create a superintendent of finance, a secretary of marine, and a secretary at war. These offices were filled, respectively, on 20 February by Robert Morris, on 27 February by Alexander McDougall, and on 30 October 1781 by General Benjamin Lincoln. McDougall declined the naval office, however, and its duties were committed to the superintendent of finance (*Journals of the Continental Congress*, XIX, 57, 125–28, 180, 203, 333–34; XX, 724–25; XXI, 1087). By adopting on 10 January 1781 the recommendations of the Committee on a Department of Foreign Affairs, Congress agreed to put a secretary at its head, but it delayed until 10 August before choosing Robert R. Livingston for that position (*ibid.*, XIX, 43–44; XXI, 851–52).

[7] On 30 September 1780 Congress agreed to a plan for drastically reorganizing the medical department of the army. Six days later Congress re-elected Dr. William Shippen, Jr. (1736–1808), of Philadelphia as director general of this department; Dr. John Cochran (1730–1807) of the same city as chief physician and surgeon of the army; and Washington's friend from Virginia, Dr. James Craik (1730–1814), as one of three chief hospital physicians. In early September, Washington had written to Jones and other members of Congress recommending Cochran and Craik to its favorable attention (*ibid.*, XVIII, 876–88, 908; Fitzpatrick, *Writings of Washington*, XX, 18–19).

[8] Richard Harrison (see Mason to JM, 2 August 1780, n. 2). Colonel Richard Kidder Meade was an aide-de-camp of Washington.

[9] On 4 October 1780 Congress instructed John Jay, U.S. minister to Spain, to insist, among other things, upon "the right of the United States of America to the free navigation of the river Mississippi into and from the sea" (*Journals of the Continental Congress*, XVIII, 900). This accorded with the instructions of the Virginia legislature to its delegates in Congress (Hening, *Statutes*, X, 537–38; Jones to JM, 19 September 1780, n. 4).

[10] When Arthur Lee (1740–1792) arrived in Philadelphia about 15 October 1780, he at once revived "the old disputes" by requesting Congress to vindicate his conduct while a commissioner of the United States at Paris (1776–1779) against the charges of his associates, Benjamin Franklin and especially Silas Deane. On 19 October Congress named JM the chairman of a committee to consider and report upon Lee's behavior in France (*Journals of the Continental Congress*, XVIII, 951–54; JM to Jones, 17 October 1780).

[11] There is no evidence that JM tried to persuade Congress to adopt this suggestion.

[12] See Jones to JM, 19 September 1780, n. 2.

[13] James Henry, after leaving Congress on 6 July 1780 as a Virginia delegate, did not return before he resigned the office in the following November (Burnett, *Letters*, V, lxiv; *Journal of the House of Delegates*, October 1780, p. 31).

[14] Mrs. Joseph Jones (*ca.* 1730–1822) was the former Mary Taliaferro. Jones may have been her second husband (King George County Court Records, Will Book, No. 3, p. 222, in Virginia State Library; *William and Mary Quarterly*,

1st ser., X [1901], 51). In 1780 James (1724–1809) and John Pemberton (1729–1795), the estate of the late Israel Pemberton (1715–1779), and Israel's son-in-law, Samuel Pleasants (1737–1807), each owned one or more houses in Philadelphia or its surrounding countryside. For this reason the particular accommodation for which JM was negotiating in Jones's behalf cannot be identified with certainty. On 21 November, however, JM informed Jones that he had engaged for the use of Jones, beginning in January, a house owned by Pleasants. This probably was Traveskan, situated two miles south of the city.

15 See Jones to JM, 19 September 1780, n. 8.

To Edmund Pendleton

RC (LC: Madison Papers).

PHILA. Octr. 3d. 1780

DEAR SIR

I had the pleasure of receiving yours of the 25 ulo. yesterday and am sorry it is not yet in my power to gratify your hopes with any prospect of a successful issue to this campaign. The reports of the approach or arrival of a French fleet continue to be circulated, and to prove groundless. If any foreign operations are undertaken on the continent it will probably be against the Floridas by the Spaniards. A Spanish Gentleman[1] who resides in this City has received information from the Governor of Cuba that an armament would pass from the Havannah to Pensacola towards the end of last month, and that 10 or 12 ships of the line and as many thousand troops would soon be in readiness for an expedition against St Augustine.[2] It would be much more for the credit of that nation as well as for the common good, if instead of wasting their time & resources in these separate and unimportant enterprizes, they would join heartily with the French in attacking the Enemy where success would produce the desired effect.[3]

The inclosed papers contain all the particulars which have been received concerning the apostacy & plot of Arnold.[4] A variety of his iniquitous jobs prior to this chef d'oevres of his villainy, carried on under cover of his military author[ity,] have been detected among his papers, and involve a number of persons both within & without the Enemies lines.[5] The embarkation lately going on at N York, and given out to be destined for Virginia or Rhode Island, was pretty certainly a part of the plot against West Point; although the first representation of it has not yet been officially c[o]ntradicted.[6] With sincere regard,

I am D Sir Yr Obt & humble servt.

J. MADISON JUNR.

[1] Probably Don Francisco Rendón, successor of Don Juan de Miralles as agent of Spain to the United States government.

[2] A false rumor was current in Philadelphia that a Spanish force numbering twenty thousand troops had sailed from Havana against British-held St. Augustine or Pensacola (Burnett, *Letters*, V, 398, n. 3; Pendleton to JM, 25 September 1780, n. 2). Bernardo de Gálvez, Spanish governor of Louisiana, captured Pensacola in May 1781.

[3] See Jameson to JM, 23 August 1780, n. 2; Samuel Flagg Bemis, *The Diplomacy of the American Revolution* (New York, 1935), p. 103.

[4] The missing inclosures were probably Philadelphia newspapers. The *Pennsylvania Packet* of 3 October contained a full account of Benedict Arnold's treachery and much correspondence concerning it. The *Virginia Gazette* (Richmond, Dixon and Nicolson) first mentioned it on 11 October, or nearly three weeks after the fateful meeting at Stony Point, N.Y., between Arnold and British Major John André to arrange for the surrender to the enemy of the patriots' key stronghold of West Point, commanded by Arnold. Congress first learned of his treason in a letter of 25 September from General Nathanael Greene (*Journals of the Continental Congress*, XVIII, 868, 876).

[5] Examples of action taken against Mrs. Arnold (Margaret Shippen of Philadelphia) and other persons suspected of treasonably assisting Arnold will be found in Fitzpatrick, *Writings of Washington*, XX, 85, 89, 90, 92, 97, 131; *Colonial Records of Pennsylvania* (16 vols.; Harrisburg, 1851–53), XII, 496, 520.

[6] JM's conjecture finds support in General Henry Clinton's letter of 11 October 1780 to Lord George Germain. In this, Clinton speaks of "an expedition to the Chesapeake" as a "feint" to "mask . . . a movement up the North River," assisted by Arnold's treachery and Admiral Rodney's ships (William B. Willcox, ed., *The American Rebellion*, pp. 462–64).

To Thomas Jefferson

Draft (New-York Historical Society). Although this undated, unsigned, and mutilated manuscript was written by Theodorick Bland, Jr., and endorsed "Rough drt of letter, from Col. Theok Bland Jr to Govr. Jefferson," its message is phrased as coming from all the Virginia delegates. Whether the letter bore JM's signature, along with Bland's and John Walker's, cannot be known since the recipient's copy is lost (Boyd, *Papers of Jefferson*, IV, 12–13), but its use of "we" and "us," unlike Bland's personal letters, justifies the inclusion of the letter here. From the news which it contains, it was written on or about 5 October 1780 (Burnett, *Letters*, V, 406, n. 2).

[PHILADELPHIA, *ca.* 5 October 1780]

SR.

Some overtures having been made to Congress, through Mr. Jay our Commissioner at the Court of Madrid, for Building Frigates in America for and on account of his Catholic Majesty and the Proposals having

been referred to the Admiralty to Confer with the Navy Boards of the
Eastern and Middle district and obtain from them estimates of what
would be the Cost of a frigate of forty Guns—and there being no Navy
Board in Virginia it was moved in Congress by the Delegates from that
State, that the Admiralty shd. also lay before Congress Estimates of the
Cost &c. of Building such frigates in Virginia in which it wd. be proper
to specify the terms, and the time it wd. take to Compleat one or more
such frigates,[1] we have thought it Proper to inform you thereof, that
proper persons may be applyed to, to make out such Estimates for
Government, in order that they may be given in to the Admiralty to
report upon [to] Congress, as we are not willing that such lucrative,
and advantageous contracts, the Execution of which must in the end
be attended with so many ad[v]antages shd. be lost to our state and
engrossed by others already so far advanced before us in the Establishing a Marine. This Estimate transmitted as early as possible will put it
in the power of the Delegates from Virginia to press its being transmitted to our Commissioner at Madrid with the Estimates from the
Other States, and the subject itself together with a speedy compliance
we have no doubt will strike you in the same important light in which
it has us. The perfect tranquility which has reigned here with regard
to news has been lately disturbed by a most extraordinary and unexpected event, no less than the sudden defection of Major Genl. Arnold
from the American Cause, and his flight to the Enemy[. He o]n the
ultimo Shamefully treacherously and ignominiously deserted the important Post at West point which Garrison he Commanded, after
having Concerted Measures with the British Adjutant Genl. Colo.
Andrè in the Quality of a Spy for delivering it up to the Enemy, with
the Blackest Circumstances of treason and Perfidy that ever enterd the
heart of any, wretch, but his own. Our Great General Washington, the
French Ambassador, and the Marquis de la fayette were to have been
his Peace offering to the Enemy. But Mr. Andre was accidentally
taken, by a Small party of Militia and is now in our Hands & has
probably before this paid his last tribute of Loyalty to his Royal Master
together with his infamous Coadjutor Joseph Smith of N. York, occa-
siond Arnolds precipitate flight on board a British Man of War which
was ready to receive him in case of Accident The Genl. and other
Gentn. above Mentioned arrived at Arnolds Quarters a few minutes
after his flight, and he has taken effectual measures to prevent further
Mischief. Arnold has wrote him a letter dated on Board the Vulture
Sloop imploring his interposition in favor of his Wife whom he has

left behind. His Papers have been seized in this City where he some time ago resided And lay open several Scenes of Vilany transacted in the Commercial way while he had the Command here between him and other Miscreants, and have laid a train perhaps for further discoveries. Quid non mortalia pectora cogis Auri Sacra fames? Every Mark of horror and resentment has been expressed by the Army at such atrocious and Complicated Vilainy, And the Mob in this City have burnt the traitor in Effigy after Exposing it through the streets with a long purse in one hand and a Mask in the other and labels descriptive of the Character thus [consigned?] to public infamy and odium. Thus with on[e act?] faded the laurels of a hero, and the apellat[ion of] Arnold must be everlastingly changed for [a representa?]tive of the Blackest infa[my].[2]

---

[1] In a long letter of 26 May 1780 from John Jay, U.S. minister to Spain, to the president of Congress, is a statement that the United States might build for Spain "light frigates, cutters, or swift sailing vessels of that size" (Wharton, *Revolutionary Diplomatic Correspondence*, III, 723). This letter was read in Congress on 14 August 1780 and referred to the Committee for Foreign Affairs (*Journals of the Continental Congress*, XVII, 727). An unspecified portion of the letter (perhaps the frigate-building matter) was referred on 21 August to Joseph Jones, George Walton, and Thomas McKean for consideration and report. The three men submitted their recommendations (not given in the printed journal and not found in Papers of the Continental Congress in the National Archives) to Congress on 2 September (*ibid.*, XVII, 802). This was shortly before Jones left for Virginia and shortly after Bland took his seat as a delegate from that state (*ibid.*, XVII, 792). On 4 October Jared Ingersoll, a delegate from Pennsylvania, informed President Joseph Reed of that state that the frigate issue would be discussed by Congress on the following day (Burnett, *Letters*, V, 405). Probably it was, even though the printed journal makes no mention either of it or of the motion of the Virginia delegates referred to in the present letter (*Journals of the Continental Congress*, XVIII, 902–6).

[2] The fact that the Virginia delegates had not heard that Major John André (b. 1751) was executed on 2 October helps somewhat to fix the date of this letter. "Joseph Smith" was Joshua Hett Smith (1749–1818), an intermediary between Major André and Benedict Arnold in the negotiations leading up to the culmination on 22–23 September of the latter's treasonable action. Smith lived near Haverstraw, N.Y., in a house belonging to his elder brother, William Smith, royal chief justice of New York (Carl Van Doren, *Secret History of the American Revolution* [New York, 1941], pp. 289, 428). According to the *Pennsylvania Packet* of Philadelphia of 3 October, the effigy of Arnold burned by a "mob" in that city four days before "had two faces emblematical of his traiterous conduct, a mask in his left hand, and a letter in his right from Belzebub." A figure of the Devil was "shaking a purse of money at the General's left ear." The Latin sentence is from Virgil's *Aeneid* (JM to Bradford, 19 June 1775, n. 3). Arnold had married Margaret ("Peggy") Shippen (1760–1803), the youngest daughter of Edward Shippen, on 8 April 1779.

Notes on Speech Regarding Vermont Lands

MS (New-York Historical Society). In James Duane's hand.

In Congress Fryday Evning 6th Octobr 1780.[1]

Mr. Maddison. Expressed his surprize that the Motion shoud be represented as unfair or indirect.[2] That he intended it to bring the true Question before Congress; for that if the District in Question was comprehended within the Jurisdiction of one or more of the United States, it must necessarily follow, that the Inhabitants coud have no Right to set up an independant State. That it had been clearly proved to lie within New York or New Hampshire; for as these States were bounded upon each other there coud be no Room between them for another Jurisdiction. That Congress by the original Union of the States must have a Superior deciding [?] power over the states and that[3]

[1] For the motion, see Resolutions respecting Vermont Lands, 16 September 1780 and n. 4.

[2] According to James Duane's notes on the debate, Samuel Huntington and Theodorick Bland, Jr., opposed JM's motion on the ground that it "was an indirect and unfair manner of deciding the Question" since "the new State" of Vermont had not been heard on its own behalf, and New York and Connecticut had each demonstrated that the other had no rightful title to the lands at issue. Bland concluded his speech by unsuccessfully moving that JM's resolution be replaced by one declaring the people of Vermont to be "an Independent State." The Duane notes are in Burnett, *Letters*, V, 408–9.

[3] Without completing his summary of JM's speech, Duane began his notes on that of Richard Howly (Ga.). Howly evidently argued that, although neither New York nor New Hampshire had rightful jurisdiction over the Vermonters, "the critical Situation of our Affairs," demanding the harmonious co-operation of the states "to oppose their common Enemy," made it premature and inexpedient for Congress to decide so controversial an issue at that time. Following his note on Howly's remarks, Duane added only, "*Mr. Ingersole* [Jared Ingersoll] That." Judging from the *Journals of the Continental Congress*, XVIII, 909, the debate ended, with no vote taken on JM's motion, "when a letter, of 2, from Ira Allen and Stephen R. Bradley, was read." These Vermont agents informed President Huntington that their commission had expired on 1 October, that they were returning to their "state," and that it would co-operate in winning U.S. independence. They closed the letter by affirming that, since Vermont had "many papers more authentic than those that have been exhibited . . . to shew our right to sovereignty," Congress should postpone rendering judgment upon the issue (NA: PCC, No. 40, I, 579). Congress did not again turn its attention to the question until 20 July 1781.

Notes on Observations of Barbé-Marbois on Western Boundary of the United States

MS (LC: Madison Papers). On 6 October 1780, having agreed two days before upon its instructions to John Jay, United States minister to Spain, Congress named a committee comprising JM as chairman, John Sullivan, and James Duane to draft a letter to Jay "explaining the reasons and principles" underlying the instructions (*Journals of the Continental Congress*, XVIII, 908). At some time between 6 and 16 October, when the committee made its report, JM took the following notes on Barbé-Marbois's "Observations sur les points contestes de la négociation entre l'Espagne et les États-Unis."

[6–16 October 1780]

Sketch of ye Observations on the boundary between the Spanish Settlements & the United States.

(by *de Marbois*)[1] [ca. 1781?][2]

The King of France though anxious to effect the Triple alliance, yet thinkg. the pretensions on both sides[3] exorbitant, did not chuse to interfere in support of either. But directed his Ministers at Phila. & Madrid to press the importance of mutual concessions[.] With this view the former represents to Congress the ne[ce]ssity of [c]on-cent[ra]ting the force agst. the common enemy, for want of which the events of the present campaign[4] have proved inadequate to the exertions. The advantages of an alliance are obvious, in case of a negociation for peace. it will be conducted with perfect harmony between the 3 allied powers—The Spaniards will be as much disposed as the french to support the just claims of U. States. They will not threaten to make a peace excluding them if the others shall be satisfied—on pretence that they are tied to France only, and had no motives to exhaust their resources for a people whose ambition prevented a treaty with a power on whom their safety depended.[5] a continental war to be dreaded by France, as it depends on the death of 2 crowned heads old & sickly and it is 18 years since she was engaged in one[6]—Hence the necessity of seeking a present peace by united efforts. another advantage of an Alliance arises from the impression an acknowledgmt. of independence[7] would make on other Powers of Europe, and on England herself.

The necessity of the Alliance being shew[n] the mea[ns] of brin[g]-ing it about are next to be considered, the observations on which are to be taken not as ministerial communications, but the private senti-

114

ments of one more impartially attached to the good of both parties, than acquainted with the pretensions of either.

Spain claims the exclusive navigation of the Mississippi; and as much I can guess that part of the continent which lies eastward of the Mississippi & formerly called the Orientalis Louisiana. On this head the following objections were suggested by the Committee to the french minister in Jany. last, when urging the necessity of satisfying Spain[8]—

Obj: 1. The Charters of the Southern States forbid such a cession.[9]

answer. The transactions of a power with its own subjects [is] not binding on another power unless communicated[,] acknowledged, and in a case like the present, unless actual possession can be pleaded. were it otherwise perpetual contests wd. prevail among the Southern powers of Europe, as they have most of them granted such [charters at sundry times] to [their subjects.] The charters of the Colonies [interfere with each other,] most of them having disputes not only with their neigh[bours, but with those] at a distance how then can they be a rule for another [power? How will it ap]pear for the states at the time they are requesting of Spain [an acknowledgment of their] independence to apply to the very record which is the proof [of their subjection? Is it] not plain that in such a case, there is no other solid [plea but actual occupation,] or at least a former public manifest possession?[10] The King of Spain however will not recur to these arguments: he will only say—those lands have been ceded 18 years ago by france to G.B. (treaty of Paris 63. art. 7) not to the Colonies. If they become the property of any common enemy, I have a full right to make the conquest of and so I do.

Obj: 2. The lands in question [are] necessary to the safety & prosperity of the States.

Ans: This is not certain. The case of Vermont, Kentucke & some Counties in Massachusets, show the danger of such ext[ensiv]e territories. It is in vain to attempt to convince eithe[r] party that their claims are agst. thei[r] interests, as they are the best judges of it—It rests therefore on the respective possibility of making the conquest, and it may be left even to a partial judge to decide on this point.

Obj: 3. Spain would take advantage of the present situation of the United States to treat with them on unequal principles.

Ans: This is the case in 99 treaties of a 100—no such inequality—rather on the side of America—Spain will acknowledge her independence and does not need hers to be so[11]—Spain will grant commercial and very likely other advantages and can not expect the same from

America. The benefits she is to reap are not of such a positive nature.

Obj: 4. If these demands were granted Spain might think herself entitled to the demand or conquest of Georgia Penobscot N. York &c.[12]

Ans: This objection is extravagant & cannot be seriously made. the most explicit assurances on this point might at any time be obtained.

Obj: 5. Such conduct in Spain neithe[r generous] nor liberal.

Ans: The Spanish Ministry have probably on this said to the French Ambassador *that the conduct of the Americans is neither*[13] *liberal nor generous*

Obj: 6. A war even a long war preferable to such conditions

Ans: A Patient extremely ill might as well say to his Phycician death is better than not to drink spirituous liquors & other things not to be found on the island where he was.

Obj: 7. The Spaniards would not suffer by the sacrifices of their own ambition. No unequal treaty can last long—the injured party will soon or later break it.

Ans: The cautiousness of Spain may be trusted to provide agst. this evil. She may perhaps upon better ground suggest the same danger to the States. They will chuse rather however to confine themselves to their right of conquest upon a country possessed[14] by their Enemy.

Obj: 8. The teritory cannot be given up with out the previous consent of the interested states.

Ans: As this argmt. is founded on the charters, if it be valid, it would prove that no treaty would be valid, unless it secured to the States [territory?] as far as the South Sea.

In this manner would reason a Minister of the [Court of Spain, and it would seem] no solid objection could be made to it. If any restricti[ons ought to be laid on these principles,] they ought to be taken from the actual settlement [of Americans on the territories] claimed by the Spaniards. By settlement is mea[nt, not temporary incursions] of a few troops, but actual occupancy supported [by the exercise of jurisdiction, and] by building of houses, clearing & inhabiting the [land, &c., without contradiction. Here an] impartial mediator might find the line to be drawn be[tween the contending parties. But I shall] Confine myself to represent to the friends of this case that[, in missing the present fair opportunity of ob]taining solid & lasting advantages to run after a shadow & a chimerical object, they expose themselves to the everlasting reproaches of their Country.[15]

---

[1] François, Marquis de Barbé-Marbois (1745–1837), secretary of the French legation, was chargé d'affaires for some weeks in the autumn of 1780 during La Luzerne's

absence from Philadelphia (Wharton, *Revolutionary Diplomatic Correspondence*, IV, 59; *Journals of the Continental Congress*, XVIII, 836–37). The uncompromising stand in regard to the western boundary of the United States asserted by Congress in its instructions to Jay of 4 October, and their probable effect of preventing Spain from allying with the United States, as France desired, led Marbois to prepare his statement. He may have been assisted in drafting it by Francisco Rendón, agent of Spain, and by Daniel of St. Thomas Jenifer, a Maryland delegate in Congress, who wished to restrict the western limits of the "landed states," and especially of Virginia, to the Appalachian watershed (Kathryn Sullivan, *Maryland and France, 1774–1789* [Philadelphia, 1936], pp. 88–90). On the strength of a dispatch from Marbois to Charles Gravier, Comte de Vergennes, 21 October 1780, in the archives of the French Minister of Foreign Affairs in Paris, Elijah Wilson Lyon writes that Marbois, by showing his "Observations" to Madison, persuaded him to make his draft of the letter to Jay "less in the tone of the ambitious principles adopted by Virginia" in relation to its western boundary and the right of Americans to a free use of the Mississippi (*The Man Who Sold Louisiana: The Career of François Barbé-Marbois* [Norman, Okla., 1942], p. 25; see also William Emmett O'Donnell, *The Chevalier de La Luzerne, French Minister to the United States, 1779–1784* [Bruges, 1938], p. 110). Although Henri Doniol (*Histoire*, IV, 593–94) states that Marbois sent a copy of his statement to the president of Congress as well as to Vergennes, no copy of it has been found in the Papers of the Continental Congress in the National Archives.

2 This date was probably inserted by someone other than JM long after he made these notes.

3 Spain and the United States.

4 This can refer only to the campaign of 1780 and hence helps to fix the time when Marbois drafted his memoir.

5 The antecedent of the two "theys" and of the first "their" in this sentence is Spain; that of "them," "a people," and the second "their" is the United States.

6 The meaning here is not clear. Apparently the sense is that France had not fought in Europe since the Seven Years' War (its preliminary Treaty of Paris was signed on 3 November 1762) and feared to become involved in another such conflict because its outcome might hinge upon Empress Maria Theresa of Austria (d. 28 November 1780), whose death would endanger the alliance between Austria and France, and upon King Frederick the Great, whose neutrality could not be depended upon even though Prussia was a member of the League of Armed Neutrality which was aimed mainly against England. Furthermore, if France's ally, the able but ailing Charles III (1716–1788) of Spain, should die, his weakling son would be his successor.

7 Of the United States.

8 *Journals of the Continental Congress*, XVI, 114–15.

9 Above, Motion regarding the Western Lands, 6 September 1780, editorial note.

10 When Henry D. Gilpin published a three-volume collection of Madison's papers in Washington in 1840, he included these notes (Vol. I, Appendix, pp. iii–v). The manuscript was not as greatly mutilated then as now. The words or parts of words inclosed in brackets between "granted such" and "possession" are taken from Gilpin's edition.

11 That is, the advantage was really on the side of the United States for her independence would be acknowledged by Spain, whose sovereignty did not depend upon its recognition by the United States or any other nation.

12 Areas occupied in whole or in part by the British in 1780.

13 JM unintentionally wrote "nor" after "neither."

14 JM inadvertently spelled it "possessessed."

15 The comment in n. 10 applies also to this paragraph.

Motion of Virginia Delegates in Congress

MS (NA: PCC, No. 78, IX, 503). In Charles Thomson's hand.

In Congress Octr. 7th 1780

Resolved,[1] That Charles Fleming and Forster Webb[2] Esquires be and hereby are appointed Commissioners on the part of the United States either of them to indorse the bills that shall be emitted by the State of Virginia pursuant to the resolution of Congress of the 18th March last[3]

[1] Preceding this word in the printed journal is the phrase, "On motion of the delegates of Virginia" (*Journals of the Continental Congress*, XVIII, 910–11). "Extract from the minutes—Chas Thomson Secy" is written at the end of the manuscript.

[2] Foster Webb. Charles Fleming (*ca.* 1731–*ca.* 1793) resigned in December 1778, after serving for nearly three years as captain, major, and lieutenant colonel of the Virginia continental line. At least by January 1781 and thereafter until the surrender of Cornwallis, he was again in the field as a lieutenant colonel of militia. On 3 January 1782 he resigned the office to which he had been appointed by this resolution. In the early years of the Revolution he was a resident of Cumberland County, but he moved to Chesterfield County and lived there until his death. He was a brother of Judge William Fleming of Virginia's Supreme Court of Appeals (F. B. Heitman, *Historical Register of Officers of the Continental Army*, p. 177; *Virginia Magazine of History and Biography*, XXIII [1915], 242; XXIV [1916], 208–10; Fleming to president of Congress, 3 January 1782, NA: PCC, No. 78, IX, 499; *Journals of the Continental Congress*, XXII, 76).

[3] See Jefferson to JM, 26 July 1780, n. 2; below, Motion regarding Virginia Currency, 11 October 1780. President Huntington wrote to Jefferson on 10 October 1780, informing him of the appointment of Webb and Fleming (*Calendar of Virginia State Papers*, I, 378).

From Edmund Pendleton

Tr (LC: Force Transcripts).

Virga. Octobr 8. 1780

Dr Sir:

I have yr obliging favr of the 26th past, I know not when my first letter, after you kindly accepted my proposed correspondence, should have reached you, but be assured I have not miss'd a week since, nor shall I unless sickness prevents me, being a very Punctual tho' not an entertaining correspondent; at this time I have not a word of foreign or domestic Intelligence to communicate, except that we had a report on Thursday last of a large fleet of British Ships arrived in Our Bay

& that they were landing their Men at Portsmouth. But as I have heard nothing further of it & the Govr had no Account of such an Invasion on Fryday, I take it for granted the story is without foundation.[1] I might indeed fill my paper if I was to trace Graves & Rodney thro' the Various excursions my fancy has framed for them, but blank paper will give you as much Satisfaction as such a Reverie would.

What do you think of Government having advertised the time & place for the Execution of each condemn'd Rioter in Britain?[2] It is a challenge to the Mob to come forth, & confirms me in a former opinion, that the despotism adopted at the commencement of the present Reign had a much more extensive Object than America & was intended to reach the whole Empire. I think I forse[e] it begun in Britain & that it will be prosecuted there whatever is the fate of America. And considering the number of Crown officers & Pensioners with the Creditors of Government & all their various Connections, It seems to me they will have a better chance of Succeeding there than here; so we can keep clear of their horid Tyrany, they may settle the other point amongst themselves. I am

Dr. Sr Yr Affe & Obt Servt

EDMD. PENDLETON

[1] Pendleton's information was premature. The invading force of General Alexander Leslie appeared in the Chesapeake on 20 October rather than on the fifth (Boyd, *Papers of Jefferson*, IV, 54; JM to Jones, 19 September 1780, n. 2).

[2] During the anti-Catholic riots in London headed by Lord George Gordon, in early June 1780, about 450 people were killed or wounded and much property was destroyed. Pendleton probably derived his information about this disorder from the *Virginia Gazette* (Richmond, Dixon and Nicolson) of 4 October 1780.

From Joseph Jones

RC (LC: Madison Papers).

SPRING HILL 9th. Octr. 1780

DEAR SR.

I think you acted very prudently in declining to press on the part of Virginia the Resolutions I left for the Consideration of Congress, had I been present I should have done the same as I had no intention when they were offered that Virginia should appear anxious about them whatever my opinion might be as to their propriety or Justice. I meant to leave them to the Candor of Congress and to those impartial reflections which ought ever and upon such great questions I trust will generally govern their Councils. I wished also to feel the pulse of that Body upon these points and to know the reasons that governed their resolutions[;] that if the resolutions were any of them rejected and the ground upon which they were overruled good[,] the Assembly of Virga. might in their deliberations on the subject perhaps be influenced by like considerations.[1] I thought I could discover a strong propensity among some of the members to give independence to the people of Vermont. This affair ought to be a warning to Congress how to act in similar situations in future—to be remiss and indecisive upon such pretensions as these serves only to support and not discourage the claimants. it does more[,] it shews the weakness or wickedness of Government and must ultimatly produce dishoner and contempt.[2] I have sent forward your letter to the auditors and inclosed my account whereby the balance due to me is £3000 which I have directed to be applied to your use and requested the money might be forwarded to you as speedily as possible as I well knew you wanted it. the fourth of the eight thousand pounds drawn for is included in the three thousand pounds and so I have informed the Auditors so that when Meade's orders are paid you must take on my account two thousand pounds. Out of Mrs. House's account of 8,000 som[e] odd dols. is to be deducted what I advanced for Wine, 5/ hard money overpaid at the former settlemt. and the money advanced by me for the Family the amount of which I gave you in the first instance and Mrs. Trist in the second.[3] I shall go off to Richm[ond] if Mrs. Jones gets tolerably well abt. the middle of next week, from whence you shall regularly hear from me. Have no reasons been assigned by the Minister[4] for the disappointments respecting the expected reinforcement. if there are any that are worthy notice I should be glad to be furnished with them that I may do Justice to the good intentions of France and to their exertions in the common cause which some are but too apt to suspect upon the present occasion and though I am not among the number I must confess I am at a loss how fully to satisfy the doubts of some and to silence the insinuations of others who ground their observations upon the transactions of the present year and particularly the promised reinforcemt.

I have mentioned this matter in Confidence to you that if you think it proper you may take occasion to intimate to the proper persons how much it would contribute to the satisfaction of the Friends of the alliance to be able to give some satisfactory reasons for our disappointments not only of the aid to come to the Continent but of our expectations of advantages to be obtained over the Enemy by the combined

Forces in the W. Indies, in short their inactivity there as well as in Europe. These I know are delicate matters, but they are such as we ought to know as well for our future government as for silencing those who throw out insinuations injurious to France.

Be pleased to present my Compliments to Mr. Pleasants and inform him he shall receive an answer from me respecting his House soon after my arrival at Richmond which I expected wou[ld] be the beginning of this month from the usual time of the Assemblys meeting but their adjourning to a later day has prevented my doing it so soon a[s] I intended. In the mean time will you be pleased to sound Mr. Pemberton as to his House and the terms if he is inclined to let it with stable room for four Horses a chariot house Garden and small Pasture with such furniture as he can spare, this information I shall thank you for as soon as possible.[5] The Report here is that Congress has suspended Gates from his Command untill his Conduct is inquired into.[6] Our Recruits I am told are going on to the Southern camp. Our Militia I believe are returned and another Division is I understand preparing to take their place.[7] with great esteem I am

Dr Sr. yr. aff Friend [&] Servt.

Jos: Jon[es]

Compliments to the Delegation.

---

[1] Jones's comment to this point in his letter is upon his resolutions of 6 September (*q.v.*) relating to Virginia's claims to territory west of the Appalachians. His remarks could have been in response to those in JM's letter to him of 19 September (*q.v.*), but JM may have discussed the subject further in a now missing letter which he apparently wrote to Jones on or about 25 September (JM to Virginia Auditors, 25 September 1780, n. 4).

[2] Above, Resolutions respecting Vermont Lands, 16 September 1780.

[3] Jones's accounts (Burnett, *Letters*, V, 412–13, n. 3) must have been forwarded in JM's letter of 25 September to the Board of Auditors of Virginia (*q.v.*). The £3,000 Virginia currency, which Jones borrowed from JM upon leaving Philadelphia in early September, was to be repaid in connection with Jones's settlement with the auditors. Two-thirds of this debt was discharged by transferring to JM £2,000 standing to Jones's credit with George Meade and Company, a Philadelphia merchant concern; the £1,000 balance was sent from Virginia (below, Expense Account as Delegate in Congress, 20 December 1780, n. 2). On the House-Trist boarding house, see Jones to JM, 19 September 1780, n. 8.

[4] Anne César, Chevalier de La Luzerne.

[5] See Jones to JM, 2 October 1780, n. 14.

[6] On 5 October Congress resolved to have a "court of enquiry" review Major General Horatio Gates's conduct as commander of the southern army and directed Washington to appoint a new commander "until such enquiry be made" (*Journals of the Continental Congress*, XVIII, 906). Although Washington named Major General Nathanael Greene on 14 October, Greene did not take active command until 4 December (Fitzpatrick, *Writings of Washington*, XX, 181–83; John Richard

Alden, *The American Revolution, 1775–1783* [New York, 1954], p. 236). On 2 August 1781, Gates wrote Thomas Jefferson that "A Motion for rescinding the Resolve of the 5th: of October has been several Times made in Congress, but once to my Astonishment was prevented being carried by a Mr: Maddison of this State, a Gentleman I do not know, and who I am satisfied does not know me" (Boyd, *Papers of Jefferson*, VI, 110). The only such motion recorded was that of James Mitchell Varnum on 24 May 1781 (*Journals of the Continental Congress*, XX, 533 n.).

7 Governor Jefferson's correspondence in early October frequently mentions the movement of troops from Virginia to the southern army (Boyd, *Papers of Jefferson*, IV, 5–24, *passim*).

To Joseph Jones

RC (LC: Madison Papers).

PHILADA. [1780, Oct. 10]¹

DEAR SIR

I received yesterday yours of the 2d. inst: Some of the questions mentioned in it I anticipated in my last. The clause of the resolutions you left on the table relating to Indian purchases is still undetermined. Many attempts have been made to bring the Vermont dispute to an issue, but the diversity of opinions that prevail on one side & the dilatory artifices employed on the other have frustrated them. All the evidence has been heard and a proposition for including it within the jurisdiction of some one of the states debated for some time, but the decision was suspended. An arrangement of the Army founded on G: Washington's letter, has passed Congress and is now with the Genl. for his observations on it. It includes a recommendation to the States to fill up their quotas. No arrangement of the Civil departments has taken place. A new medical system has been passed. Shippen is again at the head of it. Craig & Cochran have not been forgotten. The instructions relating to the Mississippi have passed entirely to my satisfaction. A committee is now preparing a state of the reasons & principles on which they stand.² Dr Lee³ has not yet arrived.

No military or naval intelligence has come to hand since my last except a further report that a very large embarkation is actually going on at N. York. It will be prudent for Virginia not to neglect the precautions necessary for her defence in case she should be the object of it.⁴

André was hung the 2d. inst: He submitted to his fate in a manner that shewed him to be worthy of a better one. His coadjutor Smith will soon follow him. The Hero of the plot, it is *said* is to be made a Brigadier and employed in some predatory expedition suited to his genius & his thirst for pelf. It is said with more probability that his baseness is heartily despised by those who have taken advantage of it, and yt. some resentment is mixed with their contempt on account of the loss of their darling officer.[5]

Our domestic controversy is still sub judice. This day I believe will certainly decide it in its present stage. If it should be unfortunate it will be carried into the Court of Errors. Some propositions founded on an amiable seperation have been made on the part of Bulkley but they were so pregnant with ruin to the old lady that her friends could not advise her to accede to them.[6]

Your compliments were presented to the family as you desired, and are returned with very great sincerity. I hope your lady and son have by this time recovered, and that no other impediment will keep you from the Assembly when it meets, or from returning hither as soon as it rises.[7]

I am dr Sir Yr. Affecte friend & Servt

JAMES MADISON JR.[8]

[1] This date was inserted by someone else, probably long after JM wrote the letter. Although this letter is undated, the contents of its first paragraph make certain that JM wrote it after the evening session of Congress of 6 October, when the committee on the free navigation of the Mississippi River was appointed, and before the vote on the western territory issue was taken on 10 October. Knowing Jones's lively interest in this latter question, JM would almost surely have reported the vote if he had known it. The fact that his letter of 10 October to Pendleton contains approximately the same information, and even some of the same expressions as this one, suggests that both letters were written on that day.

[2] JM omits mention of his own membership on this committee with John Sullivan and James Duane (*Journals of the Continental Congress*, XVIII, 908). Following this sentence in the letter is a bracket which complements one just before the third sentence in this paragraph. As already noted in the case of earlier letters, these brackets were added many years later by JM or someone of his family to designate what should be extracted for publication. For comment upon the matters mentioned in this paragraph, see Jones to JM, 2 October 1780, nn. 2, 3, 5–7, 9, 10; and Notes on Speech regarding Vermont Lands, 6 October 1780. JM's reference to "my last" in the second sentence of this paragraph suggests a now missing letter to Jones, probably dated 3 October.

[3] Arthur Lee.

[4] See JM to Jones, 19 September 1780, n. 2; and Pendleton to JM, 8 October 1780, n. 1.

[5] See Virginia Delegates to Jefferson, 5[?] October 1780, n. 2; and JM to Pendleton, 10 October 1780, nn. 4 and 5.

[6] See Jones to JM, 19 September 1780, n. 8. Insofar as the editors have been able to ascertain, the primary sources needed to clarify this matter fully are no longer

extant. Whether Joseph Bulkley had been the husband of Mrs. House (the "old lady") is not beyond doubt, but there is no question that, based upon some prior close relationship, he was pressing in the courts his claim to her boarding house, or at least to its furniture, at Fifth and Market Streets. Bulkley was evidently the more eager to gain control of this property because his own creditors insisted upon their due. Some of the furniture belonged neither to Mrs. House nor to Bulkley but to her roomers, including John Morin Scott and James Duane of New York, William Sharpe of North Carolina, Isaac Motte of South Carolina, and JM and Jones of Virginia. Until Scott left Congress for his home about 14 November, his activities on behalf of Mrs. House included speaking for her before a court and preventing Bulkley from pestering her at home. "The Genl's victory," mentioned by JM in his letter of [24?] October to Jones (*q.v.*), brought Mrs. House only temporary relief because Bulkley appealed the judgment. Upon Scott's departure, James Duane took over as her principal champion. When Bulkley won in a higher court, a deputy sheriff on 30 November attempted on Bulkley's behalf to inventory, or perhaps even to remove the furniture, in the boarding house. Duane protested directly to President Joseph Reed of Pennsylvania that day, calling attention to "our publick Characters Priviledges and exclusive Right to occupy that House" and taking the high ground that "the Reasons for protecting in all nations, the Persons Houses & Effects of foreign Ambassadors apply with at least equal Force to the Members who constitute the general Government of the United States" (*Pennsylvania Archives*, 1st ser., VIII, 629–30). Reed replied politely but upheld the officer in his duty to execute the verdict of the court (Reed to Duane, 1 and 19 December 1780, New-York Historical Society: James Duane Papers). Having removed some of the furniture, but apparently not taking any owned by a boarder, the sheriff advertised it to be sold "by Public Vendue" on 29 December 1780 in order to satisfy one of Bulkley's creditors (Duane to Reed, 16 December 1780, *Pennsylvania Archives*, 1st ser., VIII, 659; *Pennsylvania Packet*, 19 December 1780). At least insofar as JM and his fellow boarders were concerned, the matter was concluded by 3 February 1781. On that day Duane wrote Scott that although Bulkley had succeeded in taking "the few goods" belonging to Mrs. House, the rest of the furnishings had been secured from his grasp. Duane implied that since Bulkley was about to be imprisoned for debt, "he will give us no further trouble" (New-York Historical Society: James Duane Papers).

⁷ See Joseph Jones to JM, 2 October 1780, and [24?] October 1780. An attack of malaria kept Jones from reaching Richmond for the session of the Virginia legislature until 31 October. This was over two weeks after the scheduled date of convening, but a quorum did not assemble until 6 November. Although the legislature continued to meet until 2 January 1781, Jones left for home about the middle of the preceding month and delayed resuming his seat in Congress until 29 January (Worthington C. Ford, ed., *Letters of Joseph Jones*, pp. 40, 63; *Journal of the House of Delegates*, October 1780, pp. 3–7, 81; *Journals of the Continental Congress*, XIX, 94).

⁸ An unknown "WS," probably of Fredericksburg, Va., wrote to Jones on the wrapper of this letter, informing him of the patriot victory at King's Mountain, S.C., on 7 October. This note is printed in Burnett, *Letters*, V, 417, n. 2, and Jones relayed its news to JM in his letter of [24] October (*q.v.*). Congress apparently first heard of the victory on the 23d (*Journals of the Continental Congress*, XVIII, 963). "WS" may have been William Smith (1746–1802), a native of Gloucestershire, England, who became a Fredericksburg merchant and embraced the patriot cause (Catherine Lindsay Knorr, ed., "Marriage Bonds and Ministers' Returns, Fredericksburg, Virginia, 1782–1850. Also Tombstone Inscriptions from St. George Cemetery, 1752–1920" [mimeographed; Pine Bluff, Ark., 1954], p. 84).

To Edmund Pendleton

RC (LC: Madison Papers).

PHILA. Octr. 10th. 1780

DEAR SIR

Your favor of the first Inst. came safe to hand yesterday. The inclosed was sent to Mr. Pendleton who is still in town.[1]

All we know of the several fleets in the American Seas is that Rodney with a few ships at N. York, the remainder having joined Graves & Arbuthnot whom we know nothing about: Ternay is still at Rhode Island. The main french fleet under Guichen left the West Indies about the time first mentioned with a large fleet of Merchantmen under its convoy, and has not since been heard of. The residue of the french fleet is in the W. Indies but we do not hear of their being any way employed. It is said an English expedition is preparing at Jamaica against some of the Spanish settlements. The Spanish expeditions against the Floridas I believe I mentioned in my last.[2]

We have private accounts through a channel which has seldom deceived that a very large embarkation is still going on at N. York. I hope Virginia will not be surprised in case she should be the meditated victim[3]

Andrè was hung as a spy on the 2d. inst. Clinton made a frivolous attempt to save him by pleading the passport granted by Arnold. He submitted to his fate in a manner that showed him to be worthy of a better one. His coadjutor Smith will soon follow him.[4] The Hero of the Plot, although he may for the present escape an ignominious death must lead an ignominious life which if any of his feelings remain will be a sorer punishment. It is *said* that he is to be made a Brigadier and employed in some predatory expedition against the Spaniards in which he may gratify his thirst for gold.[5] It is said with more probability that his baseness is universally despised by those who have taken advantage of it, and yt some degree of resentment is mixed with their contempt on account of the loss[6] of their darling officer[7] to which he was accessory. With sincere regard

I am Dr. Sir Yr obt humbl Ser[vt.]

JAMES MADISON JNR.

1 Judge Henry Pendleton.
2 British Admirals George B. Rodney, Thomas Graves, and Marriot Arbuthnot (*ca.* 1711–1794), and French Admirals the Chevalier de Ternay and Luc Urbain

du Bouexic, Comte de Guichen (1712–1790). See Jameson to JM, 23 August 1780; Pendleton to JM, 25 September 1780, n. 2; JM to Pendleton, 3 October 1780.

³ See JM to Jones, 19 September 1780, n. 2.

⁴ After a court-martial acquitted Joshua Hett Smith, the army delivered him to New York civil authorities for trial. Escaping from their custody, he fled to the British in New York City (Fitzpatrick, *Writings of Washington*, XX, 103, 111 and n. 88, 262 and n. 16; Virginia Delegates to Jefferson, [*ca.* 5 October 1780], n. 2).

⁵ General Clinton appointed Benedict Arnold, "col[onel] of a reg[iment], with the rank of brigadier gen[eral]" (draft of Clinton's letter to Lord George Germain, 11 October 1780, in William B. Willcox, ed., *The American Rebellion*, pp. 465–66). Arnold's "predatory expedition" of early 1781 was against Virginia rather than "the Spaniards" (*ibid.,* pp. 236–37).

⁶ JM wrote and crossed out "occasioned by him" after "loss."

⁷ Major John André, Clinton's adjutant general.

Motion Regarding Virginia Currency

Printed text (*Journals of the Continental Congress*, XVIII, 916).

[11 October 1780]

On motion of Mr. [James] Madison, seconded by Mr. [Theodorick] Bland,

Ordered, That the letter, of 27 September,¹ from Governor Jefferson, with the copies of the acts of the legislature of Virginia enclosed therewith, be referred to the Board of Treasury, to enable them to ascertain and insert in the bills to be emitted by the said State, pursuant to the resolutions of Congress, of the 18 of March last, the time of the passing of the act adopting the said resolutions.²

¹ Jefferson's letter to President Huntington was read in Congress on 9 October 1780 (*Journals of the Continental Congress*, XVIII, 912; Boyd, *Papers of Jefferson*, III, 669–70).

² For the background of this motion, see Jefferson to JM, 26 July 1780, n. 2; and Motion of Virginia Delegates, 7 October 1780. The legislature of Virginia on 14 July adopted two acts in compliance with the resolutions of Congress of 18 March 1780 (*Journal of the House of Delegates*, May 1780, pp. 87–89).

Draft of Letter to John Jay, Explaining His Instructions

Draft (NA: PCC, No. 25, I, 239–49). This letter in JM's hand constituted the report of the Madison (chairman)-Sullivan-Duane committee appointed on 6 October (above, Notes on Observations of Barbé-Marbois, [6–16 October 1780], head-note). Submitted to Congress on 16 October, the letter was agreed to the next day in slightly amended form, as indicated below. The version printed in the *Journals of the Continental Congress*, XVIII, 935–47, differs unimportantly in punctuation, capitalization, and spelling from the following reproduction of the letter from its manuscript. This letter is in the form of a commentary upon the instructions to Jay, United States minister to Spain, adopted by Congress on 4 October, after being drafted by a committee of which JM's colleague Joseph Jones had been a prominent member (*ibid.*, XVIII, 900–902; Jones to JM, 19 September, n. 4, and 2 October 1780, n. 9).

[17 October 1780]

The Committee appointed to draught a letter to the Ministers Plenipotentiary at the Courts of Versailles and Madrid, explaining the reasons and principles on which the instructions to Mr. Jay of the 4th. inst: are founded[1] report the following to Mr. Jay, a copy of which with the resolution directing the draught, to be also inclosed to Dr. Franklin.

Sɪʀ

Congress having in their instructions of the 4th. inst: directed you to adhere strictly to their former instructions relating to the boundaries of the United States,[2] to insist on the navigation of the Mississippi for the Citizens of the United States in common with the subjects of his Catholic Majesty, as also on a free port or ports below the Northern limit of W. Florida & accessible to Merchant ships, for the use of the former; and being sensible of the influence which these claims on the part of the United States may have on your negociations with the Court of Madrid, have thought it expedient to explain the reasons and principles on which the same are founded, that you may be enabled to satisfy that Court of the equity and justice of their intentions.

With respect to the first of these articles by which the river Miss. is fixed as the boundary between the Spanish settlements and the United States, it is unnecessary to take notice of any pretensions founded on a priority of discovery, of occupancy or on conquest. It is sufficient that by the definitive treaty of Paris 1763 Art. 7 all the territory now claimed by the United States was expressly and irrevocably ceded to the King of G. Britain—and that the United States are in consequence of the revolution in their Government entitled to the benefits of that cession.

The first of these positions is proved by the treaty itself. To prove the last, it must be observed that it is a fundamental principle in all lawful Governments and particularly in the constitution of the British Empire, that all the rights of sovereignty are intended for the benefit of those from whom they are derived and over whom they are exercised. It is known also to have been held for an inviolable principle by the United States whilst they remained a part of the British Empire, that the Sovereignty of the King of England with all the rights & powers included in it, did not extend to them in virtue of his being acknowledged and obeyed as King by the people of England or of any other part of the Empire, but in virtue of his being acknowledged and obeyed as King by the people of America themselves; and that this principle was the basis, first of their opposition to, and finally of their abolition of, his authority over them.[3] From these principles it results that all the territory lying within the limits of the States as fixed by the Sovereign himself, was held by him for their particular benefit, and must equally with his other rights and claims in quality of their sovereign be considered as having devolved on them in consequence of their resumption of the Sovereignty to themselves.[4]

In support of this position it may be further observed that all the territorial rights of the King of G. Britain within the limits of the United States accrued to him from the enterprizes, the risks, the sacrifices, the expence in blood and treasure, of the present inhabitants and their progenitors. If in latter times expences and exertions have been borne by any other part of the Empire in their immediate defence it need only be recollected that the ultimate object of them was the general security and advantage of the empire, that a proportional share was borne by the States themselves, and that if this had not been the case, the benefits resulting from an exclusive enjoyment of their trade have been an abundant compensation. Equity and justice therefore perfectly coincide in the present instance with political and constitutional principles.

No objection can be pretended against what is here said, except that the King of G. Britain was at the time of the rupture with his Catholic Majesty possessed of certain parts of the territory in question, and consequently that his C—M. had and still has a right to regard them as lawful objects of conquest.[5] In answer to this objection it is to be considered, 1st. that these possessions are few in number and confined to small spots. 2. that a right founded on conquest being only coextensive with the objects of conquest, cannot comprehend the circumjacent territory. 3. that if a right to the said territory depended on the conquest of the British posts within it the United States have already a more extensive claim to it, than Spain can acquire, having by the success of their arms obtained possession of all the important posts and settlements on the Illinois and Wabash, rescued the inhabitants from British domination, and established civil government in its proper form over them. They have moreover established a post on a strong and commanding situation near the mouth of the Ohio.[6] Whereas Spain has a claim by conquest to no post above the Northern bounds of W. Florida except that of the Natches, nor are there any other British posts below the mouth of the Ohio for their arms to be employed against. 4. that whatever extent ought to be ascribed to the right of conquest, it must be admitted to have limitations which in the present case exclude the pretensions of his Catholic Majesty.[7] If the occupation by the King of G. Britain of posts within the limits of the United States as defined by charters derived from the said King when constitutionally authorized to grant them, makes them lawful objects of conquest to any other power than the United States, it follows that every other part of the United States that now is or may hereafter fall into the hands of the Enemy is equally an object of conquest. Not only N. York Long Island & the other islands in its vicinity, but almost the entire states of S. Carolina and Georgia, might by the interposition of a foreign power at war with their Enemy be for ever severed from the American Confederacy, and subjected to a foreign yoke. But is such a doctrine consonant to the rights of nations or the sentiments of humanity? does it breathe that spirit of concord and amity which is the aim of the proposed alliance with Spain? would it be admitted by Spain herself if it affected her own dominions? Were for example a British armament by a sudden enterprize to get possession of a seaport a trading town or maritime province in Spain and another power at war with Britain should before it could be reconquered by Spain wrest it from the hands of Britain, would Spain herself consider it as an extinguishment of her just pretensions? or would any impartial nation consider it in that light? As[8] to the Proclamation of the King of G. Britain of 1763 forbidding his governors in N. America to grant lands westward of the sources of the rivers falling into the Atlantic Ocean, it can by no rule of construction militate against the present claims of the United States. That Proclamation, as is clear both from the title and tenor of it, was intended merely to prevent disputes with the Indians, and an irregular appropriation of vacant land to individuals; and by no means either to renounce any part of ye cessions made in the treaty of Paris, or to affect the bounderies established by antient charters. On the contrary it is expressly declared that the lands and territory prohibited to be granted, were within the sovereignty and dominion of that crown, notwithstanding the reservation of them to the use of the Indians.[9]

The right of the United States to western territory as far as the Mississippi having been shewn there are sufficient reasons for them to insist on that right as well as for Spain not to wish a relinquishment of it.

In the first place the river Mississipi will be a more natural, more distinguishable and more precise boundary than any other that can be drawn eastwardly of it; and consequently will be less liable to become a source of those disputes which too often proceed from uncertain boundaries between nations.

Secondly. It ought not to be concealed that although the vacant territory adjacent to the Mississippi should be relinquished by the United States to Spain, yet the fertility of its soil, and its convenient situation for trade might be productive of intrusions by the Citizens of the former which their great distance would render it difficult to restrain and which might lead to an interruption of that harmony which it is so much the interest and wish of both should be perpetual.

Thirdly. As this territory lies within the charter limits of particular States and is considered by them as no less their property than any other territory within their limits, Congress could not relinquish it without exciting discussions between themselves & those States concerning their respective rights and powers which might greatly embarrass the public councils of the United States and give advantage to the common enemy.

Fourthly. The territory in question contains a number of inhabitants who are at present under the protection of the United States and have sworn allegiance to them. These could not by voluntary transfer be subjected to a foreign jurisdiction without manifest violation of the common rights of mankind and of the genius and principles of the American Governments.

Fifthly. In case the obstinacy and pride of G. Britain should for any length of time continue an obstacle to peace a cession of this territory rendered of so much value to the United States by its particular situa-

JAMES DUANE

JOHN MATHEWS

HENRY LAURENS

ARTHUR LEE

The Committee appointed to draught a letter to the Ministers Plenipotentiary at the Courts of Versailles and Madrid, explaining the reasons and
principles on which the instructions to Mr Jay of the 4th inst. are founded
report the following to Mr Jay, a copy of which, with the resolution directing
the draught, to be also inclosed to Dr Franklin.

Sir Congress having in their instructions of the 4th inst. directed you
to adhere strictly to their former instructions relating to the boundaries
of the United States, to insist on the navigation of the Mississippi for the citizens of the
United States in common with the subjects of his Catholic Majesty, and
also on a place below the Northern limit of W. Florida & access
to merchant ships, for the use of the former; and being sensible of
the influence which these claims may the part of the United States
may have on your negociations with the Court of Madrid, have
thought it expedient to explain the reasons and principles on which the
same are founded, that you may be enabled to satisfy that Court of the
equity and justice of their intentions.

With respect to the first of these articles by which the river Mississippi
is fixed as the boundary between the Spanish settlements and the United
States, it is unnecessary to take notice of any pretensions founded on
priority of discovery, of occupancy or on conquest. It is sufficient that by
the definitive treaty of Paris 1763 Art. 7 all the Territory now claimed by
the United States was expressly and irrevocably ceded to the King of
G. Britain — and that the United States are in consequence of
the revolution in their government entitled to the benefits of that
cession.

The first of these positions is proved by the treaty itself. To prove
the last, it must be observed that it is a fundamental principle in all
lawful governments and particularly the constitution of the British
Empire, that all the rights of sovereignty are intended for the benefit
of those from whom they are derived and over whom they are exercised.
It is known also to have been held for an inviolable principle

COMMITTEE REPORT ON NAVIGATION OF THE MISSISSIPPI

tion, would deprive them of one of the material funds on which they rely for pursuing the war against her. On the part of Spain, this territorial fund is not needed for and perhaps could not be applied to the purposes of the war and from its situation is otherwise of much less value to her than to the United States.

Congress have the greater hopes that the pretensions of his Catholic Majesty on this subject will not be so far urged as to prove an insuperable obstacle to an alliance with the United States, because they conceive such pretensions to be incompatible with the treaties subsisting between France and them which are to be the basis and substance of it. By Art. 11 of the Treaty of Alliance eventual and defensive the *possessions* of the United States are guarantied to them by his most Xn Majesty. By Art: 12 of the same treaty intended to fix more precisely the sense and application of the preceding Article, it is declared that this guarantee shall have its full force and effect the moment a rupture shall take place between France and England. All the *possessions* therefore belonging to the United States at the time of that rupture, which being prior to the rupture between Spain and England must be prior to all claims of conquest by the former, are guarantied to them by his Most Xn Majesty.[10] Now that in the *possessions* thus guarantied was meant by the Contracting parties to be included all the territory within the limits assigned to the United States by the Treaty of Paris, may be inferred from Art: 5 of the Treaty abovementioned, which declares that if the United States should think fit to attempt the reduction of the British power remaining in the Northern parts of America, or the Islands of Bermudas &c. those Countries shall in case of success be confederated with or dependent upon the United States: For if it had not been understood by the parties that the Western territory in question known to be of so great importance to the United States and a reduction of it so likely to be attempted by them, was included in the general guarantee, can it be supposed than [that] no notice would have been taken of it when the parties extended their views not only to Canada but to the remote & unimportant Island of Bermudas. It is true these acts between France and the United States are in no respect obligatory on his Catholic Majesty until he shall think fit to accede to them. Yet as they shew the sense of his Most Xn Majesty on this subject with whom his C. M is intimately allied, as it is in pursuance of an express reservation to his C. M in a secret act subjoined to the treaties aforesaid of a power to accede to those treaties that the present overtures are made on the part of the United States, and as it is particularly stated in that Act, that any conditions which his C. M shall think fit to add are to be analogous to the principal aim of the Alliance and conformable to the rules of equality reciprocity & friendship, Congress entertain too high an opinion of the equity moderation and wisdom of his C M not to suppose, that when joined to these considerations they will prevail against any mistaken views of interest that may be suggested to him.

The next object of the instructions is the free navigation of the Mississippi for the citizens of the United States in common with the subjects of his C M.

On this subject the same inference may be made from Art: 7 of the Treaty of Paris, which stipulates this right in the amplest manner to the King of G. Britain,[11] and the devolution of it to the United States as was applied to the territorial claims of the latter. Nor can Congress hesitate to believe that even if no such right could be inferred from that treaty that the generosity of his C. M would suffer the inhabitants of these States to be put into a worse condition in this respect by their alliance with him in the character of a sovereign people, than they were in when subjects of a power who was always ready to turn their force against his Majesty; especially as one of the great objects of the proposed alliance is to give greater effect to the common exertions for disarming that power of the faculty of disturbing others.

Besides, as the United States have an indisputable right to the possession of the East bank of the Mississippi for a very great distance, and the navigation of that river will essentially tend to the prosperity and advantage of the Citizens of the United States that may reside on the Mississippi or the waters running into it, it is conceived that the circumstance of Spain's being in possession of the banks on both sides near its mouth, cannot be deemed a natural or equitable bar to the free use of the river. Such a principle would authorize a nation disposed to take advantage of circumstances to contravene the clear indications of nature and providence, and the general good of mankind.

The Usage of nations accordingly seems in such cases to have given to those holding the mouth or lower parts of a river no right against those above them, except the right of imposing a moderate toll, and that on the equitable supposition that such toll is due for the expence and trouble the former may have been put to.

"An *innocent passage* (says Vattel) is due to all nations with whom a State is at peace; and this duty comprehends troops equally with individuals."[12] If a right to a passage by land through other countries may be claimed for troops which are employed in the destruction of

Mankind; how much more may a passage by water be claimed for commerce which is beneficial to all nations.

Here again it ought not to be concealed that the inconveniencies which must be felt by the inhabitants on the waters running westwardly under an exclusion from the free use of the Mississippi would be a constant and increasing source of disquietude on their part, of more rigorous precautions on the part of Spain, and of an irritation on both parts, which it is equally the interest and duty of both to guard against.

But notwithstanding the equitable claim of the United States to the *free* navigation of the Mississippi and its great importance to them, Congress have so strong a disposition to conform to the desires of his C. M that they have agreed that such equitable regulations may be entered into as may be a Requisite security against contraband; provided the point of right be not relinquished and *a free port or ports below the 31st: degree of N. L. and accessible to Merchant ships be stipulated to them.*[13]

The reason why a port or ports as thus described was required must be obvious. Without such a stipulation the free use of the Mississippi would in fact amount to no more than a free intercourse with New Orleans and the other ports of Louisiana. From the rapid current of this river it is well known that it must be navigated by vessels of a peculiar construction and which will be unfit to go to sea. Unless therefore some place be assigned to the U. S. where the produce carried down the river and the merchandis[e] [a]rriving from abroad may be reposited till they can be respectively taken away by the proper vessels there can be no such thing as a foreign trade.

There is a remaining consideration respecting the navigation of the Mississippi, which deeply concerns the maritime powers in general but more particularly their most Xn and Catholic Majesties. The Country watered by the Ohio with its large branches having their sources near the lakes on one side, and those running N. Westward and falling into it on the other sides will appear from a single glance on a map to be of vast extent. The circumstance of its being so finely watered, added to the singular fertility of its soil and other advantages presented by a new country, will occasion a rapidity of population not easy to be conceived. The spirit of emigration has already shewn itself in a very strong degree, notwithstanding the many impediments which discourage it. The principal of these impediments is the war with Britain which can not spare a force sufficient to protect the emigrants against the incursions of the Savages. In a very few years after peace shall take place this Country will certainly be overspread with inhabitants. In like manner as in all other new settlements, agriculture, not manufactures will be their employment. They will raise wheat corn Beef Pork tobacco hemp flax and in the southern parts perhaps, rice and indigo in great quantities. On the other hand their consumption of foreign manufactures will be in proportion, if they can be exchanged for the produce of their soil. There are but two channels through which such commerce can be carried on,—the first is down the river Mississippi—the other is up the rivers having their sources near the lakes, thence by short portages to the lakes or the rivers falling into them, and thence through the lakes and down the St. Lawrence. The first of these channels is manifestly the most natural and by far the most advantageous. Should it however be obstructed, the second will be found far from an impracticable [one]. If no obstructions should be thrown in its course down the Mississippi, the exports from this immense tract of Country will not only supply an abundance of all necessaries for the W. Indies Islands, but serve for a valuable basis of general trade, of which the rising spirit of commerce in France & Spain will no doubt particularly avail itself. The imports will be proportionally extensive and from the climate as well as other causes will consist in a great degree of the manufactures of the same countries. On the other hand should obstructions in the Mississippi force this trade into a contrary direction through Canada, France and Spain and the other maritime powers will not only lose the immediate benefit of it to themselves, but they will also suffer by the advantage it will give to G. Britain. So fair a prospect would not escape the commercial sagacity of this nation. She would embrace it with avidity; she would cherish it with the most studious care; and should she succeed in fixing it in that channel, the loss of her exclusive possession of the trade of the United States might prove a much less decisive blow to her maritime preeminence and tyranny than has been calculated.

The last clause of the instructions respecting the navigation of the waters running out of Georgia through West Florida, not being included in the ultimatum, nor claimed on a footing of right requires nothing to be added to what it speaks itself. The utility of the privilege asked to the State of Georgia and consequently to the Union is apparent from the geographic-representation of the Country. The motives for Spain to grant it must be found in her equity generosity and disposition to cultivate our friendship and intercourse.

These observations you will readily discern are not communicated in order to be urged at all events and as they here stand in support of the claims to which they relate. They are intended for your private information and use and are to be urged so far and in such form only as will best suit the temper and sentiments of the Court at which you reside, and best fulfil the object of them.[14]

1 Besides making minor changes in the earlier portion of this paragraph, Congress altered from here on to read, "reported a draft which was agreed to as follows" (*Journals of the Continental Congress*, XVIII, 935).

2 On 14 August 1779 Congress defined the boundaries of the United States upon which "the Commissioner . . . to negotiate a treaty of Peace with Great Britain" must insist (*ibid.*, XIV, 956–59).

3 JM's affirmation that during the colonial period the English were a people distinct from the Americans, although both owed allegiance to the same monarch, harmonizes with the opening paragraph of the Declaration of Independence.

4 Here, as well as in the later paragraph beginning "Thirdly," JM's stress upon the sovereignty of each of the thirteen states, and upon the fact that they and not the United States owned territory, squared with his position in the continuing controversy between the "big" and "little" states over the cession of the West.

5 Barbé-Marbois's "answer" to "Obj: 1" in his "Observations" bore upon this point (above, 6–16 October 1780).

6 JM of course refers to, and somewhat exaggerates the extent of, the victories of George Rogers Clark acting under a Virginia commission. In 1778–1779 he and his troops erected Fort Nelson, a settlement soon named Louisville, at the falls of the Ohio River.

7 Less than three months after the date of this letter, a Spanish military expedition captured the British post of St. Joseph on the southeastern shore of Lake Michigan.

8 The rest of this paragraph is an addition, written by someone other than JM on a separate sheet, bearing also the note—"amendment pasd to be inserted in the Blanke in the 4 page."

9 William Macdonald, ed., *Select Charters and Other Documents Illustrative of American History, 1606–1775* (New York, 1899), pp. 270–71.

10 The treaty of alliance between France and the United States was signed on 6 February 1778 (Henry Steele Commager, ed., *Documents of American History* [2d ed.; 2 vols. in 1; New York, 1940], I, 106). Under the "Family Compact" Spain entered the war later that year as an ally of France, not of the United States.

11 By the definitive Treaty of Paris, 10 February 1763, France ceded to Britain all land east of the Mississippi River except the island and town of New Orleans "provided that the navigation of the river Mississippi shall be equally free, as well to the subjects of Great Britain as to those of France, in its whole breadth and length, from its source to the sea, and expressly that part which is between the said island of New Orleans and the right bank of that river, as well as the passage both in and out of its Mouth. . . . the vessels belonging to the subjects of either nation shall not be stopped . . . or subjected to the payment of any duty whatsoever" (William Macdonald, ed., *Select Charters and Other Documents*, pp. 263–64). Shortly after the conclusion of the Treaty of Paris, Louis XV of France ceded all of the territory of Louisiana west of the Mississippi, and including New Orleans, to his uncle, Charles III of Spain.

12 A Swiss jurist, Emmerich de Vattel (1714–1767), published at Neuchâtel and London in 1758, *Le droit des gens, ou principes de la loi naturelle appliques à la conduite et aux affaires des nations et des souverains.* JM here translates a sentence

from Book III, chap. vii, paragraph 119 (James Brown Scott, ed.; 2 vols.; Washington, 1916), II, 93–94.

[13] By the Royal Proclamation of 1763, the northern boundary of the newly created province of West Florida was fixed at 31° north latitude, from the Mississippi River eastward to the Apalachicola River (William Macdonald, ed., *Select Charters and Other Documents*, p. 268).

[14] Dispatched on 28 October 1780, the instructions and this letter were received by John Jay on 30 January 1781. He later remarked that the letter stated "particularly and ably the right of the United States to the free navigation of the river Mississippi . . ." (Wharton, *Revolutionary Diplomatic Correspondence*, IV, 738; Burnett, *Letters*, V, 430–31). For a continuation of the Mississippi navigation issue, see below, Bland to Jefferson, 22 November 1780.

To Joseph Jones

RC (LC: Madison Papers).

PHILADA. Oct. 17th. 1780.

DEAR SIR

The Post having failed to arrive this week, I am deprived of the pleasure of acknowledging a line from you.[1]

Congress have at length been brought to a final consideration of the clause relating to Indian purchases. It was debated very fully and particularly, and was in the result lost by a division of the house. Under the first impression of the chagrin I had determined to propose to my colleagues to state the whole matter to the Assembly with all the circumstances and reasonings of the opponents to the measure. But on cooler reflection I think it best to leave the fact in your hands to be made use of as your prudence may suggest. I am the rather led to decline the first determination because I am pretty confident that whatever the views of particular members might be it was neither the wish nor intention of many who voted with them to favor the purchasing companies.[2] Some thought such an assurance from Congress unnecessary because their receiving the lands from the States as *vacant* & unappropriated excluded all individual claims, and because they had given a general assurance that the cession should be applied to the common benefit. Others supposed that such an assurance might imply that without it Congress would have a right to dispose of the lands in any manner they pleased, and that it might give umbrage to the states claiming an exclusive jurisdiction over them. All that now remains for the Ceding States to do is to annex to their cessions the express condition that no private claims be complied with by Congress. Perhaps it would not be going too far, by Virginia who is so deeply concerned to make it a condition of her grant that no such claims be admitted even within the grants of others, because when they are given up to Congress she is interested in them as much as others, and it might so happen, that the benefit of all other grants except her own might be transferred from the public, to a few land mongers.[3] I can not help adding however that I hope this incident in Congress will not discourage any measures of the Assembly which would otherwise have been taken for ratifying the Confederation. Under the cautions I have suggested, they may still be taken with perfect security. Congress have promoted Col. Morgan to the rank of a Brigadr. on the representations in favor of it from Govrs. Rutledge & Jefferson & Gl. Gates. The latter is directed to be made a subject of a Ct. of Inquiry and Gl Washington is to send a successor into the Southern department.[4] The new arra[n]gement of the army sent to the Genl. for his revision has brought from him many judicious & valuable observations on the subject which with the arrangement are in the hands of a Committee.[5]

The inclosed papers leave little to be added under the title of news. The Capture of British fleet mentioned in the letter from Eustatia is considered here as pretty certain.[6] The Saratoga has returned. She parted a few days before she got in with several of her prizes containing about 1000 Hhds. of rum & several hundred do. of sugar, which having been not since heard of we begin to fear have fallen back into the possession of the Enemy.[7] There is a report brought to Town by Baron Stuben that an embarkation sailed from N. Y. on thursday last but the genl has not yet confirmed it.[8] Dr. Lee has been here several days.[9] The inclosed letters were found between the pages of Vattel.[10]

General Scott's cause was decided on saturday. The inquisition was confirmed by the jury on the testimony of Fleetson who swore that the *force* was confessed to him by the General himself. Had it not been for this confession it is pretty certain the contrary evidence would have prevailed. Fortunately however after a pretty nice and tedious discussion the Inquisition was quashed by the Court, and we now stand in a secure situation.[11]

Adieu.

J. MADISON JNR.

A letter from the Continental Agt. at Statia just rcd. by the Commercial Committee reduces the Capture of the B. fleet by the Spaniards almost to certainty.[12]

¹ Brackets inclosing the first two paragraphs of this letter indicate that JM, later in his life, selected them for publication.

² In this paragraph, JM is referring to the vote in Congress on 10 October upon the report of the committee to which had been referred the western lands resolutions, introduced on 6 September by Jones and seconded by JM (Jones to JM, 2 October 1780, n. 2). The committee's report closely followed the tenor of these resolutions in that it recommended (a) that lands in the West, ceded to the United States, should be formed into "distinct republican states" to be admitted to the federal union and to be equal in "sovereignty" to each of the original thirteen states; (b) that any of the "landed states" which ceded its western lands would have the rest of its territory guaranteed to it by the United States; (c) that a ceding state which had undergone expense in holding its western territory against the British would be reimbursed by the United States (but not for the cost of its civil government there, as the Jones-Madison resolutions had stipulated); (d) that Congress could determine how ceded territory should be "granted and settled"; (e) that purchases by private persons of land from Indians in the ceded area would be invalid unless approved by the legislature of the ceding state; and (f) that Congress would not deem any private purchase as valid unless it had been approved by the legislature of the state concerned. Congress struck out b and e and then accepted a, c, and d without a recorded vote. By a vote of six states to four, with two equally divided and Delaware absent, Congress refused, however, to adopt the final proposal (Journals of the Continental Congress, XVIII, 915–16). JM's "chagrin" was the greater because his colleagues, Theodorick Bland and John Walker, deserted him on the issue and thus caused Virginia's vote to be registered with the adverse majority. Although at first he wanted to oblige them to justify their action to the General Assembly, JM decided merely to summarize, for Jones's use, the general reasons explaining the opposition vote. As mentioned earlier, Jones expected to attend the legislature in order to work for an offer of cession to the United States of Virginia's territory north of the Ohio River (Jones to JM, 19 September 1780, n. 2; and JM to Jones, 10 October 1780, n. 7).

³ JM probably had the Vandalia and Indiana land companies principally in mind.

⁴ See Jameson to JM, 20 September 1780, n. 4; and Jones to JM, 9 October 1780, n. 6; Burnett, Letters, V, 266, 270, 316.

⁵ See Jones to JM, 2 October 1780, n. 5. In his letter of 11 October, Washington commented at length upon the proposals of 3 October by Congress for the reorganization of the army. After a committee had considered Washington's suggestions, Congress amended the plan so as to embody most of them. Washington's wish to assure half pay for life to officers serving for the duration of the war was apparently his most controversial recommendation, but Congress acceded to it on 21 October, with JM among the delegates voting in its favor. Later that day, while JM was absent, Congress adopted the other amendments designed to meet Washington's objections to its original proposals (Fitzpatrick, Writings of Washington, XX, 157–67; Journals of the Continental Congress, XVIII, 931, 958–62).

⁶ Not found, but probably they were Philadelphia newspapers. The Pennsylvania Packet of 17 October contained a report from St. Eustatius of the capture of fifty-four British ships by the Spanish navy (below, n. 12).

⁷ Captain John Young, commanding the eighteen-gun sloop of war "Saratoga," brought into the Delaware River on 13 September 1780 a captured vessel with a cargo of "234 Puncheons of Rum." Young was then ordered to join the frigates "Trumbull" and "Deane" at sea (Charles O. Paullin, ed., Out-Letters of Board of Admiralty, II, 268–70). On this cruise the "Saratoga" took, and subsequently lost, "four valuable prizes" (Gardner W. Allen, A Naval History of the American Revolution, II, 510).

8 Friedrich Wilhelm Ludolf Gerhard Augustin, Baron von Steuben (1730–1794), was at this time the inspector general of the armies of the United States. The British vessels bearing Major General Leslie and his troops to Chesapeake Bay sailed from New York on 16 October (Harry M. Lydenberg, ed., *Archibald Robertson: Diaries and Sketches*, pp. 241–42).

9 Arthur Lee.

10 Letters not found. As chairman of the committee to draft a letter to John Jay, explaining the instructions of Congress to him on the western boundary of the United States, JM had found occasion to quote from Emmerich de Vattel's *Le droit des gens* (above, Draft of Letter to Jay, 17 October 1780, n. 12).

11 See JM to Jones, 10 October 1780, n. 6. "Fleetson" (Plunket Fleeson) was at this time judge of the Pennsylvania Court of Common Pleas (*Pennsylvania Magazine of History and Biography*, XXVI [1902], 341).

12 On 6 August 1780 about fifty-five British transports and merchantmen were captured off Cape St. Vincent by a combined Spanish and French fleet commanded by Don Luis de Córdova ([Louis] É[douard] Chevalier, *Histoire de la marine française pendant la guerre de l'indépendance américaine* [Paris, 1877], p. 203; Captain W. M. James, *The British Navy in Adversity: A Study of the War of American Independence* [London, 1926], p. 247). The agent of the United States on the island of St. Eustatius was Samuel Curson (*ca.* 1753–1786) of the New York firm of Curson and [Isaac] Gouverneur. He was being considered for the post of American consul at London when he was killed in a duel (J. Hall Pleasants, *The Curzon Family of New York and Baltimore and Their English Descent* [Baltimore, 1919], pp. 41–42).

From Joseph Jones

RC (LC: Madison Papers).

VIRGA. 17th. Octr 1780

DEAR SR.

We must place the taking Col. Andre among the fortunate occurrances during the present war[.] a more wicked and ruinous combination could hardly have been formed if the accounts published in the papers are generally true[;] and the three honest militiamen who rendered us the service should be rewarded[1]

An attack early the last week of the Ague and fever will prevent my being in Richmond untill next sunday at which time I determine to be there if my Families and own health will permit. We have suffered more sickness this Fall in Virginia than was perhaps ever known[.] there is scarce a Family at this late season, but are part of them sick, and one remarkable Symptom of which all complain is a constant sickness of the stomach and loathing of almost every thing offered them This is found to be obstinate and difficult to remove.[2] I hope you continue well and that the Family are so.[3]

Yr. aff Friend & Servt.

JOS: JONES.

N.B. I forgot to mention and recommend to your attention Drs. Cochran and Craig in the Medical Department as I expect from the systems being formed the appointments will take place. these are recommended to me by a good Judge of their services & qualifications.[4]

---

[1] See Virginia Delegates to Jefferson, *ca.* 5 October 1780. Jones had probably read Philadelphia newspapers forwarded to him by JM and had heard the news which would appear in the *Virginia Gazette* (Richmond, Dixon and Nicolson) of 18 October 1780. On Washington's recommendation, John Paulding (1758–1818), David Williams (1754–1831), and Isaac Van Wart (*ca.* 1758–1828), the New York militiamen who had captured Major André, were each rewarded by Congress on 3 November 1780 with a silver medal, to be presented to them by Washington, and $200 in specie, or its equivalent, annually for life (Fitzpatrick, *Writings of Washington*, XX, 133; *Journals of the Continental Congress*, XVIII, 1009–10; Frederic Shonnard and W. W. Spooner, *History of Westchester County, New York* . . . [New York, 1900], pp. 484–86).

[2] See Pendleton to JM, 1 October 1780 and n. 3; Jones to JM, 2 October 1780; and JM to Jones, 10 October 1780, n. 7.

[3] See Jones to JM, 19 September 1780, n. 8.

[4] See Jones to JM, 2 October 1780, n. 7. In his letter of 9 September 1780 to Jones, Washington had made complimentary reference to these two physicians (Fitzpatrick, *Writings of Washington*, XX, 18–19).

To Edmund Pendleton

RC (LC: Madison Papers).

PHILADA. Oct. 17th. 1780.

DEAR SIR

The Southern Post having not yet arrived, I have not the pleasure of acknowledging the receipt of your favor, which I have found you too punctual to doubt his havg. for me.

The best news I have to give you is contained in the inclosed paper in a letter from Eustatia, which comes from a person known to many Gentlemen here who say it may be fully credited.[1] The Saratoga a Continental Vessel of 16 guns is just returned from a cruise in which she took several Jamaica prizes with a prodigious quantity of rum & sugar on board. She parted from them in a fog near the coast, and as they have not yet been heard of it is feared they have fallen back into the possession of the Enemy[2]

Baron Stuben just come to town brings a report that an embarkation left N. York on thursday, but no confirmation has yet arrived from Gl. Washington or any other official source.[3] Adieu

JAMES MADISON JNR.

By a letter just recd. from the Continental Agt. at Statia by the Commercial Committee, the Capture of the British fleet by the Spaniards is brought pretty nearly to certainty[4]

1 See JM to Jones, 17 October 1780, n. 6.
2 *Ibid.*, n. 7.
3 *Ibid.*, n. 8.
4 *Ibid.*, n. 12.

From Edmund Pendleton

Tr (LC: Force Transcripts).

VIRGA. Octobr 17. 1780

DEAR SIR:

I am anxious to hear from you, since missing that pleasure last week,[1] I fear the General sickness of the Citizens has reached you. I shall be happy to learn it proceed from any other cause.[2]

The story we have of Gen. Arnold's corruption is indeed shocking to humanity & I wish much to know the utmost consequences of the discovery, as far as they are manifest & proper to be made public, for I know you too well ever to ask you to reveal even to me what yr duty, or the Interest of the States requires to be kept secret, and if I know myself I would not desire it of any One. This I wish to gratifie curiosity, & not because I feel any sore part[3] or fear the keenest probe, as I hear some have done & taken themselves away. Providence in bringing this secret mischief to light just as it was on the point of Completion, has given another Instance of its kind Interposition in favour of our just cause, which I hope will rouse all its favourers from that Apathy from which alone Our enemies can hope for success. We have just received a very agreeable pe. of Intelligence from No Carolina that Colo Sumpter has taken Colo Tarlton & all his horse but 4, with as many Infantry as made in the whole 900, having surprized them in the Village of Charlotte when they were inebriating freely upon Col Sumner's having evacuated that place & retreated towards Salisbury. The Story is not ill told & has this further confirmation that a Gentn in this county has just received a letter from his son who is in those parts, informing him that Sumner was retreating before the enemy, & Sumpter in their rear had written to General Gates to send him a speedy reinforcement, which would enable him to cut off their retreat & he doubted not to give a good Account of them; I suppose the Junquet induced him to Attack without waiting for the Succours he had called for. If this be true[4] I hope 'tis the beginning of a Flood tide in our Southern Affairs after the long Ebb we have experienced, & the rather as we hear the North Carolinians turn out very spiritedly & besides their Infantry have mounted at least 1000 good horse, and that their southern neighbours grow[n] weary of their New, Old Masters, are generally zealous to aid in their expulsion as soon as they can have a tolerable prospect of Success. Our assembly are to meet as on this day.[5] I have seen some of the Members who appear resolved to make it the business of this session to provide for the next year's campaign, which they have heretofore very improperly suspended to the May Session voting in that the raising of men at a time when they should have been in the field, May Heaven prosper their & your Councils to the putting an agreeable period to the War. I am

My Dr Sir Yr Affec & Obt. Servt

EDMD PENDLETON

[1] The "missing" letter of 3 October had reached Pendleton by 23 October when he next wrote JM (*q.v.*).

[2] The meaning of this sentence would be clearer if Pendleton had written, "I shall be happy to learn that any cause other than illness prevented you from writing."

[3] Here, in view of its unintelligibility, the transcriber may have miscopied what Pendleton actually wrote.

[4] This report appears to blend two episodes. On 21 September 1780, shortly after the evacuation of Charlotte, N.C., by the North Carolina troops of Brigadier General Jethro Sumner (*ca.* 1733–1785), North Carolina militia led by Colonel William R. Davie surprised and inflicted heavy loss upon a contingent of Lieutenant Colonel Banastre Tarleton's (1754–1833) British Legion at Wahab's Plantation, near Charlotte. Five days later, when General Thomas Sumter was at Salisbury, N.C., and Tarleton was absent from his command because of illness, Colonel Davie and his troops briefly withstood the effort of Cornwallis' army, with Tarleton's British Legion in its van, to enter Charlotte. Davie and his men were soon obliged to retreat (Christopher Ward, *War of the Revolution*, II, 738–39; Henry B. Dawson, *Battles of the United States*, I, 624–28).

[5] See JM to Jones, [10 October 1780], n. 7.

Arthur Lee to Committee of Congress

RC (NA: PCC, No. 78, XIV, 375, 378).

PHILADELPHIA Ocr 21st. 1780

GENTLEMEN[1]

I had the honor of receiv'g this day at 1 O C. P.M. a Note from you[2] desiring a sight of my Expenditures on public Account, that you may be enabled to report the proper disposition of them for Liquidation

In conformity to your desire, I now send you the Accounts, & will wait upon you immediately if it suit your conveniency, with the Vouchers referrd to in them.[3]

I have the honor to be with the greatest respect Gentlemen Yr. most Obedt. Humble Servt

ARTHUR LEE

1 On 19 October, Congress appointed JM, Thomas Bee, and Abraham Clark (N.J.) a committee to report upon Lee's letter to Congress of two days before, asking for "a full hearing at their bar upon the whole of the proceedings that concern my public conduct" while a U.S. commissioner in Paris (Jones to JM, 2 October 1780, n. 10; *Journals of the Continental Congress*, XVIII, 951–53). The postscript of this letter, not printed in the journal, reads as follows: "I have brought with me the original Vouch[ers,] to shew the manner of the expenditure in public supplies of the money entrusted to me particularly for the public use. These Vouchers I shall lay before Congress as soon as it is their pleasure to receive the[m]" (NA: PCC, No. 83, II, 302–3). This postscript is printed in Wharton, *Revolutionary Diplomatic Correspondence*, IV, 86, where the letter is misdated 7 October. After further debate, Congress decided to have the committee consider the postscript as well as Lee's request in the main text of the letter (*Journals of the Continental Congress*, XVIII, 953–54). See Lee to Committee, 27 October, and Report of Committee on Lee's letter, 1 December 1780.

2 Not found.

3 Some, at least, of these accounts and vouchers are in NA: PCC, No. 83, II, 580–606.

From Edmund Pendleton

Tr (LC: Force Transcripts).

VIRGA. Octr. 23d. 1780

DR SIR:

Since my last I have not only received yr favr. of the 10th but that of the 3d, when I supposed you had not written, also reached me after a Circuitous trip to Richmond, & removed my fears for yr want of health. I have no particulars of the Affair at Charlotte, mentioned in my former, but its authenticity seems confirm'd, & as our recruits are March'd that way, I hope we may soon have an Army in that quarter to Improve this beginning of Good fortune.[1] It will be the fault of Virginia if she is surprized by the Enemy in case they Intend an Invasion here, since they have been for some time past in daily expectation of such a Visit; how they may be prepared for it I know not, as I have not been lately from home.[2]

How do Congress bear the horid confinement of Govr. Gadsden & Cos. do they mean to retaliate, or suffer the convention troops to Riot in ease, plenty, & breathe a free & healthy Air whilst our friends are stiffled & suffocated with the stench of a prison ship, or a dungeon in St. Augustine? It is horrible to think of; unless indeed it be true that in breach of their Parole & all good faith, they had really plotted the recapture of the Town & Garrison, which cannot[3] be credited.[4]

The motions of our good Allies are Mysterious, but I yet hope may produce something beneficial before the end of the Campaign; We have a loose report that they have given the British Fleet a great wound in the West Indies, but it is too vague to be relied on. I am

Dr Sir Yr Affe & Obt Servt

EDMD. PENDLETON

50 Sail of ships are in the Bay.

[1] See Pendleton to JM, 17 October 1780, n. 3.

[2] The postscript shows that Pendleton heard, before completing this letter, that the British expeditionary force under General Leslie had arrived in Chesapeake Bay.

[3] Judging from the version of this letter in *Proceedings of the Massachusetts Historical Society*, 2d ser., XIX (1905), 117, Peter Force's copyist overlooked the word "easily" after "cannot" in the now missing original.

[4] In May 1780 Lieutenant Governor Christopher Gadsden (1724–1805) and other prominent South Carolinians who had been captured when Charleston fell to the British were released on parole. In midsummer, prior to the defeat of the patriot army in the Battle of Camden, Cornwallis suspected that some of them were breaking their parole by plotting an insurrection and sending military information to General Gates. Cornwallis thereupon imprisoned Gadsden and seventy-eight others in St. Augustine, Fla., under rigorous conditions. Gadsden's exchange was not effected until June 1781. Pendleton contrasts their hard lot with that of General John Burgoyne's troops, surrendered at Saratoga in October 1777 and interned late in 1778 in Virginia for the rest of the war (William B. Willcox, ed., *The American Rebellion*, pp. 171, 181, 183, 226, 459; Fitzpatrick, *Writings of Washington*, XX, 128; Christopher Ward, *War of the Revolution*, II, 540–42).

To Joseph Jones

RC (LC: Madison Papers). JM neglected to include the day of the month in the date line of this letter. The first paragraph, however, makes it almost certain that he was writing on 24 October. Many years later he or a member of his family bracketed the second, fourth, and fifth paragraphs with a view to their publication.

PHILADA. Octr. [24,] 1780

DEAR SIR

Your favor of the 9th. which ought to have come on Monday last did not arrive till Thursday. That of the 17th: came yesterday according to expectation.

I wish it was in my power to enable you to satisfy the uneasiness of people with respect to the disappointment in foreign succour. I am sensible of the advantage which our secret enemies take of it. I am persuaded also that those who ought to be acquainted with the cause [of] it are sensible of it; and as they give no intimations on the subject it is to be inferred they are unable to give any that would prevent the mischief. It is so delicate a subject, that with so little probability of succeeding, it would perhaps be hardly prudent to suggest it. As soon as any solution comes out you shall be furnished with it.[1]

I have informed Pleasants that you would write to him from Richmond, and on application to Pemberton was promised a written sketch of his terms which I have not yet received. if it comes before this is sealed I shall enclose it.[2]

We continue to receive periodical alarms from the Commissary's & Quarter Master's departments. The season is now arrived when provision ought to be made for a season that will not admit of transportation, and when the monthly supplies must be subject to infinite disappointments even if the States were to do their duty. But instead of Magazines being laid in[,] our army is living from hand to mouth, with a prospect of being soon in a condition still worse. How a total dissolution of it can be prevented in the course of the winter is for any resources now in prospect utterly inexplicable, unless the States unanimously make a vigorous & speedy effort to form Magazines for the purpose.[3] But unless the States take other methods to procure their specific supplies than have prevailed in most of them, their utmost efforts to comply with the requisitions of Congress can be only a temporary relief. This expedient as I take it was meant to prevent the emission of money. Our own experience as well as the example of other Countries made it evident that we could not by taxes draw back to the treasury the emissions as fast as they were necessarily drawn out. We could not follow the example of other Countries by borrowing, neither our own Citizens nor foreigners being willing to lend as far as our wants extended. To continue to emit ad infinitum was thought more dangerous than an absolute occlusion of the press. Under these circumstances the expedient of specific requisitions was adopted for supplying the necessities of the war.[4] But it is clear the success of this expedient depends on the mode of carrying it into execution. If instea[d] of executing it by specific taxes, State emissions or Commissary's & Q. master's certificates which are a worse species of emissions, are recurred to[,] what was intended for our relief will only hasten our destruction.

As you are at present a *legislator*[5] I will take the liberty of hinting to you an idea that has occurred on this subject. I take it for granted that taxation alone is inadequate to our situation. You know as well as I do how far we ought to rely on loans to supply the defect of it. Specific taxes as far as they go are a valuable fund but from local and other difficulties will never be universally and sufficiently adopted. Purchases with State money or certificates will be substituted. In order to prevent this evil and to insure the supplies therefore I would propose, that they be diffused and proportioned among the people as accurately as circumstances will admit, that they be *impress[ed]* with vigor and impartiality, and paid for in certificates not transferrible & be redeemable at some period subsequent to the war at specie value and bearing an intermediate interest. The advantage of such a scheme is this, that it would anticipate during the war the future revenues of peace, as our Enemies and all other modern nations do. It would be compelling the people to *lend* the public their commodities, as people elsewhere lend their money to purchase commodities. It would be a permanent resourse by which the war might be supported as long as the earth should yield its increase. This plan differs from specific taxes only in this that as an equivalent is given for what is received much less nicety would be requisite in apportioning the supplies among the people, and they might be taken in places where they are most wanted. It differs from the plan of paying for supplies in state emissions or common certificates in this, that the latter produce all the evils of a redundant medium, whereas the former not being transferrible can not have that effect, and moreover do not require the same degree of taxes during the war.[6]

We were informed a few days ago by Genl Washington that the fleet with about two thousand troops on board had fallen down [the river] towards the Hook, but as nothing further has since come fro[m him] on that subject I conclude they still remain there.[7] The Cork [fleet,] it is said has at last arrived amounting to upwards of 1[00 Sail.] No further account has been received here of the capture [of] the English Jamaica fleet. There has been a report today that the Prizes of the Saratoga mentioned in my last are in the river[8]

Letters from Governor Clinton mention that two parties from Canada consisting of near 1000 each had appeared on their frontier. The one by the way of Ticonderoga & lake George, the other by the way of the Oneida lake. They have already done some mischief and threaten to do a good deal more.[9]

Although the Genl.'s victory in the Supreme has sa[ved him] from

the mortification of being ejected by our late   it has not from the
vexation of being pursued by   [He] is now trying the skill of his
lawyer in framing a new a[ppeal] and means to carry the Genl. over
the whole ground [again.] The old lady is at home very ill. He has
made no attempts yet to regain her house & her effects.[10]

I am Dr Sr. Yr. Affectionate friend

J. MADISON JNR.

I shall enclose to the Govr. a copy of the proceedings of the Board
of Officers with respect to Andre's case. I suppose [you] can get a
sight of it from him[11]

A confirmation of the   Capture of the B. fleet is just recd from
Mr. Harrison at Cadiz. Some of the prizes were in that bay when he
wrote. 1000 Highland Troops for the East Indies were on board.[12]

[1] See Jones to JM, 9 October 1780. JM evidently knew that Jones would easily
fathom the hidden meaning of "our secret enemies," "those who ought to be acquainted with the cause," "the subject," and "the mischief" in this cryptic paragraph. JM possibly meant that France declined sending the greatly needed and
long-awaited additional aid in the form of soldiers and ships because of the unre-
lenting attack on Benjamin Franklin by the Samuel Adams–Arthur Lee faction
(Jones to JM, 2 October 1780, n. 10), and because congressional wrangling over
the western lands issue still held up the ratification of the Articles of Confederation.

[2] See Jones to JM, 2 October 1780, n. 14. The inclosure, if there was one, is now
missing.

[3] See Jones to JM, 2 October 1780, n. 5. Nearly every session of Congress since
JM's letter of 17 October to Jones had been marked by discussions about how to
procure and pay for food, clothing, etc., needed by the commissary and quartermaster departments (*Journals of the Continental Congress*, XVIII, 962, 964, 966,
969–72).

[4] On 18 March 1780 Congress decided to discontinue issuing continental paper
money and to rely thereafter upon currency emitted by the states and upon supplies furnished by them when requisitioned by Congress (Jefferson to JM, 26 July
1780, n. 2).

[5] Jones was a member of the Virginia House of Delegates.

[6] On the date of this letter, Congress again called upon the states, in view of "the
present want and distresses of the army" and "the calamities" which would result
from its "dissolution," to "furnish and forward, by means the most efficacious,
the supplies requested from them" (*Journals of the Continental Congress*, XVIII,
971). An equitable apportionment of the needed supplies and the payment for them
in non-negotiable, interest-bearing certificates evidently were to JM "the most
efficacious means." Virginia already had an act providing for the impressment of
needed army supplies, but it did not, and would not after amendment by the autumn
session of the legislature, embody these two features (Hening, *Statutes*, X, 233–37,
344–46).

[7] See Pendleton to JM, 23 October 1780, n. 2; Fitzpatrick, *Writings of Washington*, XX, 190; *Journals of the Continental Congress*, XVIII, 951. Bracketed words in
this paragraph, bracketed words and spaces in the second paragraph below, and the
space in the postscript represent tears in the manuscript. The editors either indicate
that they have no clue as to what was written or suggest what may once have been
where the tears occur.

8 This was a false rumor (JM to Pendleton, 17 October 1780, n. 2).

9 See JM to Pendleton, [24] October 1780, n. 2. George Clinton (1739–1812) was then governor of New York.

10 See JM to Jones, 10 October 1780, n. 6.

11 The inclosure probably was *Proceedings of a Board of General Officers, Held by Order of His Excellency Gen. Washington, Commander in Chief of the Army of the United States, Respecting Major John André, Adjutant General of the British Army, September 29, 1780* (Philadelphia, 1780). This was in Jefferson's library at the time of his death (E. Millicent Sowerby, comp., *Catalogue of the Library of Thomas Jefferson* [5 vols.; Washington, 1952–59], III, 270).

12 This postscript helps to fix the date of JM's letter, since Richard Harrison's letter of 17 August 1780 was read in Congress on 24 October (*Journals of the Continental Congress*, XVIII, 968). For the capture referred to, see JM to Pendleton, 17 October 1780, n. 4.

From Joseph Jones

RC (LC: Madison Papers).

VIRGA 24th: Octr. 1780.

DEAR SR.

I very sincerely thank you for your Friendly and regular Correspondence. when I am in Richmond which I am in hopes to be the last of this week (being sufficiently recovered from my late indisposition as to be able to take the Bark)[1] I will endeavour to make you amends by a communication from time to time of our proceedings in Assembly and such southern intelligence as may be worth mentioning.

I presume the last Post carryed you the account of our success agt. Ferguson's Party by a Body of North Carolina Militia. It is said the News came to our Governor by Express from Genl. Gates. From Richmond Genl. Mulenburgh communicated the intelligence by Express to Genl. Weedon, but no doubt the Governor has given the Predident full information. Our account was that Ferguson and 150 of the Enemy were slain, 810 prisoners with a large number of Arms taken.[2] Genl. Weedon who has hitherto remained in Fredericksburg is now under marching orders and is to set out this week from whence I conclude there are sufficient of our new levies gone forward to give him employment and to form two Brigades as Mulenburg being his Senior of course commands the first.[3] I expect you will soon have Mr. Smith with you to succeed Mr. Walker. I hope he will avoid entering into and reviving those party contentions that when he was in Congress before so much disgraced that Body and I trust the Gentlemen of our Delegation will in general check every attempt that may be made to renew former disputes or to do any thing more than what

Justice shall require. I own I have my fears Congress will again be drawn into Sects and divisions.[4] what has been done with the alliance and what with Capt. Landais?[5] In a former letter I wished to be informed what was the real cause of the disappointment that the 2d. division of the French Force did not come out, of the inactive Campaign in the W. Indies & the combined or rather the Fleets of France and Spain not combining in the British Channel. I shod. if it can be obtained be glad to hear the Sentiments of certain Gentlemen on these matters.[6] Mrs. Jones' indisposition has at length terminated in the third day Ague & Fever[.] my little Boy is some what better but his Mother is by a long and severe illness reduced to a skeliton[7] With great esteem
I am Dr Sr. Yr. Friend & Servt.

Jos: Jones.

Be pleased to forward the inclosed by the Post.[8]

[1] See Jones to JM, 19 September, n. 2, and 9 October 1780. The "bark" means cinchona bark (quinine) or a locally found substitute for it.

[2] See JM to Jones, 10 October 1780, n. 8. Brigadier Generals George Weedon (*ca.* 1730–1790) and John Peter Gabriel Muhlenberg (1747–1807) were of the Virginia militia and Virginia continental line, respectively. Since March 1780, Muhlenberg had been in charge of the defense of Virginia (Henry A. Muhlenberg, *The Life of Major-General Peter Muhlenberg of the Revolutionary Army* [Philadelphia, 1849], pp. 181–204, *passim*). At the Battle of King's Mountain, 7 October 1780, Major Patrick Ferguson (1744–1780) and 156 of his Loyalist troops were slain. The patriots captured 698 others, not including 163 badly wounded left on the field, and garnered about fifteen hundred muskets and rifles from the defeated enemy (Christopher Ward, *War of the Revolution*, II, 744).

[3] Perhaps unintentionally or because of lack of information, Jones implies that the "new levies" under Weedon and Muhlenberg were about to march to General Gates's assistance in North Carolina. This had been their aim, but General Leslie's invasion hurriedly diverted them to the Portsmouth area of Virginia in late October (Henry A. Muhlenberg, *Life of Peter Muhlenberg*, pp. 205–11, 378–79; *Calendar of the Correspondence Relating to the American Revolution of Brigadier-General George Weedon, Hon. Richard Henry Lee, Hon. Arthur Lee and Major-General Nathanael Greene in the Library of the American Philosophical Society* [Philadelphia, 1900], p. 23 [No. 16]).

[4] While in Congress in 1778–1779, Meriwether Smith had been one of the delegates opposing the coalition led by Samuel Adams and the Lees of Virginia. Although re-elected to Congress on 22 June 1780, Smith did not take his seat until 20 February 1781. John Walker left Congress on 22 November 1780 (James Curtis Ballagh, ed., *Letters of Richard Henry Lee* [2 vols.; New York, 1914], II, 69–71; *Journal of the House of Delegates*, May 1780, p. 58; Burnett, *Letters*, V, 455; *Journals of the Continental Congress*, XIX, 176).

[5] See Board of Admiralty to Nicholson, 17 April 1780, n. 6. Captain Pierre Landais (*ca.* 1731–1820), commanding the U.S. frigate "Alliance" on its voyage from France in the summer of 1780, became demented and was forcibly removed from his position by some of the crew. Arthur Lee was a passenger on the ship. Shortly after it arrived in Boston, Captain John Barry was assigned to its command and a court-martial dismissed Landais from the navy. The "Alliance" left Boston harbor

for France on 11 February 1781 (Gardner W. Allen, *A Naval History of the American Revolution*, II, 527–29, 547).

6 See JM to Jones, [24] October 1780, n. 1. The "certain Gentlemen" cannot be identified, but they may have included Washington, La Luzerne, and Arthur Lee.

7 See Jones to JM, 17 October 1780.

8 What Jones inclosed is unknown.

To Edmund Pendleton

RC (LC: Madison Papers). In its present state the original let-ter lacks its last line. In the copy below, this line is taken from Madison, *Writings* (Hunt ed.), I, 75. At the head of the letter, JM left a space between "Octr" and "1780" without filling in the date of the month. In view of what he states in the first sentence of the letter, he most likely wrote it on 24 October.

PHILADA. Octr. [24,] 1780

DEAR SIR

Your favor of the 8th. which ought to have been here on Monday week did not arrive till thursday; that of the 17th. came yesterday ac-cording to expectation. I know not how to account for your disap-pointment on the last post day having not omitted to write once since the institution of our correspondence.

Although the stroke of good fortune you mention does not appear to have been truly represented, it was only mistaken for one of equal importance which I doubt not is fully known to you by this time.[1] Our joy on this event has been somewhat abated by intelligence of an opposite complexion from the State of N. York. Two parties from Canada composed of regulars tories Canadians and Savages and amounting to about 1000 each have entered their frontiers, the one by the way of lake George, the other by the way of the Oneida lake. They have already done some mischief, and as they are pursuing their incendiary plan, will involve the inhabitants in very great distress, (it being now the eve of winter) unless a speedy check can be given to their progress. It is supposed that this expedition was intended to take advantage of the consternation in that state expected to result from the success of Arnolds treason.[2]

We had information some days ago from Genl Washington that a fleet with about 2000 troops on Board had fallen down towards the Hook, which it was supposed was destined either for Virginia or N. Carolina. As nothing further has come from the General it is to be inferred that they have not yet sailed.[3] It is said the Cork fleet consisting of upwards of 100 Sail has at last safely arrived.[4] The capture of the British fleet from Jamaica rests on the same evidence as mentioned in my last. I am Dr Sr Affec yr. obt. Servt.

[J. Madison Junr.]

PS. The President has just communicated a letter from Mr. Harrison at Cadiz confirming the capture of the B. fleet.[5] Some of the Priz[es were] in that bay when he wrote. The number taken was unknown. the fleet amounted to 60 or 70 Sail, having on board Military Stores provisions dry goods & 1000 Highland troops for the East Indies. You will have the particulars by the next post. 5 or 6 Ships also attempting to get into Gibralter with provisions have been taken by the Spanish Squadron stationed off that place. 30 Sail of French Merchantmen had arrived safe from St Domingo. The post is this moment starting adieu.

[1] See Pendleton to JM, 17 October 1780, n. 3. JM refers to the patriot victory at King's Mountain on 7 October (*Journals of the Continental Congress*, XVIII, 963). As late as 1823, JM still recalled that in 1780 it had been "the universal impression, that the victory was as critical for the public affairs as it was brilliant for those concerned in it" (JM to Francis Preston, 2 June 1823, in Madison, *Letters* [Cong. ed.], III, 320).

[2] In the late summer and autumn, the forces of Sir John Johnson, Colonel John Butler, Joseph Brant (Thayendanegea) and his Mohawks, and Cornplanter and his Senecas terrorized the New York frontier, destroying many lives and much property. By the date of JM's letter, the worst was over, and they left the area comparatively unmolested until January 1781 (*Journals of the Continental Congress*, XVIII, 964; Fitzpatrick, *Writings of Washington*, XX, 192–93; Hugh Hastings and J. A. Holden, eds., *Public Papers of George Clinton, First Governor of New York* ... [10 vols.; Albany and New York, 1899–1914], VI, 288–95, 302–9, 318 ff.).

[3] The British expeditionary force, led by General Leslie, sailed from New York on 16 October and reached Chesapeake Bay four days later.

[4] General Clinton had long expected the arrival in New York of a fleet of supply ships from Ireland. About fifty-five ships finally reached their destination on 10 November (Henry M. Lydenberg, ed., *Archibald Robertson: Diaries and Sketches*, p. 241; Fitzpatrick, *Writings of Washington*, XX, 358).

[5] See JM to Jones, [24] October 1780, n. 12.

From David Jameson

RC (LC: Rives Collection of Madison Papers).

RICHMOND Oct 25. 1780

Dr Sir

I recd. your favour without date inclosing the paper of the 10th.[1] You will see by the paper inclosed that we are invaded, since the paper went to press we are certainly informed that the Enemy have landed Men on both sides Elizabeth River. they landed with the greatest confidence—did not fire a Gun—were within speech of the people on shore. What you have in the paper is truly the substance of what intelligence we had then received It is said the Cavalry landed at Hampton had penetrated as high as the half way House[2] between Hampton & York. I fear they will do much mischief before we can collect a force sufficient to stop their progress[;] however every expedient (in our power) is in motion on both sides Jas River It is more that [than?] probable we shall now severely feel the want of Regular Soldiers of which we have next to none but in name Our affairs in the South wear a better aspect than they did but as the president has letters & papers from the Governor & from G Gates on both subjects I need not enlarge. In my last I told you the Wart. for 300,000 dollars for Georgia was paid to Mr Joseph Gray.[3] Our Assembly should have set the 16t., but there are not Members enough of either House to do business.[4] We have not £5000. in the Treasury—are we not in a most pityable situation? I am very sincerely

   Yr afe. hb St

                                                        DAVID JAMESON

   [1] JM's letter is missing. Its date, and that of the newspaper inclosed, was probably 10 October, a post day when he wrote to his correspondents in Virginia. In all likelihood he informed Jameson of much that he had written or would write to Jones and Pendleton on that day (q.v.).
   [2] The "paper" probably was the *Virginia Gazette* (Richmond, Dixon and Nicolson) of 25 October 1780, which contains a brief notice of the disembarkation of General Leslie's troops at Newport News and of their occupation of Hampton, Va. The Half-way House was an ordinary in York County on the Hampton-Yorktown-Williamsburg road.
   [3] No earlier letter from Jameson to JM, making mention of Gray, is known to the editors; nor have they found a letter from JM to Jameson inquiring about the Georgia warrant. On 13 October, Congress directed the Board of Treasury to discover to whom the $300,000 granted to Georgia on 12 February 1780 had been paid. On 23 October the Board informed Congress that, via Joseph Gray and John White (escorts employed by the Board of War) and others, the money had reached the treasury of Georgia on 13 May 1780 (*Journals of the Continental Congress*, XVIII, 920, 966–67).
   [4] On 6 November 1780, the Virginia House of Delegates was finally attended by enough delegates to make a quorum (*Journal of the House of Delegates*, October 1780, p. 7).

Thomas Jefferson to Virginia Delegates in Congress

RC (NA: PCC, No. 71, I, 495–96). Only the complimentary close and signature are in Jefferson's hand.

RICHMOND Octo. 27. 1780[1]

GENTLEMEN

I must beg the favor of you to Solicit the sending on to us immediately a good supply of Cartridge Paper & Cartouch Boxes. Nearly the whole of the former Article which we had bought at Alexandria, Baltimore &Ca. and what the Board of War sent from Philadelphia has been made up and forwarded to the Southern Army: there remains now but a few Ream to make up. I fear we have lost 2000 cartouch Boxes on the Bay which we had had made at Baltimore Our distress for these is also very great[,] muskets being really useless without them. I must entreat the greatest dispatch in forwarding these Articles

A very dangerous Insurrection in Pittsylvania was prevented a few days ago by being discovered three days before it was to take place. The Ring-leaders were seized in their Beds. This dangerous fire is only smothered: when it will break out seems to depend altogether on events. It extends from Montgomery County along our Southern boundary to Pittsylvania and Eastward as far as James River: Indeed some suspicions have been raised of it's having crept as far as Culpepper.[2] The rest of the State turns out with a Spirit and alacrity which makes me perfectly happy. If they had arms there is no effort either of public or private Enemies in this State which would give any Apprehensions[.] Our whole arms are or will be in the hands of the force now assembling.[3] Were any disaster to befall these, We have no other resource but a few scattered Squirrel Guns, Rifles &C. in the Hands of the western People.

I am with the greatest esteem Gentlemen Your most obedt. humble sert

TH: JEFFERSON

[1] This letter was read in Congress on 2 November 1780 together with one of 26 October from Jefferson to President Samuel Huntington. Both letters were "referred to the Board of War, to take order." A note to this effect by Charles Thomson on the letter of 27 October is followed by the words "Acted upon." Probably this action did not take the form of sending the supplies requested (*Journals of the Continental Congress*, XVIII, 1004; Boyd, *Papers of Jefferson*, IV, 69, 77).

[2] Although trouble with Tories in the southwestern counties of Virginia had been endemic since early 1779, their disaffection was especially serious and wide-

spread between March and October of the next year. British agents assisted the Tory leaders to enlarge the unrest in the Virginia and North Carolina back country into a full-scale uprising and possibly to draw in Cherokees as allies. An immediate objective was to gain possession of the patriots' valuable lead mines in Montgomery County, Va. Colonels William Preston, William Campbell, and Charles Lynch, aided by Colonel Benjamin Cleveland of North Carolina, the victory at King's Mountain in early October, and harsh punishment meted out to captured Tories, ended most of the overt disloyalty by mid-autumn (Louise Phelps Kellogg, ed., *Frontier Retreat on the Upper Ohio, 1779–1781* [Madison, Wis., 1917], pp. 23–26; Maud Carter Clement, *The History of Pittsylvania County, Virginia* [Lynchburg, Va., 1929], pp. 178–79; Hening, *Statutes*, X, 324–26; Jameson to JM, 25 November 1780).

[3] That is, militia to oppose the British under General Leslie in the Portsmouth neighborhood and to aid Gates's army in North Carolina.

Arthur Lee to Committee of Congress

FC (Harvard University Library).

Ocr. 27th. 1780

GENTLEMEN,[1]

The remainder of the Furniture, of which you ask the particulars,[2] consists of Knives, Forks Spoons, plates & table Linnen, with two Iron travelling bedsteds, Mattresses & Sheets. The exact quantity of these things I do not know, but they cannot be of much value; being broken Setts, & having been usd for upwards of three years.[3]

I have the honor to be with the greatest respect Gentlemen Yr. most obedt Servt.

ARTHUR LEE

[1] On the reverse of this retained copy, Arthur Lee identified the recipients by writing "The Honble Messrs Maddison, Bee & Clark." For context of this letter see above, Lee to Committee of Congress, 21 October 1780.

[2] If this request was by letter, rather than orally, it is now missing.

[3] For the report of the committee, see below, 1 December 1780.

From Edmund Pendleton

Tr (LC: Force Transcripts).

VIRGA October 30th. 1780

DEAR SIR

Since my last yr favr of the 17th has come to hand & we have a Visit from the Troops imbarked at New York. My accounts of them are very Imperfect, but they seem to have divided themselves, landing 1000 Infantry & 100 horse at Hampton & another body at Portsmouth. We have just heard that they have re-imbarked from Hampton after taking about 500 head of cattle, but whether they meant to go off or come up James River & take Possession of Wmsburg, seem'd doubtful. perhaps the paper of today may give us information,[1] and give you also a more perfect Account of the agreeable turn in our Southern Affairs, than I am able to do, having Accounts of various pieces of good fortune in that quarter said to be well authenticated, but so jumbled together and the scenes at the same time so distant, that I cant develope the Intelligence Satisfactorily. Thus Tarlton is surprized & 600 of his legion taken, but where or by whom is not said. I conjecture tis at Charlotte by Colo. Davidson, perhaps join'd by the Group of Colos who beat Ferguson at Kings Mountain. A Council of british officers & Indians are taken with many goods at Augusta in Georgia. this I suppose to be the affair of a Colo. Clarke mention'd in Dixon's last paper. 6000 French have landed & taken the Savannah, & sombody has driven Ld Cornwallis from his Dinner & some body has taken George Town. but who they are & whether the same body did both I am not inform'd, perhaps yr Accounts from Genl. Gates may be more Intelligible.[2] I think the Stroke the British Commerce hath received from the combined Fleets off Cape Finistre, must humble them a little & perhaps they may think seriously of Peace.[3] Pray is it true that a Congress of Ministers from the Belligerant as well as Several Neutral powers, is expected to be held under the Mediation of Russia? & may we expect any good from it, or is it mere amusement? Is a General Exchange of Prisoners agreed on, or only a partial one. We hear Dr Lee & Mr Izard are with you & are open & unreserv'd in their Abuse of Dr Franklin. They must have very strong proofs before they can affect the character of that great Man & Philosopher, so long & universally esteem'd for his Wisdom and Integrity, but I am more concerned for our Common Interest which must receive Injury from every Internal wrangle of this Sort.[4]

A sufficient number of our Delegates had not met to make an House on Thursday last & as many of the lower Gentn. went away on the News of the Invasion[,] I doubt they have not yet met, tho' a fortnight has elapsed since they should have met.[5] The sickly season may have Occasioned this, otherwise 'twil be difficult to Account for the Cause of such supineness at so Critical a juncture, when the consequences may be fatal. I hear the Militia March on this Occasion with great Alacrity & even Ardour, tho' I think the setting them in motion is rather slow.[6]

I hope the Prizes to the Saratoga have found their way through the Fogg to some of our ports, & not reached New York.[7] I wish you may be able to read this letter. my paper is horid but 'tis the best I can get. I am with great regard,

Dr Sr Yr Affe & Obt Servt.

EDMD PENDLETON

[1] General Henry Clinton appears to have directed General Leslie's command to penetrate Chesapeake Bay primarily to prevent Virginia and Maryland from sending military supplies and troop reinforcements to General Gates's shattered army after the Battle of Camden (JM to Pendleton, 3 October 1780, n. 6). Thanks, however, to the patriots' victory at King's Mountain and the resulting uprising of back-country settlers against the British, the pressure upon Gates was temporarily eased, and between 14 and 29 October Cornwallis' army retreated from Charlotte, N.C., to Winnsboro, S.C. For this reason, Leslie's force by late October was more urgently needed to reinforce Cornwallis than to distract Virginia and Maryland from aiding Gates. Furthermore, the surprising speed with which Virginia's militia assembled to oppose Leslie helped to convert his invasion into a localized raid, characterized mainly by his troops moving slaves, horses, and cattle from river-edge plantations to Portsmouth. By "paper of today" Pendleton probably meant the 25 October issue of the *Virginia Gazette* (Richmond, Dixon and Nicolson), due to be delivered at Edmundsbury on the date of his letter. This issue devoted only a few lines to the invasion. The versions of this letter found in Stan. V. Henkels Catalogue No. 694 (1892), p. 82, and in *Proceedings of the Massachusetts Historical Society*, 2d ser., XIX (1905), 118, read "300 horse" rather than 100. The latter figure agrees with that given by Jefferson in his letter of 25 October 1780 to Huntington (Boyd, *Papers of Jefferson*, IV, 67).

[2] The *Gazette* of 18 October erroneously noted that Colonel Elijah Clarke (1733–1799) of Georgia had driven the British from Augusta. It also mentioned a minor exploit of a contingent from Colonel William Davidson's (1746–1781) North Carolina brigade. Somehow this latter episode became merged, in the rumor reaching Pendleton, with the momentary success of Colonel William R. Davie's troops, mentioned in n. 3 of Pendleton to JM, 17 October 1780. General Gates's letter of 16–18 October 1780 to the president of Congress reported the alleged fall of Augusta as well as the equally fictitious landing of French or Spanish troops at Sunbury, Ga. (NA: PCC, No. 154, II, 299–300). Colonel Clarke would not help to recapture Augusta until June 1781, and the enemy would not evacuate Georgetown and Savannah until May and July, respectively, of that year (Christopher Ward, *War of the Revolution*, II, 813–15, 840).

[3] See JM to Pendleton, 17 October 1780, n. 4. A brief mention of this engagement is also in the *Virginia Gazette* (Richmond, Dixon and Nicolson) of 18 October.

[4] See Joseph Jones to JM, 2 October 1780, n. 10; and JM to Pendleton, 7 November 1780.

[5] See JM to Joseph Jones, 10 October 1780, n. 7.

[6] Above, n. 1.

[7] See JM to Jones, 17 October 1780, n. 7.

To Edmund Pendleton

RC (LC: Madison Papers).

PHILADA. Octr. 31. 1780

DEAR SIR

Your favor of the 23. came to hand yesterday. We received notice of the invasion of Virga. yesterday morning and more fully last evening.[1] I am sensible of the great difficulties you will have to contend with and that no practicable exertions can save the State from much injury whilst the Enemy have a total command of the Bay & rivers. The meeting of the Legislature at this juncture is fortunate. They will certainly arm the Executive with all the authorities requisite to call forth the military resources of the Country. This could be necessary at any time, but the emptiness of the Treasury makes it peculiarly so in the present moment.[2]

Congress have felt a becoming resentment of the barbarous treatment of the gentlemen in captivity at Charlestown, and have directed General Washington to require of Clinton an explanation of the matter. Nothing has yet been done in consequence of it except an application to Clinton, which as he had at that time not been officially informed of the fact, he evaded by general assurances of the humanity &c. of Cornwallis. Gen Washington had very luckily between the application & the answer received two of the Earl's bloody proclamations which he very handsomely communicated to Sr. Harry.[3]

The motions of our Allies are no less mysterious here than they appear to you. We have however experienced so many proofs of their wisdom and goodness towards us, that we ought not on slight grounds to abate our faith in them. For my own part I have as yet great confidence in both.[4]

I recollect nothing to be added to the inclosed paper,[5] except the arrival of about 2000 German & British recruits at N. York. The Cork-fleet is not yet arrived and the delay begins to make them very uneasy in that place.[6] Genl Green is appointed to command in the S. Dept. during the enquiry into Gel Gate's Conduct. He is now here on his way. Baron Stuben will accompany him.[7] With sincere regard,

I am Dr Sr. Yr. Obt. friend & Servt.

J. MADISON JUNR.

¹ JM here refers to two letters from Jefferson read in Congress on 30 and 31 October, respectively (*Journals of the Continental Congress,* XVIII, 994, 997; Boyd, *Papers of Jefferson,* IV, 58, 67–68).

² See Jameson to JM, 25 October 1780.

³ With a design to its publication, JM or a member of his family inclosed this paragraph in brackets and quotation marks many years later. On 6 October, Washington followed the instructions of Congress of about two weeks earlier by asking General Henry Clinton to confirm or deny the report that Cornwallis had confined "respectable Citizens of south Carolina on board a ship of War." Upon receiving an evasive reply, Washington sent Clinton several intercepted letters of Cornwallis and his subordinate, Lieutenant Colonel Lord Francis Rawdon, as proof of their unwarranted severity. They viewed it as justifiable retaliation against the patriots for their cruel treatment of Tories and their misconduct in other ways (Pendleton to JM, 23 October 1780, n. 4; *Journals of the Continental Congress,* XVIII, 851; Fitzpatrick, *Writings of Washington,* XX, 128 and n. 6; 147, n. 32; 194 and n. 1; and 195).

⁴ See Jones to JM, 9 October 1780, and JM to Jones, [24] October 1780, n. 1.

⁵ Not found. Probably the *Pennsylvania Packet* (Philadelphia) of 31 October.

⁶ The ships bringing the recruits had arrived at New York on 15 October (Benjamin F. Stevens, ed., *The Campaign in Virginia,* I, 281). For the Cork fleet, see JM to Pendleton, [24] October 1780, n. 4.

⁷ See Jones to JM, 9 October 1780, n. 6.

From David Jameson

RC (LC: Rives Collection of Madison Papers).

RICHMOND Nov. 4. 1780

DR SIR

I was not favoured with any letter from you by this weeks post. the post from the Northward now comes in on thursday & goes out on this day which is the reason Dixon & Co have altered their day for publishing the paper. Clarkson has not sent me a paper for two or three weeks past nor is it material whether he ever does, it is so trifling¹

Since my last some of the Enemys Vessels run up Nansemond River & landed some Men who took possession of Suffolk, & roamed at large in that neighbourhood. Our last advices from Gen Muhlenberg were from the neighbourhood of Smithfield. He had sent down a party in hope of preventing the mischiefs the Enemy were doing about Suffolk²

The report of yesterday was that the Men had again embarked, and that the Ships were moving down. It is said they are fortifying Portsmouth—what may be their intentions is still a mystery—the general opinion is, that they are waiting for orders—that they expected to meet or cooperate with Cornwallis but hearing that Ferguson was defeated

& himself obliged to retreat from Charlotte it is said a fast sailing Vessel was immediately sent out—supposed to be for fresh orders[3]

By a sensible deserter we are informed their land force is from 2500 to 3000 foot & abt. 70 horse. Their Convoy—the Romulus of 44 Guns, the Blond of 32, the delight of 16, a ship belongg. to Goodrich of 20, and two Gallies—the land forces commanded by Genl. Leslie and the Naval by Com. Gayton—that they have heavy Cannon on board and plenty of Military Stores.[4] What pity it is we cannot be aided by a few good Ships—the whole Naval & land force would fall an easy prey. The deserter says that they expected our whole force would be sent down to Suffolk & the lower parts and that they then intended to run up to Baltimore. he heard Col Fanning (his Col) say he did not doubt but he should eat his Christmas dinner in Baltimore. This Man is a native of New York—was taken at Fort Montgomery—after sometime of painful captivity inlisted in hope of finding an opporty to escape—was made a Sarjeant—escaped the next day after he was landed[5]

It is said the Vessel is taken in wch Mr Dunlap sent his printing materials.[6] There are not yet Members enough to hold an Assembly.[7] We have for two days been amused with a report that Cornwallis and his whole Army were taken—had there been truth in the report we shd ere this have had an express from that quarter

I am with esteem & respect dr Sir Yr obedt Servt

DAVID JAMESON

[1] Beginning on 4 November 1780, the weekly *Virginia Gazette* of John Dixon and Thomas Nicolson was issued on Saturdays rather than Wednesdays, as theretofore. John Clarkson (*ca.* 1753–*ca.* 1783) and Augustine Davis' *Virginia Gazette* (Williamsburg) wilted under the competition of its rival and succumbed early in December 1780 (Clarence S. Brigham, *History and Bibliography of American Newspapers*, II, 1162).

[2] See Jones to JM, 24 October 1780, nn. 2 and 3.

[3] See Pendleton to JM, 30 October 1780, n. 1. Although General Leslie re-embarked most of his troops by 15 November, he did not sail from Chesapeake Bay until a week later. His original destination was Cape Fear, N.C., but Cornwallis soon bade him proceed from there to Charleston. Leslie arrived in Charleston harbor on 14 December (Benjamin F. Stevens, ed., *The Campaign in Virginia*, I, 285–313, *passim*).

[4] Commodore George Gayton (d. 1796), the senior officer of the fleet, used the "Romulus" as his flagship. The "Blond" should be the "Blonde." John Goodrich, Sr. (*ca.* 1720–1785), and his four sons were prominent Tories of Suffolk, Nansemond County. They owned a number of merchant ships as well as a considerable acreage of land. Virginia confiscated the latter and offered it for sale in March 1780. Which of their vessels was a unit of Gayton's fleet is not known, but it may have been the twenty-gun ship commanded by John Goodrich's son Bridger, or Bridgen (*Virginia Gazette* [Richmond, Dixon and Nicolson], 4 March 1780; Lorenzo

Sabine, *Biographical Sketches of Loyalists of the American Revolution, with an Historical Essay* [2 vols.; Boston, 1864], I, 480–82). Major General Alexander Leslie (1731–1794) had commanded the light infantry at the Battle of Long Island in August 1776 and would be in command at Charleston from 1781 until its evacuation the next year (Benjamin F. Stevens, ed., *The Campaign in Virginia*, II, 442).

5 Colonel Edmund Fanning (1737–1818), a New York Tory, commanded the King's American Regiment. Governor Jefferson's dispatch of 2 November 1780 to Maryland's Governor Thomas S. Lee closely resembles the present letter in its contents and identifies the deserter as Peter Christian (d. 1791) of New York. Christian enlisted as a private in the 3d Company of the New York line on 1 January 1777 but was listed missing on 6 October 1777, the day on which Fort Montgomery, about forty miles north of New York City on the Hudson River, fell to the British. He rejoined his former regiment on 1 November 1781 (Boyd, *Papers of Jefferson*, IV, 89–90; Berthold Fernow, ed., *Documents Relating to the Colonial History of the State of New York*, XV [Albany, 1887], 223).

6 See Jefferson to Virginia Delegates, 31 August 1780, n. 3. A storm drove the vessel carrying Dunlap's press aground in Chesapeake Bay. There it was captured by the British (*Journal of the House of Delegates*, October 1780, p. 28).

7 See Jameson to JM, 25 October 1780, n. 4.

Virginia Delegates in Congress to Thomas Jefferson

Extract (Virginia State Library). This six-line plea, probably in the hand of Jefferson's clerk, is entitled, "Extract of a Lre from the Virga Delegates in Congress to his Excellency the Governour dated at Phila: Nov. 5. 1780." The letter from which this excerpt was taken is lost, but it was probably from the pen of Theodorick Bland. His financial distress appeared to exceed that of his fellow delegates, JM and John Walker. In his covering letter of 17 November, transmitting this extract, among other papers, to the speaker of the House of Delegates, Jefferson made particular reference to Theodorick Bland (Boyd, *Papers of Jefferson*, IV, 121).

[5 November 1780]

The great depreciation of money and the extravagant prices of every thing here together with the difficulty of negociating Bills renders it absolutely necessary that some stable provision shoud be made, & some fixed mode adopted for supplying us with money, other wise we shall not be able to exist. we shoud be glad to be informed on this head as soon as possible.[1]

1 Richard Henry Lee, the chairman of the committee to which the House of Delegates referred the monetary needs of the Virginia delegates and their financial accounts "against the Commonwealth" (above, Expense Account as Delegate in

Congress, [25 September 1780]), reported on 19 December that the committee had found the accounts of most of the delegates, including JM's, "fully reasonable." Upon the recommendation of this committee, the House agreed that the state treasurer ought to establish "a sufficient credit in Philadelphia" so that each delegate, at need, could draw upon his salary; and that for his "genteel support" this salary should be £2 6s. per diem in specie (or its equivalent in paper currency), plus an equal sum per diem for his traveling expenses. The Senate, however, withheld its assent to the House bill embodying these provisions (*Journal of the House of Delegates*, October 1780, pp. 21, 24, 58, 66; Burnett, *Letters*, V, 437, No. 504, n. 2; Jones to JM, 17 January 1781, n. 8).

From Joseph Jones

RC (LC: Madison Papers).

RICHMOND 5th. Nov. 1780

DEAR SR.

I thank you for your two last Letters the first I received at Home the last (Octr. 24th.) found me in this place where I have been since the 31st. ult. waiting with abt. 64 others members of the House of Delegates to make a House to proceed upon Business, but as yet we are eight or ten short and I see no likelihood of the number speedily increasing as it has not increased for three or four days.[1] For the Members who reside in the Counties upon the Sea board or contiguous thereto some excuse may be assigned and so there may for some of the Frontier Counties from the disturbances and apprehensions of the Enemy in that quarter but I am at a loss to make an excuse for those of the interior part of the State, many of whom are still absent.[2] This neglect of public Duty is the more criminal in our present situation wch. must necessarily require the exertions of the Legislature in aid of the Executive to repel the invasion of the Enemy but is exceedingly prejudicial to the common cause in delaying to adopt and prosecute with becoming spirit those measures necessary for furnishing Men and supplies to the Army. The late practice of granting certificates for supplies and transportation for the support of the Army and the intern[al] police of the respective States transferable and allowed to discharge Taxes[,] together with the late emissions of some of the States[,] however expedient and necessary the practice was found at the time all certainly tend to counteract the scheme of Finance of March the 18th[,] to increase the circulating medium[,] and precipitate our ruin. some course must be taken to stop the progress of this trafic or we never shall get the new money into circulation as the whole collections are forestalled by certificates[,] Auditors warrants[,] &c, all which now circulate as freely in payment of Taxes as the old currency, and when money is paid[,] the Collectors rather than hazard the loss of the bad Bills readily exchange the money in the Country for Certificates whereby the Treasury is almost totally deprived of money collections.

If our people knowing the public distress will not forego the advantage or convenience of present payment for their supplies they must abi[de] the consequences, but my hopes are they will submit to any Regulations the Assembly may adop[t] for raising either men[,] supplying Magazines or supporting the Credit of the Currency all of which are the great Objects we shall bend our Minds to as soon as we have a House. These are also the objects every other State should seriously attend to and in particular the puting a Stop to the circulation of the Certificates &c you mention for the measure should be general.[3] You will therefore oblige me with information what steps are taking in other States on this head—what prospect for speedily recruiting the Army and laying up Magazines to the N and middle district for the supply of the Main Army. The States never were blessed with greater plenty or had it more in their power to lay up ample Stores of provisions for the Army than at present and if the people will not lend them to the public and wait for future payment they must be taken, but they shod. be so taken as to occasion as little disgust as possible wch. a regular apportionment of specific articles may effect. some vent should be found for the surplus of the Earths productions or I fear the collection of heavy Taxes will be found oppressive and produce clamour and discontent, if their collection shall be found practicable at any rate. Whether this can be effected by internal demand and consumption I doubt and if it cannot no other mode will answer but opening the ports. In laying specific Taxes I am inclined to think double the quantity wanted shod. be required from the people as one half may be allowed for the expence of collecting[,] transporting[,] Commissaries wages[,] and the waste unavoidable besides sometimes a total loss by water and the damage in the Storehouses. These things make a specific Tax less eligible than others could it be avoided.

Letters from Mulenberg of the 2d. which arrived this morning mention the Enemy all in Portsmouth the Ships in the Rhode—different accounts as to their fortifying at Portsmouth—certain intelligence is expected every moment from Col. Gibson who is down with a party for that purpose.[4] Accounts from head quarters come in last night inform 4000 more Troops had sailed from N. York Southerly.[5] A few

JOSEPH JONES

EDMUND PENDLETON

REVEREND JAMES MADISON

THOMAS JEFFERSON

PHILIP MAZZEI

BENEDICT ARNOLD

NATHANAEL GREENE

JOHN BROWN

days past we had very flattering accounts from the South (Cornwallis and his whole Army in Captivity) the hope of its being true enough not strong in me from the imperfections of the intelligence has died away in every one for wan[t] of confirmation. One 64 and three Frigates wod. have tak[en] the whole Fleet in our Bay as there are only a 44 & 2 Frig[ates] with a 20 Gun Ship of Goodrichs. We have reason to think Dunlaps mater[ials] are in the hands of the Enemy.[6] Complimts. to the Family[7] Yrs

J. JONES

[1] See Jameson to JM, 25 October 1780 and n. 4.

[2] See Jefferson to Virginia Delegates, 27 October 1780, n. 2.

[3] See Jefferson to JM, 26 July 1780, n. 2; JM to Jones, [24] October 1780 and n. 6. Jones apparently meant that the financial measures of Congress of 18 March 1780, together with the laws of Virginia and other states enacted in compliance with those measures, had failed to halt currency depreciation, to assure popular acceptance of the new paper money at the prescribed ratio of $1.00 of the new bills for $40.00 of the old, and to yield in taxes to the state governments (and via them to the central government) sufficient income in the form of money or needed military supplies. Moreover, the people of Virginia, and of other states also, were paying their taxes in old promissory notes previously issued by state officials for goods and services. In view of the deteriorating public credit, the 40 to 1 ratio was no longer—if it ever had been—realistic. Hence, the law of Virginia providing for the emission of new interest-bearing certificates had broken down. People might of necessity accept them in payment of labor or material requisitioned by the state but, in view of their rapidly declining real value, then spent them as quickly as possible, even though they yielded 5 per cent annual interest to the holder and were to be redeemed in specie on or before 31 December 1786.

[4] See Jones to JM, 24 October 1780, n. 2; and Jameson to JM, 4 November 1780, n. 3. Colonel George Gibson (1747–1791) commanded the 1st Virginia State Regiment.

[5] This rumor was erroneous. See JM to Pendleton, 31 October 1780, n. 6, for its possible source.

[6] Jameson to JM, 4 November 1780, n. 6.

[7] The residents of JM's boarding house in Philadelphia were "the Family" (Jones to JM, 19 September 1780, n. 8).

From Edmund Pendleton

Tr (LC: Force Transcripts).

VIRGA. November 6. 1780

DEAR SIR:

My friend Mr Griffin left me this Morning by whom I sent you my best Wishes for yr health which he told me was low. I hope the Approaching Cold Season may brace up yr Nerves.[1]

I judged from yr Account of the number of the Enemy embarked from New York, that they were in pursuit of something to eat; we now hear they have pick'd up a quantum suffici[en]t to load their Vessels with Beef & Mutton & are going back to New York, where tis said Provisions were short, but this supply & that by the Cork Fleet will releive them.[2]

We have loose Accounts from the Southward that the British Army to the Amt. of 3000, are taken, that of their being surrounded by some formidable bodies of ours seems well told & renders the other not improbable.[3]

Just after yr Account of the large Invasion from Canada into the Frontiers of New York,[4] we were amused with a certain account (as 'twas called) of the taking of Quebec by the second division of the French Fleet & Army, so long expected at Rhode Island. We are since deprived of this pleasure by a flat contradiction of the Intelligence; was this mere invention, or had they any ground for circulating the Report. We had yet no House of Delegates on Saturday last, which with an Empty Treasury, are circumstances unfavourable at this juncture. Mr Henry has resign'd his Seat in Congress & I hear Mr Jones intends it. It is also said the Governor intends to resign. It is a little cowardly to quit our Posts in a bustling time.[5] I write you in a hurry being detain'd from paying you my complts til[6] I expect the post every moment. I am in all situations

Dr Sr Yr very affe Servt

EDMD PENDLETON

[1] See Jameson to JM, 13 September 1780, n. 1. Cyrus Griffin was probably on his way to Philadelphia to resume his duties as a judge of the Court of Appeals in Cases of Capture, an office to which he had been elected by Congress on 28 April 1780 (*Journals of the Continental Congress,* XVI, 397, 411; XVII, 458).

[2] On 29 October 1780, General Clinton complained that "I do not at this moment possess one month's provision with all I can collect, and I do not hear a word of our expected victualers from Cork." These victualers arrived on 10 November (William B. Willcox, ed., *The American Rebellion,* pp. 220, 469; JM to Pendleton, [24] October 1780, n. 4).

[3] This rumor was untrue.

[4] See JM to Pendleton, [24] October 1780, and n. 2.

[5] On James Henry's resignation, see Jones to JM, 2 October 1780, n. 13. Although Jones was in poor health, he did not resign; nor do his letters to JM, except for the one of 2 December (*q.v.*), suggest even a momentary inclination to do so. During the autumn of 1780, Jefferson several times expressed to friends his determination to resign "at the close of the present campaign" (Boyd, *Papers of Jefferson,* III, 643, 655; IV, 19, 53, 192).

[6] Pendleton probably meant to write "because" or some equivalent word.

To Edmund Pendleton

RC (LC: Madison Papers).

PHILADA. Novr. 7th. 1780.

DEAR SIR

Your favor of the 30 of last month came by yesterday's post, and explained a report which had amused us here for several days. It was said that some movements of the French to the Southward, had alarmed the enemy to such a degree that they had suddenly re-embarked their troops and were leaving Virginia. The re-embarkation of the detachment which had taken possession of Hampton and its vicinity was no doubt the foundation of it.[1] Our curiosity is at present almost wholly directed to the Southward and I am happy in having so intelligent and punctual a correspondent so near the principal scene of military operations.

There is I believe no doubt of an intended Congress at the Hague not of Ministers from the Belligerents but neutral powers under the auspices of Russia; and as the avowed object of it is to establish the liberty of the Seas which G. B has so little respected, and is highly approved by France & Spain as well as all the neutral Maritime powers, it must necessarily prove unfavorable to G. B. and consequently friendly to our views.[2] Congress have thought it advisable to testify their approbation of the liberal principles held out by Russia as the basis of the proposed negociation, and have accordingly by a public Act adopted them so far as to direct the Board of Admiralty to prepare instructions for their armed vessels conformable to them.[3]

Doct. Lee and Mr. Izzard particularly the latter have been here some time, and I believe are not very reserved in their reflections on the venerable Philosopher at the Court of Versailles. Mr. Izzard I understand is particularly open in his charges against him. Doctr. Lee on his arrival applied to Congress for a hearing on the subject of Mr. Deanes allegations, if any doubt remained of the falsehood & malice of them, but nothing final has been done as yet in Consequence of it. I have had great anxiety lest the flame of faction which on a former occasion proved so injurious should be kindled anew but as far as I can judge the temper of Congress is in general by no means prone to it, although there may be individuals on both sides who would both wish & endeavour it.[4] Not a word has been heard of the Saratoga's prizes.[5] A partial exchange of Prisoners we hear is agreed on, but have no official account of it. Genls. Lincoln, Thomson & du portail it is said are

165

included in it, having been set against Philips & Reidezel. I have heard but few inferior officers named, except Col. Laurens.[6]

A gentleman in Statia writes to the Commercial Committee on Octr. 3d that a Dutch war is seriously talked of at that place, that the Dutch are certainly preparing a formidable marine, and that open protection & respect is now given to American Vessels in the same manner as to those of other Independent Nations. If this fact be truly represented, and it is mentioned with strong circumstances of credibility, it is probably one of the fruits of the neutral combinations set on foot by Russia.[7]

Congress have just finished an estimate of supplies for the ensuing year requiring of the States the value of 6 Millions of Drs. in specie. The principal part of the requisition consists of specific articles, the residue in specie or the new emissions, receivable as specie.[8] If the States fulfill this plan punctually, there is no doubt that we shall go smoothly through another Campaign and if they would forbear recurring to State emissions & certificates, in procuring the supplies, it may become a permanent & effectual mode of carrying on the war. But past experience will not permit our expectations to be very sanguine. The collection & transportation of specific suppl[ies] must necessarily be tedious & subject to casualties; & the proceedings of 13 separate popular bodies, must add greatly to the uncertainty & delay. The expence attending the mode is of itself a sufficient objection to it, if money could by any possible device be provided in due quantity.[9] The wan[t] of this article is the source of all our public difficulties & misfortunes. One or two million of guineas properly applied would diffuse vigor and satisfaction throughout the whole military departments and would expel the enemy from every part of the United States. It would also have another good effect. It would reconcile the army & every body else to our republican forms of governments; The principal inconveniences which are imputed to these being really the fruit of defective revenues. What other States effect by money, we are obliged to pursue by dilatory & undigested expedients, which benumb all our operations and expose our troops to numberless distresses. If these were well paid, well fed, and well cloathed, they would be well satisfied and would fight with more success. And this might & would be as well effected by our governments as by any other if they possessed money enough as in our moneyless situation the same embarrassments would have been experienced by every government,[10]

With very sincere regard I am Dr Sr. Yrs &ca.

J. Madison Junr.

¹ See JM to Jones, 17 October 1780, nn. 6 and 12; Pendleton to JM, 30 October 1780, n. 1; and Jameson to JM, 4 November 1780, n. 3.

² See Reverend James Madison to JM, 3 August 1780, n. 3. The "intended Congress" at the Hague was not held. The maritime treaty signed at Copenhagen on 19 July between Russia and Denmark was acceded to at St. Petersburg by Sweden on 21 July and by the Netherlands on 20 November 1780 (*The Annual Register, or a View of the History, Politics, and Literature, for the Year 1781* [London, for J. Dodsley], pp. 300–303). Great Britain declared war on the Netherlands in December 1780.

³ By agreeing on 5 October to the declaration of the commercial rights of neutral nations made in the preceding February by Catherine the Great of Russia, and by adopting on 27 November instructions to the commanders of its armed ships to abide by and enforce those rights, Congress aligned with France, Spain, and the neutral powers in Europe, accepting their definitions of contraband and their position that, except for contraband, enemy goods on neutral ships and neutral goods on enemy ships were not subject to capture, and that to be legal a blockade of an enemy port must be effective (*Journals of the Continental Congress*, XVII, 802; XVIII, 864–67, 905–6, 1097–98; Wharton, *Revolutionary Diplomatic Correspondence*, III, 606–8).

⁴ See Jones to JM, 2 October 1780, n. 9; and Lee to JM *et al.*, 27 October 1780, n. 2. The paragraph to this point, as well as the final paragraph of this letter, is inclosed in brackets, indicating the portions which JM or one of his family designated, many years later, for publication. On 7 August 1780 Congress named a committee, including JM, to report upon the letter of Ralph Izard (1742–1804) of the day before, explaining his inability to fulfil his official mission as a commissioner to the Court of Tuscany (*Journals of the Continental Congress*, XVII, 701). Upon the committee's recommendation, drafted by its chairman, James Lovell, without any apparent help from JM, Congress on 9 August acknowledged Izard's "faithful endeavours" to carry out his assignment. Congress later authorized the payment of his expenses while abroad (*ibid.*, XVII, 714–15, 722; XVIII, 1086). Far more controversial was Izard's alignment while in Paris with Arthur Lee in opposing the conduct and policies of Silas Deane (1737–1789) and Benjamin Franklin. Izard arrived in Philadelphia early in August in somewhat the capacity of Lee's advance agent to arouse dissatisfaction in Congress with Franklin and Deane (Wharton, *Revolutionary Diplomatic Correspondence*, IV, 21; Burnett, *Letters*, V, 362, n. 5). For the report of the committee (with JM as chairman) on Arthur Lee's actions in Paris, see below, 1 December 1780.

⁵ JM to Pendleton, 17 October 1780, n. 1.

⁶ The long negotiations to effect an exchange of prisoners—especially of those captured by the patriots at Saratoga and by the British at Charleston—can be followed in Fitzpatrick, *Writings of Washington*, XX, *passim*. JM makes particular mention of Major General Benjamin Lincoln, Brigadier General William Thompson (1736–1781), Brigadier General Louis Lebègue Duportail (1743–1802), and Lieutenant Colonel John Laurens (1754–1782) on the American side, and of the British Major Generals William Phillips (1731–1781) and Friedrich Adolph, Baron von Riedesel (1738–1800).

⁷ Although the dispatch in question seems not to have been read in Congress, an extract from it is in the *Pennsylvania Packet* (Philadelphia) of 7 November. See also the *Virginia Gazette* (Richmond, Dixon and Nicolson) of 2 December for another letter of the same tenor from St. Eustatius. As early as November 1776, Fort Orange in that Dutch-owned island returned the salute of a U.S. naval vessel. Admiral George Rodney's capture of the island on 3 February 1781 completed the destruction wrought there by a hurricane in the preceding October (J. Franklin

Jameson, "St. Eustatius in the American Revolution," *American Historical Review*, VIII [1902–3], 691, 696, 699).

⁸ See Jones to JM, 2 October 1780, n. 4. In the present letter JM refers to an action by Congress on 4 November (*Journals of the Continental Congress*, XVIII, 1011–18). The "specific articles" comprised meat, flour, salt, and rum. By "new emissions" JM meant the paper money issued by states in accordance with the resolutions of Congress of 18 March 1780.

⁹ See JM to Jones, [24] October 1780, n. 6; and Jones to JM, 5 November 1780, n. 3.

¹⁰ At this point, without changing the comma to a period, JM crossed out a qualifying clause reading "not excepting the most absolute."

From Joseph Jones

RC (LC: Madison Papers).

RICHMD. 10th. Novr. 1780

DEAR SR.

I have your favour by the last Post.¹ We have had a House since Monday and in Com: of the whole this day have voted the raising the deficiency of our continental Troops for the War and to recruit them by a bounty which I expect will be very high but the Members in general seem to prefer that method to any other let the expences be what it will What may be the ultimate determination is yet very uncertain as there is no accounting for the whim and caprice of some but from the unanimity with which the question was carryed today (not a voice dissenting) I presage a happy issue to the business. We have recommended the bringing in the old paper currency to exchange for the new bills just arrived. by this operation if it succeeds we loose one half the Sum we expected to have the first use of but of which we have been deprived by the necessity of anticipating the Taxes by which channel alone the old money could come in, and now from an empty Treasury and the amazing expence incurred by calling forth men to oppose and repel the invasion and the pressing necessity for money it will be unavoidable I fear, the making a further emission and which was also resolved this day in Committee² Every one seems to be sensible of the evils of this measure but they see or think they see greater evils in our present situation will result to the Community from the want of money than from the increase of it, and indeed I can not see a way of carrying on our operations at this juncture so indispensably necessary withot. money. of the evils that present themselves we think we choose the least.

On the fourth instant one of our Light Horsemen met and closely interrogated a suspected person whose concious Guilt at length manifested itself and induced the Horseman to search him when he found in his poss[ess]ion a Letter written on very thin or silk paper from Genl. Lessly to Ld. Cornwallis informing his Lordship he had taken Post at Portsmouth and waited his orders. The person apprehended is it seems a Citizen employed by Lessly who informs Cornwallis he was to receive a hansome reward if he succeded in his embassy[.] unfortunately for the Embassador he was in a fair way to receive the Compliment of the Bowstring alias the halter on the 8th. instant.[3] Three other Fellows were apprehend[ed] yesterday abt. ten miles below this place the one a Sergeant of British Grenediers, the others Soldiers and all Deserters from the Barracks the last Summer and got into New York. they were part of the British Army at Portsmouth and it is supposed were on their way to the Barracks whether sent with written or verbal instructions has not yet come out.[4] Our Force below on each side James River must be Formidable. ten thousand of the Militia were I am informed ordered out but the draughts from sevl. Counties have been countermanded as soon as satisfactory information was obtained of the strength of the Enemy[.] six thousand it is thought will be a number very sufficient to secure us agt. the Armament now at Portsmouth. It is supposed this party was to have attempted a junction with the Army under Cornwallis somewhere in North Carolina but our present Force in the Field here and the unpromising [prospects?][5] that present themselves to Cornwallis in the South will prove strong impediments to the execution of the project.[6] Our Militia are commanded by our supernumerary and other experienced officers. Col. Lawson has a Corps of abt. 700 volunteer Horse and Infantry—abt. 300 of them under my nephew Col Monroe compose part of the light Infantry commanded by Col. Gibson.[7] If the Enemy stay as by the intercepted Letter it wod. seem they mean to do there must soon be skirmishing if nothing more but I hope our people will be cautious untill they are somewhat used to skirmishing of venturing to more general action. I inclose you an answer to Mr. Pleasants, which you will be pleased to deliver unless you can engage for me Pembertons House upon moderate Terms with Coach house Stabling for four Horses and the use of a small Pasture with the Gardens with a Hay loft and as much furniture for Kitchen and House as he can spare. Pembertons place is more convenient and would suit me rather better than the other but is I fear not so healthy wch. is a great object not only to myself but to Mrs. Jones who has this Summer undergone a long and tedious illness from wch. she is not yet recovered having terminated in the third day Ague and Fever. I know not what sort of House on the inside Pembertons is and wish if you are likely to engage for it you wod. take the trouble of looking into the house. If his demands are unreasonable I wod. at any rate like Pleasants's. You will observe I propose to pay the Rent quarterly wch. Mr. Pleasants required shod. be all paid at the commencement of the year[.] if he will not consent to this I will agree to pay the first Quarter at the Commencemt. and so proceed on to the first of November.[8] Mr. Henry I believe returns to Philadelphia as I hear nothing of his intention to resign.[9] he sent to the Treasurer for £8000 to enable him to set out but could not obtain it. I have done what I could since I have been here to forward money to the Delegates but could not effect it. Mr. Jameson yesterday informed me they wod. be able speedily to send you a supply. Our accounts have not yet been before the Assembly but expect them to day or Monday. The account from the Books shod. be stated and sent forward agreeable to the resolves. I shall endeavour to get matters so settled as that our supply be regular.[10] With Compliments to the Gent. of the Dele[gation] and the Family at Mrs. Houses[11]

I am yr[s] sincerely

Jos: Jones.

[1] Probably a 31 October letter, now missing.

[2] *Journal of the House of Delegates*, October 1780, p. 14; above, Motion regarding Virginia Currency, 11 October 1780, n. 2; Jones to JM, 5 November 1780, n. 3; JM to Pendleton, 7 November 1780.

[3] Benjamin F. Stevens, ed., *The Campaign in Virginia*, I, 299. The captured letter is shown in facsimile opposite p. 91 of Boyd, *Papers of Jefferson*, Vol. IV, and was printed in the 11 November issue of the *Virginia Gazette* (Richmond, Dixon and Nicolson). Forwarded by Jefferson, the letter was read in Congress on 17 November (*Journals of the Continental Congress*, XVIII, 1066).

[4] By "the Barracks," Jones meant those at Winchester and near Charlottesville in which the captured British "convention troops" were quartered. Because of the invasion by General Leslie's force, Jefferson had arranged to move most of these prisoners to Fort Frederick in Maryland (Pendleton to JM, 23 October 1780, n. 4; Boyd, *Papers of Jefferson*, IV, 109–10).

[5] Jones omitted whatever word he intended to write after "unpromising."

[6] See Pendleton to JM, 30 October 1780, n. 1; Jameson to JM, 4 November 1780, n. 3.

[7] See Jones to JM, 5 November 1780, n. 4. Robert Lawson (*ca.* 1748–1805), of Prince Edward County and formerly of the Virginia continental line, commanded militia at this time. He served on the Council of State and in the legislature for periods during the 1780's and moved to Kentucky in 1789. After serving over three years in the continental line, Major James Monroe, later President of the United States, continued as a militia officer. Colonel George Gibson was his commander.

8 See Jones to JM, 2 October 1780, n. 14; JM to Jones, [10 October 1780], n. 7.

9 Jones was mistaken. See Jones to JM, 2 October 1780, n. 13.

10 See JM to Virginia Auditors, and Expense Account as Delegate in Congress, 25 September 1780; Jones to JM, 9 October 1780, n. 3; Virginia Delegates to Jefferson, 5 November 1780, n. 1; Jefferson to Virginia Delegates, 14 November 1780.

11 See Jones to JM, 19 September 1780, n. 8; JM to Jones, [10 October 1780], n. 6.

From Edmund Pendleton

Tr (LC: Force Transcripts).

VIRGA Novr 13. 1780

DEAR SIR

I have yr favr of the 31st past & am pleased to hear the former Account of the Arrival of the Cork fleet proved premature, since we are so bad Christians as to be gratified with the distress of our Enemies. It was probably the transports with their new levies which were mis, taken for the others.[1]

The Enemy here have collected a handsome recruit of Provisions, but whether they mean to carry them to their friends at New York, or to stay here and consume the stock, yet remains a doubt, since their continuing to fortifie at Portsmouth & the Great Bridge, indicate the latter, & yet their numbers if we are not deceived in them forbid such a conjecture.[2] I have heard nothing certain from Genl Muhlenburg, a loose report was that they had been fighting two days, but this is destroy'd by later Accounts, perhaps the paper of to day, may give some Account of that[3] as well as the Enemy's Southern Army, who it is said have escap'd our Parties, & are like to get safe to Charles Town. The Enquiry into Genl. Gates's Conduct gives General Satisfaction, as popular prejudices against his Conduct to the Southward ran high, & such an Inquiry will Satisfie the Public of the justice or injustice of the Suspicion.[4]

It was rather unfortunate that Our Assembly at this important Juncture, could not make an House 'til last Monday (three weeks too late) for want of members. I hope they will make Amends by their Vigor and dilligence, for this great listlessness & inattention. I may truly call this a Gossiping letter, & will put an end to it by assuring you once again that I am

Yr obliged & affe Servt

EDMUND PENDLETON

¹ See JM to Pendleton, [24] October 1780, n. 4, and 31 October 1780, n. 6.
² See Pendleton to JM, 30 October 1780, n. 1; Jameson to JM, 4 November 1780, n. 3.
³ See Jones to JM, 24 October 1780, n. 3. The *Virginia Gazette* (Richmond, Dixon and Nicolson) of 11 November contained no items about Leslie's invasion. There was almost no fighting between his troops and the militia (Boyd, *Papers of Jefferson,* IV, 111, 127).
⁴ See Jones to JM, 9 October 1780, n. 6.

Thomas Jefferson to Virginia Delegates in Congress

RC (College of William and Mary Library). This covering note is in a clerk's hand. Although the signature has been cut off, the item is docketed "Gov. Jefferson's Letter to Delegs. in Congress."

RICHMOND, Nov. 14, 1780

GENTLEMEN

I do myself the pleasure of inclosing to you a draught¹ of mr. Ben: Harrison jur. and co: on messieurs Turnbull and co: merchants of Philadelphia² for 66,666⅔ dollars for which we have had transferred to mr. Harrison the Auditors warrant of aug. 9. 1780. for £20,000 Virginia money with which you stand charged in their books.³

I have the honor to be with the greatest esteem and [r]espect Gentlemen, Your most obedient & mo. hble. servant.

¹ Not found.
² William Turnbull (1751–*ca.* 1806), a merchant of Philadelphia, was also commissioner of claims in the treasury office.
³ See David Jameson to JM, 13 August 1780, n. 2. For the method of equating dollars with pounds, see above, Expense Account as Delegate in Congress, [25 September 1780], nn. 4, 8.

To Joseph Jones

RC (LC: Madison Papers).

PHILADA. Novr. 14th: 1780

DEAR SIR,

I am glad to find by your favor of the 5th. inst: recd. yesterday that your health & that of your family have admitted of your going to

Richmond. The tardiness of other members is very unfortunate and inexcusable at the present critical moment. I wish when they do meet the vigor & wisdom of their measures may make amends for it.

I do not learn that any of the States are particularly attentive to prevent the evils arising from certificates & emissions from their own treasury, although they are unquestionably the bane of every salutary arrangement of the public finances.[1] When the Estimate for the ensuing year was on the anvil in Congress, I proposed a recommendation to the States to discontinue the use of them, & particularly in providing the specific articles required. It met however with so cool a reception that I did not much urge it. The objection against it was that the practice was manifestly repugnant to the Spirit of the Acts of Congress respecting finance, and if these were disregarded, no effect could be expected from any additional recommendations.[2] The letters from G. Washington & the Com: General for some time past give a most alarming picture of the state & prospects of the Magazines. Applications to the contiguous states on the subject have been repeated from every quarter, till they seem to have lost all their force. Whether any degree of danger & necessity will rouse them to provide for the winter season now hastening upon us, I am unwilling to decide because my fears dictate the worst. The inroads of the Enemy on the frontier of N. York have been most fatal to us in this respect. They have almost totally ruined that fine Wheat Country, which was able and from the energy of their Govt. most likely, to supply Magazines of flour both for the main Army & the NW posts. The settlemt. of Schoarie which alone was able to furnish, accordg to a letter from Genl Washington 80,000 bushels of grain for public use has been totally laid in ashes.[3]

Genl Washington in a letter to Congress of the 4th inst: mentions that another embarkation was on foot at N York. In another of the 7. he says he had received no further intelligence on the subject, but had reason to think such a measure was still in contemplation.[4] From the last letter it appears that by the late exchange abt. 140 officers including Genls. Lincoln, Thomson, Waterbury & du portail & Col. Laurens are liberated, as also all our privates amounting to 476. The General had acceded to a further proposal of Clinton for exchanging almost the whole residue of our Officers for Convention Officers with out attaching any privates to them.[5]

Reports of the 2d division of the French fleet are again reviving as you will see by the inclosed paper. It is also said that Rodney has sailed from N. York with 10 Ships of the line for Europe, but if there be any reality in the first report, it is more likely he is gone out to meet the french.[6] The Cork fleet is not yet arrived, and very serious apprehensions begin to prevail at N. Y. on account of it.[7]

Mr. Walker has been detained since the expiration of his serv[ice] by an indisposition. He will set out in two or three days.[8] Col. Pendleton informs me that Mr. Henry has resigned his place in Congress and intimates his fear that you may follow his example. I hope he is mistaken in the first as I am assured by your req[uest?] concerning Pemberton that he must be in the last. If Mr. Henry however should have resigned I intreat you to see that the vacancy is judiciously filled; and if any thoughts of it have been indulged by your self, I intreat you still more strongly to dismiss them. I have not yet received an answer from Pemberton, and have not had time since yours came to hand to apply for it. I was unwilling to appear very anxious about the matter. You shall know what is to be expect[e]d from him by next Post.[9] I make no apology for inaccuracies & bad writing because you know the manner in which we are obliged to write for the post, and having been prevented by Company from doing any thing last night I am particularly hurried this morning. Dr sir,[?]

J. MADISON JR

[1] See JM to Jones, [24] October 1780, n. 6.

[2] After being debated during much of October, the state-by-state requisition of money and supplies was adopted by Congress on 4 November (*Journals of the Continental Congress*, XVIII, 1011–18). If an amendment was moved by JM at any time in the course of this discussion, it was not recorded in the journal. Unless by "certificates & emissions" he meant merely promissory notes given by state officials for requisitioned supplies, his meaning is not clear. On 26 October he had voted against striking out a provision permitting any state to pay part of its tax quota in "bills of credit of the emissions directed by the resolution of the 18 of March last" in lieu of gold or silver (*ibid.*, XVIII, 981).

[3] Many years later, JM or someone in his family inclosed this paragraph and the last sentence of the final paragraph in brackets, thus indicating the portions of the letter to be published. JM's references are particularly to Washington's letters of 21 October and 7 November, read in Congress on 27 October and 13 November, respectively (*ibid.*, XVIII, 982, 1049; Fitzpatrick, *Writings of Washington*, XX, 230–32, 311–15). The forces of Sir John Johnson, Joseph Brant, and Cornplanter ravaged the Schoharie Valley from end to end (Christopher Ward, *War of the Revolution*, II, 647–49; JM to Pendleton, [24] October 1780, n. 2.

[4] Congress listened to the letter of the 4th on 8 November and to the one of the 7th on the 13th (*Journals of the Continental Congress*, XVIII, 1031, 1049; Fitzpatrick, *Writings of Washington*, XX, 289–90, 311–15). General Clinton was hoping to send a force under Benedict Arnold to replace Leslie's in Virginia, but it did not sail from New York until 20 December.

[5] See JM to Pendleton, 7 November 1780, n. 6. Brigadier General David Waterbury (1722–1801) of Connecticut had been captured in 1776.

[6] The paper may have been the *Pennsylvania Journal* of 15 November 1780. This

issue printed a report that a ship recently arrived at Boston had crossed the Atlantic to "the latitude of Bermuda" in company with eight French war vessels. The report appears to have been false. Admiral George Rodney's fleet of fifteen ships left New York for the West Indies on 16 November (William B. Willcox, ed., *The American Rebellion*, p. 234, n. 1; Jameson to JM, 23 August 1780, n. 2).

7 The victualing ships from Cork had arrived in New York harbor on 10 November (JM to Pendleton, [24] October 1780, n. 4).

8 John Walker apparently left Philadelphia on 23 November 1780 (Boyd, *Papers of Jefferson*, IV, 136).

9 See Pendleton to JM, 6 November 1780. Someone—possibly JM in his old age—wrote "[not Patrick]" above "Mr. Henry," at his second mention. For Pemberton, see Jones to JM, 10 November 1780.

To Edmund Pendleton

RC (LC: Madison Papers).

PHILADA. Novr. 14th. 1780

Dr. Sir

Yr. favor of the 6th. inst: came to hand yesterday. Mr. Griffin by whom you appear also to have written has not yet arrived.[1]

It gives me great pleasure to find that the Enemy's numbers are so much less formidable that [than] was at first computed, but the information from N. York makes it not improbable that the blank in the computation may shortly be filled up. Genl Washington wrote to Congress of the 4th. inst: that another embarkation was going on at that place, and in another letter of the 7th. he says that although he had received no further intelligence on the subject, he had reason still to believe that such a measure was in contemplation. Neither the amount nor the object of it however had been ascertained.[2]

The inroads of the Enemy on the Frontiers of N. York have been distressing & wasteful almost beyond their own example. They have totally laid in ashes a fine settlement called Schoarie which was capable Gel Washington says of yielding no less than 80,000 bushels of grain for public consumption. Such a loss is inestimable, and is the more to be regretted because, both local circumstances, and the energy of that Govt. left little doubt that it would have been applied to public use.[3]

I fancy the taking of Quebec was a mere invention Your letter gave me first account of such a report. A different report concerning the 2d. division of the French fleet has sprung up as you will see by the inclosed paper. It is believed here by many, and some attention given to it by all. It is also said that Rodney has saild from N. York with 10

Ships for Europe. If he has sailed at all & the first report be true also, it is more likely that he is gone out to meet the french.[4]

The late exchange has liberated abt. 140 Officers and all our privates at N. Y. amounting to 476. G. Washington has acceded to a proposal of a further exchange of the Convention Officers without attaching any privates to them, which will liberate almost the whole residue of our Officers at that place.[5]

I am Sir with the highest esteem & regard Yr. Obt. friend & servt.

J. Madison Jnr.

[1] Cyrus Griffin.
[2] See JM to Jones, 14 November 1780, n. 4.
[3] *Ibid.*, n. 3.
[4] *Ibid.*, n. 6.
[5] *Ibid.* and n. 5.

George Morgan to Virginia Delegates in Congress

Copy (Virginia State Library). The original of this letter is missing. Theodorick Bland made a copy of it and also of the reply to Morgan. The delegates inclosed these in their letter of 22 November 1780 to Governor Jefferson.

Philadelphia Novr 16th 1780

Gentlemen[1]

I hope you will excuse the trouble I give you in calling your attention to a Subject, which is not only interesting to myself and Several other Citizens of America, but also to the State of Virginia, which you have the Honour to represent. It cannot be unknown to you Gentlemen that some time Since, the Indiana Company were called upon by the Honble the Senate and assembly of your State to set forth their right to a tract of Country on the Ohio which was Ceded to them by the treaty at fort Stanwix in 1768 & of the Consequent proceedings thereon.[2] You Must also as Members of the Honble. the Congress of the United States be acquainted with the Memorial of the Company to Congress on this Subject, requesting them to hear and determine the Case at the Bar of their House, as also that nothing decisive has yet taken effect in consequence of their application.[3] It is unnecessary to go further into a detail of Facts, to Introduce a proposition I have to make to you, in behalf of myself and the rest of the

Company; which is to Submit the dispute in Question between the State and the Company, to the arbitration & final Decision of Gentlemen of the first Capacity, Integrity, & Experience upon the Continent, to be Chosen by the Honble. the Congress in the Same Manner as is directed by the articles of Confederation in like Cases, between State and State.[4]

This Proposition is so Consonant to reason & Justice that I hope it will not be rejected. It cannot be the desire of the State of Virginia to oppress and ruin a Number of Individuals who never did them an Injury. there is every reason to Suppose her Councils are governd by more honorable motives If the Company have no right to the Lands in Question there will no doubt be a decision against them, the Compy will be Satisfied, & the State will be applauded for her Candor & Justice in Submitting the dispute to an Impartial discussion.

That the Indiana Company have just Pretensions to this tract of Country, is admitted by a great Number of Gentlemen of the first Character and abilities in the State of Virginia. On the Motion for Compensation to the Company the House of delegates were equally divided, untill the speaker gave the Casting Vote against them.[5] Some of the first Characters in other States and in England have declared their opinions in Support of our right and the Names of Camden, Franklin, Stockton, Glyn[,] Dagge & Henry, Cannot but Impress the Strongest Ideas of the Company's Right to the disputed Territory.[6]

If then they have pretensions which are warranted by Such respectable Opinions, why should they be refused an unprejudiced Investigation.

I do assure your Honors, that this proposition proceeds from an Ardent desire to Settle the dispute which we are so unfortunate as to have with the State, in the most Amicable manner and with the least Expence possible. It would be our Wish to decline investigating the rights of Virginia to the territorial Jurisdiction if not drove to such a step from necessity & to save ourselves and Families from Impending Destruction. The Act of Virginia for depriving the Company of their property, may possibly be viewed by the United States in a very different light, than what those who promoted it intended.

I intreat you will honor me with an answer in writing & believe me to be with the greatest respect

Gentlemen Yr. most obedt. & very Humb: Set

GEORGE MORGAN
Agent for the Indiana Compy.

177

1 JM and Theodorick Bland were the only Virginia delegates attending Congress at this time. For the general context of the issue raised in the letter, see above, Motion regarding the Western Lands, 6 September 1780, editorial note. The Indiana Company (often called William Trent and Company), of which George Morgan (1743–1810) of Philadelphia was the principal promoter, had been deeded by the Iroquois Confederacy, in November 1768, nearly two million acres in present-day West Virginia. At the same time, the Treaty of Fort Stanwix, concluded by these six tribes with Sir William Johnson, Indian agent of the Crown, included a confirmation of this grant. The grant was, of course, within the territorial limits of Virginia and west of the King's Proclamation Line of 1763 (Max Savelle, *George Morgan: Colony Builder* [New York, 1932], pp. 78–80).

2 In the May 1779 session the two houses of the General Assembly of Virginia resolved that the Indiana Company's deed was "utterly void." That session also enacted a general law invalidating all land titles within the state resting upon unauthorized purchases by individuals or companies from Indians (*Journal of the House of Delegates*, May 1779, pp. 39–44; Hening, *Statutes*, X, 97–98).

3 As agent of the Indiana Company, Morgan presented its memorial to Congress on 14 September 1779. By a narrow margin, and over the unanimous dissent of the Virginia delegation, Congress referred this petition to a committee. Recognizing the divisive nature of the issue, the committee apparently decided to delay its report. The Virginia legislature at the close of the year adopted George Mason's "Remonstrance . . . to the Delegates of the United States in Congress Assembled." Given permission to present this protest at their discretion, the Virginia delegates waited until 28 April 1780 before doing so (*Journals of the Continental Congress*, XV, 1063–65; XVI, 398).

4 In short, Morgan was assuming that the sovereign state of Virginia might consent to negotiate on equal terms with a private company. If Virginia would not agree with this suggestion, Morgan hinted in his next-to-last paragraph what his next step would be.

5 How Morgan knew that the vote had been close is not clear. The official journal does not record the yeas and nays (*Journal of the House of Delegates*, May 1779, p. 56). There is no doubt, however, that the Indiana Company had powerful supporters in Virginia (Thomas P. Abernethy, *Western Lands and the American Revolution*, pp. 220–21, 225).

6 Besides the patriots, Patrick Henry, Benjamin Franklin, and Richard Stockton (1730–1781), the former chief justice of New Jersey, Morgan refers here to Charles Pratt, Earl of Camden (1714–1794), the Lord High Chancellor, and the British lawyers Henry Dagge (d. 1779) and John Glynn (1722–1779). Camden had assured the company that its land title, based upon a deed from the Indians and a treaty with them, needed no confirmation from the Crown to add to its validity (Max Savelle, *George Morgan*, p. 80; George E. Lewis, *The Indiana Company, 1763–1798* [Glendale, Calif., 1941], p. 229; Thomas P. Abernethy, *Western Lands and the American Revolution*, pp. 143–44).

Certification to a Committee of Congress

RC (NA: PCC, No. 62, fol. 435).

[16–17 November 1780]

[At] the request of the Honble. T. Matlack Esqr. I received the enclosed papers from him Octr. 27. and have since had them in my care. The two certificates of faithful "each"[?] entry, on the margin of two[?] of the sheets by Mr. Walker were signed in my presence at the time I received them. Mr. Walker was not desired to certify the like with regard to the other passages. He observed that he was constantly present during the enquiry and had no doubt that the whole of the within minutes were a true recital of facts.[1]

J MADISON JUNR.

[1] On 3 July 1780, Congress appointed Thomas McKean the chairman of a committee of three members to investigate charges brought by the Board of Treasury against Francis Hopkinson, the treasurer of loans. His countercharges also became a part of the committee's business (*Journals of the Continental Congress*, XVII, 585, 598). On 31 July, Timothy Matlack (1730–1829) of Pennsylvania and John Walker were named to replace McKean's two committee colleagues, who had left the city (*ibid.*, XVII, 683–84). During the next two months the Hopkinson *vs.* Board of Treasury issue expanded to include additional allegations about the inefficiency or misconduct of the board and of the commissioners of the chamber of accounts, or particular members of each. Between 9 and 26 October the McKean committee conducted an elaborate inquiry. During these hearings they recorded the testimony of witnesses not only about the Hopkinson question but also about other evidences of financial mismanagement by the fiscal agents of the Continental Congress. McKean was absent during the last few days of the inquiry and from then until mid-November. On the day following the close of this investigation, these minutes were sealed and, as the above certificate states, turned over by Matlack and Walker to JM for safekeeping. JM notes that, in his presence and at that time, Walker certified to the truth of what was written on two of these sheets of minutes. They numbered fifty-three pages in all. Walker's marginal attestation on a leaf of the 25 October testimony reads: "This is a just & faithful entry of what passed on the subject to which the Paragraphs within the crotchets [brackets] relate. Jn. Walker." He also wrote in like manner on a page of the minutes of the next day (NA: PCC, No. 62, fols. 255–307, esp. fols. 283 and 297). Walker may have been asked to provide these certifications because Congress might not call upon the committee to report before his expected early departure for Virginia. Why Matlack wanted Madison, or any other "neutral" in Congress for that matter, to be the custodian of the minutes is more puzzling. The answer is suggested, however, by a statement made by Matlack on 17 November. On the day before, two of the commissioners of the Board of Treasury whose conduct had particularly been under attack presented a petition to Congress asking to be heard by the McKean committee in their own defense. Congress immediately granted this plea and, at the same time, added three new members to the committee. McKean thereupon reconvened it on the next day and evidently asked JM to turn over the minutes in his charge. When JM did so in person, he accompanied the sealed packet with the above note of certification, written on either 16 or 17 November. The minutes of the committee reveal that on 17 November, after JM's note was read, McKean "desired the former minutes to be opened and read by Mr. Matlack. To this Mr. Matlack objected, because he could not consent to have those minutes put into his hands, as it might be hereafter alledged, that he had made alterations therein" (NA: PCC, No. 62, fol. 339). Matlack's caution on this occasion probably explains why he gave the minutes to Madison for safekeeping three weeks before.

Thomas Jefferson to Virginia
Delegates in Congress

Extract (NA: PCC, No. 71, I, 523–24). This document, in Theodorick Bland's hand, is endorsed, "Extract of a letter from the govr. of Virginia dated November 17–80 referred to the Board of Treasury." To this notation was added, probably by a clerk of Congress or the Board of Treasury, "Treasury Board 21st. Decr. 1780 Make two Copies of the Order of Congress of the 15th Instant respecting Specie from the state of Virginia. One for the Audr. General and one other for the Treasurer." He erred in writing "15th" rather than "19th." Also on the cover is ciphering which transmutes £1,318 15s. specie into 263,750 dollars in continental currency. Jefferson's original letter to the Virginia delegates is lost. Bland evidently copied this long extract and presented it to Congress on 19 December 1780.

RICHMD. Novr 17th. 1780

GENTN:

With respect to the payment made on behalf of Mr. Braxton[1] into the Continental treasury in Part of our Quota of the fifteen Million tax,[2] the Executive having been Charged with the raising and remitting that money, we have thought it unnecessary to lay it before the Legislature. The Sum to be sent, was sent, partly in Money and Partly in Bills. These Bills were drawn in *Continental Dollars.* and paiable in such, and not in Specie. of this nature was Mr. Braxtons Bill desiring his Correspondent to pay so many Continental Dollars into the Treasury. If the treasurer has received payment in another kind of money at an Arbitrary rate of Exchange, this must have been either under the Rules of his office or against them. The former I can Hardly Suppose, and in the latter case it has become his own Private act, and he should be deemed to have received (no[t] £1318–15 hard Money but) 263750 dollars Continental Money as he has I Suppose given a discharge on the Bill for so much of its Contents. Had he rejected the Tender of the Hard Money would not Continental dollars have been paid? if they had not, then indeed the demand should have reverted on the State, and we would have fallen on means for compelling payment. We were really concernd on the return of our agent who Carried the Money and Bills that he did not have them regularly protested as there appeard some doubts on them. But he acted for the best in his own Judgment, and in that point of view was to be approved. I am exceedingly Sorry that this want of Punctuality has arisen in these remittances. We sold Tobo. for these Bills, which would in Much less time have produced us money here. But the responsibility and known Connection between the drawer & drawee induced us to consider them as even Better than Money which wd. have been, liable to Accidents in transportation. Had a tender of Specie been made to us here we would certainly have rejected it. But the payment being now to be transacted between the Drawee & Congress (passing us over) neither the Tender or receipt can be considerd as our act, but the former the act of the Drawee, and the latter of the Treasurer of Congress. we do not therefore think ourselves concernd immediately in this transaction. if Congress please to Consider the Payment of £1318..15 hard Money as a discharge of 263750 dollars paper which was to be paid by the drawee[,] well: if not on rejecting it he will make payment in the Specific Money he was Calld on to pay or we will resort to the Drawer and Compell such payment.

Since writing thus far I note more particularly than I had before done, that the treasurers return sais that he had *received from the Commonwealth of Virginia a Sum of Money in Specie*, &.c. this indeed stating it as the act of this Commonwealth renders it necessary for me to disavow it—which I hereby do. it was the Act of the drawee of which the Commonwealth had neither knowledge or Intimation; and this return fixing the Act on the Commonwealth instead of the Drawee is so far wrong.[3]

&c. &c.

THOS. JEFFERSON

[1] Carter Braxton.

[2] On 7 October 1779 Congress resolved that, beginning on 1 February 1780 and continuing thereafter to 1 October 1780, the thirteen states should pay each month to the Board of Treasury a total of $15,000,000. Of this monthly total, Virginia's quota was $2,500,000 (*Journals of the Continental Congress*, XV, 1150).

[3] In view of the fact that Braxton owed money to Virginia, and the state owed money to Congress, Jefferson permitted him to pay his debt to the state by remitting the amount of his obligation in continental currency to the Board of Treasury in Philadelphia. Braxton's authorization to his agent in that city also specified that the sum should be paid with this type of money. Therefore, as Jefferson points out in this letter, both he and Braxton had conformed with the letter of the tax requisition of Congress and also with the stipulation of its resolution of 18 March 1780 that $1.00 of the new state emissions (or $1.00 specie) should be accounted as an equivalent of $40.00 of the old continental currency. In other words, not they, but the Board of Treasury, had broken the law by accepting the specie offered by Braxton's agent at a 75 to 1 ratio, thus recognizing the degree of depreciation which existed in fact, even though the legal ratio was still 40 to 1. This error, in the words of the 1 November 1780 report of a congressional committee headed by Theodorick Bland, was "de-

structive to the credit of the new emission, and [would] have a fatal tendency to depreciate it" (*ibid.*, XVIII, 1003–4). Accepting this report on 15 November after it had been recommitted and somewhat amended, Congress exonerated the government of Virginia from intentional wrongdoing in the matter and invited it to choose between a return of the specie or having it accepted at 40 to 1 (*ibid.*, XVIII, 1057–58; NA: PCC, No. 136, IV, 621, 623, 635). Jefferson, of course, had not heard of this action when he wrote to the delegates, although he may have been informed by them, or by one of them, of the 1 November version of the committee's report. As soon as Bland laid Jefferson's letter before Congress on 19 December, JM moved that the Board of Treasury should record the transaction so that "the State of Virginia may not be included in it" (see below, Motion on Accounts of Carter Braxton, 19 December 1780).

From Joseph Jones

RC (LC: Madison Papers).

RICHMOND 18th. Nov. 1780

DEAR SR.

I have your favour by the last Post and very sincerely wish the Statia news may prove true but I cannot yet believe the Dutchmen will go to War.[1] The Generals Greene and Steuben are here on their way to the Southward.[2] from that quarter we are destitute of intelligence and from the Army to the Eastward in this State we have nothing material to mention. The Enemy still at or near Portsmouth and our People at convenient distance on the South side James River between Suffolk and Portsmouth—both Armies eating their bread and Beef in quiet withot. any quarreling that we hear of.[3] The design that was formed to attack abt. 200 of the Enemy at an out Post since called in, miscarried by the disagreement between Colonels Gibson and Parker about Rank—a fair and perhaps the only opportunity our people will have of striking the Enemy to advantage and which has been lost by a contention abt. Rank.[4] it was not so between the five Colonels whose Militia united to attack Ferguson for there the Command was given to Campbol by several Colonels himself only a Lieutenant Colonel.[5]

In a private Committee we have gone through the outlines of a Bill [to] supply the deficiency of our quota of the Continental Army for the War. The mode a bounty of a Negro not younger than ten or older than 40 years for each Recruit—these to be required from all Negro holders having twenty and upwards in their possession in the proportion of every twentieth Negro at such prices as settled by the

Bill in hard money to be paid for in eight years[,] the payment to commence the fifth year with an Int. of five P Ct. to go in payment of Taxes. The persons furnishing the Negros to be Exempted from future draughts unless upon invasion or insurrection and if they do not by a certain period voluntarily surrender them compulsion to be used. This plan if it can be so digested in the Bill as to appear practicable in execution will I believe produce the Men for the War and from what I can learn be palatible to the Delegates whatever it may be to the Senate. strong objections certainly lie agt. it and the Negro holders in general already clamour agt. the project and will encounter[?] it with all their force but you know a great part of our House are not of that Class or own so few of them as not to come within the Law shod. it pass. The scheme bears hard upon those wealthy in Negros as that property is sacrificed to the exoneration of other property. It is in nature of a loan to the State and will aid the public exigence for money—but will not I am pretty certain come under the denomination of the ancient mode of *benevolence*. Though determined to join in any scheme that shall be practicable for raising Men for the war I confess I am no great friend to the one I have stated though in Com: I have given it my assistance toward making it perfect as a majority of the Com: adopted the Plan. but my notion is and I think the mode wod. be more just and equally certain in procuring the Men to throw the Militia into divisions as by the last Law and require the divisions to find a Negro of a certain Val[ue] or Age or money equivalent to that value and on failure of obtaining a Recruit by a limited time the division to be drafted with a small bounty to the Soldier whose lot it may be to serve for three years. but the Negro bounty cannot fail to procure Men for the War under either schem[e] with the draught as the dernier resort.[6] Some doubts having arisen on the construction of the Law for issuing and funding the New money under the scheme of 18th. March last a Bill was brot. in to explain and amend it. While under consideration of a Com: of the whole the Speaker proposed an amendment whereby the New Bills as well as those emitted by act of the last Session called the 2 Million Act shod. be a legal tender in payment of all Debts and that the last wch. was not payable in Taxes until twelve months hence should now be received for Taxes[.] after long debate the Comm: of the Whole divided when abt. ten appeared in favour of the amendment so that the House and Senate agreeing to the clause the New Money of Congress and the late emission of this

183

State and I suppose of course the emission of this Session will all be a lawfull tender in payment of Debts—for such is the State of things here a further emission becomes indispensable. Thus you will see the scheme of the 18th. of March will be in great measure defeated by their proceedings and not have a fair chance to produce by its vigorous execution those advantages to the public it was well calculated to effect.[7] The executive are pursuing vigorous courses[?] to lay up a sufficiency of Beef and we have authorized them to send a Comr. into North Carolina to concert with the Executive there the laying up proper supplies of Pork as it seems the Legislature of that State had prohibited the removal of that article from the state and in Virga. there will be very little Pork obtained tho' I think we have plenty of Beef and of every kind of Grain.[8]

Col. Lee has this moment received a Line from Weedon informing him the Enemy were all embarked but where for is uncertain[.] some conjectured up James River but as they are all on board they must mean to leave us.[9] Can you contrive me the Journals of Congress for Augt & September and indeed october if printed: I mentioned in my last my terms for Pemberton or Pleasants Houses. let me he[ar] from you on the subject as soon as you can.[10] Neither Smith or Henry are I believe yet set out.[11] I repeat[?] your sending a Copy of the account from the Books of the Delegates. The other accounts are not yet laid before the House by the Auditors [so] that I can give you no information how they are relished. I am charged by the Auditors with 2000 £ on acct. the 8000 drawn, in favour of George Meade & Co. and wch. you were to receive for me but I cannot find by the Treasurers accot. that he has paid the warrants. has the money been received by the Delegates. The Executive inform me a Bill for 20,000 £ has been sent for the use of the Delegation.[12] I am

D. Sr. yr. aff Friend

JOS: JONES.

[1] This letter, probably written by JM to Jones on 7 November, is missing. In all likelihood it conveyed the news from St. Eustatius which JM sent on the same day to Pendleton (q.v.).

[2] On 30 October, Congress followed Washington's recommendations by appointing Major General Nathanael Greene to succeed Major General Horatio Gates as commander of the southern army, and by directing Baron von Steuben, the inspector general of the armies of the United States, to proceed to the same headquarters (Journals of the Continental Congress, XVIII, 994–95; Jones to JM, 9 October 1780, n. 6). After five days in Richmond, Greene left on 21 November for his post in

North Carolina, but Steuben stayed behind for a time to expedite the movement of troops and supplies from Virginia to the southern army (George W. Greene, *Life of Nathanael Greene*, III, 54–63).

3 See Pendleton to JM, 13 November 1780, n. 3.

4 Colonel George Gibson and Colonel Josiah Parker (1751–1810) of Isle of Wight County (Boyd, *Papers of Jefferson*, IV, 71–72).

5 Before writing to JM, Jones may have read the 18 November issue of Dixon and Nicolson's *Virginia Gazette*. This recounts how, on the march which culminated in the victory at King's Mountain, the five colonels leading their respective contingents of Virginia or North Carolina troops chose from among their number Colonel William Campbell (1745–1781) of Washington County, Va., to be their commander (*Journals of the Continental Congress*, XVIII, 1048–49). On 10 November, the Virginia House of Delegates designated Jones the chairman of a committee to convey to Campbell the resolution of the House thanking him and his troops (*Journal of the House of Delegates*, October 1780, p. 13).

6 The terms of this bill, as stated here, were considerably changed during the prolonged debate preceding the enactment of the law on 1 January 1781. To raise three thousand soldiers to serve either for three years or for the duration of the war, this law assigned a quota to every county. A 2 per cent ad valorem property tax was established to yield the funds needed to pay each volunteer a large bounty in money upon his enlistment. The law pledged to reward him upon expiration of his service with a land bounty and, at his option, with either £60 in specie or a Negro slave between ten and thirty years of age. Unlike the measure as explained by Jones, who shared conspicuously in the passage of this law and those laws cited in the next two footnotes, the statute merely provided that this postwar bonus would "be paid for, or procured by equal assessment on property" (*Journal of the House of Delegates*, October 1780, pp. 14, 30–63, *passim*, 71–74, 79; Hening, *Statutes*, X, 326–37; JM to Jones, 28 November 1780; Jones to JM, 8 December 1780).

7 See Jones to JM, 5 November, n. 3, and 10 November 1780. By providing for the emission of from six to ten million pounds of new paper money and by declaring it, as well as the large emissions of the spring of 1780, negotiable legal tender, the legislature of Virginia (and other state legislatures taking similar action to meet their financial crises) blasted the hope of Congress that its measures of 18 March might halt the alarming depreciation of the currency. The *Journal of the House of Delegates* does not mention either Speaker Benjamin Harrison's (1726–1791) amendment or the vote on it (*ibid.*, October 1780, pp. 9–28, *passim*, 31, 41, 46; Hening, *Statutes*, X, 241–54, 321–24, 347–50).

8 On 15 November the legislature empowered Jefferson, with the advice of his council, to use any "practicable and effectual" means to collect whatever supply of beef and salt he deemed necessary. On the same day the Assembly further authorized him, in concert with the governor of North Carolina, to find a way to meet the southern army's urgent need for pork (*Journal of the House of Delegates*, October 1780, pp. 9, 10, 15, 17, 18).

9 See Jones to JM, 24 October 1780, n. 2. "Col. Lee" was probably Richard Henry Lee of Westmoreland County, a member of the House of Delegates. The "Line from Weedon" may have been the missing inclosure mentioned in Boyd, *Papers of Jefferson*, IV, 124–25.

10 See Jones to JM, 2 October, n. 14; 24 October, n. 2; and 10 November 1780.

11 See Jones to JM, 2 October, n. 13; 24 October, n. 4; and 10 November 1780.

12 See Jones to JM, 9 October, n. 3; and 10 November 1780; Virginia Delegates to Jefferson, 5 November, n. 1; Jefferson to Virginia Delegates, 14 November 1780.

From David Jameson

RC (LC: Rives Collection of Madison Papers).

RICHMOND Novem 18. 1780

DR SIR

By Post this week I recd your favour of the 7th.[1] and can offer nothing in excuse for my not enlarging on the subject of the Invasion but that I could only have said something similar to what you had from the Govr. or in Dixons paper[2]

We have had nothing worth notice from below for several days past, indeed we are not likely to know what the Enemy is about as our Army cannot approach them they being so well guarded by passes & the Water Courses of wch. they are in possn. A Flag has lately been sent to them to ask permission for some ladies to remove themselves, whose Husbands had thot. it prudent to fly. they would not grant this permission. some too have been to ask for Slaves that had gone to them, but they would not restore them. By this means & by deserters we are informed the Vessel they sent out (supposed to be for fresh orders) is returned. what is to follow we are at a loss to guess. It is reported they have lately marched some Men towards the lower parts of N. Cara. but I do not believe it. another report is that they have recd. a reinforcement. this too I disbelieve. one day it is said they are apparently preparing to go off, the next a contrary report prevails however it seems on all hands to be agreed they have been very industrious in fortifying Portsmouth We have a considerable force now collected at and below Smithfield, and some attemps will be made to annoy the Enemy but the great advantage they have over us by being possessed of the whole Navigation will I fear render our attempts of little avail[3] We have heard nothing from the Southward since the Governors last dispatches to the Prest. of Congress of the 10th.[4] The Gov. will inclose Bills for 66,666⅔ dollars for the Delegates.[5] Gen Green & the Baron Stuben with their Suite arrd here the 16th.[6] I am much pleased with the Eusta. intelligence. I hope the Dutch begin to be in earnest.[7] The Assembly have put it in the power of the Executive to seize Beef & Salt And Col Morris is placed by the board at the head of that important business.[8] I hope he will yet be able to lay in a good Stock of Provs. but the Season was too far advanced by the late meeting of the Assembly to do all that might have been done in that way.

The Delegates are considering of the mode to raise our quota of troops for the War[9]

I am with esteem dr Sir Yr obt hbe Sevt

DAVID JAMESON

PS 9 o Clock

Just as I had finished my letter an express arrd. from Gen. Muhlen-berg—the 15th. the British troops embarked—the 16t. at 11 o Clk fore-noon Portsmouth was evacuated, the works not finish and the part that was done not destroyed—many Negroes that had gone to them left in the town—the Vessels taken by them still in the harbour—the Fleet still lying in Eliza[.] River. where they mean to go next, time must dis-cover. the people in the Town say they talked of coming up James River, a very short time will determine this part[10]

19th as an express was to be sent I thot. it best to wait till this day for it rather than send by the posts. I was in hopes of giving you some further Accot. of the Enemy but it is now past 12. o Clk & no news The Express is to wait no longer—adieu[11]

1 Not found, but see JM to Pendleton, 7 November 1780, for the news which JM probably sent also to Jameson on that day.

2 The *Virginia Gazette* of Dixon and Nicolson, published in Richmond. Gover-nor Jefferson had dispatched news about Virginia and information about the southern army to the president of Congress on 3, 7, and 10 November (Boyd, *Papers of Jefferson*, IV, 92–93, 98–99, 110).

3 See Pendleton to JM, 30 October 1780, n. 1; Jameson to JM, 4 November 1780, n. 3; and Jones to JM, 5 and 10 November 1780.

4 Above, n. 2. The letter was read in Congress on 17 November (*Journals of the Continental Congress*, XVIII, 1066).

5 See Jefferson to Virginia Delegates, 14 November 1780.

6 See Jones to JM, 18 November 1780, n. 2.

7 See JM to Pendleton, 7 November 1780, nn. 3 and 7.

8 See Jones to JM, 18 November 1780, n. 8. Colonel Richard Morris.

9 See Jones to JM, 18 November 1780, n. 6.

10 Jameson refers here to Peter Muhlenberg's letter of 18 November to Jefferson (Boyd, *Papers of Jefferson*, IV, 124–25). From aboard ship, about to leave Virginia, General Leslie wrote the next day to General Clinton: "I left the Works [at Portsmouth] entire, and I still hope you will be enabled to take up this ground, for it certainly is the Key to the Wealth of Virginia & Maryland." Leslie added that most of the people seemed sorry to have him go, that they were tired of the war, and that he had "left with the Clergyman of Portsmouth 100 Guineas to be distributed in small portions to the poorer Sort, who had lossed *their all*. I think this money will be well laid out, as it shews our intention was not to distress them." As Jameson surmised, Leslie had thought of sailing up the James River but decided its channel was too uncertain to risk his ships in it (Benjamin F. Stevens, ed., *The Campaign in Virginia*, I, 299–300).

11 Jameson probably dispatched his letter to JM with the same express rider who carried Jefferson's letter of 19 November to the president of Congress (Boyd, *Papers of Jefferson*, IV, 128–29; *Journals of the Continental Congress*, XVIII, 1095).

Virginia Delegates in Congress
to George Morgan

Copy (Virginia State Library). When Theodorick Bland made this copy of his and JM's reply to Morgan's letter of 16 November 1780 (*q.v.*), he wrote at the top of it, "Copy of Answer Given to the letter Signed Jacob [*sic*] Morgan addressed to the Virginia Delegates, &.c." JM was Bland's only colleague from Virginia in Congress at that time. Bland may have transcribed this note on 22 November, since he inclosed it in the letter of that date which he penned, on his own and JM's behalf, to Jefferson (*q.v.*). Although the manner of expression in the note suggests that JM drafted it, the now missing original was apparently also in Bland's hand. In the "Minute Book of the Indiana Company," listed as item No. 558 in A. S. Rosenbach Catalogue No. 19 (November 1917) and bought by a purchaser unknown to the present editors, mention is made of a letter from Theodorick Bland (for the Virginia Delegates?) to George Morgan, 20 November 1780, "relative to the claims of Virginia." The copy which Bland inclosed to Jefferson bears no date.

[20 November 1780]

The delegates from Virginia Inform Mr Morgan in answer to his letter of the 16th Instant. That as the State they represent have finally decided on the Subject to which his proposition relates,[1] it would be manifestly improper for them to attend to it. they think it their Duty to add that if they were less precluded they could not reconcile with the respect due from every State to its own Sovereignty and honor, an appeal, from its own decisions, to a foreign tribunal, in a case which involves the Pretensions of Individuals only—and not the Rights or pretensions of any foreign State[2]

[1] See Morgan to Virginia Delegates, 16 November 1780, nn. 2 and 3.
[2] *Ibid.*, n. 4.

From Edmund Pendleton

RC (University of Virginia Library). This is apparently the only one of the many letters written by Pendleton to JM in 1780 which still exists in original manuscript form (Pendleton to JM, 27 August 1780, headnote). How it alone survived is problematical. Perhaps the neatly printed "To James Madison Nov: 20th: 1780." near its bottom margin was added by an autograph collector to whom JM gave the letter. The letter is not copied or noted in any of the several records of Pendleton's correspondence.

VIRGA. Novr. 20. 1780.

DEAR SIR

Just coming home I have but a moment to pay you my respects & preserve my Character of a *Punctual*, tho' not of an *Intelligent* Correspondent, which you partially call me in yr. favr. of the 9th.[1] as my time & matter are equally short. Not a word have I lately from the Southern Army, to join which Genl. Green pass'd Us on Wednesday last, travelling in Post haste & wth as little parade as might be.[2]

We have had a Skirmish below, in which we killed some, took 60, & lost only two.[3] I just now saw a deserter from the Enemy, a Native of the Delaware State, who says he left them Monday, that they have had No reinforcement, are about 3000, & that they were embarking either for New York or Charles Town, some sd. one, some the other.[4] I wish you health & am

Dr. Sir Yr. Affe. & Obt. Servt

EDMD. PENDLETON

[1] Pendleton's mistake for the 7th.

[2] See Jones to JM, 18 November 1780, n. 2. Pendleton's home in Caroline County was one day's journey north of Richmond. "Wednesday last" was 15 November; General Greene arrived in Richmond the next day.

[3] In view of the fact that in his letter to JM on 27 November (*q.v.*), Pendleton said there had been no such "Skirmish," he evidently was not referring to the brush near the Great Bridge on 6 November between the British and Colonel Matthew Godfrey's militia, reported in the *Virginia Gazette* (Richmond, Dixon and Nicolson) of 18 November.

[4] See Jameson to JM, 18 November 1780, n. 10.

To Joseph Jones

RC (LC: Madison Papers).

PHILADA. Novr. 21st. 1780

DEAR SIR.

Your favor of the 10th. came by yesterday's post. I[1] am glad to find you have at last got a house [of Delegates][2] and have made so auspicious a beginning, as a unanimous vote to fill up our line for the war. This is a measure which all the States ought to have begun with. I wish there may not be some that will not be prevailed on even to end with it. It is much to be regretted that you are not in a condition to discontinue another practice equally destructive with temporary enlistments.[3] Unless an end can by some means or other be put to State emissions & certificates they must prove the bane of every salutary regulation. The depreciation in this place has lately run up as high as 100 for 1, and it cannot be satisfactorily accounted for on any other principle than the substitution of certificates in the payment of those taxes which were intended to reduce its quantity and keep up a demand for it.[4] The immediate cause of this event is said to have been the sudden conversion of a large quantity of paper into specie by some Torys lately ordered into exile by this State.[5] It is at present on the fall and, I am told the Merchants have associated to bring it down & fix it at 75. The fate of the new money is as yet suspended. There is but too much reason however to fear that it will follow the fate of the old. According to the arrangement now in force it would seem impossible for it to rise above 1 for 40. The resolutions of Congress which establish that relation between the two kinds of paper must destroy the equality of the new with Specie unless the old can be kept down at 40 for 1. In New Jersey I am told the Legislature have lately empowered the Executive to regulate the exchange between the two papers according to the exchange between the old & the new, in order to preserve the equality of the latter with specie. The issue of this experiment is of consequence, and may throw light perhaps on our paper finance.[6] The only infallible remedy whilst we can not command specie, for the pecuniary embarrassments we labour under, will after all be found to be a[7] punctual collection of the taxes required by Congress.

I hope you will not forget to call the attention of the Assembly as early as[8] the preparations for defence will admit to the means of ratifying the confederation, [by a Cession of territory][9] nor to remind it of the conditions which prudence requires should be annexed to any territorial cession that may be agreed on. I do not believe there is any serious design in Congress to gratify the avidity[10] of land mongers, but the best security for their virtue in this respect will be to keep it out of their power. They have been much infested since you left us with memorials from these people; who appear to be equally alarm[e]d & perplexed. Mr. G. Morgan, as Agent for the Indiana claimants[,] after memorializing Congress on the subject has honored the Virginia Delegates with a separate attention He very modestly proposes to them a reference of the Controversy between the Company & Virginia to arbitration in the mode pointed out in the Confederation for adjusting disputes between State & State. We have given him for answer that as the State we represent had finally determined the question, we could not with any propriety attend to his proposition[,] observing at the same time that if we were less precluded we could not reconcile with the sovereignty & honor of the State an appeal from its own Jurisdiction to a foreign tribunal, in[11] a controversy with private individuals.[12]

The last account we had of the embarkation at N. York was that the Ships had fallen down to the Hook, that the number of troops as well as their destination was unknown. That Philips was to command them. The Cork fleet is I fear at last certainly arrived.[13] The 2d. Division of French fleet has not yet made its appearance. It is made a question at present whether the squadron taken for it, as mentioned in my last[,] was not a British fleet.[14] Mr. Adams in a letter of the 23 of Augt from Amsterdam received yesterday speaks of General Prevost being sent out from England with a few frigates (and it is to be supposed some land forces as he is a land officer though Mr. Adams does not expressly say as much) for Cape fear to facilitate the Operations of the Enemy in N. Carolina.[15] A New York paper of the 17th. announces the death of your worthy friend General Woodford.[16] I suppose it has reached you through some other channel before this.

I have the books of Accts. with the papers connected with them ready to go forward to the Auditors under the care of Col. Febiger who will in a day or two send off a number of Waggons for the Southward.[17] I shall soon write you on some private matters which ought not to be entrusted to a conveyance by post.[18]

I have engaged to take Pleasants house for you on the terms given in to you with the difference, that one quarter of the rent is to be paid on the first of January and remainder as it becomes due, and you are to pay for the whole year if you leave it in Novr. The first of these conditions I was authorised to make, the last I thought it better to submit to than leave you unaccomodated or on a footing of uncertainty.

You will be at liberty [to] keep it a second year on the same terms if you please[.] [I] hope you will not leave it at the time you proposed to limit the bargain to and at any rate you can only lose two months rent a little more than 4 half Joes, a sum not worth regarding in a matter of such consequence to your private convenience & perhaps to the public Service. He engages to let you have the furniture you saw in the house and *says* he will spare you any other Articles which he may not need himself, but I believe it would be prudent not [to] rely much on this resource.¹⁹

I am Yrs. Sincerely,

J. MADISON JNR.

¹ From here through the second paragraph, the text is inclosed in brackets to mark the part of the letter which, years later, JM or a member of his family selected for publication.

² This bracketed above-the-line insert, adding what would have been obvious to Jones, was probably not in the letter as originally written but was interpolated by JM at a much later date to help the expected readers of the printed extract.

³ Instead of "not in a condition to discontinue," JM first wrote, "likely to be forced to continue." JM inserted "with temporary enlistments" above the line. It is uncertain whether these were editorial emendations made by him in later years or before he mailed the letter to Jones.

⁴ See JM to Jones, [24] October and 14 November 1780; Jones to JM, 5 November, n. 3, and 10 November 1780. John Sullivan's letters of 15 November and 3 December 1780 describe the state of the currency in Philadelphia in greater detail (Burnett, *Letters*, V, 446–49, 478).

⁵ After President Joseph Reed and the council of Pennsylvania ordered David Franks and others, suspected of conniving with Benedict Arnold, to leave Philadelphia posthaste, they were charged with inventing excuses to delay their departure in order to have time to convert their paper currency into specie. On 20 November, Franks stated under oath that neither he nor anyone else to his knowledge was guilty of this charge (*Colonial Records of Pennsylvania*, XII, 495–96, 499, 547; *Pennsylvania Archives*, 1st ser., VIII, 611, 615–17).

⁶ New Jersey's action in this regard came before Congress on 24 November in the form of "a memorial and representation" from the state's legislature. Congress referred this memorial to a three-man committee including JM (*Journals of the Continental Congress*, XVIII, 1087–89). For the committee's report, see below, 23 December 1780.

⁷ Between "a" and "punctual," JM crossed out "vigorous and."

⁸ After "as," JM wrote and then deleted "possible to."

⁹ Probably many years later, for purposes indicated in n. 2, JM wrote and bracketed this phrase in pencil, above the line. See Jones to JM, 19 September, nn. 2 and 3, 9 October 1780, and 2 December 1780. George Mason had expected to attend the legislature to wield his great influence on behalf of cession, but illness confined him at home (Mason to JM, 2 August 1780, n. 3; Kate Mason Rowland, *The Life of George Mason, 1725–1792* [2 vols.; New York, 1892], II, 1–2).

¹⁰ JM first wrote "to listen to the claims" instead of "to gratify the avidity."

¹¹ Between "in" and "a," JM crossed out three or four words so completely that they cannot now be read.

¹² See George Morgan to the Virginia Delegates, 16 November 1780; Virginia Delegates to Morgan, [20 November 1780].

13 Major General William Phillips did not leave the New York City area until late March 1781. From then until his death, about two months later, he commanded the British troops in Virginia. If Cornwallis had not needed assistance in South Carolina in November 1780, and if Washington had depleted his force around New York to aid General Greene in North Carolina, General Clinton probably would have sent some of his soldiers on an expedition up the Delaware River. The reports of embarkation may have stemmed from the activity attendant upon the departure on 16 November of Rodney's ships and of two convoys—one bound for Falmouth with commercial cargoes and the other with supplies and a few troops for Cornwallis' army. The Cork fleet had arrived in New York harbor six days before (William B. Willcox, ed., *The American Rebellion*, pp. 221, 234, 254–55).

14 See JM to Jones, 14 November 1780, n. 6.

15 John Adams' letter was read in Congress on 20 November (Wharton, *Revolutionary Diplomatic Correspondence*, IV, 41–42; *Journals of the Continental Congress*, XVIII, 1072). Major General Augustine Prevost (d. 1786) had commanded in Georgia and South Carolina in 1778–1779. The rumor that he was bringing reinforcements from England persisted at least until February 1781 (Fitzpatrick, *Writings of Washington*, XXI, 295).

16 General William Woodford died as a prisoner of war in New York City on 13 November.

17 As an episode in a distinguished military record extending from the Battle of Bunker Hill in 1775 until the close of 1782, Colonel Christian Febiger (1746–1796) was named to command the 2d Virginia Regiment in September 1777. He spent most of the autumn of 1780 in Philadelphia, collecting and forwarding military supplies to Virginia and North Carolina.

18 See JM to Jones, 25 November 1780.

19 See Jones to JM, 2 October 1780, n. 14. A half joe was about $10.00. JM inadvertently wrote "conconvenience" for "convenience."

To Edmund Pendleton

RC (LC: Madison Papers).

PHILADA. NOVR. 21, 1780

DEAR SIR

Your favor of the 13th. came safe yesterday. The past week has brought forth very little of consequence, except the disagreeable and I fear certain information of the arrival of the Corke fleet. Our last account of the embarkation at N. york was that the Ships had fallen down to the Hook, that the number of troops was quite unknown, as well as their destination, except in general that it was Southwardly. It is still said that Philips is to command this detachment.¹ If the projected junction between Leslie & Corn[w]allis had not been so opportunely frustrated by the gallant volunteers at King's Mountain it is probable that Philips would have reinforced the former, as the great force in his rear would otherwise have rendered every advance hazardous. At present it seems more likely that the declining state of their Southern affairs will call their attention to that quarter. They can it is well known regain at any time their present footing in Virginia if it should be thought expedient to abandon it,[2] or to collect in their forces to a defensible point, but every retrograde step they take towards Charlestown proves fatal to their general plan. Mr: J. Adams in a letter of the 23d. of Augst. from Amsterdam received yesterday, says that Genl. Prevost had sailed from England with a few frigates for Cape fear in order to facilitate the operations of their Arms in N. Carolina, and that the Ministry were determined to make the Southern States, the scene of a very active Winter Campaign. No intimation is given by Mr. Adams of the number of troops under Genl Prevost.[3] The 2d. division of the French fleet mentioned in my last to have been off Bermuda has not yet made its appearance. It is now rather supposed to have been a British one. The death of Genl Woodford is announced in a N. York paper of the 17th. I have not seen the paper, but am told no particulars are mentioned. I suppose it will reach his friends before this will be recd. through some other channel.[4] Adieu.

J. MADISON JUNR.

[1] See JM to Jones, 21 November 1780, n. 13.
[2] Major General Leslie's force left Virginia shortly before this letter was written (Jameson to JM, 18 November 1780, n. 10).
[3] See JM to Jones, 21 November 1780, n. 15.
[4] *Ibid.*, n. 16.

Theodorick Bland, for Virginia Delegates in Congress[?], to Thomas Jefferson

RC (Virginia State Library). This letter is signed only by Bland and is in his hand. In his first two paragraphs and part of the third, however, his "we," "us," and "our" show that he clearly writes for JM, his sole Virginia colleague in Congress, as well as for himself. Although the balance of the letter expresses a point of view at variance with JM's, it is included here because JM's later defense of his own position entitles Bland to be quoted exactly. Probably in answer to JM's request, William Munford, keeper of the rolls for the Commonwealth of Virginia, sent JM on 30 September 1820 a certified copy of this letter and also of Jefferson's note of 5 December 1780 transmitting it to Benjamin Harrison, the speaker of the Virginia House of Delegates. These transcripts are now among the Madison Papers in the Library of Congress.

PHILADELPHIA Novr 22d 1780

SR.

Mr. Walker, who sets off to Virginia tomorrow, affords us this opportunity of Enclosing your Excellency a Copy of a letter Presented
to us the 16th Inst. together with a Copy of our Answer, concerning
the affair of the Indiana Compy[1]

It may not be improper to Inform Yr. Excellency and, (through yr.
Excy.) the Legislature who we suppose may be now Siting—that every
art has been and tis probable may be used, by that Company to extend
their influence and Support their pretensions—and we are Sorry to say
that we have Suspicions founded upon more than mere Conjecture,
that the land Jobb[er]s, of this Compy., the Vandalia, and the Illinois
Companies, have too great an influence in procrastinating that desireable and necessary event of compleating the Confederation, which we
hope the Wisdom, firmness, candor and Moderation of our Legislature
now in Session will remove every obstacle to[2]

We Could wish also and we think it a duty we owe to our Constituents to call their attention to a revision of our former instructions relative to the Navigation of the Missisipi—that, Should any overtures from
Spain be offerd which are advantageous to the United States, and
which might contribute not only to releive our present necessities, but
promise us peace and a firm establishment of our Independance, it
might not be considerd as an object that would counterbalance the distant prospect of a free Navigation of that River, with Stipulated ports
—which may perhaps under another form or at some more convenient
opportunity be obtaind from that Nation, in behalf of our Citizens
Settled on its Banks and Water. Having shewn the above to my Colleague Mr. Madison—he has thought it unnecessary to Join in that Part
of it relating to our Instructions on the subject of the Navigation of
the Missisipi.[3] I am Sorry to Say that notwithstanding the high Idea I
entertain of that Gentlemans good Sense, Judgment and Candor, I feel
myself, irresistably impelld by a Sense of my duty, to State a Matt[er]
& to communicate it through the Proper Channel which *may* eventually effect so greatly the Prosperity and even existence of the United
States at large—and feeling myself willing to receive the Censure of my
Constituents if I have done wrong, or their applause if I have done
Right in Suggesting to them so important a matter I am under the necessity (as to that matter) of standing alone in my opinion; which I
wd. not wish, should in the Minutest degree, be interpreted, as obtrud-
ing or dictating a measure however necessary I as an individual Rep-

resentative of the State may conceive a relaxation of our instructions on that head to be, nor do I conceive that any Member either of the Executive or Legislature of our State, who is acquainted with my wish to promote the Public good, and to conform to the Strict tenor of their instructions, can attribute my suggestion to any wish to swerve from them in my Vote in Congress, having pledged myself both in Principle and in promise Steadily to adhere to them on all occasions.[4] I have the Honor to be

Yr. Excellys Most obedt. & very H: Svt.

THEOK: BLAND

[1] See Morgan to Virginia Delegates, 16 November 1780, and their reply to Morgan, [20 November 1780]. As mentioned earlier, John Walker had been a delegate from Virginia in Congress, and was returning home.

[2] Above, Motion regarding the Western Lands, 6 September 1780, editorial note. The Vandalia Company, variously known as the Walpole Company and Grand Ohio Company, originated in 1769. Made up of prominent Pennsylvanians and Englishmen, it claimed a vast area, mainly in eastern Kentucky and present-day West Virginia. Two years earlier, a similar group, including Benjamin Franklin, had launched the Illinois Company with the hope of securing a firm title to much of the area which later became the state of Illinois. These speculations, as well as others unmentioned by Bland, disputed the validity of Virginia's title to land west and northwest of the Appalachians (Thomas P. Abernethy, *Western Lands and the American Revolution*, pp. 37–38, chaps. iii and viii).

[3] For JM's observations on the final paragraph of this letter, see JM to Jones, 25 November 1780. Bland and JM frequently voted on opposite sides of issues before Congress. Probably Bland shared his wife's dislike of JM. On 30 March 1781 she described him to Mrs. St. George Tucker as "a gloomy, stiff creature, they say he is clever in Congress, but out of it, he has nothing engaging or even bearable in his Manners—the most unsociable creature in Existance" (*Virginia Magazine of History and Biography*, XLIII [1935], 43). Bland, who had close family ties with the Lees, belonged to the Lee-Adams faction, with which JM often differed on matters of foreign and domestic policies (Charles Campbell, ed., *Bland Papers*, I, xiii–xiv, 149).

[4] In summary, Bland recommended that Jefferson ask the legislature of Virginia, then in session, to revise its instruction of 5 November 1779 which required the Virginia delegation in Congress to insist that Spain, in any treaty of alliance or commerce with the United States, acknowledge the right of Americans to a free use of the Mississippi (Jones to JM, 19 September, n. 4, and 2 October 1780, n. 9; Draft of Letter to Jay, 17 October 1780, nn. 11, 13, 14). The position of Bland, and of the many leaders in and outside of Congress who agreed with him, was a strong one. In view of the almost desperate economic and military outlook of the United States by November 1780, and especially of the states south of the Potomac River, the above stipulation of the Virginia legislature was not only unrealistic but worked to the injury of the common cause.

Many circumstances necessitated a change. (*a*) There was an alarming depreciation of currency and a scarcity of war materials. To replenish the latter and to bolster the former, aid in money and supplies from abroad, including Spain, was urgently needed. (*b*) There was the delay in the arrival from France of the "second division" of the French fleet and of increased financial subsidies or loans. (*c*) There was the widely held belief that France was laggard in these respects because the Americans, in spite of their plight, sought what Spain had no need to grant in exchange for a military alliance with the United States. (*d*) There was the success of the British army in the South, with the Georgia and South Carolina seaboards in its control, with North Carolina threatened, and with Virginia open to invasion from the sea. Military and naval aid from Spain, dispatched from Louisiana or the West Indies, might avert complete disaster in the South. (*e*) There was the strong rumor that the League of Armed Neutrality in Europe would seek to end the war on a basis of *uti possidetis*. If Great Britain should signify its willingness to accept this principle, and if Spain and perhaps even France were enticed by it, the patriot cause might collapse, and Georgia, South Carolina, and parts of the states to the north would again become English colonies. (*f*) Finally, since the free navigation of the Mississippi was of great interest mainly to the southern states, their sister states on the middle seaboard and New England might well be more active in dispatching military and other assistance against Cornwallis if the southern delegates in Congress would yield on the Mississippi issue and thereby remove what appeared to be a main impediment to help from Spain and additional help from France.

When Bland wrote, two recent occurrences in Congress had also strengthened his plea. On 18 November the Georgia delegation recommended an abandonment of the "ultimatum" of free navigation of the Mississippi, if Spain would sign a treaty of alliance granting the United States an annual financial subsidy or loan and guaranteeing not to make peace with Britain until the United States was ready to do so. Debate on these recommendations was delayed until 5 December 1780 (*Journals of the Continental Congress*, XVIII, 1070–72, 1121; for JM's connection with them, see JM to Jones, 25 November 1780). On 22 November, Congress agreed to a letter to be sent to King Louis XVI of France, describing the critical situation, mentioning the certainty that "the four southern states will now become a principal object of their [Britain's] hostilities," and asking a further loan of at least twenty-five million livres as "indispensably necessary for a vigorous prosecution of the war." Congress thereupon named James Duane, JM, and William C. Houston as a committee to draw up instructions to Franklin consonant with this letter to the king. The committee's draft, in Duane's hand and revealing no certain evidence that JM helped in its preparation, stressed the need for more warships and supplies, as well as more money, from France. Congress received the proposed instructions on 24 November and, after debating and amending them, agreed to them four days later. JM appears to have been absent from Congress at that time (*Journals of the Continental Congress*, XVIII, 1080–85, 1092, 1094, 1101–4; NA: PCC, No. 25, I, 371, 393, 395; below, Mathews to Greene, 27 November 1780, n. 2).

From Joseph Jones

RC (LC: Madison Papers). Jones's dating of this letter is so indistinct that it could be either the "24th" or "25th." References in his text to specific actions taken by the legislature on particular days make certain that he was writing on the 24th, even though JM acknowledged the letter as of 25 November.

RICHMOND 24th. Nov. 1780

DEAR SR.

I have yours of the 14th: and from my soul wish I could inform you we proceed with that vigor and despatch the urgency of the public wants require. The Bill for filling up the quota of our continental Troops has not yet been reported although we have been in a Com: upon it a fortnight. Such various opinions prevail as to the mode of raising them as well as the bounty to be given that I can hardly yet venture to say what will be the result. I think however we shall give a bounty in Negros to such Soldiers as will enlist for the War[,] the Negro not to be transfered but [or?] forthcoming if the soldier shall desert the Service[,] and in that case revert to the public to recruit another man in his room[.] If in thirty days men are not recruited by bounty for the War a draught to take place. It seems to be the prevailing opinion for three years though I expect this long period upon a draft will be opposed but I have my hopes it will be carryed for that time. This Bill will however go into the House Tomorrow or Monday.[1] we shall then take up Finance and I see clearly we shall totally defeat the scheme of the 18th. of March last by the large emissions the urgent and pressing demands of the State require and render unavoidable, I think at least 5 M. pounds.[2] almost the sole support and succour of the Southern department depend upon Virginia and perplexed and surrounded with diffi[culty] as we are there yet appears among people in general a disposit[ion] to make exertions to their utmost ability and I have my hope we shall accomplish a great proportion if not the whole required from us. methods are pursuing by the Executive[3] to obtain a good store of Beef and we have directed a Com. to go to North Carolina to concert with that Government the laying up a sufficiency of Pork as that article is rather scarce here but in much greater plenty there. The Executive will be armed with powers competent to drawing forth every resource and if we can but furnish money for transporta[tion] and other contingent charges, the great specific supplies that will be furnished will I hope keep matters in a way that will not let the army suffer for want of our assistence.[4] The Enemy have left us without leaving behind them as heretofore those marks of ravage and devastation that have but too generally attended their progress. all the unrigged vessels remain unhurt[—]no burnings and but little plundering and this when done was by the Tories in general and reprobated we are informed by Lessly & the Commodore as well as the principal officers of their army and Fleet. Surely this sudde[n] and

most extraordinary change in the behavior of the Enemy has meaning
which though we are yet at a loss to unfold will ere long be made
manifest.[5] We have no late account from the Southward[.] the last
from Gates Smallwood and Morgen speak of our Force being incon-
siderable and almost naked and frequently withot. provision. Genl.
Greene is gone forward leaving Baron Steuben here to arrange matters
with this State and then to follow him.[6] We have had a warm debate
in the House upon a Bill to explain and amend the act of the last Session for funding the New Bills of Credit of Congress under the scheme
of the 18th of March. The question agitated whr. those Bills as well as
the two million of state money issued last Session shod. be a tender in
payment of Debts and determined that they shod. be a legal tender.
H—n—y for the question & R. H. L. agt. it and both aided by their
auxiliaries took up two days or nearly in discussing the question. indeed we loose a great deal too much time in idle unnecessary debate.[7]
Mr. Blair was yesterday chosen to succeed Mr. Nicholas in the chen-
cery and Tomorrow we fill up the vacancy in the Genl. Court, wch.
I plainly see will be the lot of Mr. Fleming. I had thought of G—f—n
but found it was in vain to propose him[.][8] I expected somebody wod.
mention Mr James Henry but it has not been done. I believe that wod.
be also useless as you know the advantage a member has over an absent
person. I this day presented pet. for relief to Mr. Dunlap for his loss
but am very doubtfull whether it will be attended with success. I wish
to hear what he says abt. geting another apparetus or wher. he declines
the business altogether[.] I shod. be sorry he should do so as I am certain he wod. be very usefull to the State and will in the end find his
account in undertaking the Business.[9] Mrs. Jones I find is not yet well
of her ague and Fever wch. being of the third day will I fear continue
on her some time as it has already been her companion through the
Fall.[10] The extract of your Letter to the Govr. respecting supply of
money was laid before the House as well as Col. Blands quere for his
satisfaction upon a scruple respecting commerce. they are refd. to a
Com. and so are the Delegates accots. Mr. M. S.'s account lodged in
the auditors office occasions speculation. You would do well if not
already done to transmit a state of the accounts from the Book and in
particular M. S.s as it is said it was never examined according to custom by the Delegates. this last upon second thought shod. not come
alone[.] it will appear pointed[.] it wod. be better to get the whole
transcribed by some person and pay him charging the State. I shall
endeavour if the matter comes on before I leave Richmond to get the
Delegates Supply of money fixed upon some sure and certain fund that

they may no longer be exposed to the difficult[ies] lately experienced.[11] R. H. Lee talks of lessening the number to save the expence.[12] Compliments to the Gent. of our Delegation and believe me

    Yr. aff Friend & Sert.

Jos: Jones

[1] See Jones to JM, 18 November 1780, n. 6. Someone, but probably not Jones and possibly not JM, drew on the manuscript a pencil line under "bounty in Negros to such Soldiers" and a vertical mark in the left-hand margin bordering the lines of text running from "we shall give" to "not recruited by bounty for the."

[2] *Ibid.*, n. 7.

[3] In the manner mentioned in n. 1, "the sole" is underscored and a marginal mark gives emphasis to the lines of text beginning "support and succour" and ending "pursuing by the Executive."

[4] *Ibid.*, n. 8. A marginal line marks the text from "be armed with powers" to "and devastation that."

[5] Jameson to JM, 4 November, n. 4, and 18 November 1780, n. 10. The "Commodore" was George Gayton.

[6] See Jones to JM, 18 November 1780, n. 2. Jones probably refers to letters received by Governor Jefferson from Brigadier Generals Edward Stevens and Daniel Morgan and Major General Horatio Gates—this last letter inclosing a dispatch to him from Major General William Smallwood (1732–1792) of Maryland (Boyd, *Papers of Jefferson*, IV, 103, 112–13, 129). These letters, forwarded by Jefferson, were read in Congress on 27 November, before JM could have received the present letter from Jones (*Journals of the Continental Congress*, XVIII, 1095).

[7] See Jones to JM, 18 November 1780, n. 7. The abbreviations stand for Patrick Henry and Richard Henry Lee. The words in the manuscript beginning "a tender in payment" and ending "idle unnecessary" are underlined and a marginal, vertical line borders most of this same passage.

[8] The persons mentioned in these sentences were John Blair, Robert Carter Nicholas (1728–1780), and William Fleming (1736–1824), who, as Jones predicted, became a judge of the General Court on 28 November (*Journal of the House of Delegates*, October 1780, p. 31), and Cyrus Griffin.

[9] See Jefferson to Virginia Delegates, 31 August 1780, n. 3; Jameson to JM, 4 November 1780, n. 6; *Journal of the House of Delegates*, October 1780, pp. 28, 49–50.

[10] See Jones to JM, 2, 17, and 24 October 1780.

[11] See Virginia Delegates to Jefferson, 5 November 1780, n. 1. On 19 December 1780, when the Virginia House of Delegates resolved that most of the congressional delegates' accounts were "fairly stated and fully reasonable," it refused to approve those of Cyrus Griffin and Meriwether Smith unless each man justified the expenses for which he claimed reimbursement from the state (*Journal of the House of Delegates*, October 1780, p. 58). After Bland directed his now vague "quere" to Jefferson, the latter sent it along to Speaker Benjamin Harrison on 17 November with a covering note mentioning Bland's "difficulty . . . in reconciling his qualification as a delegate [in Congress] to the peculiar channel into which he had previously turned his private fortune" (Boyd, *Papers of Jefferson*, IV, 121). Bland probably was worried by a legislative act of 1779, requiring each delegate to take oath that he was engaging in no foreign or domestic trading other than in commodities of his "own growth or manufacture" (Hening, *Statutes*, X, 113). On 19 December 1780, the House of Delegates evidently accepted a committee's

interpretation of this statute to the effect that activities of the sort engaged in by Bland were not banned by it (*Journal of the House of Delegates*, October 1780, p. 58).

[12] By an act of the legislature in 1779, the number of delegates in Congress from Virginia was reduced from a maximum of seven to a maximum of five, "any one of which, or a majority of those present, if more than one, to give the vote of the commonwealth" (Hening, *Statutes*, IX, 388–89; X, 74–75, 163). Lee failed in his effort to reduce this maximum. In the manuscript this sentence about Lee is underscored, as is also "Gent." in the concluding sentence.

From David Jameson

RC (LC: Rives Collection of Madison Papers).

RICHMOND Nov 25th. 1780

DR SIR

I duely recd. your favour of the 14t. and am much obliged to you for forwarding my letters to my Nephew.[1] I have desired him to trouble you with his letters to me and must beg the favour of you to send them as opportunities may offer—I suppose it will not be right to frank them by Post It appears by the proceedings of a Court Martial held in Pittsylva. many were privy to and aiding in the intended insurrectn. in that County, but they were chiefly if not altogether composed of the lower rank of the people. three of them by the name of Lay, Billings & Lawless (who were the ringleaders of those tryed) were adjudged guilty of Treason, but there was error in the proceedings & they are to have another trial.[2] I much dislike the mode of trial by Ct. Martial & wish to see that only in use wch. the Constitution points out. Several persons of more note in Pittsylva. were mentd. as promoters of the insurrection And indeed in all the Counties where insurgents have appeared, Men of note have been named as abettors, but on examination few have incurred censure—*some* have been strongly suspected, but not sufficient proof The 22d. the Enemy's Ships left Hampton Road and stood down the Bay We suppose they mean to go to So. Carolina, but time must discover their destination[3] I am with great esteem

Dr Sir Yr. Mo hb Servt

DAVID JAMESON

this by the Express

---

[1] JM's letter of 14 November to Jameson is lost, but its content probably approximated what JM wrote on the same day to Jones and Pendleton (*q.v.*). Jameson's "nephew" was most likely Lieutenant Colonel John Jameson (1757–

1810) of the 2d Continental Dragoons, who was with Washington's army in northern New Jersey. He had been a member of the county's Committee of Safety in 1775 and was county clerk of Culpeper County for many years (Ephraim Orcutt Jameson, *The Jamesons in America* . . . [Boston, 1901], p. 141).

[2] See Jefferson to Virginia Delegates, 27 October 1780, n. 2. No source known to the editors identifies "Lay, Billings & Lawless," although the last two bore family names well known in Pittsylvania County (Maud C. Clement, *History of Pittsylvania County*, pp. 277, 284). They probably took advantage of the "act for granting pardon to certain offenders," adopted by the Virginia legislature on 11 December 1780 (Hening, *Statutes*, X, 324–26).

[3] See Jameson to JM, 4 November, n. 3, and 18 November 1780, n. 10.

To Joseph Jones

RC (LC: Madison Papers). Probably at the time that JM recovered this letter from Jones's nephew, James Monroe (JM to Jones, 19 September 1780, headnote), he wrote on the last page, parallel to its right hand margin, "Georgia & S. C.—uti possidetis." On 8 January 1822 JM sent a copy of the letter, together with copies of other letters relating to the same issue, to Hezekiah Niles, who published them in the *Niles Weekly Register* (Baltimore), XXI, 347–49 (26 January 1822); hereafter cited as *Niles Register*.

PHILADA. Novr. 25th. 1780

DEAR SIR

I informed you some time ago that the instructions to Mr. Jay had passed Congress in a form which was entirely to my mind. I since informed you that a Committee was preparing a letter to him explanatory of the principles & objects of the instructions. This letter also passed in a form equally satisfactory.[1] I did not suppose that any thing further would be done on the subject, at least till further intelligence should arrive from Mr. Jay. It now appears that I was mistaken. The Delegates from Georgia & South Carolina, apprehensive that a *Uti possidetis* may be obtruded on the belligerent powers by the armed neutrality in Europe and hoping that the accession of Spain to the Alliance will give greater concert & success to the military operations that may be pursued for the recovery of these States, and likewise add weight to the means that may be used for obviating a *Uti possidetis*, have moved for a reconsideration of the Instructions in order to empower Mr. Jay in case of necessity to yield to the claims of Spain on condition of her guarantieng our independence and affording us a handsome subsidy. The expediency of such a motion is further urged from the dangerous negociations now on foot by British Emissaries for detaching Spain from the war.[2] Wednesday last was assigned for the consideration of this motion and it has continued the order of the day ever since without being taken up. What the fate of it will be I do not predict; but whatever its own fate may [be] it must do mischief in its operation. It will not probably be concealed that such a motion has been made & supported, and the weight which our demands would derive from unanimity & decision must be lost. I flatter myself however that Congress will see the impropriety of sacrificing the acknowledged limits and claims of any State without the express concurrence of such State.[3] Obsticles enough will be thrown in the way of peace, if [it] is to be bid for at the expence of particular members of the Union. The Eastern States must on the first suggestion take the alarm for their fisheries. If they will not support other States in their rights, they cannot expect to be supported themselves when[4] theirs come into question.

In this important business, which so deeply affects the claims & interests of Virginia & which I know she has so much at heart, I have not the satisfaction to harmonise in Sentiment with my Colleague. He has embraced an opinion that we have no just claim to the subject in controversy between us & Spain, and that it is the interest of Virginia not to adhere to it. Under this impression he drew up a letter to the Executive to be communicated to the Legislature, stating in general the difficulty Congress might be under, & calling their attention to a revision of their instructions to their Delegates on the subject.[5] I was obliged to object to such a step, and in order to prevent it observed that the instructions were given by the Legislature of Virga. on mature consideration of the case, & on a supposition that Spain would make the demands she has done, that n[o] other event has occurred to change the mind of our Constituents but the armed neutrality in Europe & the successes of the Enemy to the Southward which are as well known to them as to ourselves, that we might every moment expect a third delegate here,[6] who would either adjust or decide the difference in opinion between us, and that whatever went from the Delegation would then go in its proper form & have its proper effect, that if the instructions from Virga.[7] were to be revi[sed] and their ultimatum reduced, it could not be concealed in so populou[s] an Assembly, and every thing which our Minister should be authorised to yield would be insisted on, that Mr. Jay's last despatches encouraged us to expect that Spain would not be inflexible if we wer[e] so, that [we] might every day expect to have more satisfactory information from him.[8] that finally if it should be thought expedient to listen to the pretensions of Spain, it would be best before we took any decisive step in the matter to take the Counsel of those who best know the interests & have the greatest influence on the opinions of our Constituents, that as you were both a member of Congress & of the Legislature & were now with the latter, you would be an unexceptionable medium for effecting this, and that I would write to you for the purpose, by the first safe conveyance.

These objections had not the weight with my Colleague which they had with me. He adhered to his first determination & has I believe sent the letter above mentioned by Mr. Walker who will I suppose soon forward it to the Governour.[9] You will readily conceive the embarrassments this affair must have cost me. All I have to ask of you is that if my refusing to concur with my Colleague in recommending to the legislature a revision of their instructions should be misconstrued by any,[10] you will be so good as to place it in its true light, and if you agree with me as to[11] the danger of giving express power to concede, or the inexpediency of conceding at all, that you will consult with gentlemen of the above description and acquaint me with the result.

I need not observe to you that the alarms with respect to the inflexibility of Spain in her demands, the progress of British intrigues at Madrid and the danger of a Uti possidetis, may with no small probability be regarded as artifices for securing her objects[12] on the Mississippi. Mr. Adams in a late letter from Amsterdam, a copy of which has been enclosed to the Governor[,] supposes that the pretended success of the British emissaries at Madrid is nothing but a ministerial finesse to facilitate the loans and keep up the spirits of the people.[13]

This will be conveyed by Col. Grayson,[14] who has promised to deliver it himself, or if any thing unforeseen should prevent his going to Richmond, to put it into such hands as will equally ensure its safe delivery.

I am Dr. Sr. Yrs. Sincerely

J. MADISON JUNR.[15]

---

[1] See Jones to JM, 2 October 1780, n. 9; JM to Jones, 10 October 1780, n. 1; Draft of Letter to John Jay, 17 October 1780; Bland to Jefferson, 22 November 1780, n. 4. Judging from the brackets which inclose the entire text, except for the place and date, the salutation, and the complimentary close, JM late in his life, or one of his family, selected this letter for publication.

[2] William Carmichael's letter of 17 July 1780 from Madrid, telling of the efforts of a British agent at the Court of Spain, was read in Congress on 16 October (Wharton, *Revolutionary Diplomatic Correspondence*, III, 865–66; *Journals of the Continental Congress*, XVIII, 931). On 20 November, Congress listened to a letter of 23 August from John Adams, written in Amsterdam, making light of the danger

that Britain could entice Spain to conclude a separate peace (*ibid.,* XVIII, 1072; Wharton, *Revolutionary Diplomatic Correspondence,* IV, 41–42).

3 JM moved that Congress await instructions of the Virginia legislature to its delegates before giving further consideration to the Georgia proposal that John Jay's instructions, binding him to insist upon the free navigation of the Mississippi River in his negotiations for a treaty with Spain, be modified (below, 8 December 1780).

4 Several heavily deleted words intervene between "themselves" and "when" in the manuscript. They seem to be "in their claims." If JM did not make this and the other alterations noted below, before he mailed the letter to Jones, he inserted them at least prior to its appearance in the *Niles Register* in 1822.

5 See Bland to Jefferson, 22 November 1780.

6 JM probably meant James Henry or Meriwether Smith, since he did not expect Jones to return until after the Assembly of Virginia had adjourned.

7 Following "Virga.," JM wrote and then crossed out "were too rigid."

8 Probably JM refers to the long dispatch of Jay on 26 May, read in part to Congress on 21 August and referred to a committee with Jones as its chairman until he left for Virginia about two weeks later (*Journals of the Continental Congress,* XVII, 754; Wharton, *Revolutionary Diplomatic Correspondence,* III, 707–34). In it, Jay commented that "if Congress remains firm, as I have no reason to doubt, respecting the Mississippi, I think Spain will finally be content with equitable regulations, and I wish to know whether Congress would consider any regulations necessary to prevent contraband as inconsistent with their ideas of free navigation" (*ibid.,* III, 725).

9 See Bland to Jefferson, 22 November 1780, n. 1. The governor transmitted this letter to the House of Delegates on 5 December (*Journal of the House of Delegates,* October 1780, p. 38; Virginia Delegates to Jefferson, 13 December 1780).

10 The words after "concur" up to and including "any" are interline replacements by JM of a passage, about two lines long, which he crossed out so heavily that it cannot be read.

11 Between "me" and "as to" are about eight illegibly deleted words.

12 Following "her" and preceding "objects" in the original manuscript is an expunged passage which appears to have been "objects and aims against the United States."

13 This sentence closely follows the opening one of John Adams' letter of 23 August, mentioned in n. 2, above.

14 On 20 November, Congress granted William Grayson (*ca.* 1736–1790), then one of the commissioners of the Board of War in Philadelphia, a month's leave of absence to enable him to visit his family in Virginia (*Journals of the Continental Congress,* XVIII, 1072). Grayson had been colonel of a continental line regiment. He became a delegate in Congress from Virginia, 1785–1787, and one of that state's first United States senators, 1789–1790.

15 For the rest of his life, JM continued to be sensitive about his participation, and that of his state, in the Mississippi-navigation issue in the 1780's. In line with this concern, he took pains to set the record straight as often as he deemed that a historian or other commentator had distorted it. Thus, when his attention was called to David Ramsay's assertion in his *The History of the American Revolution* (2 vols.; Philadelphia, 1789), II, 300–301, that the relinquishment by Congress in February 1781 of its demand that Spain acknowledge the United States' right of free navigation had come as a result of Virginia's recommendation, JM made copies of three of his letters written on the subject late in 1780 and sent them, as mentioned in the above headnote, to Hezekiah Niles. In his covering letter of 8 January 1822 (*Niles Register,* XXI, 347), he emphasized that the Georgia and South Carolina delegates

had taken the initiative in pressing for a revision of John Jay's instructions, that JM had opposed the demand, and that on 8 December 1780, when Congress was at the point of acceding to it, he effected a postponement of a vote upon it until the Virginia delegates could learn the will of their state legislature. Only after that body had decided to follow Georgia's and South Carolina's recommendations did JM reluctantly take the lead in Congress to amend Jay's instructions on the navigation of the Mississippi (Instruction to Virginia Delegates, 2 January 1781; *Journals of the Continental Congress*, XX, 551–55; Burnett, *Letters*, V, 457, n. 3). In April 1827 JM went carefully over the matter again in a conversation with Jared Sparks at Montpelier (Herbert B. Adams, *The Life and Writings of Jared Sparks* [2 vols.; Boston, 1893], II, 34–35).

John Mathews, for Committee of Congress, to Nathanael Greene

RC (William L. Clements Library, University of Michigan).

EDITORIAL NOTE

On 23 October 1780 Congress added JM and William Sharpe to the standing committee, created 8 July 1779 "to correspond with the commanding officer of the southern department," and prescribed that the committee should thereafter "keep a journal of their proceedings and correspondence" (*Journals of the Continental Congress*, IV, 807; XVIII, 963). If the committee obeyed this injunction, its journal has apparently been lost. Since most matters relating to General Gates's (after early December 1780, General Greene's) army were referred to other committees, Congress intended that this particular committee should be a secretarial rather than a policy-recommending group, largely limited in its function to relaying relevant actions by Congress to the commander of the troops in the South. When JM and Sharpe joined the committee, the only other member was the chairman, John Mathews (1744–1802) of South Carolina.

The letters of Mathews to General Greene, preserved among the Greene papers in the William L. Clements Library, University of Michigan, and published in Burnett, *Letters*, Vols. V and VI, rarely make clear whether Mathews was writing as the committee's chairman or on his own initiative. How long JM served actively on the committee is unknown. He made no mention of it in his papers. The present letter is apparently the earliest extant dispatch of the committee following JM's appointment as a member. Although the address sheet is missing, the letter is among General Greene's papers and was almost certainly directed to him.

PHILADELPHIA Novr. 27th: 1780

SIR

Inclosed is an extract of a letter of the 23d of August last lately received from Mr. John Adams. As the intelligence relates particularly to your department, we thought it necessary to be forwarded to you.[1] This is all the foreign intelligence, worth transmitting you. As to domestic, we recollect none.

No effectual means have as yet been taken for supply[i]ng the southern army with cloathing. The Committee to whom your letter (before you left Philadelphia) was refered have made no report yet.[2] Your letter of the 19th inst. is refered to another committee,[3] the result, we will give you the earliest information of.

We are sir with sincere Esteem & regard yr. most Obedt Servts. By Orders of the Committee

JNO. MATHEWS Chairman

[1] In John Adams' letter of 23 August 1780 (Wharton, *Revolutionary Diplomatic Correspondence*, IV, 41–42) the two sentences of special interest to General Greene were: "The truth is, according to my information, that orders are already sent out by the British cabinet to prosecute the war with vigor in North Carolina and Virginia the ensuing fall, winter, and spring. General Prevost is about to sail with some frigates to aid their operations on Cape Fear River." This word about Prevost was in error (JM to Jones, 21 November, n. 15). The committee (John Mathews, chairman), to which Congress on 20 November referred Adams' letter, included among its recommended actions that Washington should take "the Command of the Southern army in person." Congress tabled the committee's report (*Journals of the Continental Congress*, XVIII, 1072, 1078), and Mathews apparently did not inclose a copy of it in the above letter to Greene.

[2] Greene left Philadelphia on 3 November. Mathews most likely refers to Greene's letter of 1 November, calling the attention of Congress to the "impossibility of employing an army to advantage in winter operations without their being clothed" (NA: PCC, No. 155, I, 455). On the same day, JM and most of the other delegates, except those of Massachusetts, agreed to "cause bills of exchange to be drawn upon the Minister of these United States at the Court of Versailles, at 90 days sight, to a sufficient amount to pay for 5000 suits of cloaths for the use of the southern army; provided the same can be obtained upon reasonable terms." Congress thereupon appointed a committee "to enquire upon what terms a contract can be made for the purpose above mentioned" (*Journals of the Continental Congress*, XVIII, 999–1000). This committee had not reported when Mathews wrote his letter, and apparently it never reported. On the other hand, the dire need for clothing from France was stressed in the instructions of 28 November to Franklin, mentioned earlier (above, Bland to Jefferson, 22 November 1780, n. 4), and in those of 23 December to Colonel John Laurens, whom Congress dispatched to France on a special mission to expedite supplies. He left too late, of course, to remedy the winter's need. The Board of War, by letter of 23 December to Congress, echoed Greene's words of eight weeks before by calling attention to the "shocking situation of the Southern troops, and indeed of the whole army on the score of cloathing." Four days later, Congress authorized the board to purchase woolen cloth and blankets (*Journals of the Continental Congress*, XVIII, 1101–4, 1178, 1184–88, 1199).

[3] Two letters from Greene, both of 19 November, were read in Congress on the date of Mathews' letter and referred to a committee comprising Ezekiel Cornell (R.I.), Bland, and Mathews (*ibid.*, XVIII, 1095). Once again, Greene pointed out his desperate shortage of clothing and wagons.

From Edmund Pendleton

Tr (LC: Force Transcripts).

VIRGA Novr 27th 1780

DR SIR:

My last Account of the Enemy was the 18th. when they were all embarked, but whether with a design to leave the State or to make an impression on some other part of it was doubtful. There was something Mysterious in their leaving their Slaves on shore & some Captur'd Vessels in the harbour at Portsmouth, & indicated their having designs of further Hostility—unless they had not room for the Slaves, Nor hands to spare to man the Vessels. this uncertainty & a report of some deserters that they meant to come up James River, induced Genl Muhlenburg to move his camp higher up the River to Watch their Motions. I expect however that the Post to day will bring us an Account of their having left us. There was no truth in the story of a battle I mentioned in my last, but I believe it was true that a clever stroke of that sort, was prevented by some dispute between two officers about rank, my friend there dont name them, but report says it was Gibson & Josiah Parker.[1]

Our last Accounts from the Southward are that Ld Cornwallis being surprised at a Tory's house at dinner, Rode off thro' a hot fire of the Militia & went off immediately in a litter to Charles Town said by deserters to be Mortally wounded. That his Army was surrounded by different parties of ours all of both very hungry, except Sumpter's party who were foremost & had the picking of the Provisions. That Tarlton's horse had made a Charge upon Sumpter in his Camp, but found him so well prepared that he was glad to scamper off as quickly as his lean Cavalry could do, leaving ten killed and twenty prisoners.[2] I suppose he hoped for another surprise.

I am told the Assembly are raising a fund of Negroes & Plate as a means of recruiting our Army for the War according to your Requisition on that head, but mean to contravene your Wishes on the subject of money, intending I hear a large New Emission & to make that as well as what was emitted under the Act of last Session, and all Certificates, payable for taxes of the next year, which will of course leave so much of the old money in Circulation & stop a proportion of the New from coming forth, & so retard, if not defeat the purpose of Congress upon that great subject. I take this only from report & it may be misrepresented; or if such be the present opinion as they have yet a very thin House, it may change in the progress of laws framed on the sub-

208

ject, which is a deep & delicate one & may Heaven give them Wisdom to discover what is best & I doubt not their Integrity in adopting it.[3] I don't hear they have proceeded yet to any Elections of a Chancellor or Members to Congress. I suppose they wait to be fuller.[4] I have a horid pen & can't see to mend it, so will only add that I am

Yours Affectionately

EDMD PENDLETON

[1] See Jameson to JM, 18 November 1780, n. 10; Jones to JM, 5 November, n. 4, and 18 November 1780, n. 4.

[2] To have Cornwallis surprised at dinner was apparently a favorite item of idle gossip (Pendleton to JM, 30 October 1780). In fact, Cornwallis had recently recovered from illness and was safe at his headquarters at Winnsboro, S.C. The sentence about Lieutenant Colonel Tarleton and General Sumter may intermix two actions. On 9 November, the latter repulsed a British force under Major James Wemyss at Fish Dam Ford on the Broad River in South Carolina (*Journals of the Continental Congress*, XVIII, 1122). Eleven days later in a heavier action at Blackstock's Plantation, near the Tiger River in the same state, Sumter fought off an attack by Tarleton's troops with considerable loss on both sides. For Cornwallis' letter of 3 December 1780 to General Clinton, describing these engagements, see Benjamin F. Stevens, ed., *The Campaign in Virginia*, I, 302–9. Christopher Ward, in *War of the Revolution*, II, 746–47, tempers the pro-British bias of Cornwallis' account. See also JM to Pendleton, 19 December 1780, n. 3.

[3] See Jones to JM, 18 November 1780, nn. 6 and 7.

[4] See Jones to JM, 24 November 1780, n. 8.

To Joseph Jones

RC (LC: Madison Papers).

PHILADA. Novr. 28th. 1780

DR. SIR

Yrs. of the 18th. came yesterday. I am glad to find the legislature persist in their resolution to recruit their line of the army for the war, though without deciding on the expediency of the mode under their consideration, would it not be as well to liberate and make soldiers at once of the blacks themselves as to make them instruments for enlisting white Soldiers? It wd. certainly be more consonant to the principles of liberty which ought never to be lost sight of in a contest for liberty, and with white officers & a majority of white soldrs. no imaginable danger could be feared from themselves, as there certainly could be none from the effect of the example on those who should remain in bondage: experience having shown that a freedman immediately loses all attachment & sympathy with his former fellow slaves.[1]

I informed you in my last that I had engaged Pleasants' house for you. Pemberton would come to no agreement on the subject.[2] I have received the £2000 your share of the draught on Meade & Compy. and the residue of the draught has all been paid. I will endeavor to send you the Journals by the first opportunity. They are too heavy to go by post. I wrote to you too [two] days ago by Col. Grayson on the subject of the Mis—pi. Mr. Walker set out a few days ago, accompanied by Mr. Kinlock, who is soon to be in a very near relation to him. The Books of Accts are on the way.[3] We have enclosed to the Govr. a copy of an Act of the Legislature of Connecticut ceding some of their territorial claim to the United States, which he will no doubt communicate to the Assembly. They reserve the jurisdiction to them selves, and clog the cession with some other conditions which greatly depreciate it, and are the more extraordinary as their title to the land is so controvertible a one.[4]

The evacuation of Portsmouth was received with much satisfaction, but a story from Baltimore that it was a manoeuvre & ended in the Enemy's running up Nansemond and entrapping our army below although exceedingly improbable has thrown us into an uneasy suspence.[5] By accounts from the W. Indies there has been in the Windwd. Islands one of the most violent & desolating hurricanes ever known. The British Islands have been laid almost entirely waste, and most of their shipping with their crews lost. Such an event with the interception of the destined supply of provision by the Combined fleets in Europe, cannot fail to bring on great distress if not a general famine. The French islands have also suffered severely.[6]

The Association of the Merchants for fixing the depreciation seems likely to prove a salutary measure. it reduced it from 90 & 100 to 75 at once which is its present current rate; although it is observed that many of the retailers elude the force of it by raising the price in hard money.[7]

I am Dr Sir Yr. Affect F

J. MADISON JUNR.

[1] See Jones to JM, 18 and 24 November 1780. This appears to be JM's earliest extant statement about Negro slavery. By inclosing in brackets this paragraph, the last two sentences of the next one, and the final paragraph, JM meant to designate them for publication.

[2] See JM to Jones, 21 November 1780.

[3] All the matters in this paragraph to this point were touched upon by Jones in his 9 October and 18 November letters to JM (q.v.). "Kinlock" was Francis Kinloch (1755–1826), a delegate in Congress from South Carolina. On 22 February 1781 he married John Walker's daughter Mildred (H. D. Bull, "Kinloch of South Carolina," *South Carolina Historical and Genealogical Magazine*, XLVI [1945], 65–67).

[4] The Virginia delegates' letter to Jefferson, inclosing a copy of Connecticut's

land-cession proposal, has not been found; nor is any reference made to the matter in the journal of the October session of the House of Delegates. In October 1780 the legislature of Connecticut offered to cede to the United States all of its ungranted territory lying west of the so-called Susquehanna Company Purchase within the bounds of Pennsylvania, as defined by the Connecticut charter. Tacitly included in the offer was a transfer by Connecticut of its acrimonious boundary dispute with Pennsylvania to the United States. This circumstance and also the fact that the issue could hardly be isolated from the much larger problems of western land cessions and the Vermont lands probably explain why Connecticut's offer was not formally laid before Congress until 31 January 1781 (above, Motion regarding the Western Lands, 6 September 1780, editorial note; Resolutions respecting Vermont Lands, 16 September 1780, editorial note; *Journals of the Continental Congress*, XIX, 99–100).

⁵ See Jameson to JM, 4 November, n. 3, and 18 November 1780, n. 10.

⁶ See JM to Pendleton, 7 November 1780, n. 7. Hurricanes devastated many of the islands between 3 and 16 October. For contemporary descriptions of the destruction, see *Pennsylvania Packet* (Philadelphia), 5, 6, and 23 December 1780, and J. Dodsley's *Annual Register . . . for 1780*, pp. 292–98.

⁷ See JM to Jones, 21 November 1780. On that day a group of Philadelphia businessmen under the chairmanship of John Bayard, speaker of the Assembly, resolved to maintain 75 to 1 as the commercial exchange rate between continental currency and hard money and to brand as a "disaffected and dangerous person" anyone who insisted on a higher premium for specie (*Pennsylvania Packet*, 21 November and 11 December 1780). Some critics, however, believed that, but for the protests of the delegates to Congress and of the Pennsylvania Assembly, these same merchants would at once have "Doubled the Specie prices of their Articles" (*Pennsylvania Journal* [Philadelphia], 22 November 1780; Burnett, *Letters*, V, 473).

From Philip Mazzei

RC (LC: Madison Papers). The cover sheet is addressed to "Honble: James [Mad]ison Esqre. Member of C[o]ngress from Virginia." Below the address are several unintelligible words and also "Nantes March 20. 1781 Received & forwarded by Sir Your very obt sr[?]. Jona. Williams Jr." Along the opposite margin appears "p[er] the Luzerne Capt Bell. for Philadelphia Q [?]. D. C." Captain Thomas Bell commanded this privateer owned by Robert Morris. The bracketed words near the end of the letter were taken from the Italian transcription in Richard Cecil Garlick, Jr., *Philip Mazzei, Friend of Jefferson: His Life and Letters* (Baltimore, 1933), pp. 70–71.

pma: copia
FIRENZE 30 9bre 1780.

CARMO: AMICO,

Vi scrivo in lingua toscana perchè è più facile per me, e sarà una lezione per voi; e preferisco lo stil familiare allo scrivere in terza persona affinchè vi riesca più intelligibile, conoscendovi abbastanza filosofo

per disprezzare l'inutile cirimoniale. Ò inteso ultimamente da una breve
lettera dl. Bellini dei 4 Giugno anno corrente (l'unica da me ricevuta
d'America dopo la mia partenza) che voi siete in Congresso. L'avevo
inteso anche in Nantes dal giovanetto Little-Page, ma non in modo da
esserne sicuro. Lo credevo per altro, e ne ò parlato molte volte con Mr.
John Adams in Parigi, il quale sospirava sempre *for good members
from Virginia* e desidera ardentemente di conoscervi non avendovi
conosciuto avanti neppur per fama a motivo d[e]lla vostra giovinezza.
Ò piacere che voi siate in Congresso per la giustizia che la [Pa]tria à
reso al vostro merito e molto più per il vantaggio che la Causa comune
può ricevere dalla saviezza dei vostri consigli; ma ne compiango la
perdita nel Consiglio di Stato in Virginia. In questo vi dirò ingenua-
mente che ci contribuisce molto il mio amor proprio. La politica, le
leggi di cui rispetto sommamente trattandosi di cose altrui, e special-
mente d'affari pubblici, non voglio che entri ne'miei propri. Quando si
tratta di me stesso intendo che la Sincerità (quel mio Nume prediletto)
trionfi su tutte le altre mie qualità buone, o cattive. V[i] ripeto dunque
che il mio amor proprio contribuisce molto a farmi desiderar[e] che
voi foste tuttavia nel nostro Consiglio di Sta[to, pe]rchè mi lusingo che
avreste f[at]to i vostri sforzi per impedir ch'io fos[si stato] discreta-
mente e indecentemente negletto. Detto anche dall'istesso B[ellini, se]
per maggiore sventura Mr. Page abbia renunziato. Dio sa di che razza
[di] gente sarà ora composto il Consiglio; e il povero Governatore non
solo non avrà forse il potere di fare adottare le massime opportune, ma
riguardo a me sarà anche sospettato di parzialità. Mi ricordo quando
voi con espressioni amichevoli e patetiche mi parlavate del trionfo che
avrebbero avuto i miei nemici, e delle crudeli mortificazioni che
avrebbero sofferto gli amici, che si erano resi in certo modo responsabili
della mia condotta, se questa non avesse corrisposto alla loro aspettativa.
La memoria di ciò serve ad inasprire non poco il mio giusto risenti-
mento, vedendomi, o [per] negligenza imperdonabile; o per malignità
la più scellerata, costituito in una totale inazione, mentre con sommo
mio onore, e consolazione dei miei cari amici avrei potuto rendere
importantissimi servigi alla Patria nel tempo del maggior bisogno. Io
non so ormai quali altre scuse potere addur qua per non aver dopo tanto
tempo ricevute nuove Commissioni, o almeno la copia delle vecchie, e
neppure una risposta ad alcuna delle mie tante lettere, molte delle quali
si sa essere arrivate, e per vari bastimenti, mandandone 4 copie d'ognuna.
Non ardisco di scrivere tutti i dubbi che mi vengono in [m]ente, ma
non vi tacerò che, se il giusto riguardo, che io devo al mio propr[io
dec]oro e alla sensibilità dei miei cari Amici in Virginia, mi ridurrà mai

a [g]iustificare al Mondo la mia condotta, farà probabilmente più strepito di quel che certi vili e pusillanimi soggetti forse s'immaginano. Le testimon[ian]ze del mio zelo non solo per le incombenze a me confidate, ma per promuovere tutto ciò che puo esser'utile alla nostra gloriosissima Causa ovunque io sono stato, saranno di gran peso non sol[o] per natura loro, come per i Personagi che le faranno. Se mai però arrivasse questa per me infelice necessità farei tutti i miei sforzi per salvare il pubblico carattere, quantunque le mie offese venisser[o] da chi lo rappresenta. Vi ricorderete quanto io mi raccomandai di esser fornito d'aneddoti onorevoli per [esser]e continovamente ragguagli[a]to di tutto ciò che passa d'essenziale. Io non ò potuto neppure arrivare a sapere su che piede il Pubblico prenda denaro a cambio dopo l'ultima riforma della nostra moneta corrente, per il che siamo restati privi di molte cose utilissime e necessarie, che vari avventurieri ci avrebbero mandate. [Se] i carichi non son molto ricchi non possono sopportare le gravi spese, da ciò ne segne che gli avventurieri non potrebbe[ro coi] medesimi [va]scelli riport[are] in[dieto] che una piastre por[zione] [torn] Come è dunque sperabile che vogliano correre tanti risc[hi se n]on posso dir loro in qual maniera potrebbero impiegare il lor denaro presso di noi? Se volete veder chiaramente quanto io abbia ragion di lagnarmi, bisogna che vi diate l'inco[m]modo di leggere con ordine cronologico le 22 lettere che ò scritto al nostro Governo, ed avrei piacere che vedeste anche la lettera privata, che ò scritto in questa lingua al nostro Governatore. Spero che di tutte ne verrà alm[e]no una copia a salvamento: ne mando 3 delle private, e 4 delle pubbliche. Da queste, facendone uno spoglio, mi lusingo che potreste ricavar molte cose, che vi sarebbero di qualche uso in Congresso. Di qua è difficile ch'io possa darvi nuove interessanti, che non riceviate più presto da altre parti. Vi avverto per vostra regola, acciò ne facciate uso come giudi[c]ate proprio, che in Genova inclinerebbero a prestare il lor denaro al Congresso piuttosto che a un solo Stato, e che qua per quanto mi pare avrebbe molto peso la mia opinione. [in unintelligible cipher] Dalle mie lettere al Governo si vede in che miserabile stato devono esse[re l]e mie finanze, ma potete anche immaginarvelo dal sentire che non ò [re]cevuto finora neppure una lettera. Non mancate di ragguagliarmi dei nostri affari, e indirizzate le lettere a Mr. Mark Lynch Mercht. in Nantes, o a Mr. Adams. Mr. Page vi avrà notificata la cagione, per cui non vi ò scritto prima. Conservat[em]i la vostra carissima amicizia, e credetemi colla maggiore stima,

Vostro Umismo: Servo e Amico Vero

FILIPPO MAZZEI

first copy

FLORENCE 30 November 1780

MY VERY DEAR FRIEND

I am writing in tuscan because it is easier for me and it will be a lesson for you; and I prefer the familiar style to the third person so that I might be more intelligible to you, knowing you to be enough of a philosopher to despise useless ceremony. I have learned recently through a brief letter from Bellini[1] of 4 June this year (the only one I have received from America since my departure[2]) that you are in Congress. I had also heard this in Nantes from young Little-Page,[3] but not in such a way as to be sure of it. Nevertheless, I believed it, and I have spoken about it many times with Mr. John Adams in Paris, who always longed *for good members from Virginia.* He ardently desired to become acquainted with you, not having known of you before, not even through the renowned activity of your youth. I am pleased that you are in Congress for the honor that the Country has rendered to your merit and even more so for the advantages that our common cause can receive from the wisdom of your counsels, but I regret the loss to the Council of State in Virginia. In this regard I will tell you ingenuously that my own personal pride plays a considerable part. I do not want politics, whose principles I highly respect, especially in regard to public affairs, to enter into my personal life, when it is a matter of my honor, I believe that Sincerity (that favorite Divinity of mine) triumphs over all my other qualities, good or bad. I repeat then, that my own self-esteem contributes a great deal to my desire that you were still in our Council of State, for I am confident that you would have made an effort to prevent my being indiscreetly and indecently neglected. This also applies to Bellini who, unfortunately, might be renounced by Mr. Page.[4] God knows what kind of people the Council will be composed of now; and the unfortunate Governor[5] will perhaps not only lack the power to adopt the best measures, but in regard to me he will also be suspected of partiality. I recall when you used to speak to me in friendly and touching terms of the triumph that my enemies could have had and of the cruel mortifications my friends would have suffered, they who were made in some degree responsible for my conduct, which might not have corresponded to their expectations. The memory of this greatly arouses my just resentment, seeing myself the object of unpardonable negligence and, through such wicked malevolence, relegated to complete inaction, when to my own honor and to the consolation of my friends I would have been able to render important services to the Country in the time of great need. I do not know what other excuses I could present for not having received new commissions, or at least a facsimile of the old one, after all this time.[6] I have not even received a reply to some of my many letters. I know a number of them have reached their destination, having sent 4 copies of each one on various ships. I dare not write of all the doubts that come to my mind. I will not conceal from you, however, considering the just regard I owe to my own honor and to the sensibility of my dear friends in Virginia, that I will ever be obliged to defend my conduct to the world. It will perhaps cause more of an uproar than certain vile and pusillanimous persons suppose. The evidences of my zeal, through the duties confided to me and through the promotion of everything that can be of use to our glorious cause wherever I have been, will have considerable weight, not only by their nature, but through the important people who will bear witness to them. Therefore, if the unhappy necessity should ever arise, I would make every effort to save my public character, regardless of the effect my offenses might have. You will remember how much I used to pride myself on being made the subject of honorable anecdotes for being informed of everything of importance. I have not even been able to find out on what basis the public might obtain money for exchange since the last reform of our currency.[7] This has deprived us of many necessary and useful things that various adventurers could have supplied.[8] If the cargoes are not very profitable, they cannot meet the heavy expense, from which it follows that the adventurers, with the same ships would not be able to bring back more than a small portion for their efforts. Consequently, how can it be hoped that they would want to run such risks if I cannot tell them how they could invest their money with us? If you wish to see clearly how much cause I have for complaint, you should make an effort to read, in chronological order, the 22 letters I have sent to our Government. I would also be pleased if you could see the private letter I have written in this language to our Governor.[9] I hope that of all of them at least one copy will have been preserved: I send three of them privately and 4 by public mail. After examining one of these letters carefully, I am sure you could find many things that would be of some use to you in Congress. From here it is difficult to give you interesting news that you do not receive more quickly from elsewhere. I am advising you for your information, and you can use this as you see fit, that in Genoa they would be inclined to lend their money to Congress rather than to an individual state, and that my opinion should carry considerable weight here.[10]

It can be seen from my letters to the Government in what a miserable state my finances must be, but you can imagine my feelings at not having as yet received even one letter. Do not fail to keep me informed of our affairs, and address your letters to Mr. Mark Lynch Mercht. in Nantes,[11] or to Mr. Adams. Mr. Page will have notified you as to why I have not written to you before. May you preserve our dear friendship, and may you hold me in high esteem.

   Your Humble Servant and True Friend

PHILIP MAZZEI

[1] Carlo (Charles) Bellini.

[2] See Mazzei to JM, 13 June 1779.

[3] Lewis Littlepage (1762–1802), of Hanover County, Va., was in Nantes in 1779–1780 to learn French, preparatory to living in the household of John Jay, minister to Spain. He served in 1781–1782 as aide-de-camp to the Duc de Crillon in the French expedition against Port Mahon, Minorca, and against Gibraltar. Later he was in Turkey and, from 1784 to 1798, he held important offices under the King of Poland (Wharton, *Revolutionary Diplomatic Correspondence*, V, 785; Burnett, *Letters*, VIII, 278, n. 6; Boyd, *Papers of Jefferson*, XIII, 441; Horace E. Hayden, *Virginia Genealogies: A Genealogy of the Glassell Family of Scotland and Virginia ...* [Wilkes-Barre, Pa., 1891], pp. 402–20). See also Curtis Carroll Davis, *The King's Chevalier: A Biography of Lewis Littlepage* (Indianapolis, 1961).

[4] John Page.

[5] Thomas Jefferson.

[6] See Mazzei to JM, 13 June 1779, n. 3.

[7] What "last reform" he has in mind is doubtful but perhaps he refers to the changes made by the act of Congress of 18 March 1780 (Jefferson to JM, 26 July 1780, n. 2).

[8] That is, Europeans who would be willing to ship needed supplies to America on credit, in return for commodities or cash from there.

[9] Mazzei wrote frequently to Jefferson during the latter half of 1780, but no letter in Italian from him at that time seems to have survived. It may be true, however, that an English version of the letter, mentioned here, did reach the governor (Boyd, *Papers of Jefferson*, III, *passim*, and esp. p. 557; IV, 51–52).

[10] Four lines of manuscript in code follow this sentence. The key to the code has not been discovered. JM apparently attempted to locate a copy of the key to Mazzei's cipher for, in a letter of 29 September 1781 (LC: Rives Collection of Madison Papers), David Jameson wrote JM: "If I have received any letter from you desiring Mazzies Cypher it has Escaped me[.] The Cypher was destroyed with the Counci[l pa]pers in January." Thus the state's copy was lost when British troops under Benedict Arnold entered Richmond.

[11] Lynch had advanced money to Mazzei when he reached France in November 1779, and later acted as a transmitter of letters to him (Mazzei to JM, 13 June 1779, n. 3; Boyd, *Papers of Jefferson*, III, 311; IV, 310). This may have been the Mark Lynch who lived in New York City in 1797 (*New York Genealogical and Biographical Register*, XXXI [1900], p. 223).

Report of Committee on Letter of Arthur Lee

MS (NA: PCC, No. 19, III, 511). The report is in the hand of Thomas Bee of South Carolina.

[1 December 1780]

The Committee to whom were referred the Letter from Arthur Lee Esqr.[1] &c submit the following report.

Arthur Lee Esqr. having deposited with the President of Congress a Picture of the King of France set with Diamonds presented to him by the Minister of that Monarch on his taking leave of the Court of Versailles as a Mark of his Majesty's esteem, and intimated, that as the Picture was presented to him in consequence of his having been a Commissioner of Congress at that Court, it did not become him to retain the same without the express approbation of Congress, Resolved that he be informed that Congress approve of his retaining the Picture[2]

Resolved That Mr. Lee be further informed in Answer to his Letter that there is no particular charge against him before Congress properly supported. That Congress are sensible of his zealous & faithful Exertions to discharge the great public trust reposed in him; and that *he be assured* his recall was not intended to fix any kind of censure on his Character or Conduct abroad[3] but appeared at the time a necessary measure to put a stop to differences subsisting among their Commissioners in Europe greatly detrimental to the Interest of the United States, the particular grounds of which differences, it was not then in the power of Congress fully to Investigate.

The Committee also report That the Sum mentioned in his accounts to have been paid for Intelligence appears a reasonable charge & ought to be allowed.[4]

That the same allowance be made to his secretary, as was made to Mr Stockton who acted in that capacity to the Honble Willm. Lee Esqr.[5] and that the other Articles stated in his accounts with the Vouchers produced, be referred to the Board of Treasury for liquidation.

[1] Lee's letter of 17 October, after being spread on the journal of Congress two days later, was then referred for report to a committee of which JM was chairman (Jones to JM, 2 October, n. 10; Lee to JM, Bee, and Clark, 21 and 27 October 1780, n. 2; JM to Pendleton, 7 November 1780, n. 4). The committee's recommendations reached Congress on 30 October (*Journals of the Continental Congress*, XVIII, 994), but it delayed action upon them for about one month.

² Arthur Lee had been a commissioner of the United States at the court of Louis XVI. Lee informed Congress that his fellow commissioner, Silas Deane, had misused public funds. Although each man had staunch supporters in Congress, its members unanimously agreed on 10 June 1779 that, since Deane was back in the United States, Lee should also "repair forthwith" to Philadelphia to attend a congressional inquiry into the truth of his charges (*ibid.*, XIV, 712, 714). Lee knew of this action by mid-September (Wharton, *Revolutionary Diplomatic Correspondence*, III, 329), but he delayed his return because he was also the agent of the United States to the Spanish court. On 25 December 1779 he heard that Congress had vacated this commission on 13 October, or about two weeks after it had appointed John Jay as minister pleni-potentiary to Spain. Lee thereupon wrote to Congress that he would come home as soon as Jay arrived (*ibid.*, III, 447; *Journals of the Continental Congress*, XV, 1113, 1166). About mid-January 1780, or some ten days before Jay reached Cadiz, the Comte de Vergennes, on behalf of his sovereign, presented Lee "with a gold en-amelled snuff-box, containing the picture of the king of France, set with diamonds" (Richard Henry Lee, *Life of Arthur Lee, LL.D.* . . . [2 vols.; Boston, 1829], I, 168; Wharton, *Revolutionary Diplomatic Correspondence*, III, 462). After a long delay before taking ship from France, Lee finally arrived in Philadelphia in early October 1780 (*ibid.*, IV, 85).

³ Congress struck out the remaining lines of this paragraph before adopting the report (*Journals of the Continental Congress*, XVIII, 1115). This pallid sort of vindi-cation, unaccompanied by a blanket approval of Lee's expense accounts, naturally failed to placate him or to end his controversy with Deane and the Board of Treasury.

⁴ According to the printed journal (*ibid.*), the report of the committee ended with this sentence. The manuscript of the resolutions, however, includes the next para-graph also. It, too, was adopted by Congress.

⁵ William Lee, a brother of Arthur Lee, served as commissioner of Congress at the courts of Berlin and Vienna. Between May 1778 and December 1779 his secre-tary was Samuel Witham Stockton (*ca.* 1747–1794), who also held many offices in New Jersey, including those of secretary of the convention to ratify the Federal Constitution and secretary of state in 1794. On 14 October 1780 Congress and Stock-ton arrived at a settlement of his account (*ibid.*, XVII, 454–55; XVIII, 926–27; *New Jersey Archives*, XXV, 470 n.).

From Joseph Jones

RC (LC: Madison Papers).

RICHMOND 2d. Decr. 1780

DEAR SIR.

I have no Letter from you by this weeks Post although I expect you sent one as Mr. Griffin informs me what News there was worth com-municating, especially the contents of Mr. Adams's Letter, you had mentioned.¹ I have been much indisposed the greatest part of this week and not able to give much assistence in the business upon hand which are chiefly the Bills for recruiting the Army—and emiting and funding

I suppose six Millions of pounds.[2] The first was reported to the House near a week past and has been the subject of Debate every day. It went in a plan for giving Negro bounties[3] and has been rejected by an amendment from the word Whereas[.] the amendment proposes to give a bounty of five thousand pounds to each recruit for the war or three years[,] which is yet uncertain[,] but I expect it will be the last and this money to be demanded from all persons having assessable property above 100 £ Specie value at the rate of 2 PCt. at present it stands no lower than those having property above three hundred but I expect it will be brought to 100 £. The money or some specifics which are allowed to be paid in lieu of money are to be collected by the last [of] Janry. This collection added to the Tax to be paid by the people under the Act of the last Session will be very difficult for them to comply with but the situation of the Treasury withot. money and the demands now due from the public and the late expe[nces] occasioned by the invasion[4] will soon exhaust the new emission which will be gone as soon and as fast as they can make it for almost the whole burthen of the Southern Army will and must as Genl. Green informs us fall on this State.[5] I am in hopes the bounty of 5 will be reduced to three thousand pounds which will then for 3000 men amount to 9,000,000 an amazing Sum for a bounty. But our Legislators are timid or affect many of them to be timid abt. a draft which had better be made of ye. Militia to serve two years witht. bounty unless a very small one and that body or any other that may be necessary supplyed from the Militia by rotation to be at Camp by the time the others are to come away and to serve other two years. In the meantime let an exemption from draft or even Militia Duty out of the State be offered by the Law to every person who recruits a Soldier for the war whereby a number of our people will be constantly endeavouring to enlist Soldiers for the war and a great number I have no doubt might be so enlisted for a much less Sum than the bounty prop[osed] to be offered. If we raise the 3000 only for three years it is intended to furnish money to the officers or some proper person to take the proper occasion of enlisting as many of them for the War as they can and there are moments when most of them may be enlisted.[6] It is in contemplation to send some proper person to lay before Congress the resources of this State and its ability to maintain the Southern War in which embassy perhaps North Carolina may join that more dependence may not be placed on us than we are able to bear least a disappointment may ensue as we have no doubt the great operations of this

Winter and next Spring will be to the South. The Person is also to press the making strong remonstrences to France and Spain for their cooperation with proper Force by Sea and Land to recover S. Carolina and Georgia—a Resolution to this effect now lies on the Table.[7] Mr. Henry has sent in his resignation[.] no proposal yet of filling his place and am doubtfull whether it will be done as some think to save expence the number should be lessened. Our accounts as well as those of the preceding Delegates are before a Committee.[8] No step yet taken abt. the cession of Lands but will be taken up so soon as the recruiting and supply Bills are passed. Mr. Mason has not yet appeared and I do not expect he will this session as he has the remains upon him of a severe fit of the gout. however I have my hopes we shall obtain a cession of all beyond the Ohio.[9] Certainly if Lessly is gone to the Southward and anor. reinforcement from New York and also one expected from England in that quarter Congress or the Commander in Chief shod. send on to the Southwd. the pensylvania line before it is too late for if their reinforcements arrive they will go where they pleas[e] as our army will be unable to withstand them and the severity of the approaching Season will retard the march exceedingly of any succour by Land.[10] Mrs. Jones still continues to suffer the assaults of the Ague and Fever and she writes me it has so weakened and reduced her she fears she shall not be in condition to go north and if her state of Health shod. be such as to render her unable to travel I think I shall decline it myself.[11] Have you fixed any thing with Pemberton or Pleasants[?] if you have not and either of them are disposed to Rent upon the Terms I mentioned endeavour to make it conditional that if in a month or six weeks I shod. decline the bargain I may be at liberty as they shod. if any other offered to Rent their places.[12] As soon as I return Home or soon after you shall hear further from me upon this subject. I send for my Horses today and shall return abt. the 10th. or 12.[13] Your Letters after the receipt of this please to direct to Fredericksb[urg] untill further informed. I have [this] moment your Letter[14] wch. I expect by some mistake went on to Petersburg as this is the day for the return of the Post from there. I find you have engaged Pleasants House for me and must abide by it. I thank you for your trouble in that matter and shall be ready to return you the favour whenever in my power. I am

Yr. Aff Friend

JOS: JONES

¹ Near the close of this letter, Jones wrote that he had just received JM's letter of 21 November. In this, JM made his earliest known reference to John "Adams's Letter." And yet, in this first sentence, Jones remarks that JM "had mentioned" Adams' letter. Perhaps by an oversight, Jones neglected to say that Colonel Grayson had traveled faster than the "weeks Post" and had already delivered JM's letter of 25 November (q.v.) in which the Adams' dispatch is also referred to. Possibly, however, Jones should have added "to Cyrus Griffin" after "you had mentioned." For another reference to Adams' dispatch see Mathews to Greene, 27 November 1780, n. 1.

² See Jones to JM, 18 November, nn. 6 and 7, and 24 November 1780; JM to Jones, 28 November 1780.

³ Someone, but most probably not Jones, underlined "for giving Negro bounties" in the manuscript.

⁴ The British invasion of Virginia by Major General Leslie's troops.

⁵ In Richmond, on 20 November 1780, General Greene wrote to Governor Jefferson pointing out that "on Your exertions hang the Independence of the Southern States" (Boyd, *Papers of Jefferson*, IV, 130; Jones to JM, 18 November 1780, n. 2). Here, as remarked in n. 3, much of the passage from "Southern Army" to the end of the sentence is underlined, and the passage is further emphasized by a vertical mark beside it in the left-hand margin.

⁶ In the form passed by the Virginia General Assembly on 1 January 1781, the recruitment act differed substantially from Jones's discussion of it in this letter (Hening, *Statutes*, X, 326–37; *Journal of the House of Delegates*, October 1780, p. 79).

⁷ Although the House of Delegates adopted a resolution on 2 December to this effect and sent it to the Senate for consideration, the choice of Speaker Benjamin Harrison as special emissary to Congress and to the minister of France was not made until 27 December, and then only after Richard Henry Lee had withdrawn as rival candidate for the appointment (*ibid.*, pp. 34, 35, 65, 70, 76–77; JM to Jones, 12 December 1780; Jones to JM, 2 January 1781). In the manuscript a vertical line, probably not drawn by either Jones or JM, margins the passage from "It is in contemplation" to two lines beyond "on the Table."

⁸ This session of the Virginia Assembly did not fill the vacancy left by James Henry's resignation on 28 November as a delegate in Congress (*Journal of the House of Delegates*, October 1780, p. 31; Jones to JM, 2 October, n. 12, 18 November, and 24 November 1780, n. 11; Virginia Delegates to Jefferson, 5 November 1780, n. 1). Someone underlined the words, "Mr. Henry has" in the manuscript.

⁹ See Mason to JM, 2 August 1780; JM to Jones, 21 November, n. 9; and Motion regarding the Western Lands, 6 September 1780, editorial note.

¹⁰ See Jameson to JM, 4 November 1780, n. 3; JM to Jones, 21 November 1780, n. 13. At this time, Washington was planning to make a surprise attack upon the British in New York City and had no intention of weakening his army in order to reinforce Greene. The Pennsylvania line was establishing its winter quarters near Morristown, N.J. (Fitzpatrick, *Writings of Washington*, XX, 418, 424, 428, 447).

¹¹ See Jones to JM, 2 and 9 October, and 10 November 1780. In the manuscript a marginal line extends from "if her state of Health" to thirteen words beyond the location of n. 12.

¹² See JM to Jones, 21 and 28 November 1780.

¹³ The exact date of Jones's departure from Richmond is not known. From his letter to JM of 8 December (q.v.), he apparently intended to leave for his home five or six days later, or nearly three weeks before the Virginia Assembly adjourned.

¹⁴ JM's letter of 21 November.

From Edmund Pendleton

Tr (LC: Force Transcripts).

Virga. Decemr 4th 1780

Dr Sir

Since my last I am indebted for yr two favrs of the 14th & 21st past. Every thing wears the Appearance of confirming the Intention of the Enemy to make a Winter campaign to the Southward; The Fleet who lately left us it is said divided off the Capes part steering Eastward the Others to the South. if those & the late Embarkation from New York[1] should meet at Charles Town I fear that with the Army already there, they will recover the ground they have lost by the Spirited affair at King's Mountain, & revive the Rapidity of their progress through that State.

Our Militia are returned sickly & murmuring at the treatment they met with below, from forced Marches & too *Strict* Attention to Order, not being allowed to break their Ranks, tho' to avoid Deep Ponds of water or to drink; this brought on Pleurisies, & the death of 8 from this County[2] that I have heard of, besides many yet in danger; I fear it will have bad effects on the recruiting Service, besides the loss of some good men.

Our Assembly have made all paper money Issued or to be issued, a legal tender in Payment of all Debts. The Specific Negroe & Plate taxes are given up & we are to pay £80 P Ct on the Late Specie Valuation, in January, as a fund for raising the Soldiers at £5000 a man for 3 years service (for I understand they have no hopes of Raising them for the War) tho' I hope that term will exceed the other Indefinite one.[3] Mr Blair succeeds Mr Nicholas in the Chancery, & Mr Fleming goes into the General Court. Yr Colleague in the room of Mr Henry is not yet chosen.[4] I am Dr Sr

Yr mo. affe

Edmd Pendleton.

[1] See Jameson to JM, 4 November 1780, n. 3; JM to Jones, 21 November 1780, n. 13.

[2] Caroline County (Pendleton to JM, 11 December 1780).

[3] See Jones to JM, 18 November, nn. 6 and 7, and 2 December 1780. Pendleton evidently meant a tax of £80 in paper currency on each £100 of property valuation in terms of specie. At the 1 for 40 rate ("the Late Specie Valuation"), £100 in specie is equivalent to £4,000 paper. Two per cent of £4,000 is £80.

[4] See Jones to JM, 24 November, n. 8, and 2 December 1780, n. 8.

To Joseph Jones

RC (LC: Madison Papers).

PHILADA. Decr. 5th. 1780

DEAR SIR.

I had yours of the 25th. Ulto. by yesterdays post. I congratulate you, on the deliverance of our Country from the distresses of actual invasion. If any unusual forbearance has been shewn by the British Commanders, it has proceeded rather I presume from a possibility that they may some time or other in the course of the war repossess what they have now abandoned than from a real disposition to spare.[1] The proceedings of the Enemy to the Southward prove that no general change of system has taken place in their military policy.

We had letters yesterday from Mr. Jay & Mr. Carmichael as late as the 4 & 9th of September. Mr. Jay informs us that it is absolutely necessary to cease drawing bills on him; that 150,000 drs. to be repd. in three years with some aid in cloathing &c is all that the Court will advan[ce] for us. The general tenor of the letters is that our affairs there make little progress, that the Court is rather backward, that the navigation of the Mississippi is likely to prove a very serious difficulty, that Spain has herself been endeavoring to borrow a large sum in France on which she meant to issue a paper currency, that the terms & means used by her displeased Mr. Necke[r] who in consequence threw such discouragements on it, as in tur[n] were not very pleasing to the Spanish Minister, that Mr. Cumberland is still at Madrid labouring in concert with other Secret Emissaries of Britain to give unfavorable impressions of our Affairs, that he is permitted to keep up a correspondence by his Couriers with London, that if negociations for peace should be instituted this winter, as Spain has not yet taken a decided part with regard to America England will probably chuse to make Madrid rather than Versailles the seat of it.[2] However unfavorable many of these particulars may appear, it is the concurrent representation of the above Ministers that our disappointment of pecuniary succour at Madrid is to be imputed to the want of ability and not of inclination to supply us, that the steadiness of his Catholic Majesty is entirely confided in by the French Ambassador, and yt. the mysterious conduct of Mr. Cumberland and of the Court of Spain towards him, seems to excite no uneasiness in the Ambassador. The letters add that on the pressing remonstrances of France & Spain Portugal had agreed to shut her ports against English prizes, but that she persisted in her refusal to accede to the armed neutrality.[3]

The recipt of the foregoing intelligence has awakened the attention of the Georgia Delegates to their motion of which I informed you particularly by Col. Grayson. It has lain ever since it was made undisturbed on the table. This morning is assigned for the consideration of it, and I expect it will without fail be taken up. I do not believe Congress will adopt it without the express concurrence of all the States immediately interested. Both my principles & my instructions will determine me to oppose it. Virga. & the United States in general are too deeply interested in the subject of controversy to give it up as long as there is a possibility of retaining it. And I have ever considered the mysterious & reserved behaviour of Spain, particularly her backwardness in the article of money as intended to alarm us into concessions rather than as the effect of a real indifference to our fate or to an alliance with us. I am very anxious notwithstanding to have an answer to my letter by Grayson.[4]

We had a letter yesterday also from Mr. Adams who was at Amsterdam; and several others from him a few days before. Searl who carried despatches relating to the object of Mr. Laurens' Mission had fortunately arrived; though Mr. Adams gives no very sanguine idea of a successful result. The news of the fate of the Quebec & Jamaica fleets arrived in London pretty nearly about the same time and had a very material effect both on stocks and on ensurance.[5]

Information from the W. Indies gives a tragical picture of the effects of the tempest. Martinique has suffered very considerably in their Shipping and Seamen. The English have certainly lost the Ajax a Ship of the line & 2 frigates stationed off St. Lucie to intercept the Martinique trade with almost the whole of their crews, and there is great reason to suppose that several others which are missing have shared the like fate. St. Lucie is entirely defaced. In Barbadoes scarce a house remains entire, and 1500 lives at least are lost. One of the largest Towns in Jamaica has been totally swept away and the insland [island or inland?] otherwise greatly damaged. The Spaniards too on Cuba have not escaped, and there is a *report* that their fleet on its way to Pensacola has been so disabled & dispersed, that the expedition is for the present frustrated. This morning's paper which I this moment looked into has I perceive [a more par]ticular acct. of the disaster in W. Indies than I had befo[re read but] the St. Lucie paper says nothing of the loss of the Ajax &. but only tha[t] they were driven to sea[.] I am less confident as to the fact, though it might be intentionally omitted or not known there.[6]

It is not without reluctance that I trust this to the conveyance by post. If I had less experienced his punctuality in our correspondence or knew of a better opportunity I should act otherwise. As it is I consider the importance of your knowing the particulars from Spain as a ballance for the risk.

We have in Town at present several gentlemen of distinction from the French army. Among them the Chev: de Chatteleux the 2d. in comman[d] a man of sense politeness & letters. The Viscompt de Noailles brother in law to the Marquis de la fayette, and Baron de Montesquieu grand son to the great Montesquieu.[7] I hope I shall soon hear of your taking up the back lands & the confederation. I have not time to consult Dunlap.[8]

Adieu.

J. MADISON JR.

[1] See Jameson to JM, 18 November 1780, n. 10. The first three paragraphs of the present letter are inclosed in brackets, signifying that many years after it was written JM or one of his family selected this portion for publication.

[2] On 4 December, Congress received Benjamin Franklin's letter of 22 May from Paris, John Adams' letters of 24 August and 4 September from Amsterdam, John Jay's letter of 16 September from San Ildefonso, and William Carmichael's letters of 22 August and 6 and 9 September, also from San Ildefonso (*Journals of the Continental Congress*, XVIII, 1116, 1120). With the exception of the earlier of Adams' two letters, all these dispatches are in Wharton, *Revolutionary Diplomatic Correspondence*, III, 697; IV, 38–41, 45, 51–54, 59. Carmichael of Maryland (d. 1795) was secretary of Jay's mission to Spain, 1780–1782, and chargé d'affaires there from 1782 to 1794. Carmichael's comment about Spain's adamant stand on the Mississippi issue had reduced the optimism which JM expressed in his letter to Jones on 25 November (*q.v.* and n. 8). Jacques Necker (1732–1804) was director general of the Royal Treasury of France from 1776 to 1781, and again from 1788 to 1789. Richard Cumberland (1732–1811), although better remembered today as an English dramatist, was secretary of the Board of Trade in 1780. In that year he went to Madrid on a confidential mission designed to persuade Spain to withdraw from the war against Britain. According to Cumberland, he failed primarily because his government forbade him to suggest that Britain might be willing to return Gibraltar to Spain.

[3] See Reverend James Madison to JM, 3 August 1780, n. 3; JM to Pendleton, 7 November 1780, nn. 2 and 3.

[4] See JM to Jones, 25 November 1780 and nn. 3, 15. This was JM's "letter by Grayson." The motion of the delegates from Georgia and its context are presented in n. 4 of Bland to Jefferson, 22 November 1780.

[5] At least eleven letters from John Adams, dated between 12 June and 25 September 1780, were read in Congress on 27 and 30 November and 4 December 1780 (*Journals of the Continental Congress*, XVIII, 1095, 1107, and 1116). On 8 July 1780, James Searle (1730–1797), a Philadelphia merchant and a delegate in Congress for two years, was commissioned by the president and Assembly of Pennsylvania to seek loans and military supplies for his state in Europe (*Colonial Records of Pennsyl-*

vania, XII, 414–19; *Pennsylvania Archives*, 1st ser., VIII, 532–33). Henry Laurens had been captured at sea by the British on 3 September 1780 while under commission from Congress to seek financial loans in the Netherlands. The British imprisoned him in the Tower of London. JM derived his word about "the Quebec & Jamaica fleets" from John Adams' letter of 4 September to Congress (Wharton, *Revolutionary Diplomatic Correspondence*, IV, 45). For notes about these naval actions, see JM to Pendleton, 19 September 1780, n. 1; JM to Jones, 17 October 1780, n. 7.

⁶ See JM to Jones, 28 November 1780, n. 6. Although the British lost thirteen naval vessels in the hurricanes, the seventy-four-gun "Ajax" was merely one among the many which suffered damage (*Letter-Books and Order-Book of George, Lord Rodney, Admiral of the White Squadron, 1780–1782* [2 vols.; New York, 1932], II, 90–94; Wm. Laird Clowes, *The Royal Navy: A History from the Earliest Times to the Present* [7 vols.; Boston, 1897–1903], III, 479 n., 513).

⁷ Bearing letters of introduction from Washington to the president of Congress, François Jean, Chevalier de Chastellux (1734–1788), Louis Marie, Vicomte de Noailles (1756–1804), and Chastellux's aide-de-camp Charles Louis de Secondat, Baron de Montesquieu (*ca.* 1755–1824)—all officers of the French forces at Newport —arrived in Philadelphia shortly before the date of JM's letter (Fitzpatrick, *Writings of Washington*, XX, 403–6). Chastellux dined with the southern delegates, including "Maddison," on 13 December (*Travels in North-America in the Years 1780–81–82 by the Marquis de Chastellux* [New York, 1828], pp. 143–44).

⁸ John Dunlap (Jefferson to Virginia Delegates, 31 August 1780; Jameson to JM, 4 November 1780, n. 6).

To Edmund Pendleton

RC (LC: Madison Papers).

Philada. Decr. 5th. 1780

Dr Sr.

I have your favor of the 27th. ulto. and congratulate you on the deliverance of our Country from the distresses of actual invasion. The spirit it has shewn on this occasion will I hope in some degree protect it from a second visit.

Congress yesterday received letters from Mr. Jay & Mr. Carmichael as late as the 4 & 9th of Sepr. The general tenor of them is that we are not to rely on much aid in the article of cash from Spain, her finances & credit being scarcely adequate to her own necessities, and that the B. emissaries are indefatigable in misrepresenting our affairs in that kingdom and in endeavouring to detach it from the war. The character however of the Catholic king for steadiness and probity, and the entire confidence of our allies in him, forbid any distrust on our part. Portugal on the pressing remonstrances of France & Spain has at length agreed to shut her ports agst. English prizes but still refuses to accede to the armed neutrality. Mr. Adams writes that the fate of the Quebec and Jamaica fleets arrived at London nearly about the same time and had a very serious effect on all ranks as well as on stocks and ensurance.[1]

Our information from the W. Indies gives a melancholy picture of the effects of the late tempest. Martinique has suffered very considerably both in shipping & people. Not less than 600 houses have been destroyed in St. Vincents. The Spaniards in Cuba also have not escaped, and it is *reported* that their fleet on its way from the Havannah to Pensacola has been so disabled & dispersed as to defeat the expedition for the present. On the other side our Enemies have suffered severely. The Ajax a ship of the line and two frigates stationed off St Lucei [Lucia] to intercept the Martinique trade are certainly lost with the greatest part if not the whole of their crews; and there is great reason to believe, that several other capital ships that have not been since heard of have shared the like fate. The Island of St. Lucie is totally defaced. In Barbadoes a[lso], scarce a house remains entire and 1500 persons at least have perished. One of the largest towns in Jamaica has been totally swept away and the island otherwise much damaged. The consequences of this calamity must afford a striking proof to G. Britain of her folly in shutting our ports against her W. India commerce and transferring the advantage of our friendship to her Enemies.[2]

I am Dr. Sir yrs. sincerely

J. Madison Junr.

[1] See JM to Jones, 5 December 1780, nn. 2, 5.
[2] *Ibid.*, n. 6.

Samuel Nightingale, Jr., to Virginia Delegates in Congress

Printed text (Charles Campbell, ed., *Bland Papers*, II, 39). From the salutation, Nightingale addressed his letter to Bland and JM, the only delegates from Virginia then in Congress, rather than to Bland alone. The editor of the *Bland Papers* either decided to print only an extract of the letter or could print no more because the rest of it was missing or illegible.

Providence, December 6th, 1780

Gentlemen,

I[1] this day received your favor, dated the 14th October, inclosing a letter from his Excellency Governor Jefferson, dated the 28th of the same month, also a letter to the Hon. John Foster, which I have delivered him.[2] Due attention shall be paid to them.

I am very sorry to hear your state is invaded by a powerful enemy, but hope you will soon be able to dislodge them.

Observe you design the goods belonging to the state of Virginia which came in the schooner Committee, shall be transported by land; and that you request me to do something, but am not able to tell what, as that part of your letter was entirely worn out before I received it. The small arms are very badly packed, having nothing between them and considerable play in the boxes. I shall consult some person that is acquainted with the manner of packing arms, and endeavor to get them packed properly, as it must be for your interest, and presume you will justify me in so doing. I sent a letter to his Excellency Governor Jefferson, dated 22d of November,[3] inclosing an invoice of that half of the goods which is stored for the former owners, to your care. By it you will see the marks and numbers which were found on the goods when. . . .[4]

[1] Samuel Nightingale, Jr. (1741–1814), member of a prominent mercantile family in Providence, R.I., was an active patriot in his city even as early as the time of the Stamp Act (Gertrude Selwyn Kimball, *Providence in Colonial Times* [Boston, 1912], pp. 294–99, 321, 367–68).

[2] John Foster was judge of the Court of Admiralty of Rhode Island (John Russell Bartlett, ed., *Records of the State of Rhode Island and Providence Plantations, in New England*, IX [Providence, 1864], 55). None of the letters mentioned in this paragraph is known to be extant. Either Nightingale or the editor of the *Bland Papers* probably erred, since it is unlikely that a letter from the delegates of "14th October" would inclose one from Jefferson, dated 28 October.

[3] Printed in Boyd, *Papers of Jefferson*, IV, 143–44.

[4] The main subject of this letter was long-lasting and puzzling, both to Jefferson and the Virginia delegates in Congress. The schooner "Le Comité," bound from Nantes, France, to Virginia with munitions, clothing, salt, and other much needed supplies purchased by that state, was captured by a British ship off Cape Henry and soon recaptured by two American privateers. On 26 September, after they brought their prize to Providence, the ship and one half of its cargo were sold at public auction. Under the prize law, the other half was still the property of Virginia. How to convey this half from Providence to Richmond is the problem discussed in the present letter, and will arise frequently hereafter in letters from or to Madison and the other Virginia delegates as late as 1 May 1781. For the next mention of the subject, see Jefferson to Virginia Delegates, 18 December 1780.

From Philip Mazzei

RC (LC: Madison Papers). Water stains have entirely elimi-
nated the last four lines of this letter and largely blotted out
what appears to have been the first eight lines.

FIRENZE, [7. 10]bre 1780

CARMO: AMICO

[Questa serv?]irà di supp[lemento alla pr?]ecedente d[el 30 del pas-
sato?] unicamente   [un'aneddoto che potrebbe causare una revolu-
zione?]

della Regina [d'Ungheria]
della guerra [al me questo?] ultimo   [L'Imperatore è tutto di?]
contrario   nel'occhi il Rè [di Prussia in?] posse[so a?] mig[lior]
parte della Silesia. Non è contento del   della Francia   [in] tempo
delle dispute intorno alla Baviera, e Seguet[asse?] una guerra in Germania, se la Francia e l'Inghilterra ci si mescolassero inclinerebbe a col-
legarsi colla seconda. Se potessi dirvi da chi sono Stato informato delle
disposizioni dell'Imperatore considerereste come una dimonstrazione
geometrica. Come tale potete annunziarla al Congresso, e quando vi
piaccia potete comunicare anche Le mie congetture che Sono le Se-
guenti. Il Rè di Prussia non può essere unito all'Imperatore, e La Russia non Si Staccherà dalla Prussia. Gli Olandesi, medessimi Giudei d'Eu-
ropa, prenderanno schiaffi e calci in culo in infinito prima di romper
La Neutralità, che è sempre vantaggiosa al Loro interesse, non ostante
le prese che gl'Inglesi fanno dei Loro Bastimenti; ed [essen?]do forzati
ad entrare in guerra, non converrebbe Loro di mettersi contro La Russia e La Prussia, dalle quali potrebbero essere si facilmente oppressi. La
Russia à 30 Vascelli di Linea, e l'Imperatore non ne à uno; e Se La Dani-
marca si unisse all'Inghilterra, La Svezia che non Sarà disgiunto dalla
Francia non è inferiore in forze marittime. Gli affari di Germania non
posson progiudicare ai vantaggi, che potremo ricavar dall'Italia Se
prendiamo i passi opportuni, quantunque il Granduca, fratello dell'Imperatore, per ragioni

Vostro Umilmo. Servo e Amico Vero

FILIPPO MAZZEI

229

FLORENCE, [7 December] 1780[1]

DEAR FRIEND

This will serve as a supplement to my preceding letter of the 30th of last month[2]   a story that could produce a revolution

of the Queen of Hungary
of the war [and in this latter regard it appears to me that the Emperor is completely opposed   the King of Prussia?] in possession of the greater part of Silesia. He is not satisfied with   of France in the time of the disputes over Bavaria, and [should?] a war in Germany follow, if France and England were to become involved in it, he would be inclined to ally himself with the latter.[3] If I were to tell you by whom I have been informed of the inclinations of the Emperor, the result could be regarded as a geometrical demonstration. You can announce it to the Congress as such, and when you wish, you can also communicate my conjectures, which are as follows. The King of Prussia cannot be united with the Emperor, and Russia will not detach herself from Prussia.[4] The Dutch, those Jews of Europe, will accept an infinite number of slaps and kicks in the posterior before breaking their Neutrality,[5] which is always advantageous to Their interests, in spite of the fact that the English seize Their Ships; and being forced to enter a war, it would not profit them to place themselves in opposition to Russia and Prussia, by whom they would easily be defeated. Russia has 30 Ships of the Line, and the Emperor does not have even one; and if Denmark should unite with England, Sweden, which will not detach herself from France, is not inferior in maritime forces. The affairs of Germany cannot be detrimental to the advantages that we will be able to procure in Italy if we take the proper steps, though the Grand Duke, the brother of the Emperor,[6] for reasons

Your Humble Servant and True Friend

PHILIP MAZZEI

[1] In a letter to JM on 13 March 1782 (misdated the 15th as printed on pp. 77–80 of Richard C. Garlick, Jr., *Philip Mazzei*), Mazzei recalled that in his letter of 7 December 1780 he had commented about the "death of the Queen of Hungary and . . . the political system of the Northern Powers." This remark serves to date the present letter and also to make almost certain that its completely illegible third line mentioned Maria Theresa's death late in November 1780.

[2] See Mazzei to JM, 30 November 1780.

[3] Probably the sense of what Mazzei wrote was something as follows: "This supplementary letter will deal only with the possible effects of Maria Theresa's death

in bringing about a revolutionary realignment of European powers. Emperor Joseph II, the successor of Maria, is completely opposed to having King Frederick the Great of Prussia possess most of Silesia. The Emperor was not satisfied with the conduct of France during his largely unrewarding dispute (1777–1779) with Frederick the Great over the Bavarian Electorate issue. If Joseph's hope of recovering Silesia, mostly lost to Frederick in 1742, should precipitate a new war between Austria and Prussia, and if France and England become involved in the conflict, Joseph will be inclined to ally with England rather than France."

4 Mazzei's analysis was not trustworthy. There was no war between Austria and Prussia over Silesia. Joseph II and Catherine the Great of Russia co-operated between 1781 and 1783 in an attempt to dismember the Ottoman Empire but were unsuccessful largely as a result of the skilful diplomacy of the French foreign ministeɪ Charles Gravier, Comte de Vergennes.

5 Here Mazzei had in mind the League of Armed Neutrality. As mentioned above, Britain declared war on the Netherlands a few days after the date of this letter (Reverend James Madison to JM, 3 August 1780, n. 3; JM to Pendleton, 7 November 1780, nn. 2 and 3).

6 The Grand Duke of Tuscany from 1765 to 1790 was Leopold I. In 1790 he succeeded his brother, Emperor Joseph II of Austria. For the hoped-for "advantages" to accrue to Virginia from the mission of Mazzei, see his letter to JM, 13 June 1779, n. 2.

Motion on Instructions to John Jay

MS (NA: PCC, No. 36, I, 115). The manuscript, in JM's hand, is endorsed, "Motion from the Delegates of Virginia, Decemr 8th: 1780 postponed."

[8 December 1780]

Whereas the propositions moved by the Delegates from Georgia and taken into consideration on the 5th. instant:[1] do essentially affect the claims of Virginia as defined & recognized by Congress in their instructions both to their Minister Plenipo: for negociating peace & their Minister Plenipo: to the Court of Spain;[2] which claims the State of Virginia has expressly instructed their representatives in Congress to insist upon; and it has been urged as a reason for agreeing to the propositions above mentioned that the change of circumstances which has taken place since these instructions were given on the part of Virginia may have changed the sense of that State with regard to the object of them; Resolved yt. the further considerations of the said Propositions be suspended untill such of the Proceedings of Congress and of the communications from their Ministers in Spain as relate to this matter together with the said propositions shall have been transmitted by the Delegates from Virginia to the Legislature of that State, and their ultimate sense thereon be made known to Congress.[3]

[1] *Journals of the Continental Congress*, XVIII, 1070–71, 1119, 1121.

[2] After "Spain" in the manuscript, the following words are crossed out: "as well as directly contravene the instructions given by the State of Virginia to its Delegates in Congress."

[3] See Jones to JM, 2 October, n. 9; Draft of Letter to Jay, 17 October and n. 14; Bland to Jefferson, 22 November and n. 4; JM to Jones, 25 November 1780 and nn. 3, 8, and 15; Virginia Delegates to Jefferson, 13 December 1780.

From Joseph Jones

RC (LC: Madison Papers).

RICHMOND 8th: Decr. 1780

DEAR SR.

I have yours of November the 28th. by the Post and wish I could inform you the assembly had yet fixed the plan of recruiting our quota of Continentals but such various opinions and modes are proposed that great delay has been the consequence. The present proposition is a bounty of 5000 for the War 2500 for three years if it comes to a draft for that period—the whole to be collected from the Taxable property by the last of Janry—each division to cloath the Soldier and find him a Beef. It is expected this mode will raise us 3000 Men and as many Beeves to feed them. Whether this will pass I cannot pretend to say but am told it is the most agreeable of any thing that has been proposed.[1] My speaking thus doubtfully proceeds from my nonattendance in the House this week being confined by a slight but lingering Fever. I am somewhat better today and hope in a few days to be in the house again though I shall continue a very short time having sent for my Carriage to go home. The Finance Bill was under consideration of the Com: of the whole yesterday. I have not heard whr. they got through it. These finished[,] the next great object will be to take up the question of ceding the back Country.[2] This I want done before I go and also to have some mode fixed for the Deputies being regularly supplied. I mean to take a few days of next week for these purposes before I set out. I have already requested your future Letters to be addressed to me at Fredericksburg untill I give you notice of my being abt. to leave Virga. for Pensylvania This I expect yet to do as by the last Post Mrs. Jones informs me she and my Son Are both upon the mend[.] you need not Therefore if not already done say anything to Mr. Pleasants as I expect Mrs. Jones may be prevailed upon her health being in some measure restored to venture North.[3]

The Negro scheme is laid aside upon a doubt of its practicability in any reasonable time and because it was generally considered as unjust, sacrificing the property of a part of the Community to the exoneration of the rest, it was reprobated also as inhuman and cruel. how far your Idea of raising black Regiments giving them freedom wod. be politic in this and the Negro States deserves well to be considered so long as the States mean to continue any part of that people in their present subjection as it must be doubtfull whether the measure wod. not ultimately tend to increase the Army of the Enemy as much or more than our own for if they once see us disposed to arm the Blacks for the Field they will follow the example and not disdain to fight us in our own way and this wod. bring on the Southern States probably inevitable ruin[.] at least it wod. draw off immediately such a number of the best labourers for the Culture of the Earth as to ruin individuals, distress the State and perhaps the continent when all that can be now raised by their assistance is but barely sufficient to keep us joging along with the great expence of the war. The Freedom of these people is a great and desireable object[.] to have a clear view of it wod. be happy for Virginia but whenever it is attempted it must be I conceive by some gradual course alowing time as they go off for labourers to take their places or we shall suffer exceedingly under the sudden revolution which perhaps arming them wod. produce.⁴ Adieu I hope my head will be easier when I next write

affly yrs.

Jos: Jones.

Majr. Lee is now here on his way to the South. The Army we are told is very weak in that quarter and we hear the Enemy are reinforcing from New York. I am apprehensive all Virga. can do will not be sufficient to make head agt. them if it be true what is said that they will be eight thousand strong. Cloathing and Blankets are exceedingly wanting in our Army. for want of these not above 400 of 800 and upwards of our new levies can yet go forward since the Enemy left us.⁵

---

¹ See Jones to JM, 2 December 1780.
² See Jones to JM, 18 November, n. 7, and 2 December 1780. In the House of Delegates the "bill for procuring a supply of money for the exigencies of the war" passed on the date of this letter; the proposal "to lodge a sufficient credit in Philadelphia" to furnish "the delegates their pay" was discussed on 19 December 1780; and the land-cession bill passed on 2 January 1781 (*Journal of the House of Delegates*, October 1780, pp. 41, 58, 80).
³ See Jones to JM, 2 October, n. 14, and 2 December 1780, n. 13; JM to Jones, 21 November 1780.
⁴ See Jones to JM, 18 and 24 November and 2 December 1780; JM to Jones, 28

November 1780. In the manuscript, someone underlined the second word in this paragraph and ran a vertical line down its left-hand edge, beside the first five lines, ending with the words "how far." Near the close of the paragraph, the six lines beginning "of the war" and ending "sudden revolution" are similarly marginated.

[5] Lieutenant Colonel Henry ("Light-Horse Harry") Lee was graduated in 1773 from the College of New Jersey. In early December 1780 he was in Richmond collecting supplies for his cavalry battalion (Lee's Partisan Corps) before leading it south to join General Greene's army (Boyd, *Papers of Jefferson*, IV, 188–89). Lee was a delegate in Congress from 1785 to 1788, the governor of Virginia from 1791 to 1794, and a Federalist member of the United States House of Representatives from 1799 to 1801. General Robert E. Lee was his son.

From Edmund Pendleton

Tr (LC: Force Transcripts).

VIRGA. Decr 11, 1780

DEAR SIR

I take up the Pen merely to ask you how you do? Having nothing foreign or domestic to entertain you with; I have not even heard a word from the Assembly this two weeks; Yes I have one very unlucky circumstance to mention which tho' it may seem of little consequence, I fear will have important effects in [the[1]] future. Our militia[2] who turn'd out with the greatest alacrity are return'd with the most rivited [?] disgust, which is communicated to all others, so that it is announced in all Companies, that they will die rather than Stir again. They were very sickly & many died below, on their way back & since their return, all which they attribute to the Brutal behavr. of a Majr Mcgill, a Regular Officer,[3] who had the command of them in their March down; besides forced & hasty Marches, which will hurt raw Men, they alledge that he wantonly drove them thro' Ponds of Water wch might have been easily avoided, & would not allow them time to eat, thus travelling in their wet cloaths, they contracted laxes[4] & Pleurisies, which proved fatal. This disgust I fear will prove a prohibition to the recruiting our Continental Quota[5]—if it produces none other bad effects. I am

Dr Sr Yr Affe

EDMD PENDLETON

[1] As in the version of this letter, copied from the now missing original, printed in the *Proceedings of the Massachusetts Historical Society*, 2d ser., XIX (1905), 121–22.

[2] Pendleton means the Caroline County militia, which were called out to resist the British invasion of the Portsmouth area of Virginia from late October until about

20 November (Jameson to JM, 25 October, n. 2, and 18 November 1780, n. 10; Pendleton to JM, 30 October 1780, n. 1).

3 Probably Charles Magill who, after service in the Virginia continental line, became a major in a state line regiment. Governor Jefferson apparently held him in high esteem, gave no hint that he was "Brutal," and had used him, and would again use him, to maintain liaison with the patriot army in North Carolina (Jameson to JM, 30 August, n. 1; Pendleton to JM, 4 December; Boyd, *Papers of Jefferson,* IV, 243, 647–48).

4 Diarrhea.

5 See Jones to JM, 18 November 1780 and n. 6.

John Mathews, for Committee of Congress, to Nathanael Greene

RC (William L. Clements Library, University of Michigan).

PHILADELPHIA Decr. 12th: 1780

SIR,

The inclosed extracts appear as sufficiently interesting, to induce us to forward them to you. The reiterated information we have lately received from different quarters leave little room to doubt, that the Southern States, will be the grand theatre of war this ensuing winter and spring.[1]

The Waggons with stores for the army under your command, with two Companie[s] of Artificers, are now on their way to join you.

Nothing has been as yet done to supply your troops with cloathing. Capt. Jones had sailed with the cloathing, but being dismast[ed] a few days after he got to sea, was obliged [to p]ut back to be refitted. By a letter recei[ved] yesterday from Mr. Williams at Nantz; he informs us, that the Vessels will be ready to sail again in a few days. They will have on board, [already?] made and materials sufficient for making, 20,000 suits of cloaths, with some hats, stockings, shirts, Overalls, Shoes & Stocks and barrels & locks, for 20,000 muskets, & 100 Tons of Saltpetre.[2]

The article of intelligence contained in the inclosed extracts, respecting Portugal seems to be pretty well [sustained?] by subsequent advices.[3]

We have received no late intelligence of the enemies movements at New York. They appear to be quiet at present.

We are sir with much Respect & Esteem Yr. most Obet. Servts. By Order of the Committee[4]

JNO. MATHEWS Chairma[n]

¹ The principal inclosure was the copy of an extract from a letter of 17 October 1780 by an unknown correspondent—probably an Englishman—to Arthur Lee. The other was a copy of Lee's note of 7 December, transmitting the extract to the president of Congress (William L. Clements Library, University of Michigan). Besides mentioning Henry Laurens' imprisonment in the Tower and the accession of the Netherlands and Portugal to the League of Armed Neutrality (JM to Jones, 5 December 1780 and n. 5), the letter to Lee stated that Henry Clinton had asked to be relieved of his command if he could not be reinforced with ten thousand men, that a vessel bearing an assurance to Clinton of the government's approval of his conduct and of its determination to send him assistance as soon as possible had left England on 10 October, that steps were already being taken to raise "nine new Regiments of foot and one of Horse," that the belligerent powers in Europe were "busily preparing for another campaign," that "Ten Ships of the Line are now about sailing from Brest with about 5000 troops, some say to reinforce Monsieur Ternay, and others, that they are for the West Indies," and that the British would concentrate on North Carolina and Virginia in the coming campaign. The comments about Clinton are apparently based on his letter of 25 August 1780 to Lord George Germain and upon Germain's reply of 13 October (William B. Willcox, ed., *The American Rebellion*, pp. 454–55, 467–68). If Lee's correspondent had the letter of 13 October in mind, obviously he was incorrect about the date on which it left by ship for America. The writer of the letter to Lee may also have raised false hopes by his mistaken information regarding the French reinforcements assembling at Brest.

² See Mathews to Greene, 27 November 1780, n. 1; JM to Jones, 12 December 1780, n. 7. For Williams, see n. 5 of the next item.

³ See Virginia Delegates to Jefferson, [12] December 1780.

⁴ JM was a member of the committee "to correspond with the commanding officer of the southern department" (Mathews to Greene, 27 November 1780, editorial note).

Virginia Delegates in Congress
to Thomas Jefferson

RC (Virginia State Library). All of this letter, including its text and the address on the cover sheet, is in JM's hand, except for Theodorick Bland's signature at the close.

PHILADA. Decembr. [12,]¹ 1780

We have the honor to enclose your Excellency a Resolution of Congress of the 6th. instant relating to the Convention troops[,]² also a copy of a letter from G. Anderson found among the dead letters in the post office and communicated to Congress by the Postmaster. If there should be occasion for the original of the letter it shall be transmitted on the first intimation.³

An Irish paper informs us that Henry Laurens Esquire was committed to the Tower on the 6th. of October by a warrant from the

Secretarys of State on suspicion of High Treason. All the despatches entrusted to the same conveyance unfortunately fell into the hands of the Enemy at the same time.[4]

A letter from Mr. Jonathan Williams dated at Nantz, Octr. 17. confirms an account received several days ago, of the Ariel commanded by P. Jones, Esqr. & containing cloathing &c for the Army being dismasted & obliged to return into port. The effect of this delay will be severely felt by the troops who have already but too much reason to complain of the sufferings they have been exposed to from a want of these necessaries.[5]

The same letter from Mr. Williams as well as some others received within a few days give us reason to believe that Portugal has at length yielded to the solicitations of the Neutral Powers & to the remonstrances of France & Spain so far as to accede to the general object of the former and to exclude the English from the privileges which their vessels of War heretofore enjoyed in their ports.[6] we have received Payment of the Bill drawn by Mr. Benjn. Harrison.[7]

we [are?] with perfect respect Yr. Excellys most obedt. & very Hum[ble] Servts.

JAMES MADISON JUNR.
THEOK. BLAND JR.

[1] In the third paragraph, the delegates mention Jonathan Williams' dispatch of 17 October. This was read in Congress on 11 December (*Journals of the Continental Congress*, XVIII, 1141). This fact as well as the close resemblance between what JM wrote to Joseph Jones on 12 December (*q.v.*) and what is in the present letter seems to justify assigning the same date to it.

[2] The two inclosures mentioned in this paragraph have not been found. Congress resolved "That such of the Convention troops as are not already removed from the barracks near Charlotteville" to Fort Frederick in Maryland remain at Charlottesville (*ibid.*, XVIII, 1123; Pendleton to JM, 23 October 1780, n. 4; Jones to JM, 10 November 1780, n. 4).

[3] On George Anderson, see Henry to Virginia Delegates, 23 May 1780, nn. 1 and 4.

[4] See JM to Jones, 5 December 1780, n. 5.

[5] See Mathews to Greene, 27 November 1780, n. 2; JM to Jones, 12 December 1780, n. 7. Jonathan Williams, Jr. (1750–1815), grandnephew of Benjamin Franklin, was serving at Nantes as commercial representative of the United States envoys to France. Although Arthur and William Lee's charges that Williams had been involved in dishonest financial transactions were not sustained, they exacerbated the factionalism between the Lee and Deane-Franklin supporters in Congress. Later in his career, Williams became a distinguished army engineer and the first superintendent of the United States Military Academy.

[6] See JM to Jones, 5 December 1780.

[7] See Jefferson to Virginia Delegates, 14 November 1780. In his accounts under date of 6 December, JM entered, "To do [cash] recd from Turnbull & Co—23691 [dollars]" (Expense Account as Delegate in Congress, 20 December 1780).

To Joseph Jones

RC (LC: Madison Papers). The cover sheet bears the penciled note, "returned by Mr. M." JM probably added this many years later, after retrieving this letter, among others, from Jones's nephew, James Monroe.

PHILADA. Decr. 12th. 1780

DEAR SIR

Agreeably[1] to your favor of the 2d. instt. which came to hand yesterday I shall send this to Fredericksbg. I am sorry that either your own health or that of your lady should oblige you to leave the legislature before the principal business of the Session is finished. I shall be still more sorry if either of these causes should disappoint my hopes of your return to Philada. at the promised time.[2] I am the more anxious for your return because I suppose it will supersede the proposed measure of sending an envoy to Congress on the business you mention. If the facts are transmitted by the Speaker of the Assembly or the Executive, may they not be laid before Congress with as much efficacy by the established representatives of the State as by a special messenger? and will not the latter mode in some measure imply a distrust in the former one, and lower us in the eyes of Congress & the public?[3] The application to the Ct. of France has been anticipated. Congress have even gone so far as to appoint an Envoy Extraordinary to solicit the necessary aids. Col. Laurens was invested yesterday with that office. I leave the measure to your own reflection.[4] How far it may be expedient to urge Spain to assist us before she is convinced of the reasonableness of our pretensions, ought to be well weighed before it be tried. The liberty we took in drawing on her for money excited no small astonishment, and probably gave an idea of our distress, which confirmed her hopes of concession on our part. Accts. rcd. since my last repeat her inflexibility with regd. to the object in question between us. It is indispensable that we should in some way or other know the *Ultimate* sense of our Constituents on this important matter.[5]

Mr. Laurens is certainly in captivity. An Irish paper tells us he was committed to the tower on the sixth of Octr. under a warrant from the three Secretaries of State.[6] Portugal has acceded to the neutral league so far as to exclude the English from the privileges her armed vessels have heretofore enjoyed in her ports. The Ariel with P. Jones & the cloathing &c. on board was dismasted a day or two after she sail'd & obliged to put back into port.[7] If G. Washington detaches no further aid to the Southwd. it will be owing to the reduction of his force by the expiration of enlistments. The Pennsylvania line is mostly engaged for the war and will soon form almost the whole of the army under his immediate command.[8]

Mr. Sartine, it seems has been lately removed from the administration of the naval department, in consequence of his disappointing the general hopes formed from the great means put into his hands. When it was mentioned to me by Mr. M——s.[9] I took occasion to ask whether the deception with regard to the 2d. division ought to be ultimately charged upon him, observing to him the use the Enemies of the Alliance had made of that circumstance. From the explanation that was given I believe the blame rests upon his head, and that his removal was the effect of it in a great measure; though it is possible he may like many others have been sacrificed to ideas of policy, and particularly in order to cancel the unfavorable impression which the disappointment left on America. A high character is given as might be expected of his successor the Marquis de Caster, particularly with respect to those qualities in which Mr. Sartine is charged with having been most deficient.[10]

I am yrs. sincerely

J. MADISON JNR.

[1] The brackets which inclose the entire text of this letter signify that JM, in his old age, or a member of his family selected the letter for publication.

[2] See Jones to JM, 8 December 1780. What "the promised time" was is unknown, but probably it was after the legislature of Virginia adjourned, or early in the new year.

[3] See Jones to JM, 2 December 1780, n. 7.

[4] The appointment of Colonel John Laurens as "minister . . . to the Court of Versailles for the special purpose of soliciting aids . . . and forwarding them to America without loss of time" (*Journals of the Continental Congress*, XVIII, 1130, 1141) was, from one standpoint, an episode in the long struggle in Congress between the partisans of Arthur Lee and Ralph Izard on the one side and those of Silas Deane and Benjamin Franklin on the other (Jones to JM, 2 October 1780, n. 10; JM to Pendleton, 7 November 1780, n. 4; Mathews to Greene, 27 November 1780, n. 2; and Report on Letter of Arthur Lee, 1 December 1780, n. 2). On the day before he wrote Jones, JM was named to a committee to "prepare a draught of a commission and instructions to" Laurens. For its report, see under date of 23 December 1780.

[5] "Our pretensions," of course, refers chiefly to the freedom to use the Mississippi (JM to Jones, 5 December 1780, and nn. 2 and 4; Virginia Delegates to Jefferson, 13 December 1780). On 9 December, when William Carmichael's letter of 25 September from San Ildefonso was read in Congress, its members learned that the king of Spain "would never relinquish the navigation of the Mississippi, and that the ministry regarded the exclusive right to it as the principal advantage which Spain would obtain by the war" (Wharton, *Revolutionary Diplomatic Correspondence*, IV, 70).

[6] See JM to Jones, 5 December 1780, n. 5.

7 Shortly after sailing for the United States, Captain John Paul Jones, commanding the sloop of war "Ariel," encountered a severe gale near the French coast on 8–11 October. With much difficulty he succeeded in bringing the greatly damaged ship back to Lorient. Repairs to the vessel delayed his departure for America until 18 December 1780 (Samuel E. Morison, *John Paul Jones*, pp. 304–7).

8 See Jones to JM, 2 December, n. 10. On 9 December Washington wrote Jefferson: "It is happy for us, that the season will probably compel both Armies to continue in a state of inactivity; since ours is so much reduced by discharging the Levies, which composed a considerable part of it, even before their time of service expired; this expedient we were forced to adopt from the present total want of flour" (Fitzpatrick, *Writings of Washington*, XX, 447).

9 Probably François de Barbé-Marbois.

10 Charles Eugène Gabriel de la Croix, Marquis de Castries (1727–1801), replaced Antoine R. J. G. G. de Sartine (1729–1801) as the French Minister of Marine on 14 October 1780. In a letter of 3 December to the president of Congress, Franklin merely stated that Sartine's removal "does not affect the general system of the court, which continues favorable to us" (Wharton, *Revolutionary Diplomatic Correspondence*, IV, 179). By "2d. division," JM meant the long-hoped-for second fleet, in addition to that of de Ternay, still blockaded at Newport, R.I.

To Edmund Pendleton

RC (LC: Madison Papers). Besides Pendleton's docketing identification, the cover sheet bears the following notes: (*a*) "omit" in JM's hand, signifying that he decided to exclude the letter from his papers being assembled for publication; (*b*) "cop.," probably a jotting by William C. Rives's clerk after transcribing it for inclusion in Madison, *Letters* (Cong. ed.); and (*c*) "changes in French Cabinet," a reminder in the hand of Rives of what particularly interested him in the letter.

PHILADA. Decemr. [12][1] 1780

DEAR SIR.

I had the pleasure of yours of the 2d.[2] instant yesterday. We have not heard a word of the fleet which lately left Cheasapeake. There is little doubt that the whole of it has gone to the Southward.[3]

Our intelligence from Europe confirms the accession of Portugal to the Neutral league; so far at least as to exclude the English from the privileges which their Vessels of War have hitherto enjoyed in her ports. The Ariel commanded by P. Jones which had on board the cloathing &c. which has been long expected from France was dismasted a few days after she sailed and obliged to return into port; an event which must prolong the sufferings which our army has been exposed to from the delay of this supply. Mr. Sartine, the Minister of the french Marine has been lately removed from the admi[ni]stration of that departmt. His successor is the Marquis de Caster, who is held out to us as a man of greater activity & from whom we may hope for more effectual co-operation.

An Irish paper informs us that Mr. Laurens was committed to the Tower on the 6th. of Octr. by the three Secretaries of State on suspicion of high treason. As the warrant with the names of the Secretaries subscribed (with some other particulars) is inserted, no hope remains of the fact being a forgery.[4]

With very sincere regard, I am Dr. Sir Yr Obt Servt.

J. MADISON JUNR.

[1] As indicated by the first words of JM's letter of 12 December to Jones (q.v.), and by the first words of this one to Pendleton, JM heard from each of these men in the same mail. Since the news in his reply of 12 December to Jones closely resembles what he here writes to Pendleton, he almost certainly penned this letter on that date also.

[2] Error by JM for "4th."

[3] In the left-hand margin, written parallel to the edge of the paper and alongside this paragraph, are the following barely legible words, apparently in JM's hand, "& with Leslies tro[o]ps" (Jameson to JM, 4 November 1780, n. 3). This marginal addition may, of course, have been added by JM many years after he wrote the original letter.

[4] For editorial comment about the matters touched upon in the two final paragraphs of this letter, see JM to Jones, 12 December 1780, nn. 6 through 10.

Virginia Delegates in Congress to Thomas Jefferson

RC (Henry E. Huntington Library). With the exception of Theodorick Bland's signature, this letter is in JM's hand. At JM's request, William Munford, keeper of the rolls of the Commonwealth of Virginia, sent him a transcript of the letter, attested on 31 August 1819 to be "a true copy of a document communicated by Governor Jefferson to the General Assembly." This copy, from which JM had a transcript made for publication in *Niles Register*, XXI (1821–22), 349, is among JM's papers in the Library of Congress. Late in life, he also selected this letter for inclusion in the first edition of his papers.

PHILADELPHIA December 13th. 1780

SIR

The complexion of the intelligence received of late from Spain, with the manner of thinking which begins to prevail in Congress with regard to the claims to the navigation of the Mississippi,[1] makes it our duty to apply to our constituents for their precise full and ultimate sense on this point. If Spain should make a relinquishment of the navigation of that river on the part of the United States an indispensable condition of an Alliance with them, and the State of Virginia should adhere to their former determination to insist on the right of navigation, their delegates ought to be so instructed not only for their own satisfaction, but that they may the more effectually obviate arguments drawn from a supposition that the change of circumstances which has taken place since the former instructions were given may have changed the opinion of Virginia with regard to the object of them. If on the other side any such change of opinion should have happened, and it is now the sense of the State that an Alliance with Spain ought to be purchased even at the price of such a cession if it cannot be obtained on better terms it is evidently necessary that we should be authorized to concur in it. It will also be expedient for the Legislature to instruct us in the most explicit terms whether any and what extent of territory on the East side of the Mississippi and within the limits of Virginia, is in any event to be yielded to Spain as the price of an Alliance with her. Lastly it is our earnest wish to know what steps it is the pleasure of our Constituents we should take in case we should be instructed in no event to concede the claims of Virginia either to territory or to the navigation of the abovementioned river and Congress should without their concurrence agree to such concession.

We have made use of the return of the Honble. Mr. Jones[2] to N. Carolina to transmit this to your Excellency, and we request that you will immediately communicate it to the General Assembly.[3]

We have the honor to be with the most perfect respect & esteem Yr. Excelly's Most Obt. & humble servants,

JAMES MADISON JUNR.
THEOK: BLAND

[1] Above, Motion in Congress on Instructions to John Jay, 8 December 1780, and footnotes for the context of this letter.

[2] Willie Jones (1740–1801), a delegate in Congress from North Carolina, is not mentioned in its journals after 11 December (*Journals of the Continental Congress,* XVIII, 1140). In a letter to Joseph Jones on 19 December 1780 (*q.v.*), JM remarked that he supposed Willie Jones "will not be at Richmond till nearly Christmas."

[3] When Jefferson laid this letter before the House of Delegates on 25 December, the matter was referred "to the committee of the whole House on the state of the Commonwealth." See below, under date of 2 January 1781, for the resolution of the General Assembly instructing the Virginia delegates in Congress on this issue.

Matthias Halsted to Virginia
Delegates in Congress

RC (Virginia State Library). Halsted's signature at the close of his statement is followed by an unsigned addendum of five lines in a different and unknown hand. The docketing note on the cover sheet erroneously attributes the statement to "Mathew Halstead."

[17 December 1780]

The Subscriber Matthias Halsted[1] of Elizabeth Town in the State of New Jersey, Who was a Prisoner of War & Confined in the Sugar House Prison in the City of New York, from the 25th Day of March untill the 27th Day of September last, Hereby Represents & Declares; That Charles Williamson Esqr. & Lieut. John Smith, Both of Princess Ann County in the Common Wealth of Virginia; were During that time Confined in the same prison[;] That the Subscriber was Informed by the said Williamson & Smith that they & John Hancock Esqr. of the Said Princess Ann County, had been held in Close Confinement from the time of their Captivation Which was in May 1779, sometimes in the Sugar House Prison & sometimes in the Provost Prison,[2] in which last Mentioned place the said John Hancock was Confined During the Confinement of the Subscribers in the Sugar H[ouse;] That the above named Mr. Williamson had Ap[plied?] to the British Commissary General of Priso[ners?] for a Parole to Return to Virginia, to Effect his Exchange, & the Exchanges of the Other Gentlemen above Named, to Which no satisfactory Attention has been paid; That he (Mr. Williamson) had been Informed that Neither of the Above Named Gentlemen would be Exchanged or Liberated until a Colonel Elligood[3] in Virginia, should Either be sent into the British lines, Set at Liberty in Virginia, or some treaty Concluded Respecting him; That upon Mr. Williamson Requesting a Proposal in form[?] Respecting Col. Elligood, he was Informed Proposals must be made from this side; That the foregoing were Assigned as Reasons, for their not being Exchanged for some persons sent from Virginia with Proposals for them, Together with the following Reason, that the Persons sent from Virginia were Naval Prisoners, they Citizens, Consequently in Different Departments; That from Prisoners Who had left the Different Prisons in New York since the first of this Month, The Subscriber has learned the above Named Gentlemen Remain in the Situation before Described; That their Situation is truly Distressing; friendless,

Moneyless, with an Allowance scarcely sufficient to support Nature, And too far Distant from home to procure Any supplies from thence —That in Making this Representation, the Subscriber has no Other Motive than the feelings of humanity toward persons suffering for their Attachment to their Country's Interest, Whose Distress is Encreased by the Inattention of their Country to them; And his Anxious [De]sire to Procure the liberation of all in their situation, particularly of those Who Appear to Merit Attention; And That in Describing their Distressed Situation, The Subscriber is Restrained by a Parole from saying so much as Might with great Propriety be urged and from Which he could be withheld by no Other Consideration. In full Testimony of all Which I hereunto subscribe my Name at Philadelphia the 17th December 1780.[4]

MATTHIAS HALSTED

The Above representation is made to the Honl. the Delegates of Virginia, who are desired to remember that Mr. Halstead is a Prisoner on Parole, his Name on that Acct. it is expected will be kept a Secret.

[1] Matthias Halsted (1736–1820) had resigned as quartermaster of the 1st New Jersey Regiment in August 1776. Staten Island Tories took him captive during their raid into Elizabethtown on 24 March 1780 (Edwin F. Hatfield, *History of Elizabeth, New Jersey: Including the Early History of Union County* [New York, 1868], pp. 484–85). In 1781, when he was a brigade major and aide to Major General Philemon Dickinson of the New Jersey militia, Halsted again displayed interest in captives of the British by bringing charges (which he later failed to support) against Mr. John Adam, deputy commissary of prisoners (Fitzpatrick, *Writings of Washington*, XXII, 73, 213, 423–24).

[2] To which of the sugar houses, used for the storage of rum, molasses, sugar, etc., on the city's wharves, Halsted refers is not known. There were also a number of provost or common jails for the incarceration of criminals in times of peace. Halsted may mean the most notorious of these prisons—the one situated at the northeast corner of City Hall Park and known for many years after the Revolution as the Hall of Records (Hugh Hastings and J. A. Holden, eds., *Public Papers of George Clinton*, V, 192 n.; VI, 722 n.; James Grant Wilson, ed., *The Memorial History of the City of New York, from its First Settlement to the Year 1892* [4 vols.; New York, 1892–93], II, 540). Williamson, Smith, and Hancock, all prominent civilians and active in the affairs of Lynnhaven Parish in Princess Anne County, were probably taken by the British during Commodore Sir George Collier's invasion of Virginia in May 1779 (George Carrington Mason, ed., *The Colonial Vestry Book of Lynnhaven Parish, Princess Anne County, Virginia, 1723–1786* [Newport News, Va., 1949], pp. 94, 114–26; above, Henry to Jay, 11 May 1779 and notes). They may have been captured to insure loyalists in Princess Anne County of kind treatment or, perhaps, to be exchanged for loyalists held by the patriots. Charles Williamson (*ca.* 1747–1797) became a justice of the peace in 1777, and was appointed the next year a commissioner to supply provisions to women whose husbands were in continental service, and a co-commissioner (with John Hancock, Sr.) to administer the estates of several British subjects (Princess Anne County Court Records, Will Book, No. 2, pp. 83–85, and Minute Book, No. 10, pp. 179, 246, both on microfilm in Virginia State

Library; H. R. McIlwaine *et al.*, eds., *Journals of the Council of the State of Virginia* [Richmond, 1931——], II, 245). John Hancock, Sr. (*ca.* 1732–*ca.* 1805), had been intermittently since 1762 a justice of the peace and was his county's presiding justice at the time of his capture. He had been sheriff in 1772 and was to serve for four years between 1786 and 1804 as a member of the House of Delegates (*Bulletin of the Virginia State Library*, XIV [1921], 61; Earl G. Swem and John W. Williams, eds., *A Register of the General Assembly of Virginia 1776–1918 and of the Constitutional Conventions* [Richmond, 1918], pp. 24, 40, 44, 63). John Smith (*ca.* 1741–1815) was frequently a constable after 1770. There is no evidence that he ever held a military rank (Princess Anne County Court Records, Minute Book, No. 9, p. 1, and Will Book, No. 3, p. 119). Although the date of their release is unknown, they were probably the three men on whose behalf the Virginia delegates moved for support from Congress on 22 December (*q.v.*).

3 Jacob Ellegood (Elligood, Alligood) (b. *ca.* 1740), a leading Tory landowner of Princess Anne County, was lieutenant colonel of Virginia militia in 1775 when he accepted Governor Dunmore's commission to raise the Queen's Loyal Virginia Regiment, the first royal partisan corps organized during the Revolution. It consisted of about five hundred Tories recruited in Princess Anne and Norfolk counties. Ellegood was captured at the Battle of Great Bridge on 9 December 1775, and remained a prisoner until April 1781, when he was paroled after much negotiation. He continued on the roster of Lynnhaven Parish, where he had been a justice of the peace, until November 1778, when he was replaced as a lay official because he was "out of the county." In 1788 he returned briefly to Virginia, where his wife had remained in order to safeguard the property interests of a minor son. Then he moved to New Brunswick (Boyd, *Papers of Jefferson*, III, 665; IV, 164, 622 n., 644 n.; V, 428; *Virginia Magazine of History and Biography*, XIV [1906–7], 252 n.; George C. Mason, ed., *Colonial Vestry Book of Lynnhaven Parish*, pp. 98–109; *Tyler's Quarterly Historical and Genealogical Magazine*, V [1923–24], 144; "Transcript of the Manuscript Books and Papers of the Commission of Enquiry into the Losses and Services of the American Loyalists . . . in the Public Record Office of England, 1783–1790," LVIII, 72–92, in the New York Public Library).

4 Athough the present location of this manuscript (see headnote) permits little doubt that JM and Bland forwarded it to Jefferson, no reference to it has been found in the papers of JM or Jefferson. The preceding footnotes furnish evidence of the release of the four principals named in the document but not as the result of exchanging Ellegood for the other three men. See Board of War to Virginia Delegates and Motion of Delegates, [22 December, 1780].

Thomas Jefferson to Virginia Delegates in Congress

Translation (Thomas Jefferson Memorial Foundation). Jefferson's original letter is probably not extant. This French version, translated and copied by a person or persons unknown, was in all likelihood sent from Philadelphia on 2 January 1781 by the Chevalier de La Luzerne in his letter to Chevalier Charles René D. S. Destouches, who commanded the French fleet at Newport, Rhode Island, after Admiral de Ternay's death on 15 December 1780. A translation of La Luzerne's letter from the French original, but incorrectly dated 2 January 1780, is in Charles Campbell, ed., *Bland Papers*, II, 30–31.

A RICHMONT le 18. Decemb. 1780.[1]

MESSIEURS

J'ai pris les informations nécessaires pour connoitre les rades d'ou les vaisseaux de guerre François qu'on stationneroit cet hiver dans notre Baye pourroient proteger le plus efficacement son commerce, etre le plus en sureté et avoir la meilleure retraite. Celles *d'Hampton* et *d'York* sont les seules qui commandent l'entrée de la Chesapeak; aucun vaisseau ne peut y pénétrer sans être vu de l'une ou l'autre de ces deux places. La rade D'Hampton est plus à portée des caps d'environ une heure ou une heure et demi de navigation et par cet avantage l'emporte de beaucoup: mais d'autres considérations la rendent très inférieure à celle d'York. Les vaisseaux ne sont pas dans la première parfaitement à l'abri des tempetes; on n'y peut recevoir aucune assistance de la terre contre une supériorité maritime, si petite qu'elle soit; un Vaisseau de ligne ne peut remonter plus haut qu'à environ huit milles de *Burwell's Ferry* et une frégate qu'à *Jamestown*, sans s'alleger; il est vrai qu'en prenant ce dernier parti, elle pourroit s'avancer Jusque par de la *Hoods*, ou elle seroit en toute sureté. D'York-town au contraire, on a également vue sur la Baye quoiqu'on en soit un peu plus éloigné; le port y est parfaitement sur pendant tout l'hyver; les batteries de la place peuvent par une coopération sauver de la nécessité de faire retraite devant une petite supériorité de Force, et si la retraite étoit indispensable, l'on a quatre brasses d'eau jusqu'à *portopotank*, 25 miles audessus d'York et 6. au dessous de *West-point* ou la rivière a un mile et demi de large, mais ou le chenal n'a que 150. Verges et s'etend le long de la rive du nord. Il y a une barre à cet endroit ou ne trouve que 18. pieds d'eau quand la marée est haute. cette derniere profondeur se soutient jusqu'à *Cumberland* sur *la pamunkey* et jusqu'à *King and queen Court house sur la Mattapany*. À Cumberland la rivière a 100. ou 120 yards de large, à King et queen Court house elle en a 250. et ces deux places sont dans le coeur du pays. Il paroit d'après cela que des Fregates auroient une retraite sure à tous égards; mais que des vaisseaux de ligne ou tous autres tirant plus de 18. pieds d'eau ne seroient pas dans le même Cas. On peut d'ailleurs se procurer plus facilement à York town qu'à Hampton les rafraichissement necessaires et toutes ces considérations paroissent devoir lui obtenir la préférence.

J'ai l'h. d'E. & &.

Signé   TH. JEPHERSON.

---

[1] Above this line and separated from it by a horizontal line is written, "Traduction de la lettre du Gouverneur de Virginié aux délégués de cet état en congrés."

At RICHMOND the 18. Decemb. 1780.

GENTLEMEN:[1]

I have gathered the information necessary to become acquainted with the roadsteads from which the French warships that will be stationed this winter in our bay can most effectively protect its commerce, be safest, and have the best harbor.[2] Only those of *Hampton* and *York* command the entrance of the Chesapeake; no vessel can enter there without being seen from one or the other of these two places. Hampton roadstead is only an hour's or an hour and a half's sail from the capes and this is very much of an advantage: but other considerations make it very inferior to that of York. In the first of these places ships are not completely protected from gales; nor can they receive any assistance from land against a superior naval force, however slight that superiority may be. A ship of the line can not go farther up stream than about eight miles from *Burwell's Ferry*[3] and a frigate only to *Jamestown*, without unloading; it is true that by doing the latter it can move up even beyond *Hoods*,[4] where it would be in complete safety. On the other hand one may keep an equally good watch on the Bay from Yorktown although one's view from there is a little more distant; the harbor there is completely safe all during winter; the batteries at that site can cooperate to make unnecessary a retreat before a slightly superior force, and if the withdrawal were to be indispensable, there are four fathoms of water as far as *portopotank*,[5] 25 miles above York and 6 below *West-point*[6] where the river is a mile and a half wide, but where the channel is only 150 rods [wide] and extends the length of the north bank. There is a bar at that place where the water is only 18 feet deep at high tide. This latter depth continues up to *Cumberland* on *the pamunkey* and up to *King and queen Court house* on the mattapany. At Cumberland the river is 100 or 120 yards wide, at King and queen Court house it is 250 and these two places are in the *heart* of the country. In view of this it appears that frigates would have in every respect a secure haven; but that ships of the line or all others drawing over 18 feet of water would not be in the same circumstances. Moreover, necessary supplies can be procured more readily at Yorktown than at Hampton and all these considerations ought to make it the preferred location.

I have the h[onor] of b[eing] & &

signed TH. JEPHERSON[7]

[1] JM and Theodorick Bland, Jr.
[2] In his letter of 2 January [1781] to Destouches, mentioned in the headnote, La

Luzerne stated that the Virginia delegates had informed him in writing (letter missing) about the fate of "Le Comité" and of their concern about getting its cargo from Rhode Island to Virginia (Nightingale to Virginia Delegates, 6 December). La. Luzerne hoped that Destouches agreed with de Ternay's aim "to establish a strong blockade off and near the Chesapeake bay." La Luzerne suggested that if this were done, one of the French warships could carry to Virginia the cargo aboard "Le Comité" belonging to that state. La Luzerne added: "To this I subjoin an order [30 December 1780, q.v.] of the delegates of Virginia, addressed to Mr. Samuel Nightingale, that he deliver to your order the articles in his care. These delegates assure me, that Virginia will spare no pains to render the requisite situation agreeable to the ships which you may judge fit to be charged with this blockade." The blockade would also render the "very essential service" of protecting the commerce of Virginia and Maryland.

3 On the James River about six miles from Williamsburg.

4 On the James River across from Weyanoke.

5 Portopotank Creek flows into the York River and is part of the boundary between Gloucester and King and Queen counties.

6 West Point, about forty miles from Chesapeake Bay, is on the peninsula where the Pamunkey and Mattaponi rivers meet to form the York.

7 This letter appears to be an answer to a missing letter from JM and Bland in which they forwarded to Jefferson the dispatch of 22 November from Nightingale to him (Nightingale to Virginia Delegates, 6 December 1780).

Motion on Accounts of Carter Braxton

MS (NA: PCC, No. 36, IV, 521). Written by JM. The motion is endorsed by Charles Thomson, "Mr. Bland[,] Mr. Madison."

[19 December 1780]

On motion of Mr. [James] Madison, seconded by Mr. [Theodorick] Bland, *Ordered*,[1]

That so much of the sd. letter as respects the receiving in specie, at the rate of 75 cont: drs. for 1. of specie into the Continental Treasury be referred to the Board of Treasury & that they be directed to have the transaction stated in their books & in the books of the Treasurer in such manner that the state of Virginia may not be included in it.[2]

1 This opening portion is copied from the *Journals of the Continental Congress*, XVIII, 1174.

2 For the context of the motion, see Jefferson to Virginia Delegates, 17 November 1780 and n. 3.

To Joseph Jones

Printed text (Madison, *Papers* [Gilpin ed.], I, 76–77). The manuscript is now lost. Besides the text below, JM probably added the news about the army mentioned in his letter of the same date to Edmund Pendleton (*q.v.*).

PHILADELPHIA, December 19th, 1780.

DEAR SIR,

Yours of the eighth instant came to hand yesterday. I was sorry to find the Assembly had not then taken up the recommendation of Congress on the subject of the western lands. Its being postponed so late will, I fear, prevent the result of their deliberations from being communicated to Maryland before the rising of their Legislature; in which case much time must be lost, unless their Delegates be authorized to accede to the Confederation, on a cession satisfactory to themselves,— a liberality of proceeding hardly to be expected from that State, after the jealousy and reserve it has shown.[1] I am no less sorry to find so little progress made in the plan for levying soldiers. The regular force for the southern department must be principally, it seems, contributed by Virginia, the North Carolina Assembly having broken up without making any effectual provision of that sort. One would have supposed that the fatiguing service exacted of the militia in that State, would have greatly facilitated such a measure, and yet that is assigned as the obstacle to its practicability.[2]

I wish anxiously to hear from you on the subject stated in my letter by Grayson, and in my subsequent one by the post. Circumstances which I do not choose unnecessarily to hazard by the post, have made it expedient to lay the matter before the Assembly, that their former instructions may not be invalidated by a supposed effect of a change of situation, or may be rescinded if real. This went by W. Jones, Esquire, on his return to North Carolina, who, I suppose, will not be at Richmond till nearly Christmas. I wish it could have reached the Assembly before your leaving it.[3]

---

[1] See Jones to JM, 2 and 8 December 1780. JM's "fear" was unwarranted since the Maryland Assembly on 2 February 1781 authorized its delegates in Congress to ratify the Articles of Confederation (*Journals of the Continental Congress*, XIX, 138–40).

[2] The legislature of North Carolina had adjourned about three months before. It had accomplished little except to levy a tax, collectible in grain, and to create a Board of War which failed to operate effectively (*State Records of North Carolina, 1777–1790*, XIV, 378, 387, 390).

[3] The matter about which JM wished "anxiously to hear" was the position of the Virginia legislature on the Mississippi navigation issue in its relation to negotiating a treaty with Spain (JM to Jones, 25 November 1780; Virginia Delegates to Jefferson, 13 December 1780 and n. 3).

To Edmund Pendleton

RC (LC: Madison Papers).

PHILADA. Decr. 19th. 1780

DEAR SIR

You preserve your character for punctuality so well that I always have the pleasure to begin with acknowledging the receipt of a favor from you. That of the 11 instant came to hand yesterday. As the sufferings of your Militia are ascribed to the conduct of their Commanding Officer, I hope the disgust will be only local.[1] A general disgust would be a very serious misfortune.

We are informed from good authority that an embarkation is taking place at N. York. From the number of Regiments & Corps mentioned, it probably consists of about 4000 troops. Knyphausen & Philips it is said are to have the command of them. Their course will without doubt be directed to the Southern States.[2]

We have a probable story from the Southward, corroborated by a paper from N. York, that Tarlton has had an encounter with Sumpter, in which he lost upwards of 100 men including the wounded, & received a mortal wound himself. Sumpter is said to have been wounded but slightly and to have lost one man only. The personal wound of Tarlton is omitted in the N. Y. Paper, but his loss otherwise is represented as greater than our own account makes it.[3]

I am Dr Sr. Yrs. sincerely

J. MADISON JUNR.

[1] See Pendleton to JM, 11 December 1780.

[2] The source of JM's information was probably Washington's letter of 13 December to President Samuel Huntington, read in Congress on 18 December 1780 (Fitzpatrick, *Writings of Washington*, XX, 468–69; *Journals of the Continental Congress*, XVIII, 1156). On Lieutenant General Baron Wilhelm von Knyphausen, see JM to Jefferson, 23 June 1780, n. 1; on Major General William Phillips, see JM to Jones, 21 November 1780, n. 13. The troop embarkation was the outset of the British expedition, led by Brigadier General Benedict Arnold, to Virginia late in December. Knyphausen remained in New York, and Phillips did not reach Virginia to supersede Arnold in command until late March 1781 (Benjamin F. Stevens, ed., *The Campaign in Virginia*, I, 310–11, 375).

3 The engagement between Tarleton and Sumter occurred on 20 November at Blackstock's Plantation, S.C. Tarleton emerged unscathed; Sumter with a bullet in his right shoulder. The exact number of casualties cannot be ascertained. The patriots apparently lost three killed and four wounded; the British, about fifty (Christopher Ward, *War of the Revolution*, II, 746–47; Pendleton to JM, 27 November 1780, n. 2). The *New York Gazette, and Weekly Mercury* of 18 December 1780 carried a report of the battle by "Lieutenant McLeod of the Royal Artillery."

Expense Account as Delegate in Congress

MS (Virginia State Library). In this instance, unlike on 25 September (*q.v.*) when JM forwarded an expense account to the Virginia Auditors of Public Accounts, he either wrote no covering letter to them or it has been lost. The statement given below covers the quarter from 20 September to 20 December 1780 and is taken from a double-size master sheet on which Madison recorded his debits and credits as a delegate from December 1779 to 20 March 1781. Also in the Virginia State Library is the ledger page for Madison of the Auditors of Public Accounts of his state. Among his papers in the Library of Congress are two sheets in his hand—one headed "Expences from the 20th of Sepr. 1780" and the other, "Money received from the 20th Sepr. 1780." Entries on this retained copy or on the auditors' ledger page which help to clarify the quarterly statement, given below, are mentioned in the notes.

[Dr.]			[Cr.]	
1780	From Sepr. 20—to Decr. 20-1780			[Dollars]
To Balance on last settlement.........	9962⅓ Dollars[1]	By Board & Lodgs. including liqrs & Co.[7] from Sepr 20..........		18889
Ocr. 17 / Nov. 1 / Novr 8 To Cash recd. of Geo. Meade & Co. for draught on the Auditors in their favor..	1780 Decr. 20 6666⅔[2]	By incidental expenses not included the above.....		800[8]
[Nov. 14][3] To do. recd of—Graatz[4] in part of a draught on the Auditors in their favr. (my share 10,000).........	4000[5]	By expence of two Horses at public Stables.....		2827⅓[9]
Decr. 6. To do recd from Turnbull & Co......	23691[6]	By extra do. during occasional scarcities of forage there................		1370⅔[10]
	44320	By 5¼ Cord of Wood.........		276[11]
		By Candles—276—washing 1025—Barber 350.....		1641[12]
		By allowance for 91 days at 20 Drs. per day......		1820[13]
				30,028[14]
		By advance to Robt Jewel for cloathg. food & medicine for 6 sick Sailors belongg. to Virga. exchanged at N. Y................		2760[15]
		By Cash pd. for box to inclose the Books of the Delegates sent to Virga. under the care of Col. Febiger[16]		30
				32818
		Balance................		11502
				44320[17]

1 See Expense Account as Delegate in Congress, 25 September 1780—the next to last entry in the credit column.

2 This figure represented a fairly complicated transaction. The auditors sent to the Virginia delegates a draft for £8,000 Virginia currency in favor of George Meade & Co. of Philadelphia. This amount at 3⅓ for 1 equaled $26,666⅔ in continental money, to be divided evenly between the four delegates—Theodorick Bland, Joseph Jones, JM, and John Walker. Hence each would receive $6,666⅔. But in this figure another settlement was also involved. When Jones left Philadelphia in September 1780, he borrowed the equivalent of £3,000 Virginia currency from JM (Jones to JM, 9 October 1780, n. 3). Jones arranged to clear two-thirds of this debt by having £2,000 paid from the amount which Virginia owed to him. Thus, although Madison received from Meade & Co. $5,000 on 17 October, $3,678 on 1 November, and $4,655½ on 8 November, or $13,333⅓ in all, only one half of this total was a payment to him by Virginia. The other half was "on acct of JM & J[oseph] J[ones]" and hence not chargeable against JM by the auditors (JM's retained copy of his financial accounts, mentioned in headnote). Jones cleared the £1,000 remainder of his obligation by sending JM that amount from Virginia.

3 Date omitted on both JM's master sheet and his retained copy. Date taken from auditors' ledger page.

4 Michael Gratz of Philadelphia.

5 In the letter from the Virginia delegates to the auditors, 11 September 1780, a draft of $30,000 receivable from Gratz is mentioned. Each of the three delegates (Walker had left Congress) was to receive $10,000 of it. JM drew $4,000 on 14 November and the rest early in 1781 (Receipt to Gratz, 3 January 1781; Expense Account as Delegate in Congress, 27 March 1781, in Virginia State Library).

6 See Jefferson to Virginia Delegates, 14 November 1780. The auditors' ledger page records 78, 92, and 100 to 1 as the depreciation rate allowed for the Meade, Gratz, and Turnbull drafts, respectively. Thus this Turnbull payment to JM amounted only to £71 1s. ($23,691 ÷ 3.33 ÷ 100).

7 This may be an abbreviation for "company" or a symbol for "etc."

8 Here JM appears to have reduced to a round number what he recorded in his retained copy as "Fruits &c. prior to 25th. of Ocr . . . . 200" and "To Fruits &c & wine . . . . 658⅓."

9 On his retained copy, no sum appears for "To Horses & Stablage."

10 This figure is the approximate total of the following five entries on his retained copy: "Sepr. 28. 3 Bushels of Oats at 30 drs. per Bushel . . . . 90"; "Octr. 7. 12 do [Bushels] . . . . 300"; "Novr. 2. 5 Bushels of Oats at 28 drs . . . . 140"; "Novr. 24. To Oats . . . . 180"; and "Decr. 18th To 20 Bushels of Oats at 33 drs . . . . 660." These add up to $1,370. Having undercharged for fruits and wine (above, n. 8), he may have felt justified in adding an extra two-thirds of a dollar here so as to make his total expenses for the quarter amount to an even number of dollars.

11 On his retained copy JM wrote "Octr. 25. 5¼ Cords of wood at £175 with cartage &c. . . . . 267.0." Multiplying £175 by 5¼ and dividing the result by 3.33 equals approximately 276. JM evidently noted the erroneous total on his retained copy but, without changing it, he merely entered the correct sum on the copy for the auditors.

12 This amount should have been $1,651 ($276 + $1,025 + $350). And yet, JM once again varied from an entry in his retained copy. There he recorded, "To Barber . . . . $300." There also are these entries: "Novr 28. To washing . . . . 575"; "Dec 19 . . To washing . . . . 450"; and "Novr. 7—To 12 lb. Candles at 23 drs . . . . 276." Hence his charges for washing and candles on his quarterly statement and on his retained copy are in agreement.

13 The per diem allowance had been fixed by the Virginia General Assembly

(Expense Account as Delegate in Congress, 25 September 1780, n. 5). JM kept no record of this item on his retained copy.

14 The sum of the seven figures above the horizontal line is 27,624 rather than 30,028. The difference of 2,404 resulted from four errors made by JM in his computation. First of all, he clearly arrived at 30,028 by adding the itemizations on his retained copy and then mistakenly assumed that the items on his copy for the auditors would total the same amount. Second, when he added the items on his retained copy, he misread 267.0 (see n. 11 above) as 2,670. Hence on this one item he was in error by 2,403. Note 11, above, also points out that his retained copy differed by 9 from his copy for the auditors. Finally, as indicated in note 12, the 276, 1025, and 350 on his retained copy, by being erroneously totaled on the copy for the auditors as 1,641, rather than 1,651, resulted in a difference of 10 between the two copies. Thus, 2,403 minus 9 plus 10 equals 2,404, which was the net amount of JM's overcharge. Judging from the ledger page for JM in the account book of the auditors, they failed to detect his error either in his candles-washing-barber entry or in his addition of the seven figures mentioned at the beginning of this note.

15 Robert Jewell (d. 1781) was warden of the "new jail" at 6th and Walnut streets in Philadelphia, where war prisoners were often confined (*Pennsylvania Magazine of History and Biography*, XLI [1917], 411–12; John F. Watson, *Annals of Philadelphia and Pennsylvania in the Olden Time* . . . , revised by Willis P. Hazard [3 vols.; Philadelphia, 1927], III, 179–80; *Journals of the Continental Congress*, XVII, 676–77).

16 Colonel Christian Febiger.

17 Although it is reasonable to believe that these expenses were approved by the Auditors of Public Accounts for submission to the legislature of Virginia, no documentary evidence of this fact is known to exist. In late December 1780, when JM's quarterly statement probably reached Virginia, the legislature was rushing its business to completion in the face of the news of an invasion of the state by British troops under Brigadier General Benedict Arnold. There is no mention in the General Assembly's journal for the closing days of that session or for the subsequent session from 2 to 22 March 1781 of the accounts of the delegates in Congress for the last quarter of 1780. On the other hand, JM had over $30,800 placed to his credit in Philadelphia by Virginia in February 1781 (Expense Account as Delegate in Congress, 27 March 1781, in Virginia State Library). This would hardly have been done if his accounts for the preceding quarter had not passed muster with the state authorities.

Virginia Delegates in Congress to William Livingston

RC (New York Public Library). The text of this letter is in Madison's hand. The letter and its address sheet have become separated—the former is in the Emmet Collection and the latter among the papers of William Livingston.

PHILADA. Decr. 21st. 1780

SIR[1]

We received this morning a letter[2] subscribed by Peter Thornton informing us that he is the son of a gentleman in Virginia, that he lately made his escape from N. York and is now detained by your Excellency till some testimony shall be given by the Delegates from Virga. in his favor. Although we are total strangers to the youth, and are very imperfectly informed of his case, yet as we have no reason to doubt his being the son of the gentleman he calls his Father, whom we know to be of respectable character & family and firmly attached to the independance of this Country, we venture to request your Excellency to permit him to proceed on his journey to Virginia[.][3] If on his arrival here we shall have reason to suspect the reality of his professions, we shall take the necessary steps to frustrate the views of Impostors.

We have the honor to be with the highest respect & esteem Yr. Excelly's. Most Obt. & humb Servts.

JAMES MADISON JUNR:

THEOK: BLAND

[1] William Livingston, a member of the Continental Congress from 1774 to 1776 and of the Constitutional Convention of 1787; governor of New Jersey from 1776 until his death in 1790.

[2] Not found.

[3] Jones to JM, 17 January 1781. Almost nothing is known about Peter Thornton except that he was a son of Anthony Thornton, Jr. (1726–1782), of Caroline County. Anthony had served as sheriff of Caroline County, a judge of its court, and a member of its Committee of Safety. Peter appears to have been about twenty-two years of age. Why he had been in New York and how he escaped are questions as unanswerable as what became of him later (Caroline County Court Records, Order Book, 1785–1787, I, 85, photostats in Virginia State Library; T[homas] E. Campbell, *Colonial Caroline: A History of Caroline County, Virginia* [Richmond, 1954], pp. 264, 266, 269). A letter of 18 December 1780 from the chief justice of the Supreme Court of New Jersey, David Brearley, to Governor Livingston stated that Brearley had furnished Thornton with a pass to proceed from Freehold to Trenton, N.J. Once Thornton arrives at Trenton, Brearley continued, the governor might decide to enable him to reach the delegates of Virginia in Congress, but he "ought by no means to be permitted" to go to that state without the sanction of its "proper authority" (MS in Papers of William Livingston, New York Public Library). The governor evidently counseled Thornton to seek from Madison and Bland a note directed to Livingston, expressing their readiness to receive Thornton in Philadelphia. Livingston received the note, but what happened to Thornton thereafter is unknown.

Board of War to Virginia Delegates in Congress and Motion of Delegates

Printed text (*Journals of the Continental Congress*, XVIII, 1181–82). The letter of 21 December from the Board of War has not been found, but it is summarized in the *Journals*, preceding the motion made the next day. For the possible context of this item, see Matthias Halsted to Virginia Delegates, 17 December 1780, and n. 2.

[22 December 1780]

The delegates for Virginia laid before Congress a letter, of 21, from the Board of War, stating that there are three gentlemen citizens of Virginia who were taken in arms as voluntier militia men and carried to New York, that the enemy have admitted them to their paroles, that they are now here and want money to carry them home; that there is no provision made by Congress for persons in their circumstances; Whereupon,

On motion of the delegates of Virginia,

Ordered, that the Board of War[1] advance to those three gentlemen so much money as may be absolutely necessary to enable them to proceed to Virginia, and charge the same to the said State.

1 The motion at first specified the Board of Treasury, but this is crossed out.

Commission of John Laurens and Amendment to His Instructions

MSS (NA: PCC, No. 25, I, 397, 401–4). The proposed commission is in JM's hand. Except for a sentence by John Mathews of South Carolina, the instructions were penned by John Sullivan of New Hampshire. They are printed in the *Journals of the Continental Congress*, XVIII, 1184–88. Congress tabled JM's proposed amendment.

Much of the background and immediate context of the decision by Congress on 11 December to send Colonel John Laurens of South Carolina on a special mission to France has already been the subject of editorial comment (Bland to Jefferson, 22 November 1780, and nn. 3 and 4; JM to Jones, 25 November 1780, n. 15; Report on Letter from Arthur Lee, 1 December 1780, and nn. 2 and 4; Motion on Instructions to Jay, 8 December 1780). To a considerable extent the dispatch of the Laurens mission resulted from a merging of three issues of much concern to JM since the early autumn of 1780: (*a*) the desperate need of the southern states for greater military aid against Cornwallis' army; (*b*) the desire of the South Carolina and Georgia delegates for assistance from Spain, even at the price of relinquishing the right to navigate the Mississippi River; and (*c*) the drive by the Lee-Adams faction in Congress, assisted by the return of Ralph Izard and Arthur Lee from Europe, to have Benjamin Franklin ousted as minister plenipotentiary at the Court of Versailles.

The voting records of the delegates, even upon matters allied with these topics, did not always form a consistent pattern. The pressure of crosscurrents arising from other problems and the need to compromise, so that action could be taken on divisive issues, sometimes blurred the primary alignments within Congress. Thus, JM was occasionally on the same side of a question with Samuel Adams and the other Massachusetts delegates, and in opposition to his friend James Duane of New York, with whom he normally worked in accord.

Although JM recognized the seriousness of the military situation in the Carolinas and Georgia, he opposed gaining Spanish help by abandoning the right of states with sea-to-sea charters to use the Mississippi freely. Furthermore, he was as convinced of Franklin's integrity as of his lack of responsibility for the delay by France in sending additional military supplies (especially clothing) and warships. On these matters, as already indicated, he and Theodorick Bland, his sole colleague from Virginia in Congress between 23 November 1780 and 29 January 1781, did not see eye to eye.

On 25 October 1780, in response to a request from Franklin, Congress decided to dispatch a consul to France "whose duty it shall be, in addition to his consular functions, to receive and forward all supplies to be obtained in that kingdom for the use of the United States, and to assist in directing our naval affairs." Two weeks later, having been nominated by John Walker of Virginia, Colonel William Palfrey of Massachusetts, recently paymaster general of the continental army, was appointed (*Journals of the Continental Congress*, XVIII, 976–78, 1041 n., 1136–37). Even though the Lee-Adams faction had wanted Franklin removed rather than assisted, it applauded the choice of Palfrey. Early in 1781 he was lost at sea on his way to France.

Shortly after the Palfrey appointment, the critical military situation in the South brought the anti-Franklin group in Congress welcome allies. The resolutions of 18 November of the Georgia delegation, insofar as they related to Mississippi navigation and the hoped-for alliance with Spain, have already been noted. Not mentioned before was the resolution proposing that an "Envoy extraordinary be appointed to go to the Court of Versailles, to make, in concert with Mr. Franklin, the public representations of the United States," and that he be entrusted also with the dispatches for Jay (*ibid.*, XVIII, 1070–71). In this fashion, the entente between the two dissident groups, however dissimilar their separate aims, was first made public.

Although conclusive documentary evidence cannot be cited, there is no reason to doubt that Madison, and others in Congress sharing his views, sought to shelve this proposal indefinitely. If adopted, it would amount to a censure of Franklin and a dilution of his authority. During late November the "Envoy extraordinary" suggestion was not debated. Congress, on the contrary, apparently sought palliatives designed to quiet the Georgia and South Carolina delegates and the anti-Franklin faction. These took the form of a letter to Louis XVI pleading for more assistance; of additional instructions to Franklin, drafted by a committee of which JM was a member, directing Franklin to co-operate with Palfrey and to heighten his own efforts to get military and financial help posthaste from France; and of a proposal, advanced many times before and tabled once again on this occasion, to appoint "a secretary to the commission of our Minister Plenipotentiary at the Court of Versailles" (*ibid.*, XVIII, 1080–85, 1101–4, 1106, 1113).

Perhaps these diversionary tactics might have succeeded if JM and his committee on Arthur Lee's letter of 17 October had not persuaded Congress on 1 December to adopt a report which stopped far short of commending Lee for his conduct in Europe (Report on Letter of Arthur Lee, 1 December 1780, and esp. n. 4). Thereafter the "Envoy extraordinary" issue came quickly to a head. On 8 December, Congress, without a recorded vote, agreed to a motion by John Sullivan, seconded by Thomas Bee, to dispatch "an envoy extraordinary" to solicit aid "in conjunction with our Minister Plenipotentiary" at Versailles. Alexander Hamilton was Sullivan's choice for the mission. Three other candidates were also brought forward, including John Laurens, the nominee of Richard Howly (*Journals of the Continental Congress*, XVIII, 1130, 1138). Howly and his fellow delegate from Georgia, George Walton, had moved the resolutions of 18 November mentioned above. John Laurens, a son of Henry Laurens who was then imprisoned in the Tower of London, had been educated in England and had served with distinction in the patriot army. In the autumn of 1779 he had been the unsuccessful nominee of Elbridge Gerry (Mass.) for appointment as a "Minister plenipotentiary at the Court of Versailles," and before the close of that year had declined the offer of Congress to make him secretary to the United States minister to France (*ibid.*, XV, 1115, 1128, 1160 n., 1172–73, 1183, 1366; Burnett, *Letters*, IV, 538–41).

On 11 December 1780, a letter from Arthur Lee, written four days earlier, was read in Congress. Besides expressing dissatisfaction with the refusal of Congress to recognize the value of his services abroad, he denounced Franklin in unequivocal terms. After referring this second letter to a committee, of which Bland was chairman, Congress declined to follow the wishes of JM and others to reconsider its decision of 8 December to appoint a special envoy to France. John Laurens was at once unanimously chosen for this post (*Journals of the Continental Congress*, XVIII, 1139–41; Wharton, *Revolutionary Diplomatic Correspondence*, IV, 182–86; JM to Jones, 12 December 1780, and n. 4). Also on the same day, John Sullivan, JM, and John Mathews were delegated the task of laying before Congress a draft of Laurens' commission and instructions.

Occurrences in Congress during the next twelve days affected the work of this committee, reported on 23 December. As already noted, JM and Bland on 13 December wrote to Jefferson requesting him to have the Assembly of Virginia confirm or modify the instructions to its delegates in Congress about the navigation of the Mississippi. Two days later, the Bland committee, in its first report on Arthur Lee's letter of 7 December, recommended that Congress follow Lee's proposal to send an envoy "to reside at the Court of the Empress of Russia." Without a recorded vote, Congress immediately agreed and appointed Duane, John Witherspoon (N.J.), and JM as a committee to draft the envoy's commission and instructions. Significantly, Richard Howly at once nominated Lee for the mission, but he had to compete with Duane's choice of Francis Dana of Massachusetts and John Mathews' of Alexander Hamilton. On 18–19 December Congress selected Dana and agreed to his commission and instructions, apparently drafted by Duane (*Journals of the Continental Congress*, XVIII, 1155–57, 1164, 1166–73). Possibly because Duane and JM were on the committees to draft commissions and instructions for the envoys both to France and to Russia, they decided to divide the tasks, with JM bearing the main load of the former and Duane of the latter.

On 21 December, Duane carried a motion through Congress to alter "the stile and title of the minister" to be sent to France. Thereupon JM introduced, and Duane seconded, a motion to delete the words "envoy extraordinary" from the Sullivan resolution of 8 December, partially quoted above. In quick order, JM and his fellow delegates of like mind succeeded in substituting "minister" for that title and in deleting "in conjunction with our Minister Plenipotentiary at that court." Perhaps, however, the excision of this phrase was not displeasing to the Lee-Adams faction. Lack of a record of the "yeas and nays" leaves this point in doubt. Consequently, the Sullivan resolution, as amended, read as follows: "Resolved that a minister be appointed to proceed to the Court of Versailles for the special purpose of soliciting the aids requested by Congress, and forwarding them to America without loss of time" (*ibid.*, XVIII, 1177–78). Thus the way was cleared for a consideration of the draft of Laurens' commission and instructions.

[23 December 1780]

[Commission]

The United States of N. Hampshire &c.[1] to John Laurens Esqr.

We reposing especial trust & confidence in your fidelity zeal prudence and abilities have nominated & constituted, and by these presents do nominate & constitute you our Minister[2] for the special purpose of proceeding to the Ct. of Versailles & representing to his Most Xn[3] Majesty, the present state of our public affairs, with the necessity & mutual advantage of his maintaining a naval superiority in the American seas, and also of soliciting from Him[4] and forwarding to the United States, certain aids in money & stores according to an Estimate herewith delivered to you,[5] the better to enable us to prosecute the war with vigor, and co-operate with the Aims of our Ally with effect. In witness whereof &c.[6]

[Proposed Amendment to Instructions]

You will before your departure confer with the Minister Plenipo: of his Most Xn Majesty to the United States[7] and with the Honble. Major General the Marquis de la fayette on the general subject of your Mission and avail yourself of such information & advice as may tend to facilitate its success. You will also apply to the Commander in chief for his opinions & information respecting the State of the Army, & the most effectual mode of rendering the co-operation of France[8] [& o]f the United States during the next campaign, decisive against the common Enemy.[9]

---

[1] In the formal commission "N." becomes "New" and instead of "&c" there appear the names of the states arranged in their geographical order from north to south. Following "Georgia," there are the words "in Congress assembled—To John Laurens, Esquire, Greeting."

[2] Following "Minister" JM wrote and deleted "to the Court of Versailles." Obviously the phrase necessarily belonged a few words farther on and there was no reason for repeating it.

[3] "Christian."

[4] JM first wrote "his Majesty." Someone unknown struck this out and replaced it with "Him."

[5] Not found.

[6] The commission, as adopted by Congress, has as its final paragraph, "Witness his excellency Samuel Huntington, esquire, President, the 23d day of December, in the year of our Lord, 1780, and in the 5th year of our independence," signed by Huntington and countersigned by Charles Thomson, secretary of Congress.

[7] Chevalier de La Luzerne.

[8] Following "France," are the deleted words in JM's hand, "the aim of his Most Xn Majesty."

[9] Across the manuscript of this amendment appear two large X's and in the left-hand margin is the word "postpond," written by Charles Thomson. Although Congress did not adopt this amendment, it inserted in the instructions a direction to Laurens, "if it should not retard your voyage," to confer with the persons listed by JM, and also with "the commanders in chief of his Most Christian Majesty's fleet and army at Rhode Island." Having adopted the commission and amended instructions, Congress on the same day (23 December) appointed JM as one of a committee of three "to confer with the honble J. Laurens on the subject of his mission." Three days later, following the Christmas recess, JM was also named to a committee of five "to confer with the honble the Minister of France on the subject of Mr. Laurens' mission" (*Journals of the Continental Congress*, XVIII, 1193). As a belated and rather too obvious effort to soften the blow against Franklin, Congress on 27 December agreed upon "Additional Instructions to Dr. Franklin," notifying him that Laurens had been "instructed, and it is well known to be his own disposition, to avail himself of your information and influence, And Congress doubt not that the success of this measure will be much promoted by the assistance he will derive from you." Stricken by Congress from the proposed draft of these "Additional Instructions" was an affirmance by that body of its "high sense" of Franklin's "experience, wisdom, love of your country, and the esteem entertained for you by the Court at which you reside" (*ibid.*, XVIII, 1198–99). Although evidence of the fact

does not appear in the journals of Congress, the committee to confer with Laurens fulfilled its mission, while the one appointed to talk with La Luzerne was probably equally diligent. On 1 January 1781, President Huntington sent to Laurens his commission, his instructions, and various other papers to take to France (Burnett, *Letters*, V, 500–503, 506–7). He embarked at Boston on the continental frigate "Alliance" on 11 February and reached Lorient on 9 March 1781 (Wharton, *Revolutionary Diplomatic Correspondence*, IV, 252, 317).

Committee Report on Memorial of New Jersey Legislature

MS (NA: PCC, No. 41, VII, 64).

EDITORIAL NOTE

On 24 November 1780 Congress appointed James Duane, JM, and William C. Houston a committee to report upon a document read in Congress on that day and often called the "New Jersey Remonstrance" (*Journals of the Continental Congress*, XVIII, 1087–89; JM to Jones, 21 November 1780, and n. 6). In this memorial Governor William Livingston in Council and the "House of Assembly," under date of 20 November, pointed to the fact that, since the resolutions of Congress of 18 March (Jefferson to JM, 26 July 1780, n. 2; Jameson to JM, 16 August 1780, n. 5) were not workable in practice, New Jersey had repealed its enforcement act requiring the state treasurer to exchange the new currency issue at $1.00 for $40.00 of the old continental money and to receive the new notes at this same ratio in payment of taxes to the state. In other words, the 1 to 40 rate could not be maintained in the face of a simultaneous market place ratio of 1 to 80 or 90. To require that taxes be paid at the legal rate had caused New Jersey citizens great loss. The memorial recommended that, "as there is a necessity . . . [to have] . . . an uniformity in the value of the money issued by the several States," Congress ask them to rescind their enforcement acts. The balance of the remonstrance, after stressing the inability of New Jersey to pay its money quota to Congress as long as the farmers were obliged to accept certificates rather than currency from the army quartermasters and foraging agents, urged rectification of the existing injustice whereby the citizens of New Jersey were forced to provide far more than their due proportion of the food needed by the troops, while the people of some states were largely immune from impressments of this kind.

[23 December, 1780]

[Resolved] That Although Congress highly approve of the zeal and attention to the public interest manifested by the Legislature of New Jersey in their attempt to fix & preserve the value of their quota of the bills of credit emitted pursuant to the Resolutions of the 18th. of March last; yet as the measures they have adopted for the purpose are fundamentally repugnant to the general tenor of those resolutions on the vigorous execution of which Congress place their Chief reliance for carrying on the war, they can not comply with the desire of the said State that an adoption of their measures should be recommended to the other States, but on the contrary earnestly recommend to the Legislature of N. Jersey to rescind the same[1]

---

[1] With the exception that "to rescind the same" was replaced by "as well as the other States, to devise such wise and vigorous remedies as will produce the great and salutary purposes intended by the said act," this passage by JM became the opening paragraph of the majority report of the committee (NA: PCC, No. 20, I, 307). The other two paragraphs were evidently the handiwork of Duane. Houston seems to have dissented, because he drafted a version considerably less critical of the action taken by his state of New Jersey (*ibid.*, No. 41, VII, 61; printed in *Journals of the Continental Congress*, XVIII, 1192, n. 1). Congress tabled the report. When it was finally taken up on 24 August 1781, Congress decided not to act upon it.

To Edmund Pendleton

RC (LC: Madison Papers).

PHILADA. Decr. 26. 1780

DEAR SIR

I have your favor of the 18th. inst: inclosing another relating to Capt: C. Taylor with a certificate of his situation, to which I shall pay the necessary attention but cannot undertake to predict certain success.[1]

The Danish Declaration with the step taken in consequence by the Ct. of London mentioned in the inclosed are the chief news of this week.[2] There is a *report* that Arnold is gone up the Sound with 4000 troops towards N. London.[3] Wishing you the compliments of the Season

I am Dr Sr. Yours Sincerely

J. MADISON JUNR.

---

[1] Neither Pendleton's letter nor the "certificate" has been found. "C. Taylor" was probably Craddock Taylor (b. *ca.* 1754) of Orange County, a ship captain. Taylor evidently had been captured and paroled by the British and Pendleton was interested in effecting his exchange (Pendleton to JM, 5 February 1781; and JM to Pendleton, 13 February 1781). In 1763, JM and Taylor had been fellow students in Donald Robertson's school (*Virginia Magazine of History and Biography*, XXXIV [1926], 142). By 1783 he had again gone to sea and his name does not reappear in Virginia records (David John Mays, *Edmund Pendleton, 1721–1803* [2 vols.; Cambridge, Mass., 1952], II, 206).

[2] See JM to Pendleton, 7 November 1780, n. 2. The missing inclosure was probably the 19 and 23 December issues of the *Pennsylvania Packet* (Philadelphia).

[3] This was a false rumor since Brigadier General Benedict Arnold and his British troops reached Hampton Roads, Va., four days after the date of this letter. A force under Arnold burned New London, and Groton as well, on 6 September 1781 (Christopher Ward, *War of the Revolution*, II, 626–28, 868).

George Mathews and Christian Febiger to Virginia Delegates in Congress

RC (NA: PCC, No. 78, XVI, 109–10). Addressed to "Colonel Bland, and Mr Maddison. Present"

PHILADELPHIA December 28. 1780

GENTLEMEN

Some doubts arises with us, whether, under the late Acts of Congress for arranging the Army of the United States,[1] the Officers of the State of Virginia that have been, or now are Prisoners of War on Long Island,[2] may be equally intituled to their Rank in that Line, (agreable to their Standing in the Army,) with those Officers who have never experienced the distresses of Captivity, or even those that are prisoners at the Southward:[3] We therefore request that you will use your endeavours to have a Resolve passed by Congress, giving, (or rather confirming) that right; and we flatter ourselves no difficulty will be in your way on a Subject of such equal Justice, as we think ourselves Justifiable in Saying that it is the wish of the Officers of that Line; that the Prisoners have the same Rank when exchanged, which they would have been intituled to had they never been taken; and that their will be but few Officers more than will complete their Line agreable to the new arrangement.[4]

We are, Gentlemen, with due respect Your Most Obedient and Humble Servants.

GEO. MATHEWS Col.[5]
CHRISTIAN FEBIGER[6]
Colo 2nd Va Regt

[1] On 3 and 21 October Congress adopted a series of resolutions providing for a structural rearrangement of the army (*Journals of the Continental Congress*, XVIII, 893–97, 958–62). Neither these resolutions nor Washington's long comment upon some of them (Fitzpatrick, *Writings of Washington*, XX, 157–67) mentioned the issue raised in this letter.

[2] Negotiations between Washington and Clinton for exchanging the prisoners

held by the British in the New York City neighborhood for the "Convention troops" in barracks in Virginia and Maryland had been in progress for many weeks (*Journals of the Continental Congress*, XVII, 704–6; Fitzpatrick, *Writings of Washington*, XX, 314–15, 324–25, 330–31, 375–77, 443–44).

3 Principally those captured by the British when Charleston surrendered on 12 May 1780.

4 For JM's motion following the submission of this letter to Congress, see Motion on Seniority in Army, 1 January 1781.

5 George Mathews (1739–1812) was colonel of the 9th Virginia Regiment when he was captured by the British at the Battle of Germantown in October 1777. He was temporarily released on parole during 1780 to assist in the negotiations for an exchange of prisoners (Fitzpatrick, *Writings of Washington*, XVII, 342, 352, 408–10, 475–76; XX, 443). Following the Revolution and his removal from Virginia to Georgia, Mathews served (1789–1791) as a member of Congress from Georgia and as its governor in 1787 and again in 1793–1796. Early in 1812, President Madison angered Mathews by disavowing his attempt to drive Spain from East Florida.

6 Febiger resumed his command of the 2d Virginia Regiment during the Yorktown campaign of 1781. From 1789 until his death seven years later he was state treasurer of Pennsylvania.

Virginia Delegates in Congress to Samuel Nightingale, Jr.

RC (Rhode Island Historical Society). Although the cover sheet is missing, this note was almost certainly addressed to Nightingale. It is in Theodorick Bland's hand except for JM's signature.

PHILADELPHIA Dcr. 30th [1780]

SR.

Please to deliver to the Order of Monsr. de Touche,[1] Commander in Chief of the Squadron of his Most Christian Majesty now at Rhode Island, the Arms, Amunition Cloathing Medcines and other Articles, imported in the Comite on account of the State of Virginia and oblige Sr.[2]

Yr. most obedt. H. Sets

JAMES MADISON JUNR.

THEOK: BLAND

1 Captain Charles René Dominique Sochet Destouches (1727–1793) had succeeded to the command of the French ships at Newport on the death of Admiral Ternay, on 15 December 1780, and he remained in command until the arrival in May 1781 of Admiral Jacques Melchior, Comte de Barras-Saint-Laurent. A captain since 1772, Destouches was promoted to commander in 1782 and rear admiral in 1792 (Baron Ludovic de Contenson, *La Société des Cincinnati de France et la guerre d'Amérique 1778–1783* [Paris, 1934], p. 271).

2 See Nightingale to Virginia Delegates, 6 December 1780, and nn. 1 and 4; Jeffer-

son to Virginia Delegates, 18 December 1780, headnote, and n. 1. Below the signatures is the following order: "the things mentioned are to be delivered to Mr. dubose [?] agent of the French fleet at providence [.] newport the 26t january 1781. [signed] Destouches." Since this letter of the Virginia delegates was handed to La Luzerne for inclosure in his dispatch of 2 January 1781 to Destouches (Charles Campbell, ed., *Bland Papers*, II, 30–31, where it is incorrectly dated 2 January 1780), the latter probably added his postscript before the letter reached Nightingale. For "Mr. dubose," see Nightingale to Virginia Delegates, 15 February 1781, n. 2.

Motion on Instructions to George Washington

Printed text (*Journals of the Continental Congress*, XIX, 2).

[1 January 1781]

That so much of the letter from Mr. Adams[1] as relates to the probable operations of the enemy against the southern states be transmitted to the Commander in Chief;[2] and that he be informed that it is the desire of Congress that he should immediately make such a distribution of the forces under his command, including those of our allies under the Count de Rochambeau as will most effectually counteract the views of the enemy and support the southern states.

[1] Although John Adams had warned Congress in a letter of 23 August 1780 that the British were planning an all-out campaign against Virginia and North Carolina in 1780–1781, he felt certain that the continued support of France and Spain could be relied upon (Wharton, *Revolutionary Diplomatic Correspondence*, IV, 41). On 1 January the report on this letter by a committee was discussed and recommitted. During the debate, JM presented this motion, which was seconded by Thomas Bee.

[2] On the motion of William Sharpe, the remainder of the resolution was struck out. Only Virginia, South Carolina, and Georgia voted to retain this portion. On the motion of Thomas Burke (N.C.), it was replaced by the words "And that he be desired to give his opinion to Congress on the expediency of ordering the forces of his Most Christian Majesty, now at Newport in Rhode Island, to take post in Virginia" (*Journals of the Continental Congress*, XIX, 2–3).

Motion on Seniority in Army

Copy (NA: PCC, No. 41, II, 174). Copy of resolution signed "Extract from the Minut[es,] Geo. Bond Depy Secy."

January 1st. 1781

Resolved, That in the new arrangement of the Army it is the sense of Congress, that the Officers of the continental lines, who have been exchanged since the said arrangement or are now in captivity ought to be considered and arranged according to their respective ranks in the same manner with those who have not been Prisoners.[1]

[1] Moved by JM, seconded by John Sullivan, and adopted by Congress. For the context of the motion, see Mathews and Febiger to Virginia Delegates, 28 December 1780, and n. 1.

Virginia Delegates in Congress to Thomas Jefferson

RC (Virginia State Library). Written by Theodorick Bland and signed by Bland and JM. Docketed by a clerk, "Col Blands Lr. inclosg Baron de Arendt's Jany 81." Arendt's letter of 30 December 1780 "A L'Honorable Assemblée du L'Etat de Virginie" is also in the Virginia State Library.

PHILADELPHIA Jany 1st. 1781

SR.

We have been Hond. with Your Excellencys favor in answer to ours concerning the Safest and best Harbor &c. &c. which has been duely communicated, through the proper Channel,[1] and we beg leave to inform you that we have endeavord to improve the intended design into a mode for obtaining a more Speedy and safe Conveyance of the Cargoe of the Comite to Virginia (should it take place,) than a land Carriage would be and hope it will meet with yr. approbation, as it appeard to us the most eligible method, we have venturd to adopt it without particular Instructions for so doing.[2] Monsr. L___ has promised to use his endeavors to have our request complied with.[3] We have the Honor of transmiting to Yr. Excellency a Proposal from a Baron D'Arendt. He Speaks of a Commission with which he is charged but we have not as yet seen his Commission or powers, we have seen Mr. Wm. Lee's written request to him to endeavor to negotiate the Sending of Arms, Linen, &c. with Mr. Wm. Lee's promise to him in writing that if he Succeeded he shd. be handsomely rewarded by the State of Virginia, but if not he shd. be Entitled to receive from that State twenty five Louis D'ors for his trouble;[4] all these things we offer to Yr. Excellency at his request, (being ourselves Ignorant of the whole transaction except as stated above) and wait your Orders thereon.

In a letter from his Excy. Genl. Washington dated New Windsor

Decr. 27th. 1780 we have the following Intelligence—"Another embarkation has taken place at New York supposed to consist of two thousand five Hundred land forces, whose destination is not yet known the fleet fell down to the Hook on Wednesday last."[5] *Our* Conjecture is that they are destined to the Southward, and indeed all the Enemy's political & military manoeuvres seem to indicate their Intention of making a Vigorous effort against the Southern States, this Winter. We are Sorry to inform yr. Excellency that we receive very little Authentic Intelligence of the Steps which are taking to counteract those vigorous operations, that we are in a great measure uninformd of the progress that has been made in raising the new army, and on what terms, of what has been, and will be, done in establishing Magazines for its Support, and above all, of the measures persuing to cancell the old money and give an effectual Support to the new, by providing for its punctual and final redemption with Specie. This is a crisis at which we conceive a most assiduous application to these great objects to be necessary, and (next to the completion of the Confoederacy which is perhaps the Basis of the whole) of the first importance to America therefore highly importing us to know, as the measures of so large a state as ours cannot but have considerable effects on the other states in the Union.

We have the honor to be with the greatest respect Yr obt. & humble Servants.

JAMES MADISON JUNR.
THEOK: BLAND

1 See Jefferson to Virginia Delegates, 18 December 1780, answering their letter to him of about 6 December.

2 See Nightingale to Virginia Delegates, 6 December 1780, and 15 February 1781.

3 The delegates wrote La Luzerne on 1 January, urging that a frigate from the French squadron at Rhode Island bring the arms to Virginia. This letter has not been located but is described in Bland to Jefferson, 9 February 1781 (Boyd, *Papers of Jefferson*, IV, 567–68). La Luzerne wrote on 2 January to Chevalier Destouches, commander of the French squadron at Rhode Island, to seek his co-operation in this matter (Jefferson to Virginia Delegates, 18 December 1780, n. 1).

4 Henry Leonard Philip, Baron d'Arendt, had been colonel of the continental German Battalion. In a letter of 30 December 1780 from Philadelphia to the Virginia Assembly, he admitted that he had failed to carry out the mission, entrusted to him by William Lee, to open up a trade in cloth and ammunition from Prussia in exchange for tobacco and other goods from Virginia. Nevertheless, Arendt had found that the Prussian Director General of Maritime Commerce, although fearing undue losses from British capture of the proposed cargoes at sea, was sufficiently interested to request more specific information about how the business could be transacted. After pointing out that his expenses had far exceeded twenty-five guineas, Arendt asked to be reimbursed by at least that sum, in accord with Lee's promise to him

in letters of 3 and 5 July 1779. Jefferson agreed to grant to Arendt the sum asked for, even though he was convinced of Virginia's inability to trade with Prussia. On 4 April 1781 Congress added JM to a committee appointed to consider Arendt's unsettled claims against the United States. Congress eventually granted Arendt full pay as a colonel to 1 January 1781 and assured him of whatever further rewards might be bestowed upon officers of his rank and service (*Journals of the Continental Congress,* XIX, 143–44, 180–81, 353; XX, 589, 740–42; NA: PCC, No. 78, VII, 359–60; Jefferson to Virginia Delegates, 26 January 1781).

⁵ Washington to president of Congress (Fitzpatrick, *Writings of Washington,* XXI, 22). This is a summary, rather than a direct quotation. The expedition, commanded by Benedict Arnold, numbered about sixteen hundred troops and was directed against Virginia (William B. Willcox, ed., *The American Rebellion,* p. 235). New Windsor is near Newburgh, N.Y.

From Edmund Pendleton

Tr (LC: Force Transcripts).

VIRGA Jany 1st 1781

DEAR SIR

I have forfeited my reputation for punctuality, by omitting to pay you my Respects by last post, Which being Christmas day, I had fancied the rider would not move, but he did so, & without my letter. I am afraid you'l say it would have been no loss, If I had repeated the Mistake to-day, since I have not a Sylable of Intelligence foreign or domestic, except that we have housed a fine Crop of Corn, such as was never seen in Virginia before, & have hitherto had a charming winter. The account of Sumpter's Success agt Tarlton, & of Colo Washington's Compleat surprise of the Enemy, at least a party of them, are our last Accounts from the Southward,¹ & I do not hear on what ground our Assembly fix'd the recruiting Bill which changed shapes as often as Proteaus.² It is said they adjourned on Saturday last.³ I am glad to hear that the embarcation at New York was only taking place when you wrote your last letter,⁴ as we had supposed the reinforcement were already at the Southward—as it is, we have some more time for preparation. I fear not enough. pray what do you think of our New Appointment of something I know not what to call him, to Congress?⁵ Accept the Complts of the Season, & my wishes for your enjoyment of health & every Felicity, who am

Dr Sr Yr Affe & Obt Servt

EDMD PENDLETON

¹ See JM to Pendleton, 19 December 1780, n. 3. Early in December, Colonel William A. Washington, utilizing a "Quaker gun," a log propped on the stumps of three of its limbs to simulate a cannon, forced the surrender of a Tory outpost at Rugeley's Mills, S.C. Gen. Nathanael Greene's letter of 7 December, containing inclosures describing military operations in the South, reached Congress on 28 December 1780 (*Journals of the Continental Congress,* XVIII, 1199; Greene's letter and inclosures are printed in the *Pennsylvania Packet* [Philadelphia], 30 December 1781).

² The sea god Proteus assumed many different shapes to avoid capture. The bill "for recruiting this State's quota of troops to serve in the continental army" was revised several times during December before being enacted by the Assembly on 1 January 1781 (Jones to JM, 18 November, n. 6, and 2 December 1780; *Journal of the House of Delegates,* October 1780, pp. 36–63, *passim,* 78–79; Hening, *Statutes,* X, 326–37).

³ The Virginia Assembly adjourned on 2 January 1781.

⁴ JM to Pendleton, 19 December 1780.

⁵ Pendleton here grudgingly refers to Benjamin Harrison, appointed by the Assembly on 23 December 1780 as Virginia's special delegate to present its military needs to Congress, to Washington, and to La Luzerne (Jones to JM, 2 December 1780, n. 7; JM to Jones, 12 December 1780; Jones to JM, 2 January 1781).

From Joseph Jones

RC (LC: Madison Papers).

2d. Janry 1781

DEAR SR.

I was not in a condition to visit Fredericksburg the last week or you should then have been informed that Mr. Braxton has taken the Warrant upon the Treasurer and agreed to give Bills payable in Philadelphia for the amount of 110,000 £.¹ Mr. Fitzhugh was to bring them up but is not yet arrived unless he came yesterday wch. may be the case as Braxton wrote me it was expected they would rise on Saturday last.² That however is I think doubtfull as I am pretty certain they wod. if possible take up the question of the back Lands as well as the Mississippi affair with Spain.³ It seems their was a Ballot for a Person to repair to Congress and the General,⁴ in consequence of the Resolution I before mentioned to you, the day Braxton wrote, and the House being divided between the Speaker & R. H. Lee the question could not be decided as the Speaker being the person in question could not [vote] in his own case[.] after much debate and perplexity Lee withdrew his Pretensions so that Harrison stood elected.⁵ Braxton says the old Fellow was so disgusted with the vote that he believed he wod. resign his appointmt. Shod. that be the case I question whether any one undertakes the Embassy especially as it is in great part superseded by

Col. Laurens's appointmt.[6] No doubt but the Delegates in Congress by proper Instructions could have done every thing this Agent can do but as he was to attend the Gener[al] and our Delegation thin[7] it was thought be[st] to appoint some person not of the Delegation as he wod. be necessarily absent for some time on the visit to Head Quarters. I told Mr. Henry[8] the Father of the proposition I had no doubt but every proper measure was already taken and that I did not believe any good wod. result from it further than might be expected from the State[9] the Commonwealth could give of its ability to comply with the requisitions of Congress[,] that if more was laid upon her than she could bear some other course might in time be taken to supply what she wod. likely fall short, but this could be done by a representation of the matter by the Executive to the Delegates as well as in any other way. I have not heard the issue of the Report on the Delegates accounts and their future allowance.[10] If nothing unforeseen prevents I shall I hope be able to leave this abt. the 12th. instant for Philadelphia. Mrs. Jones's third day Ague and Fever still pursues her and she is so reduced as to be scarsely able to take exercise wch. makes it rather disagreeable to leave her but as she has agreed to try the Northern air next Spring if in her power and several things are wanting to prepare for Housekeeping it makes a trip on my part necessary previous to her going as she cannot venture into the City untill I could make the proper provision for fear of the smallpox.[11] It is to be hoped the removal of Sartine[12] and the introduction of this new man of distinguished ability into the managemt. of the naval departmt. of France will produce a more active and vigorous prosecution of the War in favour of America than we have yet experienced. I fear from the great delays in the Assembly our new Levies will be late in the Field.[13] adieu.

Yrs. very truly.

JOS: JONES.

[1] Evidently Carter Braxton had not fully discharged his debt to the state of Virginia (Jefferson to Virginia Delegates, 17 November 1780, and n. 3).

[2] The "they" in this sentence is the General Assembly. In the House of Delegates, William Fitzhugh and Jones were the members from King George County.

[3] On 2 January 1781, the date of its adjournment, the General Assembly adopted resolutions dealing with these two subjects (*Journal of the House of Delegates,* October 1780, pp. 80–81; Instruction from Virginia Legislature, 2 January 1781). Following this sentence in the manuscript are two short parallel lines, approximately perpendicular to the text. Identical marks follow the sentence ending "in any other way" later in the letter. Who inserted these marks and for what reason are unknown.

[4] George Washington.

[5] Richard Henry Lee and Benjamin Harrison, speaker of the House of Delegates,

each received forty votes on 22 December 1780, when a joint session of the two houses of the General Assembly balloted to elect the special delegate already mentioned (Jones to JM, 2 December 1780, n. 7; JM to Jones, 12 December 1780; *Journal of the House of Delegates*, October 1780, p. 65).

[6] Harrison, "the old Fellow," was then about fifty-five years old. On the mission of John Laurens, see Commission and Instructions to Laurens, 23 December 1780.

[7] JM and Theodorick Bland were the only delegates from Virginia in Congress at this time.

[8] Patrick Henry (*Journal of the House of Delegates*, October 1780, p. 35).

[9] As so often in the writings of this period, the word "state" is used as the equivalent of "statement."

[10] See Expense Account as Delegate in Congress, 25 September, n. 5, and 20 December 1780, n. 13; Virginia Delegates to Jefferson, 5 November 1780, n. 1.

[11] See Jones to JM, 2 October 1780, n. 14. Jones resumed his seat in Congress on 29 January 1781 (*Journals of the Continental Congress*, XIX, 94).

[12] See JM to Jones, 12 December 1780, n. 10.

[13] See Pendleton to JM, 1 January 1781, n. 2.

Virginia Delegates in Congress to Samuel Nightingale, Jr.

RC (Rhode Island Historical Society). Written and franked by JM. Addressed to "Samuel Nightingale Esqr. Providence Rhode Island." Docketed by Nightingale, "Messrs Madison & Bland, Letter dated Jany 2nd 1781 also an Order from them for the Virginia Goods whic[h] is Delivered Jany 31st 1781."

PHILADA. Jany. 2d. 1781

SIR

We have been honored with yours of the 6th. Ulto. and in behalf of the State we represent are greatly obliged by the attention you have been pleased to pay to their interest in the Comitè and her Cargo,[1] a continuance of which we must request. We conceived when we last wrote that a speedy and safe conveyance of the arms ammunition cloathing & other Articles might be obtained by land.[2] To that end we obtained an order of Congress to the Board of War directing them to order the Quarter Master General or his Deputy to send them on as expeditiously as possible and also a requisition of Congress to the State of Rhode Island, to cause the residue of the arms that were adjudged to the recaptors, to be purchased and sent on.[3] We have now hopes of as certain and a more speedy conveyance for them & therefore have to request you that (if they are not already sent forward by the first intended mode of conveyance) they may be delivered to our order, which you will probably receive soon after the receipt of this.[4] You will oblige us by taking triplicate receipts for the Articles you may deliver, one of which to be sent to the Governor of Virginia, another to us & the third to be kept by yourself. We are in behalf of the state we represent,

Yr. Most Obt. & humble servants

JAMES MADISON JUNR
THEOK. BLAND

[1] See Nightingale to Virginia Delegates, 6 December 1780 and n. 4, 15 February 1781.

[2] Letter has not been found (Nightingale to Virginia Delegates, 6 December 1780, n. 2). The delegates wrote Nightingale on 30 December, but by then they had already decided to have the goods carried to Virginia by sea.

[3] The order to the Board of War and the requisition on Rhode Island passed on 2 October 1780 (*Journals of the Continental Congress*, XVIII, 890).

[4] See Virginia Delegates to Nightingale, 30 December 1780; Jefferson to Virginia Delegates, 18 December 1780, n. 2.

To Edmund Pendleton

RC (LC: Madison Papers).

PHILADA. Jany 2d. 1781

DEAR SIR

Yesterday's post was the first that has failed to bring me a line from you since our correspondence commenced. I hope it has not been owing to any cause which concerns your health.

We had it yesterday from under Genl Washington['s] hand that another embarkation is actually departed from N. York, amoun[ting] to abt. 2500 troops. There is little d[oubt] that they will steer the same course with the preceding detachments.[1] Congress are under great anxiety for the States agst. which this accumulating force is to be directed and the more so as the principal means of their defence is so little in their power. It is not so much the want of men as the want of subsistance arms & cloathing which results from the want of money that gives the greatest alarm. A disposition appears to do every thing practicable for their relief and defence.[2]

Mr. Harrison writes from Cadis that the Combined fleets in that port, including 18 Ships from the W. Indies under Guichen, amounted to 68 Ships of the line. He offers no conjecture as to the manner in which they will be employed.[3]

I am Dr Sir Yrs Sincerely

J. MADISON JUNR.

1 See Virginia Delegates to Jefferson, 1 January 1781, n. 5.

2 See Motion on Instructions to Washington, 1 January 1781.

3 The letter from Richard Harrison, *de facto* American consul at Cadiz (Mason to JM, 2 August 1780, n. 2), may have been dated either 12 or 30 September 1780. Extracts from letters written in Cadiz on those dates appeared in the *Pennsylvania Journal* of 3 January 1781, but the paper did not name the correspondent. If Harrison wrote either or both of these letters, JM must have seen a more complete version, because some of the information which he reports to Pendleton is not in the published extracts.

Instruction from Virginia General Assembly to Its Delegates in Congress

Printed text (*Journal of the House of Delegates,* October 1780, pp. 80–81).

[2 January 1781]

Resolved, That the navigation of the river Mississippi ought to be claimed by Virginia only, as co-extensive with our territory, and that our delegates in Congress be instructed to procure for the other States in the Union, the free navigation of that river as extensively as the territorial possession of the said States reaches respectively. And that every further or other demand of the said navigation be ceded, if insisting on the same is deemed an impediment to a treaty with Spain.

Provided, That the said delegates use their endeavor to obtain, on behalf of this State, or other States, having territory on the said river, a free port or ports below the territory of such States respectively.[1]

1 For the background of this motion, see the following 1780 items: Draft of Letter to Jay, 17 October and nn. 11, 14; Bland to Jefferson, 22 November and n. 4; JM to Jones, 25 November and nn., 5 December and n. 2, 12 December, n. 5; Motion on Instructions to Jay, 8 December; Virginia Delegates to Jefferson, 13 December; Commission and Instructions to Laurens, 23 December, editorial note.

To Michael Gratz

MS (Historical Society of Pennsylvania).

Jany 3d. 1781

Recd. of Mr. Michael Gratz four thousand eight hundred and thirty seven continental dollars, being part of ten thousand dollars due on a draught in his favor by the Virginia delegates on the Auditors of that

State, four thousand dollars having been received before.[1] the remaining ballance eleven hundred sixty three.[2]

J. MADISON JUNR.

[1] On 14 November 1780 (Expense Account as Delegate to Congress, 20 December 1780).

[2] This reference to a balance still due does not square with JM's entry for 3 January in his statement of 27 March 1781 to the Virginia auditors (Virginia State Library). In the latter, it appears that on 3 January he received from Gratz $6,000 rather than $4,837. Probably he consolidated two transactions in the account sent to the auditors, although in fact he had drawn the balance of $1,163 sometime between 3 January and 27 March 1781.

Christian Holmer to Virginia Delegates in Congress

MS (NA: PCC, No. 41, IV, 153).

[*ca.* 3 January 1781][1]

The Honourable Gentlemen Delegates from the Common Wealth of Virginia.

Your Most Humble Memorialist Shew that he in August last year, Acquainted the Honourable Congress, and Delegates from Virginia[2] his Circumstances and Condition in Health as in Wanting every Thing Nessesary, and beg'd to be help whit a part for which he have Ventered his life Spend in your Service his Fortune, lost his Health, Cripled and unfit to Earn any thing, but by Colonel Muhlenberg[3] a Member of Congress Received a Answer Un exspected, that the Resolve was I Should wait the[re] was no money; Pray I beg you to Consider if a Major can Seport him Self with One Shilling a day for Three Ration and Sixty Two and a half Dollar in Gold or Silver According to promiss a month if that is not enough to make any officer Run in Debt I leve to your own Genereose Consideration; for to Seport me Self I must Sell one thing after a other to I am most Ruind and Nou But Waiting 6 or 7 Months before one Shilling a day Can be paid, is that Just, Right, or Generouse, I will leve it to God and the world. Shall I as I exspect go to Goal for my own Money and Suffer Missery in my Weekniss of Body, the Almighty God I hope will Soon Relieve me, but my Complain Shall Appear for his Throne Against Unjustice done me on Earth. Pardon my free writing Gentlemen for Dead is a Nothing to Compare Against that Miserable life I must leve in, all for my

True and Faithfull Service pass Five years. One Hundred Pound hard money or the Exchance is all what I at present time Want[,] pass Sixty Thousand dollars is due me, if Such Sum of 100 Pound may be Granted as a avance or part of my due, that I may Cleare my Self as a Honest man for the world I shall be Extremly Glad and Thankfull. if not I beg a Answer to or from, that I may give me Self up to my Creditors, and Acquaint the world of my Suffering.

I Remain with the Greatest Regard Honourable Gentlemen Your Most obedient and most Humb. Serv.

CHRISTIAN HOLMER.

Majr. in the Virginia Artillary Continental Armee.[4]

[1] The petition is undated, but it was presented to Congress on this day. Probably, as the next note suggests, Christian Holmer was in Philadelphia and penned his plea very shortly before it was laid before Congress. Even though the Treasury office believed Holmer deserving of relief, it seems not to have been extended by Congress at this time (NA: PCC, No. 136, V, 9; *Journals of the Continental Congress*, XIX, 15, 34–35).

[2] This memorial, addressed to Congress rather than to the delegates of Virginia, was dated 22 August 1780 and read to Congress on that day. Holmer was then in Philadelphia, as he would also be on 13 March 1781, when his third petition to Congress for back pay from August 1780 was finally granted (*ibid.*, XVII, 755; XIX, 254; NA: PCC, No. 41, IV, 135; No. 42, III, 401).

[3] Frederick Augustus Conrad Muhlenberg (1750–1801), a member of the Continental Congress from Pennsylvania. He would be the first speaker of the House of Representatives and serve in that body from 1789 to 1797.

[4] On 30 November 1776 Congress elected Holmer to be the major of Colonel Charles Harrison's artillery battalion, ordered to be raised in Virginia (*Journals of the Continental Congress*, VI, 195). About three years later, although he was the oldest officer of his rank in the 1st Artillery Regiment of that state, he was denied promotion because, as Washington wrote, his "qualifications as an officer [are] far below mediocrity" (Fitzpatrick, *Writings of Washington*, XV, 96). Judging from his memorial of 22 August 1780, Holmer had suffered other misfortunes, including losing his horses, partial blindness resulting from illness, lameness sufficient to unfit him for further active duty, creditors threatening to imprison him for debt, and no money with which to satisfy them and to pay his way back to Virginia. "I am undone," he declared, "and in my Old Age must suffer Misery for Fightin for America Liberty" (NA: PCC, No. 41, IV, 135). By the summer of 1781, he was in Richmond, asking the state government for money because he was obliged "to sell one thing after a other to maintain me with." "Old Holmer," as Colonel Christian Febiger then called him, seems to have been granted a half year's pay. Without avail, he sought help from Washington on 13 December 1782, and died about six months later (*Calendar of Virginia State Papers*, II, 211, 322; III, 498; Fitzpatrick, *Writings of Washington*, XXVI, 8 and n. 13).

John Mathews, for Committee of Congress, to Nathanael Greene

RC (William L. Clements Library, University of Michigan).

PHILADELPHIA Jany 4th: 1781

SIR,

The inclosed extracts from Genl. Washingtons letter of the 13th & 27th. Ulto. and from Mr. Houston's of the 30 Ulto. & newspapers will give you all the information from this quarter, worth communicating,[1] except that the fleet from New York, is sailed; what it's destination is, we are at present uninformed. 'tis said Portsmouth in Virginia.[2]

There are now 1500 coats, some vests, & overalls, making up for the southern army, & blankets are also procured for them: all of which will be forwarded without loss of time. And we hope with more care than has hitherto been done so as they may arrive safe.[3]

The resolve of Congress of the 1st. inst. is only the foundation of what is to be done for your department. the result, we will as early as possible inform you of.[4]

We are sir with much Esteem & Regard Yr. most Obedt. servts. By Order of the Committee

JNO. MATHEWS Chairman

P.S. We will thank you for a copy of our last letter, having forgot to keep one[5]

---

[1] The inclosures are missing, and the newspapers and letter of William C. Houston have not been identified. The dispatches of 13 and 27 December were laid before Congress on 18 December 1780 and 1 January 1781, respectively (*Journals of the Continental Congress*, XVIII, 1156; XIX, 1). The extracts sent to Greene were probably copies of Washington's remarks about the embarkation in, and departure of British troops from, New York harbor, presumably with a southern destination (Fitzpatrick, *Writings of Washington*, XX, 468–69; XXI, 22). If the excerpts dealt with these matters, however, they were forwarded by Mathews and his committee merely to make doubly sure that Greene received the news, for Washington had dispatched the information directly to Greene at the same time that he reported it to Congress (*ibid.*, XX, 465–66; XXI, 21–22).

[2] Benedict Arnold's expeditionary force sailed from Sandy Hook on 20 December, arrived for the most part at Hampton Roads ten days later, proceeded up the James River without delay, and occupied Richmond on 5 January 1781 (William B. Willcox, ed., *The American Rebellion*, pp. 236–37; Boyd, *Papers of Jefferson*, IV, 259).

[3] Greene wrote on 28 December 1780 to the president of Congress that "the small force that I have remaining with me are so naked & destitute of every thing, that the greater part is rendered unfit for any kind of duty" (NA: PCC, No. 155, I, 499).

[4] Motion on Instructions to Washington, 1 January 1781.

[5] Probably the letter of 12 December 1780 from Mathews and his committee (*q.v.*).

Committee Report on Relief to Prisoners

MS (NA: PCC, No. 19, VI, 329–30). Written by JM. Docketed by clerk "Report of Comee. on report of Comee. on letters from Gen. Washington of Decr. 8th &c. Read & Passed Jany 8th. 1781."

[8 January 1781]

The Committee to whom was referred the Report of a Committee on Letters from Genl Washington &c.[1] report the following Resolutions.

Resolved, That it be earnestly recommended to the States from N. Hamshire to N. Carolina inclusive to procure & forward to the Treasurer of the U. States or to their Commissy of Prisoners appointed to reside in N York by the first day of March next for the use of the officers in captivity at that place and on Long Island[2] & to be charged to the United States the following sums respectively in specie or bills of exchange on N. York[3] viz N. Hamshire 2,319. Massachussetts 13,334. Rhode Island 1,160 Connecticut 9,855 New York 4,347. New Jersey 5,217. Pennsylvania 13,334. Delaware 987. Maryland 9,159. Virginia 14,492 No Carolina 5,796.[4]

Resolved that it be permitted to such of the said States as can not provide their respective proportions within the limited time, in specie or bills as aforesaid, to export to N York Lumber boards scantling Iron Hemp Tar or pitch to be consigned to the American Commissary of Prisoners sending them, in sufficient quantity to procure the same.[5]

That to prevent a repetition of the distresses to which the want of Specie has exposed the Officers of the United States in Captivity, it be further recommended to the States above named to procure & transmit to the Treasurer of the United States half yearly during the war reckoning from the first day of March next, the sum of ____ Dollars in specie in the proportions above assigned. The same to be[6] credited to the sd States respectively.

[1] In his letter of 8 December 1780 to the president of Congress, Washington explained that he could not proceed further in his negotiations with General Henry Clinton for the exchange of prisoners until an arrangement had been agreed upon concerning the expenditures of each belligerent for subsisting and otherwise caring for the captives taken from the other (Fitzpatrick, *Writings of Washington*, XX, 443–44). The "&c." stands for a letter of 16 December, with its inclosures, from three of those captives held on Long Island—Brigadier General James Irvine of Pennsylvania, Colonel John Ely of Connecticut, and Colonel George Mathews of Virginia. Having been chosen in November 1780 by their fellow prisoners of commissioned

rank to present their hard situation to Congress and ask it for immediate relief and support, these three officers gained their temporary release on parole from Clinton. He assured them that Congress or the state governments might send various commodities to New York City, where the proceeds from their sale could be used to pay the prisoners' debts and provide for their future subsistence. Clinton stipulated only that these goods should be sold at fixed prices, so as not to undercut the Tory merchants in that city, and that he be permitted to provide relief in a similar way to the convention prisoners in Virginia and Maryland (NA: PCC, No. 78, XII, 195–96, 199–200, 203–9). Thereupon the three officers proceeded to Philadelphia, addressed the above-mentioned letter of 16 December to Congress (*ibid.*, No. 78, XII, 191–94), and included with it their correspondence with the British military authorities. On 18 December Congress referred these documents, together with Washington's dispatch of 8 December, to John Sullivan, John Mathews, and Theodorick Bland. On 6 January 1781, the day that their report was read, Congress assigned it for reconsideration by JM, Joseph Montgomery (Pa.), and Jesse Root (Conn.). Judging from the resolutions here given, Congress had deemed the briefer report of the Sullivan committee too mild in tone and not sufficiently specific in content (*Journals of the Continental Congress*, XIX, 31 and n. 2).

2 Here JM wrote and crossed out "the sum of 80,000 dollars."

3 Following "York," JM wrote and then deleted "in the following proportions."

4 Only to this point was the report acceptable to Congress. Each of the remaining two paragraphs is lined out in the published journal (*ibid.*, XIX, 38–39) and marked out with a rough cross in the manuscript. Although Jefferson had been informed as early as 12 October 1780 that the British would permit tobacco to go to New York for this purpose, Congress resisted the proposal as "an absolute breach of faith" pledged to France (Boyd, *Papers of Jefferson*, IV, 33–34, 550, 656).

5 The meaning becomes clearer when the sentence's final comma is shifted to follow "Prisoners" and when "the same" is replaced by "the quota mentioned above."

6 Following "to be," JM struck out "charged to the United."

John Mathews, for Committee of Congress, to Nathanael Greene

RC (Historical Society of Pennsylvania). Address sheet missing.

PHILADELPHIA Jany. 9th: 1780.[1781][1]

SIR,

We are desired by Congress to transmit you the inclosed resolutions.[2]

Nothing new has transpired since we last wrote, informing you of the departure of the British fleet from New York, except that in less than forty eight hours after their sailing, there was a most violent storm, which we have the best reason to imagine they had to encounter. This circumstance we flatter ourselves, will be attended with many advantages, as it will necess[a]rily cause delay on their part, & give the longer time for your reinforcements coming in. And further, that our Express, will reach you before they can, & although the notice of their approach may be short, yet it will be of consequence.[3]

We are Sir with much Esteem & Regard Yr. most Obedt. servts. In behalf of the Committee

JNO. MATHEWS Chairman

<hr>

[1] The contents of this letter permit no doubt that the year should be 1781 and that Mathews was addressing General Greene in the name of the committee of which JM was a member (Mathews to Greene, 27 November 1780, editorial note).

[2] Inclosures missing. Early in January, Congress adopted several resolutions on issues relating to the quartermaster's department when Greene had been quartermaster general, and on supplying equipment for the southern army (*Journals of the Continental Congress*, XIX, 10–13, 19–20, 23–24, 26–27, 35–36, 40).

[3] A gale on 26 and 27 December 1780 scattered the ships carrying Benedict Arnold's troops from New York to Chesapeake Bay. Although most of them reached there on 30 December, three transports bearing four hundred soldiers were delayed in arriving until five days later (William B. Willcox, ed., *The American Rebellion*, pp. 236–37; Christopher Ward, *War of the Revolution*, II, 868).

To Thomas Jefferson

RC (Virginia State Library).

PHILADA. Jany 9th. 1781

SIR

The inclosed extract of a letter from General Washington No. 1 will give your Excellency a more particular account of the late embarkation from N. York than has been before obtained.[1]

On thursday last Congress were informed by General Potter & Col. Johnston who came expresses for the purpose that a general mutiny of the Pennsylvania line stationed near Morris Town apart from the rest of the Army had broken out on the morning of New Year's day.[2] Every effort was used by the Officers to stifle it on its first appearance but without effect. Several of them fell victims to the fury of the Mutineers.[3] The next information came from Genl Wayne who wrote from Princeton whither the troops had marched in regular order on their way to Philada. as they gave out, with a determination not to lay down their arms nor return to their obedience till their grievances should be redressed. They did not suffer any of their Officers to remain with them except Genl Wayne and Colns: Steuart & Butler and these they kept under a close guard, but in every other respect treated with the utmost decorum.[4] The greivences complained of were principally a detention of many in service beyond the term of enlistment & the sufferings of all from a deficient supply of Cloathing & subsistance & long arrearage of pay. Several propositions & replies on the subject of redress passed between a deputation of Sergeants on the part of the Troops & General Wayne, but without any certain tendency to a favorable issue.[5] The Affair at length took a very serious aspect and as a great proportion of that line are foreigners and not a few deserters from the British Army, and as they shewed a disposition to continue at Princeton from whence a refuge with the Enemy who it was said were coming out in force to avail themselves of the situation of things, was very practicable, it was thought necessary to depute a Committee of Congress with powers to empl[o]y every expedient for putting a speedy end to it.[6] The President of the State with a number of Gentlemen from this place also went up to interpose their influence.[7] The inclosed copy of a Letter from the Committee No. 2 with the paper No. 3 referred to in it are the last accounts received of the matter.[8] The manner in which the offers of [the] emissary of Clinton were received & treated is a very auspicious circumstance & will probably in its impression on the enemy fully balance the joy & encouragement which this event tended to give them.[9]

Col. Bland being one of the Committee does not join me in this

I have the honor to be with great respect & esteem Yr. Excelly's obt. & hum. serv

JAMES MADISON JNR.

His Excelly. The Govr. of Virginia

[1] Of the three inclosures in this letter, JM designates as "No. 1" the copy in his hand of the third paragraph of Washington's dispatch of 2 January 1781 to the president of Congress, bearing upon the size and composition of the British expeditionary force commanded by Benedict Arnold (Mathews to Greene, 4 January 1781). Since JM's inclosure is merely an accurately copied extract from a letter readily available in printed form (e.g., Fitzpatrick, *Writings of Washington*, XXI, 51), it is not reproduced here.

[2] Judging from the printed journal, the news reached Congress on Wednesday, 3 January 1781. That evening Congress appointed John Sullivan, John Witherspoon, and John Mathews "to confer with the supreme executive of the State of Pennsylvania, on the subject matter of the intelligence received this day." Two days later Samuel John Atlee (Pa.) and Theodorick Bland were added to this committee (*Journals of the Continental Congress*, XIX, 20, 25). The "expresses" were James Potter (1729–1789), brigadier general of the Pennsylvania militia and soon-to-be vice-president of that state's Supreme Executive Council, and Francis Johnston (1749–1815), colonel of Pennsylvania's 5th Regiment, continental line, and later the sheriff of Philadelphia County.

[3] On 1 January, the "tranquility of winter quarters," about which Washington wrote that day to Timothy Pickering (Fitzpatrick, *Writings of Washington*, XXI, 41), was suddenly ended by the mutiny. During the uprising, resulting in the displacement of the commissioned officers by a board of sergeants, one of the officers and one mutineer were killed and two officers were wounded (*ibid.*, XXI, 56 n.;

Harry Emerson Wildes, *Anthony Wayne: Trouble Shooter of the American Revolution* [New York, 1941], p. 227).

4 Brigadier General Anthony Wayne (1745-1796) of the Pennsylvania line reported the mutiny to Washington on 2 January, and wrote to Congress about it six days later. Wayne's dispatch was not read in Congress until the day after JM penned the present letter to Jefferson (Fitzpatrick, *Writings of Washington*, XXI, 56 n., 64-65; *Journals of the Continental Congress*, XIX, 41). Since no earlier message from Wayne to Congress about the mutiny has been found, JM may refer to a letter of 4 January from Major General Arthur St. Clair to the president of Congress, inclosing copies of the terms asked for by the committee of sergeants on that day, and of Wayne's reply thereto. St. Clair's letter, presumably with these inclosures, was laid before Congress on 6 January (NA: PCC, No. 152, IX, 439-46; *Journals of the Continental Congress*, XIX, 30). Although St. Clair wrote from Trenton, the Wayne inclosures were dated at Princeton, about ten miles away. Colonels Walter Stewart (1756-1796) and Richard Butler (1743-1791) were both of the Pennsylvania line. Stewart, sometimes called "the handsomest man in the American army," became a Philadelphia merchant after the Revolution (*Pennsylvania Magazine of History and Biography*, XLVII [1923], 275). Butler, a brigadier general and United States agent for Indian affairs, met his death when St. Clair and his troops were ambushed by the Indians in the Ohio country.

5 For this correspondence, see *Pennsylvania Archives*, 2d ser., XI, 660-63, 671-72, 687-88, 696.

6 Above, n. 2.

7 Joseph Reed, president of the Supreme Executive Council of Pennsylvania, headed the group of prominent residents of Philadelphia which left that city with General Potter on 5 January to go to Princeton, where the mutineers had encamped. Most of the committee from Congress followed the next day (Carl Van Doren, *Mutiny in January* [New York, 1943], pp. 98-100).

8 JM's inclosure "No. 2," with the exception of a few unimportant word omissions, is a verbatim copy of John Witherspoon's letter from Trenton, 7 January 1781, written in the name of the committee of Congress, to "the President of Congress." Congress received this report on 8 January (*Journals of the Continental Congress*, XIX, 32; NA: PCC, No. 152, IX, 447). It is printed in Burnett, *Letters*, V, 515-16. JM's inclosure "No. 3" is a faithful copy of General Henry Clinton's undated notice addressed "To the Person appointed by the Pennsylvania Troops to lead them in the present struggle for their Liberties and Rights," offering to receive the mutineers on generous terms within the British lines. For this invitation, see Samuel Hazard, ed., *The Register of Pennsylvania* ... (16 vols.; Philadelphia, 1828-35), II, 167; or *Calendar of Virginia State Papers*, II, 149-50.

9 JM here refers to what Witherspoon had written in his letter mentioned in n. 8. The mutineers not only spurned the offer of General Clinton but turned over his emissary and the emissary's guide to President Reed. These two men, John Mason and James Ogden, were hanged on 11 January (*Pennsylvania Archives*, 2d ser., XI, 702; *Journals of the Continental Congress*, XIX, 82).

To Edmund Pendleton

RC (LC: Madison Papers). The address sheet is missing, but JM, probably late in life, wrote "To Mr. Pendleton" at the top. Pendleton docketed the letter "James Maddison Esq Jan. 9th. 1781."

PHILADA. Jany 9th: 1781

Dr Sr.

I have again the pleasure to begin with acknowledg the receipt of a favor from you, that of the 1st. inst: having come to hand yesterday.

On Thursday last Congress were informed by Genl. Potter & Col. Johnston who came Expresses for the purposes that a general mutiny had broken out on the morning of New Year's day in the Pennsylvania line which was cantoned near Morris Town apart from the rest of the Army. Every effort was used by the Officers to stifle it in its infancy but without effect. Several of them fell victims to the fury of the Mutineers. The next information came from Gen Wayne who wrote from Princeton whither the troops had marched in regular order on their way to Philada. as they gave out with a determination not to lay down their arms nor return to their obedience till a redress of grievances should be obtained. They suffered none of their officers to be among them except Genl Wayne & Cols. Steuart & Butler and these they kept under close guard, but in every other respect treated with the utmost decorum. The grievances complained of were principally a detention of many in service beyond the Term of Enlistment & the sufferings of all from a deficient supply of cloathing and subsistence and the long arrearage of pay. Several propositions & replies on the subject of redress passed between a deputation of Sergeants in behalf of the Troops & Genl Wayne but without any certain tendency to a favorable issue. The affair at length began to take a very serious countenance and as a great proportion of that line are foreigners & not a few deserters from the British Army and as they shewed a disposition to continue at Princeton from whence a refuge with the Enemy who it was said were coming out in force for the purpose, was at any moment practicable it was thought necessary, notwithstanding the humiliation of the step to depute a Committee of Congress with powers to employ every expedient for putting a speedy end to the discontents. The President of the State with a number of Gentlemen from this place also went up to interpose their influence. By a letter from the

Committee who had proceeded as far as Trenton recd. the evening before last, it appears that the President who was ahead & had written in to Genl. Wayne was likely to have a confidential reception. The Committee also[?] write that an Emissary of Clinton who had appeared among the Soldiers with a paper setting forth the folly & danger of adhering to a cause which had already brought so much misery upon them, promising a protection under the British Govt. a body of troops to cover their escape, & payment of all arrears due from Congress, was siezed & given up to Genl. Way[n]e Who handed him with his guide over to the President of this State, who placed them under the custody of his light-horse. This circumstance not only presages a fortunate issue to the Mutiny, but is such a proof of attachment to the Country in the most trying situation as must effectually repress the joy & encouragement which the Enemy had taken from this threatening event.[1] The late detachmt from N. York which a letter from Fredg.[2] says is in Chesapeak is abt. 1600 strong & commanded by Arnold.

I am Yrs Sincerely

J. MADISON JUNR.

[1] For editorial clarification of the persons and events mentioned in this letter, see the footnotes of JM to Jefferson, 9 January 1781. JM probably wrote to Pendleton at somewhat greater length about the mutiny because he did not send him copies of the three documents contained in his dispatch to Jefferson.

[2] In the *Pennsylvania Journal* of 10 January 1781 is an extract from a letter written eight days before by an unnamed person living at Fredericksburg, Va., stating that "about 48 sail of vessels arrived in our Bay, Saturday evening last, supposed from New York."

To Nathanael Greene

Incomplete printed copy from Stan. V. Henkels Catalogue No. 988 (29 January 1909), item 699. The original manuscript was sold in 1940 to a private collector by Parke-Bernet Galleries, Inc., of New York City (Catalogue No. 223 [30 October–1 November 1940], item 559).

Jan. 13, 1781

I enclose you an extract of a letter from General Washington of the 2d instant,[1] giving a more precise account of the embarkation from New York on the 20th ulto. than has been before obtained. On the night of the 1st instant a mutinous spirit which had been for some time working in the Pennsylvania Line of the Army broke out with such violence that the utmost efforts of the Officers were insufficient to suppress it. Two of them unhappily fell victims to the fury of the Mutineers, after completely shaking of[f] all military authority they proceeded in an entire body and in regular order to Princeton with an intention as they gave out to come on to this city and with a determination neither to lay down their arms nor return to their obedience until their grievances should be redressed. These consisted principally in the detention of many in service beyond the term of enlistment, and the sufferings of all from deficient supplies of cloathing and provisions, and the long arrearage of pay, contrary to their first plan they declined coming to this place and established their encampment at Princeton, where they entered into negotiations with Genl. Wayne, Lt. Cols. Stuart & Butler (the only officers they suffered to remain among them and whom they kept under close confinement, although in every other respect they treated them with the utmost decorum) on the subject of redress. The nature of some of their demands and the manner of their proceeding gave at length a very serious countenance to the affairs, and as the proximity of Princeton to a place of junction with the Enemy was surmised to be the probable motive of their stopping at that place, as it was confidently alleged that the Enemy were coming out in force to avail themselves of the event, and as many of the troops were foreigners & not a few deserters from the British Army it was thought best to appoint a Committee with full powers to take the necessary steps for quieting the disturbance as speedily as possible. In consequence of the appointment the Committee judged it advisable to proceed immediately to meet the Troops. The President of the State with several other Gentlemen from this place had set out for the same purpose a little time before the[m?] The information since received both from the forces & the latter is, that the President had met with a confidential reception from the troops, that they had given up to him & Genl. Wayne, an emissary and guide from Clinton with a flattering invitation to them to take sanctuary from their miseries & the resentment of those who had usurped the public authority, under the British Government, that they had been prevailed on to come forward as far as Trenton where an accommodation of principles of equity was pretty far advanced & in a sure train of being soon completed, & that the emissary & guide were under sentence of death, and would be executed yesterday morning.[2]

[1] See JM to Jefferson, 9 January 1781, for footnotes to supplement the information contained in the present dispatch.

2 The fact that JM wrote this letter to Greene is fairly conclusive proof that he was still a member of the committee "to correspond with the commanding officer of the southern department" (Mathews to Greene, 27 November 1780, editorial note). The committee's chairman, John Mathews, was absent from Philadelphia at this time as a member of the committee investigating the mutiny of the Pennsylvania troops. Mathews apparently did not return to Congress until 18 January (*Journals of the Continental Congress*, XIX, 71). Although JM probably viewed his letter as a message from the committee, Greene replied to it on 1 April 1781 as though it had been a personal communication from JM alone (William L. Clements Library, University of Michigan).

Thomas Jefferson to Virginia Delegates in Congress

FC (Virginia State Library).

RICHMOND Jany. 15. 1781.

GENTLEMEN

I called on Mr. Anderson the Writer of the letter to Capt Trot which you were pleased to inclose to me and desired he would explain the foundation on which he had written that letter. His explanation I now inclose you,¹ from which you will be able to collect only thus much that his application on behalf of Mr. Trot was utterly rejected and nothing said which could authorize him to suppose we should wink at his loading his Vessel with Corn. He has trimmed up an Answer for me of which I only wish to be acquitted till it can be understood.²

I must at the same time acknowledge to you with candor that considering the neutral light in which Congress have placed the Bermudians and the extreme want of Salt here we have at various times permitted them to bring in Salt and exchange it with Government at the [E]x. of one Bushel of Salt, for two at first and afterwards three of Corn: and sometimes for Tobacco. We have been rigorous in allowing no more to be carried out than was procured by exchange in this way.³ You cannot be made more sensible of the necessity which forces us to this Barter, than by being assured that no further back than the Counties adjoining the Blue-ridge Salt has sold lately for from 4 to 500 £ the Bushell.

(Signed)   T. J.

¹ Neither this inclosure nor the earlier letter from the delegates has been found.
² For George Anderson, see Patrick Henry to Virginia Delegates, 23 May 1780, n. 1. Captain Perient Trott (*ca.* 1736–post-1793) was a member of a prominent Ber-

muda family with both marital and commercial ties with North America. Probably his ship was the "Truce," which was reported to be in the Chesapeake in August 1780 (*Bermuda Historical Quarterly*, X [1953], 25; *Virginia Gazette* [Williamsburg, Clarkson and Davis], 19 August 1780). Although from early in the war the Continental Congress had forbidden trade with the British, it had always excepted commerce between Bermuda and the United States from its ban. Thus, even its rigidly prohibitive ordinance of 27 March 1781 forbade "the capture or condemnation of any vessel belonging to any inhabitant of Bermudas, which, being loaded with salt only, may arrive in any of these United States, on or before the first day of May next" (*Journals of the Continental Congress*, XIX, 316). To relieve the desperate shortage of salt in Virginia late in 1780, the General Assembly authorized the "agent" of the governor "to export to the island of Bermudas, any quantity of Indian corn not exceeding six thousand barrels, in payment for any quantity of salt that can or may be obtained for the same" (Hening, *Statutes*, X, 377). Apparently the Bermudians alone could engage in this trade (Boyd, *Papers of Jefferson*, IV, 466). The offense of Anderson and Trott evidently had been their determination to ship corn to Bermuda without importing salt or without a permit from the governor's agent.

³ On 19 February 1781, Benjamin Harrison informed Jefferson that the French minister seemed "extremely averse" to having "the Bermuda and Irish trades" opened because they would "prove injurious to the common cause." "I shall leave," Harrison continued, "these matters to our Delegates who I am confident will use their endeavors to have them put on a proper footing" (*ibid.*, IV, 656).

To Edmund Pendleton

RC (LC: Madison Papers).

PHILADA. Jany. 16th: 1781

DEAR SIR

I[1] was very glad at not being disappointed in my expectations of a favor from you by yesterday's post.[2] Several reports in quick succession of the arrival & progress of the predatory band under Arnold had rendered us exceedingly anxious to hear the truth & particulars of the matter. Some letters by the post tell us that the Governor with Baron Steuben was wholly engaged in removing & securing the arms & ammunition. If so he was better employed than in writing to Congress on the subject, which from his usual punctuality was expected.[3] The enterprise against Richmond at this season was certainly an audacious one and strongly marks the character which directed it. Having been long sensible that the security of the country as high up as tide water reaches has been owing more to the ignorance & caution of the enemy than to its own strength or inaccessibleness, I was much less astonished at the news than many others. To those who are strangers to the sparse manner in which that country is settled & the easy penetration afforded by its long navigable rivers, the rapid and unopposed advances of the

Enemy appear unaccountable & our national character suffers imputations which are by no means due to it.[4]

Congress have yet received no official report of the result of the conciliatory measures taken with the revolted Soldiers at Trenton. From oral & circumstantial evidence There is no doubt that they have been successful. A discharge of a part from the service & a supply of cloathing & money to the rest is the price of their submission.[5] This much considered in itself was required by justice & is consequently consistent with dignity. But considered with respect to the circumstances attending the negotiation, there is but too much ground to suspect that it will be attributed to our fears, & is therefore not a little mortifying. Happily the example, as we understand by a letter from Genl Washington recd. yesterday had not infected the other parts of the Army.[6] As the same causes however which engendered this malignant humour in the Pennsylvania line are known to exist in the other lines, we cannot be sure that the same effects will not yet take place in the latter unless they be speedily removed. As one step towards it Congress are endeavoring to profit of the alarm which this event must have excited in the States by calling upon them for the means of immediately furnishing some pay to the troops of their respective lines.[7]

You ask me what I think of the Delegate Extraordinary to Congress?[8] I wish you had told me what you think of such an appointment. It is pretty certain I believe that people in general will not consider it as a proof of confidence in the ordinary Delegation. As Mr. Jones who I believe possesses the confidence of his Country & I am sure will have as much weight in Congress as any man that will be sent on such an occasion, will come about the same time, & having attended the Legislature will be as well informed in every point of view I can not deny that the appointment appears to me to be at least a supernumerary one.[9] I wish the good effects of it may shew that I am mistaken.

The trade of this City has just suffered a very severe blow. No less than seven fine vessels have been taken out of an Outward bound fleet & carried into N. York.[10]

I am Dr Sir Yrs. very sincerely

JAMES MADISON JUNR.

The Emissary from Clinton with his guide were executed on Saturday morning last.[11]

[1] Evidently selecting this letter for publication, JM or a member of his family, many years later, put a bracket before the "I" and a companion bracket after the

postscript. With the exception of the complimentary close and JM's name, the entire letter is published in Madison, *Papers* (Gilpin ed.), I, 79–81.

2 Not found. Pendleton likely had written on 8 January.

3 JM most probably had read in the *Pennsylvania Journal* of 10 January the extract from a letter written two days before by an unknown correspondent in Fredericksburg. This informant, however, erroneously reported that Jefferson and Steuben had preserved the stores and records by moving them to Manchester before the forces of Benedict Arnold occupied "West Ham." On the contrary, the British destroyed some of the stores and public documents at Westham, along with the foundry there. Most of the firearms cast into the James River by the militia to prevent their capture were soon recovered. Arnold's foray, obliging Jefferson to abandon Richmond for a few days, naturally prevented him from writing to Congress or the Virginia delegates during the emergency. The British entered Richmond on 5 January, burned its few makeshift public buildings, and withdrew the next day. Jefferson returned to the town on 8 January (Boyd, *Papers of Jefferson*, IV, 259, 326; Dumas Malone, *Jefferson the Virginian*, pp. 336–40). Jefferson's letter of 10 January to Congress was received eight days later (*Journal of the Continental Congress*, XIX, 70).

4 In similar vein, Washington commented in his letter of 6 February 1781 to Jefferson that "considering the situation of your state, it is to be wondered you have hitherto suffered so little molestation" (Fitzpatrick, *Writings of Washington*, XXI, 191).

5 JM's "evidence" was substantiated by the committee on the mutiny when it reported to Congress on 24 January 1781 (*Journals of the Continental Congress*, XIX, 79–83).

6 In his letter of 6 January 1781 to the president of Congress, Washington warned that the patience of other troops than those of the Pennsylvania line might also become exhausted. Hence it would be "far better to meet them with a part of their just dues, than to put them to the necessity of demanding them in a manner disreputable . . . to the service and the Cause, and totally subversive of all military discipline" (Fitzpatrick, *Writings of Washington*, XXI, 64–66).

7 On 15 January 1781 Congress agreed upon a circular letter to the states, attributing the mutiny to their failure to comply with the requisitions of Congress and urging "great and spirited exertions" immediately (*Journals of the Continental Congress*, XIX, 58–61).

8 See Pendleton to JM, 1 January 1781; Jones to JM, 2 January 1781.

9 See Jones to JM, 2 December 1780, n. 13, and 2 January 1781, n. 11; JM to Jones, 12 December 1780.

10 On 10 January 1781 the *Pennsylvania Journal* reported that, about five days before, the British had captured off the Delaware capes one American ship inbound from Hispaniola and six ships outbound from Philadelphia.

11 JM should have written "on Thursday" rather than "Saturday" (*Journals of the Continental Congress*, XIX, 82).

From Joseph Jones

RC (LC: Madison Papers). Address sheet is missing, but the letter's context and its presence in the Madison Papers permit no doubt that JM was the recipient.

17th. Janry 1781[1]

Dr. Sr.

I was in doubt whether to write you by this post or not as I intend seting out in a day or two for Philadelphia and should probably have the pleasure of taking you by the hand before my Letter wod. arrive but as we have yet in this quarter recd. no certain account of the departure of the Enemy and it is reported they intend paying us a visit up Potomack I may possibly delay my Journey a few days to see the event of this affair.[2]

We hear they have done great injury to the Houses of Col. Harrison of Berkely and carryed away all his valuable Negros.[3] If they attempt to visit Fredericksburg I believe they will have reason to repent the Enterprise as there now is there and in the Neighbourhood a considerable Force and a further reinforcemt. expected to Day. I have I confess no expectatio[n] they will come up Potomack River. their Force is inadequate to any attack where the Country has been previously alarmed which is here and I believe in most other parts[4] the case. If they do us any injury it must be by plundering private persons of their property along the Shores and receiving the Negros who may run away and join them. It is not improbable this days Post may bring us information of their departure.[5] I hav[e] a Letter from Col. Anthony Thornton f[or] you with I presume the Cash inclosed you advanced his Son.[6] The Assembly have come to a set [of] Resolutions relinquishing to the United States[7] the Lands beyond the Ohio upon certain conditions. They have also changed the allowance to the Delegates to 46/ specie P day.[8]

I am Dr. Sr. Yr. aff Friend & Sevt.

Jos: Jones

Be pleased to renew a Ticket in the Lottery for Mrs. H. Battaile No. 12153 a price of 40 doll and for J. J. the number inclosed.[9]

---

[1] Besides this date line, placed by Jones at the end of the letter, JM also dated it— "1781, Jan. 17."

[2] Although it is not known when Jones left his home near Fredericksburg to go to Philadelphia, he resumed his seat in Congress on 29 January. Allowing at least a

week for the trip, he could not have delayed his departure long after writing this letter. Benedict Arnold and his troops evacuated Richmond on 6 January and, "without a whiff of gunpowder," returned to Portsmouth where they entrenched and encamped for the winter (Boyd, *Papers of Jefferson*, IV, 259; Christopher Ward, *War of the Revolution*, II, 869).

3 Berkeley, the estate of Benjamin Harrison, speaker of the House of Delegates, was on the James River below Richmond. As late as 1783, he was still trying to recover his slaves, or at least their value (Fitzpatrick, *Writings of Washington*, XXVI, 364, 370, 401).

4 Following "parts," Jones wrote and deleted "of the Country."

5 Jones, of course, was overly sanguine. The British continued to harry Virginia until the surrender of Cornwallis in October 1781.

6 Virginia Delegates to Livingston, 21 December 1780, n. 3.

7 Jones had written "Congress," but then changed it to "United States."

8 See Virginia Delegates to Jefferson, 5 November 1780, n. 1. Jones was mistaken. Hening's *Statutes* does not include this law, and there is no mention of its passage in the *Journal of the House of Delegates*. Furthermore, in his financial statement to the Virginia auditors on 27 March 1781, JM continued to show his per diem expense allowance at the old rate of $20.00 (MS, Virginia State Library). Also see Burnett, *Letters*, VI, 192.

9 The first lottery "for defraying the expences of the next campaign" was provided for by Congress in November 1776 (*Journals of the Continental Congress*, VI, 917, 959–64). In May 1780, as an economy measure, Congress authorized the managers of the fourth lottery to accept renewals from persons who wanted to retain the same tickets which they had held as participants in the third lottery. Although the drawing of the fourth lottery's winning tickets began on 2 April 1781, it was not completed for over a year; and the lucky holders were not paid until long after (*ibid.*, XVII, 459–60; XIX, 123, 304; XXI, 1200; XXII, 151; XXIII, 543–44, 824). "Mrs. H. Battaile" may have been Hannah Battaile (1718–*ca.* 1793), the widow of Nicholas Battaile of Caroline County and a sister of JM's paternal grandmother (T. E. Campbell, *Colonial Caroline*, pp. 380, 479).

Thomas Jefferson to Virginia Delegates in Congress

RC (NA: PCC, No. 71, II, 21–26). Docketed "Richmond January 18th 1781 Letter from Govr. Jefferson of Virginia to the Delegates of the State. so much as relates to a supply of ammunition & military stores Referred to the Board of War." Only the complimentary close and signature are in Jefferson's hand. A clerk's copy of this letter is in the Executive Letter Book, Virginia State Library.

RICHMOND Jan. 18. 1781.

GENTLEMEN,

I inclose you a resolution of Assembly directing your Conduct as to the navigation of the missisippi.[1]

The loss of powder lately sustained by us (about 5 tons)[2] together with the quantities sent on to the Southward have reduced our stock very low indeed. We lent to Congress in the course of the last year (previous to our issues for the Southern army) about ten tons of powder. I shall be obliged to you to procure an order from the board of war for any quantity from five to ten ton to be sent us immediately from Philadelphia or Baltimore, and to enquire into & hasten from time to time the execution of it. The Stock of Cartridge paper is nearly exhausted.[3] I do not know whether Captn. Irish or what other Officer should apply for this.[4] It is essential that a good stock should be forwarded & with out a moments delay. If there be a rock on which we are to split, it is the want of Muskets, bayonets & cartouch boxes. The occurrences since my last to the President are not of any magnitude.[5] three little rencounters have happened with the enemy. in the first General Smallwood led on a party of two or three hundred Militia and obliged some armed vessels of the enemy to retire from a prize they had taken at Broadway's,[6] and renewing his attack the next day with a 4 lbr. or two (for in the first day he had only muskets) he obliged some of their Vessels to fall down from City point to their main fleet at Westover. The enemy's loss is not known. ours was 4 men wounded. One of the evenings during their encampment at Westover & Berkeley their Light horse surprized a party of about 100 or 150 Militia at Charles City Courthouse killed & wounded 4. & took as has been generally said about 7 or 8. On Baron Steuben's approach toward Hood's they embarked at Westover; the wind whi[ch] till then had set directly up the river from the time of their leaving James Town, shifted in the moment to the opposite point. Baron Steuben had not reached Hood's, by 8 or ten miles when they arrived there. They landed their whole army there in the night Arnold attending in person. Colo Clarke (of Kaskaskias) had been sent on with 240 men by Baron Steuben, & having properly disposed of them in ambuscade gave them a deliberate fire which killed 17 on the spot & wounded 13. they returned it in confusion by which we had 3 or 4 wounded. & our party being so small & without bayonets, were obliged to retire on the enemy's charging with bayonets. They fell down to Cobham, from whence they carried all the tobacco there (about 60 hhds.[)] and the last intelligence was that on the 16th they were standing for Newports news.[7] Baron Steuben is of opinion they are proceeding to fix a post in some of the lower Counties. Later information has given us reason to believe their force more considerable than we at first supposed. I think since the arrival of the three transports which had been separated in a Storm, they may be considered as about 2000 strong[.][8] their naval force according to the best intelligence is the Charon of 44 guns, Commodore Symmonds;[9] the Amphitrite, Iris, Thames, & Charles town Frigates, the Fowey of 20 guns, 2 Sloops of war, a privateer Ship & 2 brigs. We have about 3700 militia embodied, but at present they are divided into three distant encampments: one under General Weedon at Fredericksburg for the protection of the important works there;[10] another under General Nelson[11] at & near Wmsburg; & a third under Baron Steuben at Cabbin Point.[12] as soon as the enemy fix themselves these will be brought to a point.

I have the honor to be with very great respect Gentlemen Your most obedt. servt

TH: JEFFERSON

[1] See Instruction to Virginia Delegates, 2 January 1781.

[2] Destroyed at Westham by the British troops under Benedict Arnold (JM to Pendleton, 16 January 1781, n. 3). This letter was read in Congress on 29 January and, as mentioned in the headnote, a portion of it was referred to the Board of War (*Journals of the Continental Congress*, XIX, 95).

[3] On 29 January 1781, Jefferson informed Benjamin Harrison that four of the "five to ten Tons" of powder asked of Congress must be at Fort Pitt by 1 March if they were to be of any use to George Rogers Clark in his expected expedition against Detroit (Boyd, *Papers of Jefferson*, IV, 467; Motion of Virginia Delegates, 19 February 1781).

[4] Captain Nathaniel Irish (1737–1816), probably a Pennsylvanian (*Pennsylvania Archives*, 5th ser., III, 1085), and certainly a member of Benjamin Flower's Artillery Artificer Regiment, had been on detached duty since August 1780 as continental commissary of military stores in Virginia, and for a month beginning 20 January 1781 he also acted for that state in the same capacity. Thereafter he remained in Virginia in charge of the "laboratory," in or near Richmond, of the continental line (Boyd, *Papers of Jefferson*, IV, 417, 518, 619, 658; V, 96, 232). A "laboratory" was an ammunition factory.

[5] Jefferson probably refers to his two dispatches to President Samuel Huntington on 15 January rather than to his brief covering note to him written two days later (Boyd, *Papers of Jefferson*, IV, 366–70, 386).

[6] Broadway is on the Appomattox River, near its junction with the James River, while most of the other places mentioned later in this letter (City Point, Westover, Berkeley Charles City Court House, Hood's Point, Jamestown, Cobham, and Newport News) are on or near the James River, between Richmond and Chesapeake Bay.

[7] Soon after Benedict Arnold's troops landed in Virginia, Major General Steuben suspended his efforts to collect and forward reinforcements and supplies to General Greene and, in Jefferson's words, "descended from the dignity of his proper command to direct our smallest movements" (*ibid.*, IV, 298, 335). The episodes involving the militia under Major General William Smallwood have not been identified. If a British report can be believed, a small body of their troops on 8 January 1781 surprised a considerable force of Virginia militia making merry in the Charles City

Court House tavern, killed or wounded "upward of twenty" of them, and took eight prisoners (Henry B. Dawson, *Battles of the United States,* I, 645–46). Colonel George Rogers Clark, soon to become a brigadier general of the Virginia state line, was in Richmond at the start of Arnold's invasion, making plans to lead an expedition against Detroit (Boyd, *Papers of Jefferson,* IV, 424).

[8] Even when the missing "three transports," carrying some four hundred troops, succeeded in reaching Chesapeake Bay, the force under Arnold was only sixteen hundred strong. He had used about half that number in his raid on Richmond (Christopher Ward, *War of the Revolution,* II, 868; Benjamin F. Stevens, ed., *The Campaign in Virginia,* II, 228).

[9] In October 1781 Captain Thomas Symonds (d. 1793) was to sign the Articles of Capitulation at Yorktown, when the British ships of war surrendered because of their blockade by the French fleet. Symonds' own ship, "Charon," was burned on 10 October by French shells.

[10] The principal "works" at Fredericksburg were the iron foundry of Colonel James Hunter and the state "manufactory of arms," which was then under the management of Major Charles Dick.

[11] General Thomas Nelson.

[12] Cabin Point is at the northwestern edge of Surry County, about three miles southwest of the James River.

From Reverend James Madison

RC (LC: Madison Papers).

Jany. 18th. 81.[1]

DEAR COL.

I intended to have sent you a Letter by ye. last post, but failed of an oppy. and by this Time I suppose you have heard thro' many Channels of ye. Loss of our Capitol, & ye Disgrace of Virginia. True it is that Arnold with not more than 1500 men landed at Westover, marched within 24 Hours after ye Time of landing to Richmond, destroyed whatever was considered as public Property with all ye. Rum in ye Place, proceeded to ye Foundary destroyed there a considerable Quantity of Arms & ammunition, returned ye Next Day, without scarce a Gun being fired at him: The Families within ye Sphere of his Action have suffered greatly.[2] Some have lost 40, others 30, every one a considerable Part of their Slaves. The Speaker's House they made use of as Barracks for a Day or two.[3] It is said they have ruined there every Thing they could lay their Hands upon. Williamsburg, where we remained, was not, fortunately for us, an object worthy of their attention. They landed upon their Return below Hog Island, and marched it is said to Smithfeild, but we have not yet heard what has been ye Consequence: It is expected they mean to secure themselves at

Portsmouth, or carry on their predatory Plan up Potowmack, taking Fredericksbg in their way, or indeed making ye Iron Works there a principal object.[4]

Such is ye. unequal war wh. we wage—and such too, wh. is by far a more melancholy Reflexion, is ye. improvident Spirit of this Country! But I fear this is only ye Beginning of Sorrows, or ye. Prelude to Something more important. For may it not reasonably be conjectured, that their Intention is[5] first to cut ye Sinews of Opposition by destroying our Arms &c. and then attack us in Force?

But you will ask, what has become of ye former Spirit of Virga. I assure you, I beleive, it is still as high as ever, it neither slumbers, nor sleeps.[6] The Militia turn out with great Readiness, when called upon. They[7] have upon this Occasion shewn a Zeal & Heartiness for ye Common Cause, wh. I fear'd was almost extinguished But our dispersed Situation, ye want of proper Arrangments will, unless Experience teaches[8] us Wisdom, ever expose us to similar Misfortunes.

The University is a Desart. We were in a very flourishing way before ye first Invasion. we began to collect before ye last, but we are now entirely dispersed. The Student is converted into ye Warrior, some of ye Professors thought it prudent to retire. Your Brother has not returned since ye first Invasion.[9]

It is scar[c]e worth sending you Information of ye Plan I spoke of, but it is, that I am gradually undergoing a Conversion, and I think, if Constitution will stick by me, I shall in less than a year exchange my present Profession for a more fashionable one at least; I hope, (for that is ye main Reason of most Conversions) for a more profitable one too. The Law is disagreable—but Divinity & Philosophy in ye Bargain will starve a Man in these Times.[10]

Yrs affecty

JM

---

[1] Above this abbreviated date, JM wrote "1781." Under the "81," he docketed the letter with the words, "Madison Js. Revd."

[2] See JM to Pendleton, 16 January 1781, n. 3; Jefferson to Virginia Delegates, 18 January 1781.

[3] See Jones to JM, 17 January 1781, n. 3.

[4] Hog Island, in Surry County, is on the James River southeast of Williamsburg. Smithfield, in Isle of Wight County, is on Pagan Creek near its junction with the James River and about eleven miles by land from Hog Island. For the ironworks at Fredericksburg, see Jefferson to Virginia Delegates, 18 January 1781, n. 10.

[5] Reverend James Madison wrote "is" above a deleted "was."

[6] "Behold, he that keepeth Israel shall neither slumber nor sleep" (Psalms 121:4).

[7] "But," as the opening word of this sentence, was deleted.

8 Before "teaches," a "shall" and also a "will" above it were crossed out.

9 While he was a student at William and Mary, William Madison, nineteen years old in 1781, may have roomed in the home of Reverend James Madison (*The History of the College of William and Mary from Its Foundation, 1660, to 1874* [comp. by faculty; Richmond, 1874], p. 97). Athough the faculty, and perhaps a few students also, had assembled once again by 7 March 1781, the college was obliged to close later that year for about twelve months. During that time its buildings were occupied successively by British troops and those of France and the United States. On 27 September 1781 Dr. James Thacher, a surgeon in the continental army, wrote that the institution was "capable of accommodating three hundred students, but the tumult of war has broken [it] up" (*William and Mary Quarterly*, 1st ser., I [1892–93], 264; XVI [1907–8], 59; *History of the College of William and Mary* [1874], p. 51).

10 The writer appears to be referring to a "Plan" which he had mentioned to JM in a conversation or in a now missing letter rather than to the publication project discussed in the letter of 3 August 1780 (*q.v.*). Judging from his remarks to JM in a letter on 9 March 1781 (LC: Madison Papers), Reverend James Madison may have given thought to becoming a lawyer. If this was his "Plan," he abandoned it.

Virginia Delegates in Congress to Thomas Jefferson

RC (New York State Library, Albany). Except for JM's signature, this letter is entirely in the hand of Theodorick Bland.

PHILADELPHIA Jany 23d. 1781

SR.

It is with much concern that we have learnt from Your Excellencys and the Baron de Steubens letters to Congress,¹ the Misfortunes² our Country has sufferd from the Invasion under the command of the detestable Arnold, and that he has ventured with impunity even to our Capitol.³ we have some reason to Imagine that the same plan of operations which induced Clinton to send him there will occasion him to remain in our Bay and continue that alarm to our state and Maryland which he has so successfully begun in order to Harrass our Militia encrease our expences, waste our resources destroy our Magazines and Stores when he finds it practicable, and by thus distracting us prevent our sending the necessary Succours to the Southern Army. This Sr. is a game we are open to at every period of our short enlistments, and in a great measure exposed to for want of a Militia organized to take the field, a few Gun boats or Galleys, and some good fortifications in the most advantageous Situations on our Rivers for defence, but this late event has renderd this so obvious, that we are fully persuaded our

Country will now see the necessity of adopting arrangements very different from what have been of late trusted to. We have been anxiously expecting to hear that some steps were taken at Rhode Island in Consequence of our application to the Minister—but it is more probable you will hear before we do[.] shd. that event take place, which we have spared no pains to have accomplished; and of this we have little doubt shd. it be found practicable;[4]—Nothing new has happend here since we last wrote.[5]

The Judge of the Admiralty of this State has given us notice that there are three Negroes Tom Hester & Celia confined in Goal here in consequence of a condemnation of the Vessel in which they were taken. They say they are the property of a certain Money Godwin of Norfolk in Virginia, that their Master went off with the British fleet under Leslie and gave them permission to do the same, on which they went on board the Vessel in which they were taken. If on enquiry your Excellency shall find these facts to be truly stated, we shall with pleasure execute your instructions for securing the slaves for those to whom [they] shall be adjudged.[6]

We have the honor to be with the utmost respect Yr Excelly's Most Obt. & humble servants

James Madison Junr.

Theok. Bland

1 Steuben's letters of 8 and 11 January were read in Congress on 18 and 22 January, respectively, while Jefferson's of 10 January was read on the 18th (*Journals of the Continental Congress*, XIX, 70, 74; Boyd, *Papers of Jefferson*, IV, 330, 333–35).

2 After this word, Bland wrote and deleted "and disgrace."

3 See JM to Pendleton, 16 January, n. 3; Jones to JM, 17 January, n. 2; Jefferson to Virginia Delegates, 18 January 1781, n. 7.

4 The matter here referred to was the cargo of the ship "Le Comité" (Nightingale to Virginia Delegates, 6 December 1780 and n. 4, 15 February 1781; Virginia Delegates to Nightingale, 2 January 1781 and nn.).

5 See JM to Jefferson, 9 January 1781.

6 If, as seems likely, Francis Hopkinson (1737–1791), judge of the Court of Admiralty of Pennsylvania, notified the Virginia delegates of this matter by letter, it has not been found. Although the Tory Money Godwin remains merely a name, he may have been a member of the family long and prominently identified with Nansemond County and the Norfolk neighborhood. And yet, no trace of a name even remotely resembling Money Godwin has been found in Norfolk municipal or county records. The escaped slaves may have invented the name of a fictitious master as a delaying tactic. General Leslie and his British troops evacuated Portsmouth about 19 November 1780 (Jameson to JM, 18–19 November 1780, n. 10). On 3 February 1781 Jefferson asked Colonel Thomas Newton of Norfolk, a commissioner of the Navy Board of Virginia, to ascertain the facts about Godwin and the three Negroes (Boyd, *Papers of Jefferson*, IV, 521). Jefferson apparently did not instruct the delegates, as they here suggested that he might wish to do.

To Edmund Pendleton

RC (LC: Madison Papers). Mathematical notations by Pendleton appear on the cover sheet.

PHILADA. Jany 23d. 1781

DEAR SIR

I have nothing new this week for you but two *reports:* the first is that very great discontents prevail in N. York among the German Troops for causes pretty similar to those which produced the eruption in the Pennsylvania line. It is further said on this head that a party of 200 have deserted from Long Island & gone to Rhode Island.[1] The other report is that the British Minister either has or proposes to carry a bill into Parliamt. authorising the Commanding officer in America to permit & promote a trade with us in British Goods of every kind except Linens & Woolens. This change of system is said to be the advice of some notable refugees with a view to revive an intercourse as far as possible between the two Countries, & particularly to check the habit that is taking place in the consumption of French Manufactures. Whatever their public views may be it is certain that such a plan would open fine prospects to them in a private view.[2]

We have recd. no fresh or certain information of the designs of F. and Spain in assembling so great a force at Cadiz. There does not appear to be any object in that Quarter except Gibralter. Should the attempts be renewed agst. that place, it will prove that the former has not that absolute sway in the Cabinet of the latter which has been generally imagined. Nothing would have prevailed on the French to recall their fleet from the Islands at the time they did but the necessity of humouring Spain on the subject of her hobby horse.[3]

I am glad to hear that Arnold has been at last fired at. It sounded a little unfavorably for us in the ears of people here that he was likely to get off without that proof of a hostile reception. If he ventures an irruption in any other quarter I hope he will be made sensible that his impunity on James River was owing to the suddeness of his appearance & not to the want of spirit in the people.[4]

I am Dr. Sir Yrs sincerely

J. MADISON JUNR.

---

[1] JM's information appears to have been erroneous. The origin of it has not been identified. On the other hand, in early January, contingents of Hessian troops had moved from Staten Island to Long Island. General Clinton named Major General

Riedesel, shortly after his release as an American prisoner of war in October 1780, to command the British and Hessian troops on Long Island. On 22 February 1781 Riedesel issued a proclamation, promising a conditional pardon to all deserters who returned to duty (Bernhard A. Uhlendorf, trans. and ed., *Revolution in America: Confidential Letters and Journals, 1776–1784, of Adjutant General Major Baurmeister of the Hessian Forces* [New Brunswick, N.J., 1957], p. 405; William Leete Stone, trans., *Memoirs, and Letters and Journals, of Major General Riedesel, during his Residence in America* [2 vols.; Albany, 1868], II, 88–89, 92).

2 Perhaps JM had already heard the rumor reported on 27 January 1781 in the *Pennsylvania Packet* (Philadelphia): "We are told from pretty good authority, that the first business of the new parliament will be to enable the ministry to enter into a treaty with America, the consequences of which may easily be foreseen. The majority of the cabinet are for settling matters in any way they can." This report seems to have stemmed from a letter written in London on 21 October 1780. See Jefferson to Virginia Delegates, 15 January 1781, n. 3.

3 Gibraltar was "an excellent ally of the English," serving to divert much French naval and military aid from the United States during the latter half of the Revolution. In fulfilment of a pledge to help Spain recover the stronghold from the British, France for over three years, beginning in August 1779, co-operated with Spain in besieging Gibraltar. The negotiations under way during all of 1781 between France and Spain to mount a joint and irresistible assault by land and by sea upon the rock culminated in the formidable but unsuccessful efforts under the leadership of the Duc de Crillon during the summer and autumn of 1782 (Doniol, *Histoire*, V, 14–26).

4 The now missing letter of 15 January from Pendleton to JM may have mentioned skirmishing in Virginia between the militia and Benedict Arnold's troops. The Philadelphia newspapers reported nothing to this effect until the 30 January issue of the *Pennsylvania Packet*. Also see Jefferson to Virginia Delegates, 18 January 1781.

Thomas Jefferson to Virginia Delegates in Congress

FC (Virginia State Library).

RICHMOND January 26th 1781.

GENTLEMEN

I shall now beg leave to answer your Letter of the first inst. which inclosed a Paper from Baron de Arendt.[1] Mr. William Lee was some Time ago invested with a special Agency from this State, having received however no instructions from him of his having engaged any other Person to transact any Part of it, we are uninformed as to his Stipulations with the Baron de Arendt. If he has left the particular one for twenty five Louis unfulfilled we think ourselves bound to discharge which we will do in such Sum of paper money as may purchase that quantity of hard money in Philadelphia for there being no hard money here there is no fixed exchange. If you will therefore settle this

Sum with him we will make the Remittance either in money or by answering a Bill or otherwise as shall be most practicable. After a variety of Trials to effect the cloathing of our Troops and procuring of military Stores and failing in them all a particular Institution has been adopted here for those Purposes.[2] into this Channel all our means must be turned to enable it to be effectual. Our Situation is too well known to suppose we have any Thing to spare. It is therefore not in our Power to enter into the Commerce with Prussia proposed by the Baron de Arendt however desirous we are of opening a Communication with that respectable State and willing under every other Circumstance to effect it by great Sacrifices were Sacrifices necessary. Should the Subject of Prussia chuse to adventure on Private Trade with our Citizens every Facility and encouragement in our Power will be certainly afforded. As the Speaker Harrison sets out within three or four Days for Philadelphia and can so much more fully explain to you by words the Steps taken for supporting our Opposition to the common enemy.[3] I shall decline answering that Paragraph of your Letter and beg leave to refer you to him.[4]

(Signed)   TH JEFFERSON

P S   We have no Letters of Marque left[.] be so good as to send us some by the first Opportunity.[5]

1 See Virginia Delegates to Jefferson, 1 January 1781, n. 4. For about two months before the date of this letter, the Prussian baron had been in Philadelphia—and he remained there until February 1782—seeking from Congress the money which he insisted was due him for his services as a colonel (NA: PCC, No. 78, VII, 331–62, 407, 410, 435–52).

2 Jefferson here refers particularly to the act of the October 1780 session of the General Assembly for "supplying the army with clothes, provisions, and waggons" (Hening, Statutes, X, 338–43, 376–78). This measure directed each county and municipal "corporation" to supply a specified number of "suits of clothes," consisting of "two shirts of linen or cotton, one pair of overalls, two pair of stockings, one pair of shoes, one wool, furr, or felt hat, or leather cap." Jefferson charged Colonel William Davies of the 1st Virginia Continental Regiment with the enforcement of this measure, including the assembling of cloth, of old shoes to be repaired, and of leather for making new ones (Boyd, Papers of Jefferson, IV, 414–15, 445–47, 453).

3 If this period in the manuscript is changed to a comma, the meaning will be clarified.

4 Benjamin Harrison, bearing this letter to the Virginia delegates, reached Philadelphia on 11 February (Pendleton to JM, 1 January 1781, n. 5; Boyd, Papers of Jefferson, IV, 589; Virginia Delegates to Jefferson, first letter of 13 February 1781).

5 See Jefferson to Virginia Delegates, 22 February 1781, n. 2.

Virginia Delegates in Congress
to Thomas Jefferson

RC (LC: Continental Congress Miscellany). In Madison's hand,
except for signatures of Jones and Bland.

PHILADA. Jany. 30th. 1781

SIR

We were honored yesterday with your Excellency's favor of the
15th. inst: inclosing Mr. Anderson's explanation of his letter to Capt.
Trott, and that of the 18th. enclosing instructions as to the Mississippi
& requesting sundry military supplies, in promoting which no exertions shall be omitted on our part. Your Excellency's letter to Congress
on the subject of the Convention Prisoners & the unequal apportionment of the general resources with respect to the two great Departments was also received yesterday and referred to a Committee.[1] The
Resolutions of the General Assembly ceding the Territory N. West of
the Ohio to the United States was laid before Congress at the same
time.[2] Although nothing has been yet done declaratory of their sense
of them and although they are not precisely conformable to the recommendations of Congress on the subject, we flatter ourselves that the
liberal spirit which dictated them will be approved & that the public
will not be disappointed of the advantages expected from the measure.[3]
We have pretty good though unauthenticated information that Maryland has already acceded to the federal Union.[4]

Since the extinguishment of the Mutiny in the Pennsylvania line,
some commotions founded on similar complaints have taken place in
that of New Jersey. But we have the pleasure to inform you that the
prudent & seasonable remedies applie[d] have re-established order &
discipline among the troops.[5]

We have the honor to be with the most perfect esteem & regard Yr
Excelly's. Most Obt. servts.

Jos. JONES.
JAMES MADISON JUNR.
THEOK. BLAND

---

[1] Jefferson's letter of 15 January 1781 to President Samuel Huntington was the
one in question (Boyd, *Papers of Jefferson*, IV, 369–70; *Journals of the Continental
Congress*, XIX, 95). The "two great Departments" were the military forces in the
south and in the middle states.

[2] Jefferson inclosed a copy of these resolutions, adopted by the General Assembly

of Virginia on 2 January, in his letter of 17 January 1781 to President Samuel Huntington (Boyd, *Papers of Jefferson*, IV, 386–88; *Journals of the Continental Congress*, XIX, 96). For the background of these resolutions, see Motion regarding the Western Lands, 6 September 1780 and nn.; Jones to JM, 2 October 1780, n. 2; JM to Jones, 17 October, n. 2, and 28 November 1780, n. 4.

³ The terms of cession offered by Virginia were hedged with so many qualifications that JM understates by remarking that the proposals did not "precisely" conform with the resolve of Congress on 6 September 1780 "to press upon those states which can remove the embarrassment respecting the western country, a liberal surrender of a portion of their territorial claims" (*Journals of the Continental Congress*, XVII, 806). JM was overly sanguine about the probability that the delegates in Congress would view the offer of Virginia as "liberal." They and the Assembly of Virginia did not reach common ground on the issue until about three years later.

⁴ This premature rumor was also reported in the *Pennsylvania Journal* of 31 January. The decision of the Maryland Assembly to accept the Articles of Confederation occurred two days later. On 12 February the Maryland delegates informed Congress that they were empowered to sign the document on behalf of their state. The affixing of their signatures was part of the ceremonies on 1 March whereby Congress formally proclaimed the Articles to be in effect (*Journals of the Continental Congress*, XIX, 138–40, 213–23). These ceremonies had been devised by a committee, appointed on 22 February, composed of George Walton, John Mathews, and JM. Following the main portion of its report, drafted by Walton, is a supplementary paragraph, also in his hand, recommending that Congress adjourn after the formal exercises to enable its members and the honored guests to "drink a glass of wine [to] 'The United States of America.' A keg of biscuit, in the room of cake." Following "cake," JM placed an asterisk and then quipped in a footnote, "Does it mean the Cake room" (NA: PCC, No. 23, fol. 29; *Journals of the Continental Congress*, XIX, 191–92). Insofar as the record shows, this sally was JM's only "contribution" to the work of the committee. His good humor may not have been unqualified. The Maryland Assembly had explicitly pointed out in its resolutions that, by ratifying the Articles, the state "doth not relinquish, or intend to relinquish, any right or interest she hath, with the other united or confederated states, to the back country ... and ... that no article in the said Confederation, can or ought to bind this or any other State, to guarantee any exclusive claim of any particular State, to the soil of the said back lands, or any such claim of jurisdiction over the said lands or the inhabitants thereof" (*ibid.*, XIX, 139). These reservations, of course, boded ill for the acceptance by Congress of Virginia's offer of cession of 2 January 1781.

⁵ Encouraged by the success of the Pennsylvania mutineers (Virginia Delegates to Jefferson, 9 January 1781), three New Jersey regiments marched from their winter quarters to Trenton on 20 January. Washington adopted stern measures and sent Major General Robert Howe with a detachment of New England troops to force their submission. One of the leaders from each mutinous regiment was courtmartialed and two of them were hanged. The rest of the men returned to duty (Fitzpatrick, *Writings of Washington*, XXI, 132–33, 156–57).

Motion on Navigation of Mississippi

MS (LC: Continental Congress Miscellany). Entirely in JM's hand. Docketed by Charles Thomson, "Motion, Respecting the Mississipi by the delegates of Virginia Feby. 1. 1781."

[1 February 1781][1]

The Delegates from Virginia have received an instruction from the General Assembly of that State[2] which authorises them to inform Congress, that the zeal of their Constituents to promote the general object of the Union and to remove as far as depends on them every reasonable obstacle to the speedy conclusion of an Alliance between his Catholic Majesty & these States has so far prevailed over all considerations of a particular interest, that they have consented to withdraw the claim urged in their former instructions to their Delegates on the subject,[3] to the navigation of the river Mississippi, except of such part thereof as forms their Western boundary: provided such cession shall be insisted on by Spain; and relying on Congress for their utmost endeavours to obtain for that & the other States having territory on the said river a free port or ports below such territory. In pursuance of the object of this instruction the Delegates aforesaid propose that the following letter of instruction be immediately transmitted to the Minister Plenipotentiary of the United States at the Court of Madrid.

Sɪʀ

Congress having, since their instructions to you of the ___ day of ___[4] relative to the claim of the United States to the free navigation of the river Mississippi & to a free port or ports below the 31st. degree of N. Latitude resumed the consideration of that subject, & being desirous to manifest to all the world & particularly to his Catholic Majesty the moderation of their views, the high value they place on the friendship of his Catholic Majesty and their disposition to remove every reasonable obstacle to his accession to the Alliance subsisting between his M. C. Majesty & the U. States, in order to unite the more closely in their measures & operations three powers who have so great a Unity of Interests, & thereby compel the common Enemy to[5] a speedy just & honorable peace, have resolved, and you are accordingly hereby instructed to recede from the instructions above referred to, so far as they insist on the free navigation of that part of the river Mississippi which lies below the 31st degree of N. L and on a free port or ports below the same; provided such cession shall be unalterably insisted on by Spain, and provided the free navigation of the said river above the said degree of N Latitude shall be acknowledged & guaranteed by his C Majesty to the Citizens of the United States in common with his own subjects. It is the Order[6] of Congress at the same time that you exert every possible effort to obtain from his C. Majesty the Use of the river aforesaid with a free port or ports below the said 31st. degree of N. Latitude for the Citizens of the United States,[7] under such regulations & restrictions only as may be a necessary safeguard against illicit commerce.[8]

[1] Although this is the date on the docket, the printed journal of the Continental Congress contains no reference to this statement and proposed letter until 15 February.

[2] See Instruction to Virginia Delegates, 2 January 1781 and n. 1; Virginia Delegates to Jefferson, 30 January 1781, n. 2.

[3] See Bland to Jefferson, 22 November 1780, n. 4. Instead of the word "urged," JM first wrote "stated" and then deleted it.

[4] See Draft of Letter to John Jay, 17 October 1780. On 15 February 1781, when Congress agreed to this proposed letter, these blanks were filled in with "the 29th September, 1799, and 4 of October, 1780" (*Journals of the Continental Congress,* XIX, 152). If the printed journals are accurate, it was on 28 (not 29) September that Congress first instructed Jay to stand firm at Madrid for "the free navigation of the river Mississippi into and from the sea." Congress reaffirmed this instruction on 4 October 1780 (*ibid.,* XV, 1119; XVIII, 900).

[5] After "to," JM wrote "bestow" and then crossed it out.

[6] Here JM first wrote "*command,*" and above it he put "directed." He crossed out the latter and substituted "order," but neglected to delete "*command.*"

[7] Following "States," JM at first wrote "having territory therein." By striking out these qualifying words and then inserting "United" before "States," he significantly changed the extent of the concession which Jay was to "exert every possible effort" to obtain.

[8] As printed in the journal, "I am, &c. S. Huntington, *President*" follows "commerce." Congress adopted the letter by a vote of seven state delegations. Three states, Massachusetts, Connecticut, and North Carolina, were opposed and New York was equally divided. The votes of New Jersey and Maryland were lost because each had only one delegate in Congress (*ibid.,* XIX, 153–54). Jay received the instruction on 18 May 1781 (Wharton, *Revolutionary Diplomatic Correspondence,* IV, 740).

Motion on Impost

MS (NA: PCC, No. 36, IV, 263). In JM's hand. Endorsed "Motion for Amendment."

[3 February 1781]

That it be earnestly recommended to the States, as indispensably necessary to the support of public credit and the prosecution of the war, immediately to pass laws laying an impost of 5 PerCt. ad valorem on all goods wares & merchandises imported into them respectively after the 1st. day of May next from any foreign port Island or plantation,[1] to vest Congress with full power to collect & to appropriate the same to the discharge of the principal & interest of all debts already contracted or which may be contracted on the faith of the United States during the present war, and to give to the Officers which shall be appointed by Congress to collect the said impost all the legal authorities necessary to the[2] execution of his duty.[3]

[1] Following "plantation," JM struck out what appears to have been "excepting the West [Indies?]."

[2] He wrote and crossed out "punctual" after "the."

[3] A motion, introduced in Congress on 3 February by John Witherspoon, to ask the states to empower that body to superintend the "commercial regulations of every State" and to give it an "exclusive right of laying duties upon all imported articles," occasioned a vigorous debate. Although the resolution was voted down in its original form by a vote of five states to four, it was then considerably amended and adopted by a vote of four to three. As passed, however, it still asked the states to allow Congress to levy for the use of the United States a 5 per cent *ad valorem* import duty after 1 May 1781 on all goods of foreign origin, excepting a few specified articles such as munitions, clothing, and salt. Joseph Jones, who had recently resumed his seat in Congress, joined JM on each of the two divisions to override Bland's vote of "Aye" and thereby record Virginia in opposition to the proposal. Judging from JM's substitute motion, here given, he was against lodging in Congress the power to levy the duty, although in favor of having it collected by congressional appointees and used to help restore the financial credit of the United States. The printed journal indicates neither at what stage of the debate JM introduced his motion (granting that it was ever introduced) nor whether it came to a vote (*Journals of the Continental Congress*, XIX, 105–6, 110–12; JM to Pendleton, 29 May 1781 in Madison, *Writings* [Hunt ed.], I, 136–38).

Committee Report on Tax Status of Friendly Aliens

MS (NA: PCC, No. 20, I, 9–10). Report entirely in JM's hand. Docketed "Report of the Committee on Presidt. Ware's letter of the 20th. of Novr. 1780 part passed Feby 5. 1781."

[5 February 1781]

The Committee to whom was referred the letter of the 20th. day of Novr. 1780 from Presidt. Ware with the papers enclosed[1] having considered the subject to which they relate,[2] and consulted the best sources of information within there power as to the law of Nations thereon, Report,

That it does not appear that any principle or usage established among the most friendly powers, or the spirit or tenor of any particular conventions among such powers & still less any article or clause in the Treaties between his most Xn Majesty & the United States, authorize a claim of exemption by the subjects of the former residing in America from any taxes or imposts on their property,[3] common to the Citizens of the latter and to the subjects of other nations.

That Alien friends appear to be entitled by their residence to exemption from all military & other personal services except in certain critical situations, from all taxes laid directly on their persons, and in general from all such other taxes as in their nature have immediate relation to Citizenship, and are incompatible with the duties they owe to their lawful[4] Sovereigns

With respect to the particular case of Monsr. Delatour a french subject residing in N. Hamshire stated to Congress by President Ware, the Committee are of opinion that the tax on his stock in trade of which he complains, being common to the Citizens of that State and no wise incompatible with his character of a French subject, is liable to no objection; unless such effects be included in his computed Stock as lie out of that State, to which distinction careful attention ought to be paid.[5]

The Committee further report as their opinion that as the general Law of Nations does not define with any degree of precision the privileges[6] and obligations of foreigners with respect to taxes & imposts, and as the Treaties subsisting between France & the U. States contain no particular regulations on that subject, and as it is of the utmost consequence to the inter[est] of commerce & to harmony of intercourse between the U. States & their Allies, that some precise & permanent rules thereon founded on equity liberality & reciprocity should be speedily settled, it is expedient that the Minister Plenipotentiary at the Court of Versailles should be author[ized] to open a negociation with that Court for such purpose, and that a Committee be appointed to prepare the necessary instructions for his conduct therein.[7]

---

[1] Meshech Weare (1713–1786) was president of the Executive Council of New Hampshire during most of the Revolution. The missing inclosures in his letter of 20 November 1780 to John Sullivan, a New Hampshire delegate in Congress, were a committee report of the state's General Assembly on the matter at issue (see n. 2) and a copy of a letter from La Luzerne to Monsieur Celeire de La Tour. On 11 December 1780 Congress referred Weare's letter to JM, Thomas Bee, and Sullivan. The absorption of Congress in more important problems, and Sullivan's chairmanship of the congressional committee appointed on 3 January 1781 to deal with the mutiny of the Pennsylvania continental line, delayed the submission of the com-

mittee's report to Congress until 5 February. During the committee's deliberations, it consulted La Luzerne (NA: PCC, No. 64, fols. 152–53, 156; Burnett, *Letters*, V, 480–81, 499, 549; *Journals of the Continental Congress*, XVIII, 1140; XIX, 116).

2 De La Tour, a French merchant resident in Portsmouth, had refused to pay the tax levied by the town upon his wares on the ground that he was exempt under the terms of the Treaty of Amity and Commerce concluded between the United States and France on 6 February 1778. Unable to contravert de La Tour's argument, especially since it had the support of the French minister, the town officials appealed to the legislature, and it, via President Weare and Sullivan, to Congress. Although Weare mentioned Article XIII as the portion of the Treaty of Amity and Commerce needing interpretation by Congress, a later paragraph in his letter shows that he had intended to refer to Article XI (*Treaties and Conventions Concluded between the United States of America and Other Powers since July 4, 1776 . . .* [comp. for Department of State; Washington, 1889], pp. 299–300).

3 Following "imposts," JM first wrote "laid on their property within the United States."

4 JM wrote "lawful" over a deleted "respective."

5 This paragraph was a part of JM's report, even though the type size used for it in the printed journal suggests that it was an addition by Congress itself. In the left-hand margin of the manuscript report opposite this paragraph, Charles Thomson wrote "passd." The printed journal makes it evident that Congress adopted the recommendations up to the end of this paragraph but postponed action upon the balance of the report (*Journals of the Continental Congress*, XIX, 116–17). Judging from the silence of the printed journals, this postponement never ended.

6 JM at first wrote "rights."

7 In early February, in accordance with its resolution of 10 January 1781, Congress gave consideration to the appointment of a Secretary of the Department of Foreign Affairs. The office remained unfilled until the following August, but in February some of the delegates favored Madison for the post. After surmising that Madison would likely be chosen, Thomas Burke added in a letter, probably written on 6 February: "he is a young Gentleman of Industry and Abilities, but I fear a little deficient in the Experience Necessary for rendering immediate Service in that department. however his local Situation makes him more desireable to the Southern Gentlemen . . ." (Burnett, *Letters*, V, 562–63; Jones to JM, 2 October 1780, n. 6).

From Edmund Pendleton

Tr (LC: Force Transcripts).

VIRGA Feby 5th 1781

DEAR SIR

I congratulate with you upon the very Agreable Intelligence from the South, of which you will have a full account ere this reaches you.[1] I think Ld Cornwallis's Army must be broken & can only depend for safety upon that at Cambden under Genl Lesly,[2] & could we immediately fill up our line for the War, I think the termination of that evil would not be far distant. I have heard Arnold & his crew have left Us, but don't know the certainty—[3] Nor what purpose the Assembly are to meet the 1st. of March—unless it be on the subject of money or that any circumstance respecting the recruiting the men, may make it necessary. perhaps times appointed for measures, may have elapsed during the Invasion & require new directions.[4]

Our friend Craddock Taylor wishes to know if there are any hopes of his speedy exchange—there are some Seamen at Winchester who would answer the purpose, if they can be applied to it, but that you know best.[5] My Nephew Mr Harry Pendleton is here & desires his Complts to you.[6] It is said that in Morgan's engagement the Militia behaved to a Charm—dealing out their Bayonets with all the Spirit & Dexterity of Veterans, let them have credit for it. My Complts to Mr Jones I will be ready to write him next week.[7] I am

Dr Sr Yr Affe & Obt

EDMD PENDLETON

[1] Pendleton refers to the severe defeat, inflicted 17 January 1781 by Brigadier General Daniel Morgan's force, largely made up of southern militiamen, upon Lieutenant Colonel Banastre Tarleton's troops at the Cowpens in western South Carolina. Although each side numbered only about eleven hundred troops, the victory, like that at nearby King's Mountain in October 1780, came most opportunely to boost patriot morale. Hence its importance cannot be judged merely in statistical terms. Virginians were the more elated by the news because their militia, in contrast to its conduct at the Battle of Camden, fought bravely while two heroes of the battle, Morgan and Lieutenant Colonel William Washington, were fellow citizens. Congress first learned of the victory on 8 February from General Nathanael Greene's dispatch of 24 January, inclosing Morgan's report to him of five days earlier (*Journals of the Continental Congress*, XIX, 129).

[2] In his report of 17 March 1781 to Lord George Germain (Benjamin F. Stevens, ed., *The Campaign in Virginia*, I, 355–56), Cornwallis wrote: "The unfortunate Affair of the 17th of January, was a very unexpected and severe blow; for besides reputation, our loss did not fall short of 600 men. . . . That General Greene might be uncertain of my intended route [into North Carolina], as long as possible, I had left General Leslie at Camden. . . . I employed the 18th in forming a junction with him, and in collecting the remains of Lieut-Colonel Tarleton's Corps. . . ."

[3] The rumor was false. Arnold and his troops were at Portsmouth in winter quarters. Pendleton may have been misled by a report of 1 February from Fredericksburg to the effect that all the British troops and ships in Chesapeake Bay had been ordered back to New York City. This report was printed in the *Pennsylvania Packet* of 13 February.

[4] Pendleton guessed correctly.

[5] Convention troops were being held at Winchester.

[6] Judge Henry Pendleton of South Carolina.

[7] When Joseph Jones resumed his seat in Congress on 29 January, Pendleton began writing one week to Jones and the next to JM (*Journals of the Continental Congress*, XIX, 94).

Thomas Jefferson to Virginia
Delegates in Congress

FC (Virginia State Library).

RICHMOND Febry 7th. 1781.

GENTLEMEN

The Courier d'Europe a vessel from Penet & Coy.[1] having on board military stores for this state was chased into Boston by the enemy in the summer of 1779. They were principally Artillery Stores, too bulky and heavy for us to think of bringing them on by land. By the loss of our papers we are unable to furnish an invoice of them but they are in the hands of a Mr. J. Bradford in Boston[2] who I suppose can furnish you with one. If you can get them on board any part of the French Fleet which may at any time be coming here, it would be eligible: otherwise I would beg the favour of you to have them disposed of to the best advantage for the public.[3]

I am with very great respect & esteem Gentm. Your most. Obt. & Mst. hmbl St.

T. J.

[1] See Mazzei to JM, 18 June 1779, n. 2.
[2] See Report of Board of Admiralty, 29 March 1780, n. 4.
[3] Over a year later John Bradford was still trying to sell the military supplies, but they were then worth little more than scrap iron (Bradford to Virginia Delegates, 20 March 1782, in *Calendar of Virginia State Papers*, III, 104).

Virginia Delegates in Congress
to Thomas Jefferson

RC (Virginia State Library). Except for the signatures of Joseph Jones and Theodorick Bland, the letter is entirely in the hand of JM and franked by him. A clerk, however, docketed it, "Colo T. Blands Letter Feby 81."

PHILADA. Feby. 13th. 1781

SIR

By the Speaker Harrison who arrived here the day before yesterday we were honored with your Excellency's favor of the 26th. Ulto. We shall communicate your answer to the Baron d'Arendt, and if his claim against the State be supported by proper evidence shall take the best steps in our power to discharge it[1]

A Vessel just arrived from Cadiz has brought Congress two letters from Mr. Carmichael, from one of which dated Madrid Novr. 28th. 1780. the following is extracted: "From the best information I have been able to collect I am sorry to tell you, that the nation (British) will be able to borrow the sum demanded for the expenditures of 1781, which with the usual vote of credit at the end of the session will amount to 16 Millions sterling at least. The scheme of the Ministry to effect this is not yet public but I am told it will be on similar conditions to that of the present year. 92,000 men are voted for the marine, and I have reason to think a considerable reinforcement will be sent early to the Southward and that agreeable to a proposition of Sr. J. Amherst[2] the Enemy means to occupy and fortify strongly a post near the Mouth of Chesapeak from which, with a strong Garrison & naval force, they hope to interrupt the navigation of the bay and by frequent incursions prevent the States of Maryland & Virginia from sending supplies of men &c &c. to the Carolinas Among the troops mentioned to be embarked there are three regiments of Light Dragoons. Your servants nearer G. B. will however give you more accurate information. I am persuaded that our Ally will take early measures for defeating these designs. This latter information is derived indirectly from conversations with men in a situation to be well informed."[3] Private letters by the same conveyance add that the blockade of Gibraltar was continued with great vigor, and that the Garrison began to be severely distressed.[4]

We have the honor to be with great respect & esteem Yr. Excelly's. obt & hume servants

Jos: Jones

James Madison Junr.

Theok. Bland Jr

[1] See Jefferson to Virginia Delegates, 26 January 1781, nn. 1 and 4.

[2] Sir Jeffrey Amherst (1717–1797), a British commander-in-chief during the French and Indian War, had declined a field command in the Revolution but served in England as an adviser on military affairs in North America.

[3] See JM to Pendleton, 23 January 1781, n. 3. The brig "Virginia," arriving at Philadelphia on 11 February, forty days out of Cadiz, delivered official letters of 28 November and 19 December to Congress from William Carmichael. JM's information is taken from the first of these dispatches. Both are printed in Wharton, *Revolutionary Diplomatic Correspondence*, IV, 164–68, 198.

[4] See JM to Pendleton, 23 January 1781, n. 3. The "private letters" have not been identified. Carmichael's letter of 28 November 1780 to "Dear [Richard?] Harrison" (Dolley Madison Memorial Association, Guilford College, N.C.) does not mention Gibraltar.

Virginia Delegates in Congress
to Thomas Jefferson

RC (Virginia State Library). Written by Theodorick Bland and signed by Bland and Joseph Jones.

PHILADELPHIA Feby. 13 1781

SR.

We are Just informd from Genl. Varnum a Member now in Congress from Rhode Island that he has received Certain Intelligence that the Culloden of 74 Guns is drove on Shore and all her Crew except 17 men Perishd. the London of 90 Guns is driven out to Sea dismasted and two other 64 Gun Men of War Were dismasted entirely and all their Guns thrown over board in the late Storm.[1] Since writing the above We have procured the acct. from Genl. Varnum in his own hand, which We have the Honor to Enclose.[2] it is moreover added that on hearing the above the Enemy at N. York sent orders to Arnold to retreat from Virginia.[3] Heavenly Storm[.] we are Yr. Exclys Most obedt. Serts

JOS: JONES
THEOK: BLAND

[1] James Mitchell Varnum (1748–1789), a continental officer on active service, 1775–1780, but a delegate in Congress from Rhode Island at the time of this letter. The source of Varnum's information about the gale on 22 January, which scattered and damaged the British blockading fleet in Long Island Sound, is unknown. As early as 31 January the *Pennsylvania Journal* (Philadelphia) carried a rumor about the havoc wrought by the storm. The *Journal* of 14 February reported that "a gentleman arrived yesterday from Rhode Island" with news of the wrecked ships (Burnett, *Letters,* V, 567 and n. 3). The present letter exaggerates the extent of the loss in ships. The "Culloden" was wrecked, but its crew and stores were saved; the "Bedford" and "America," although severely damaged, managed to limp back to port (William B. Willcox, ed., *The American Rebellion,* pp. 249–50 and n. 2). Jefferson probably heard the news from Washington before the delegates' letter arrived (Fitzpatrick, *Writings of Washington,* XXI, 191–92).

[2] Inclosure not found.

[3] The delegates were reporting a false rumor which appeared in the *Pennsylvania Packet* (Philadelphia) of 13 February.

To Edmund Pendleton

RC (LC: Madison Papers).

PHILADA. Feby. [13][1] 1781

DEAR SIR

I have your favor of the 5th. instant by the post. Col. Harrison arrived here yesterday,[2] and as he mentions no circumstance which indicated an intended departure of the Enemy I am afraid your intelligence on that subject was not well founded. Immediately on the receipt of your former letter relating to an exchange of C. Taylor[3] I applied to the Admiralty department, and if such a step can be brought about with propriety, I hope he will be gratified, but considering the tenor of their treatment of naval prisoners, and the resolutions with which it has inspired Congress, I do not think it probable that exchanges will go on easily, and if this were less the case, a mere passenger under the indulgence too of a parole, can scarcely hope to be preferred to such as are suffering the utmost hardships and were made prisoners in public service.[4]

A vessel arrived here a few days ago from Cadiz which brings letters of as late date as the last of Decr. Those that are official tell us that England is making the most strenuous exertions for the current year, & that she is likely to be but too successful in the great article of money. The Parliament have voted 92000 seamen, and a considerable land reinforcement for their Southern Army in America is also sd to be in preparation. Private letters by the same conveyance mention that the blockage of Gibralter is going on with alacrity, and that the garrison is in such distress as flatters the hope of a speedy capitulation.[5]

If Mr. Pendleton your nephew is still with you be pleased to return him my compliments.[6] With great respect I am

Dr Sr. Yr. Obt. servant

J. MADISON JNR.

[1] In his reply of 5 March (LC: Force Transcripts) Pendleton referred to this letter as "of the 13th past" and he docketed it with that date. On the other hand, in his second sentence JM alluded to the arrival of Benjamin Harrison "yesterday." JM probably thought that Harrison had reached Philadelphia on the 12th, not knowing of his arrival late the evening before. At the outset of the second paragraph, JM mentions "a vessel" coming "a few days ago." This was the "Virginia," which docked at Philadelphia on 11 February. If JM had been writing on the 12th, he would hardly have referred to the 11th as "a few days ago."

[2] See Pendleton to JM, 1 January 1781, n. 5.

[3] Craddock Taylor. The date of the "former letter," now missing, was 18 December 1780 (JM to Pendleton, 26 December 1780).

[4] On 5 January 1781, Congress voted to stop exchanging captive navy personnel until Great Britain returned to America the United States seamen held as prisoners overseas. On 29 January Congress superseded this resolution with another which sanctioned as harsh a treatment of prisoners from the British armed services as was meted out by the British to their captives from the American army or navy (*Journals of the Continental Congress*, XIX, 28, 96–97).

[5] See Virginia Delegates to Jefferson, first letter of 13 February 1781, n. 4.

[6] Henry Pendleton.

Samuel Nightingale, Jr., to Virginia Delegates in Congress

Draft (Rhode Island Historical Society).

PROVIDENCE Feby 15th 1781

GENTN.

I Recd your Favor of 2nd Jany, and your Order for the Goods, in my hands, in favor of Monsr. La Touch,[1] and have Deliverd them to his Agent Monsr Dubosy[2] ye 31st Jany last as Pr a Rect Inclosed,[3] and hope they will arrive in Virginia in good order. Monsr. Dubosy refused to give a Rect for the paritcular Articles, as he had not seen them. In your Order you mention that I should send the Amunition there was but little and that Clamed by Monsr. Couloux La Vigna, and it was Delivered him.[4] There is some Chinces & Velvets & Thick felts that was marked MR yet in my hands, it is supposed these belong to Mr. Robert Morris of Philadelphia,[5] There is also the Cordage & Sole Leather, (all the rest are sent by the above conveyance) These are articles that cannot be much wanted in Virginia, and there is some charges to pay here, I propose selling these for that purpose, and as soon as they are sold shall send you an Acct of them, with the Bills that are now unpaid. I have had much more Trouble with these goods than to receive goods from any Person, and sell them, as I attended the whole time of unlading & Storeing them, takeing there marks & Numbers, opening and makeing an Invoice of the whole, then Packing them up untill after Coart, Gitting Evidences, attending the Tryal at the Admiralty Coart, dividing the goods, and makeing Invoices of the division, Packing up the goods again, giveing Copies of all the Invoices and other papers to remain in the Admiralty office, Settling with the Recaptors not without Difficulty &c &c—For which I propose Chargeing Two & one half Pr. Ct. Commissions, Five Pr. Ct. is the customary Commissions in the New England States.

I sent a Letter to His Excelency Govr. Jefferson with these goods, inclosing Monsr. Dubosy Rect, also a general Invoice mentiong the Number of pieces [of] Broad Colth, Serges, Linnens, and all the things that was deliverd them.[6] A more particular Invoice I before sent you. I now send you a Copy of the Invoice of the whole Cargo that came in the Schooner Le Committe to Providence, with some Accounts & bills[.][7] I did not pack the Arms in Straw, as I Proposed to you some time past, but was ready to do it, if they went by land; but it was not necessary as they went by water.[8]

Messrs Madison & Bland

[1] Destouches. For an identification of "the Goods," see Nightingale to Virginia Delegates, 6 December 1780, n. 4.

[2] See Virginia Delegates to Nightingale, 30 December 1780, n. 2. "Dubosy" may have been Denis Jean Florimond Langlois de Montheville, Chevalier du Bouchet (1752–1826), deputy adjutant general of the French army in the United States.

[3] Not found.

[4] Coulaux la Vigne (Vigna), resident in Philadelphia, represented Penet, d'Acosta Frères et Cie of Nantes, which claimed ownership of "Le Comité" and its stores. Shortly after the schooner and its stores had been sold at public auction on 26 September 1780, Vigne presented a power of attorney to the judge of the Admiralty Court of Rhode Island, sufficiently convincing to award him "the neat Proceeds of all that was sold" (Boyd, *Papers of Jefferson*, IV, 143). The cargo, of course, had not been sold.

[5] Robert Morris, partner in the important banking and trading firm of Willing and Morris and soon to be superintendent of finance.

[6] In the Rhode Island Historical Society is Nightingale's retained copy of his letter of 31 January 1781 to Jefferson. Attached to the letter is a copy of a statement listing as the property of Virginia delivered to "Dubosy," forty-five chests of arms, six casks, five boxes, and eight bales of unspecified "Merchandize," and three casks, three boxes, and one bale of unidentified "Medicines." An equal quantity of Virginia's goods had been awarded by the Admiralty Court to the American privateers that had retaken "Le Comité" at sea from its British captors. In addition to the above articles Nightingale mistakenly sent on to Virginia two other "Parcels of Medicines" marked "CV." On 9 April 1781, Jefferson returned these to the Virginia delegation in Congress for delivery to their rightful owner, Coulaux la Vigne (Boyd, *Papers of Jefferson*, V, 395).

[7] Inclosures not found.

[8] See Nightingale to Virginia Delegates, 6 December 1780. Nightingale had first written and crossed out the following sentence: "I wrote you some time past that I Intendid to git the Arms repacked, I found it would be attended with considerable Expence, on that Account I did not meddle with them, as a little expence would fit them to go by water, (which I got done before they went away) but I should not have sent them by land, before they were in proper order[.]" On 9 February, Theodorick Bland informed Jefferson by letter that, thanks to the efforts of the Virginia delegates and especially to his own efforts, the arms owned by Virginia aboard "Le Comité" were at last in the hold of a French frigate "intended to be sent" to Chesapeake Bay (Boyd, *Papers of Jefferson*, IV, 567). The ship never reached Chesapeake Bay, and the arms had to be landed at Philadelphia. From there the Virginia delegates forwarded them by land (*ibid.*, V, 326, 550–51).

Motion of Virginia Delegates in Congress

Printed text (*Journals of the Continental Congress*, XIX, 173–74).

[19 February 1781]

On motion of the delegates of Virginia;

Ordered, That the quartermaster general be and hereby is directed to transport to Fort Pitt four tons of powder, to be delivered to the order of the State of Virginia, and for which the said State is to be accountable; that the expence of such transportation be charged to the said State,[1] and that a warrant be issued by the Board of Treasury, in favour of the said quartermaster general, on the treasury of Virginia, for twelve hundred dollars, in bills emitted pursuant to the resolution of 18 March last, for which the said State is to be credited.[2]

[1] See Jefferson to Virginia Delegates, 18 January 1781, and H. R. McIlwaine, ed., *Official Letters of Virginia Governors,* II, 338. The delegates probably introduced this motion after hearing about Jefferson's needs as reported to them orally by Benjamin Harrison (Virginia Delegates to Jefferson, 13 February 1781). On 13 April 1781, Richard Peters, secretary of the Board of War, informed the president of Congress that four tons of powder for the use of General George Rogers Clark were en route to Fort Pitt (NA: PCC, No. 60, fol. 29). A letter of 18 February from "the Western Department," read in Congress on 13 March 1781, reported that Fort Pitt (Pittsburgh) was in a "ruinous and defenceless" state and that its hungry and ill-equipped garrison consisted of part of a Pennsylvania and part of a Virginia regiment, as well as "a small detachment of Artillery and some independent companies" (*Journals of the Continental Congress,* XIX, 254, 279–80).

[2] For the act of 18 March 1780, see Jefferson to JM, 26 July 1780, n. 2.

Virginia Delegates in Congress to Thomas Jefferson

RC (Virginia State Library). Written by Theodorick Bland but signed only by JM and Joseph Jones. Docketed by a clerk, "Virga. Delegates Lr. Feby 81."

PHILADELPHIA Feby. [20?],[1] 1781

SR.

Since our last in which we informd Yr. Excy of the Arrival of Col. Harrison in this City,[2] his Applications to Congress have been referd to a Special Committee—and the necessary Steps are taking to Answer the wishes and wants of the Southern States, and of our State in particular as far [as] is practicable in the present Situation of affairs.[3] we doubt not but that Gentn. will give you full Information of the Progress he has made in the Special Business for which he has been Sent.[4]

We are happy to Inform you of the Arrival of Capt. Paul Jones in the Ariel from France. This event would have been a much more pleasing one had he brought the cloathing so long and anxiously expected—his Cargo is however by no means useless as it Consists of about thirty Ton of Powder.[5] It is Conjectured that by this time Count D'Estaing is arrived in the West Indies with twenty two sail of the Line[6]—and we are in great Hopes before this reaches you that a Ship of the Line from the fleet of our Allies in Rhode Island and three frigates will be in our Bay in order to cooperate with our Troops, in taking Ample Vengeance on Mr. Arnold, for his treasons, perjuries Robberies and depradations. accounts being received in this Town that they saild from Rhode Island immediately after the Storm & that Monsr. Destouches had taken effectual measures to Block up the Remaining Vessels of the Enemy in Gardners Bay. we have sanguine hopes that this Expedition will not be fruitless, and that our Allies will find us in a Condition effectually to cooperate with them, as their aid will enable us to draw our whole force to a point.[7] One of the frigates above mentiond will bring the Arms and Stores which were retaken in the Comite;[8] which will perhaps not be an unseasonable aid. we have enclosed Yr. Excellency two New York Papers for your perusal containing Arnolds account of his Victories and Captures[9]

Mr. Hays informed us this morning he should be ready to set out for Virginia with the printing materials in abt. a week.[10] We are with great respect

Yr. Excelcys obed Servts.

JOS: JONES.
JAMES MADISON JUNR.

P.S. since writing the above we have authentic information that one seventy four with two Frigates & a Cutter sailed from Rhode Island on the eigth for Chesapeak Bay[11]

[1] Dating this letter the 20th seems to be warranted because (a) the 20th was Tuesday, and the delegates usually wrote to the governor on that day of the week; (b) they knew of the recommendations of the committee appointed to confer with Benjamin Harrison, and its report was submitted to Congress on the 19th; and (c) John Paul Jones reached Philadelphia on the 18th. On the other hand, comments in n. 6, below, will indicate why the letter possibly was written a few days after the 20th.

[2] See Virginia Delegates to Jefferson, first letter of 13 February 1781.

[3] On 13 February, Congress appointed a committee of six men, with Samuel Adams

as chairman and JM as one of the members, to confer with Harrison. The committee's report, debated and largely agreed to by Congress on 20 February, recommended "as absolutely necessary" an increase of the army in the south to ten thousand men, with adequate transportation, arms, clothing, and other equipment, and a levy upon almost all of the qualified manpower and matériel from Pennsylvania south to Georgia in order to achieve this purpose. On 24 February, Congress adopted the remaining recommendation of the committee, that the British prisoners should be moved at once from Virginia to a more northern state (*Journals of the Continental Congress*, XIX, 142, 160, 176–78, 193).

4 In his letter of 19 February to Jefferson, Harrison qualified his report of success by adding, "I foresee very great difficulty in their [Congress] carrying their resolutions into effect, they being extremely poor and their credit but low." He also stated that the Virginia delegates, or at least some of them, were opposing his efforts to have Congress remove the British prisoners from Virginia (Boyd, *Papers of Jefferson*, IV, 655–57).

5 See Jameson to JM, 16 August, n. 7, and 13 September 1780, n. 4. In a close vote in Congress on 19 February, JM joined with other delegates to defeat a motion to have Jones examined at a *public* session of Congress to ascertain why "cloathing and arms belonging to these United States" were detained in France. Jones convinced the Navy Board that he was not responsible for the detention and that a brigantine carrying clothing as part of its cargo had been captured by the British because, contrary to his orders, it had sailed from France in advance of the "Ariel." On 27 February, having complimented Jones upon "his distinguished bravery and military conduct" and his brilliant victory over the British ship of war "Serapis," Congress resolved that Franklin should inform Louis XVI of its willingness to have him award the cross of military merit to Jones (*Journals of the Continental Congress*, XIX, 175–76, 200, 319). Probably it was at this time that JM gained his "slight and transient" acquaintance with Jones and became convinced that Jones's "heroism will fill a very brilliant page" in the history of the American Revolution (JM to John H. Sherburne, 28 April 1825, in the U.S. Naval Academy Museum, Annapolis).

6 The conjecture was in error. Comte d'Estaing (1729–1794) was still in command of the French fleet besieging Gibraltar. Although a report, dated 18 January 1781, in Martinique did not appear in print until the 27 February issue of the *Pennsylvania Packet*, it could have been known in Philadelphia as early as the 20th. This report told of a victory won by Estaing's fleet over that of Rear Admiral Samuel Hood. By not specifying where this engagement had taken place and by adding that the remnants of Hood's command had reached St. Lucia, this report conveyed the mistaken impression that Estaing was in the West Indies area.

7 Gardiner's Bay, an arm of Long Island Sound at the eastern end of Long Island, was the base of the British fleet blockading the French men-of-war in Rhode Island ports. For "the Storm," see Virginia Delegates to Jefferson, 13 February 1781, n. 1. Thanks to its crippling effect upon the enemy, Destouches felt able to weaken his naval force by sending the sixty-four gun "L'Eveillé" and two frigates under the command of Captain Arnaud Le Gardeur de Tilly to Chesapeake Bay. When Tilly reached there on 11 February and found that Arnold's vessels had withdrawn into water too shoal for him to follow, he soon sailed back to Rhode Island. On his return voyage, however, Tilly captured the forty-four gun "Romulus" as well as several British privateers and provision ships (*Providence Gazette; and Country Journal*, 3 March 1781; Wharton, *Revolutionary Diplomatic Correspondence*, IV, 267). Washington was greatly disappointed because of the small size of the French squadron and its failure to take French troops to Virginia (Fitzpatrick, *Writings of Washington*, XXI, 372–73).

8 See Nightingale to Virginia Delegates, 15 February 1781. The frigate bearing the

cargo from "Le Comité" did not sail with this squadron. In his letter of 19 February to Jefferson, Benjamin Harrison stated that he would leave money with the Virginia delegates to cover the cost of freighting this cargo from New Castle, Del., to Fredericksburg, if the French frigate could not land it at Yorktown (Boyd, *Papers of Jefferson*, IV, 656).

9 Inclosures not found. One of them was probably the extra edition of Rivington's *Royal Gazette* of 3 February.

10 See Jefferson to Virginia Delegates, 31 August 1780 and n. 3. After the first shipment of printing equipment to Virginia by John Dunlap and his partner, James Hayes, Jr. (1760–1804), had been captured by the British in October 1780, the General Assembly encouraged the printers to try again. Hayes arrived in Richmond with his press in March 1781 (Boyd, *Papers of Jefferson*, V, 193, 386).

11 As stated in n. 7, above, "L'Eveillé" was of sixty-four rather than seventy-four guns. This vessel, together with the two frigates and cutter, was back in a Rhode Island port by 25 February (*Pennsylvania Packet* [Philadelphia], 6 March 1781).

Thomas Jefferson to Virginia Delegates in Congress

RC (NA: PCC, No. 71, II, 45–46). Docketed, "Feby 22 1781 Letter from Govr. Jefferson of Virginia—Read 26th." FC is in Virginia State Library: Executive Letter Book.

In Council Feby 22d. 1781

GENTLEMEN

The object of the inclosed Memorial of Messrs. Stodder, Kerr & North being attainable by Congress only and proper to be the Subject of a representation from them I take the Liberty of transmitting it to you that Justice may be done to the parties interested.[1]

I have the honor to be with great respect—Gentlemen your mo. ob. Hble Servant.

TH: JEFFERSON

P.S. We are and have long been without Letters of Marque[2]

1 David Stodder, George Kerr, and William North and Company, apparently a partnership of blockade-runners, sent an undated memorial to Jefferson and the Virginia Council of State, complaining that their ship, the "Renown," had been captured in August 1780 by the British while in the neutral Dutch port of St. Martin where, in accordance with the "law of nations," the governor had guaranteed to protect the vessel (Jameson to JM, 30 August 1780). A part of its cargo consisted of ninety hogsheads of tobacco. The petitioners requested Jefferson to forward their plea to Congress if Virginia was unable to recover damages for them from the government of the Netherlands. On 26 March Congress agreed to JM's motion by directing that the memorial be sent to John Adams at Amsterdam with instructions to seek redress from the States General (*Journals of the Continental Congress*, XIX, 312). The memorial

with accompanying protests and affidavits is in NA: PCC, No. 41, IX, 133–51. David Stodder (d. 1781) was a shipbuilder and shipowner of Gosport, Va. From 1777 to 1779, a David Stodder of that port was employed by the continental agent as "Master Builder" of the two thirty-six-gun frigates being constructed at Gosport in Norfolk County (H. R. McIlwaine, ed., *Official Letters of Virginia Governors*, I, 95, 102, 256; II, 9; NA: PCC, Marine Committee Letter Book, 1776–1780, fols. 182, 202, 205; NA: PCC, No. 136, II, 215, 531; *Journals of the Continental Congress*, X, 326, 338). George Kerr (*ca.* 1745–1784) was a Sussex County merchant (Sussex County Court Records, Will Book D, p. 257, microfilm in Virginia State Library). William North (*ca.* 1750–1822) was a merchant from Norfolk County (Norfolk County Court Records, Audit Book, No. 5, p. 177, microfilm in Virginia State Library).

² Twenty-four letters of marque, in fulfillment of the request of Jefferson to the Virginia delegates on 26 January (*q.v.*), had been dispatched to him by Charles Thomson, secretary of Congress, on 19 February 1781 (*Calendar of Virginia State Papers*, I, 526).

Amendment to Committee Report on Hartford Convention

MS (NA: PCC, No. 33, fol. 427). Undated. Endorsed by Charles Thomson, "Amend proposd." The amendment is in JM's hand.

[*ca.* 23 February 1781]

to report to Congress thereon, except such as in the opinion of the Committee require order to be taken by the respective departments, which the Committee shall lay before Congress in the first instance with such their Opinion.¹

¹ After commissioners from the four New England states and New York, meeting at Hartford in mid-November 1780, sent a copy of their proceedings to Congress, that body referred them on 12 December 1780 to a committee of five members, composed of John Mathews as chairman, JM, and three others (*Journals of the Continental Congress*, XVIII, 1141). During its deliberations the committee evidently decided to disregard the most provocative recommendations of the Hartford Convention—namely, that, whenever all other expedients had failed, Congress should call upon Washington to use troops to force a state to provide its due quota of soldiers, money, or supplies to the common cause. One recommendation of the committee, included in its report which Congress debated and recommitted on 23 February, was "that for the dispatch of business a committee of three members of Congress, of whom the president shall always be one, be appointed to receive all public dispatches addressed to Congress, and that they be authorized to refer them to such of the departments as are proper to consider them" (*ibid.*, XIX, 155–56, 190). Although the journal is silent, JM probably offered his amendment during that debate as a substitute for the following words, which came immediately after the portion just quoted: "either to report to Congress or take order on them as the case may require. Except such of them as in their opinion demand the immediate and more particular attention of Con-

gress, which shall accordingly be laid before Congress, at their first meeting after receipt of the same." This section was stricken out by Congress (*ibid.*, XIX, 156). Although the committee remained in existence at least as late as 6 March (*ibid.*, XIX, 235), there is no evidence that it ever submitted a revised report to Congress. As a result of the inauguration of the government under the Articles of Confederation on 1 March, Congress appointed two important committees—one "to revise the rules for conducting business in the United States in Congress assembled" and the other, including JM, to prepare a plan to enable Congress to execute its rightful authority under the Articles of Confederation (*ibid.*, XIX, 225, 236; XX, 469–71, 476 ff.). Their assignments, so similar to those of the committee on the recommendations of the Hartford Convention, may have served to end that committee's existence.

INDEX

NOTE: Persons are identified on pages cited below in boldface type. Identifications made in Volume I are noted immediately after the person's name.

The Papers of James Madison

DESIGNED BY JOHN B. GOETZ
COMPOSED BY THE UNIVERSITY OF CHICAGO PRESS
IN LINOTYPE JANSON WITH DISPLAY LINES IN
MONOTYPE JANSON AND CASLON OLD STYLE
PRINTED BY THE UNIVERSITY OF CHICAGO PRESS
ON WARREN'S UNIVERSITY TEXT, A PAPER WATERMARKED
WITH JAMES MADISON'S SIGNATURE AND MADE EXPRESSLY
FOR THE VOLUMES OF THIS SET
PLATES PRINTED BY MERIDEN GRAVURE COMPANY
MAP DRAWN BY FRANZ ALTSCHULER
BOUND BY BROCK AND RANKIN IN COLUMBIA BAYSIDE LINEN
AND STAMPED IN GENUINE GOLD